THE ART SPY

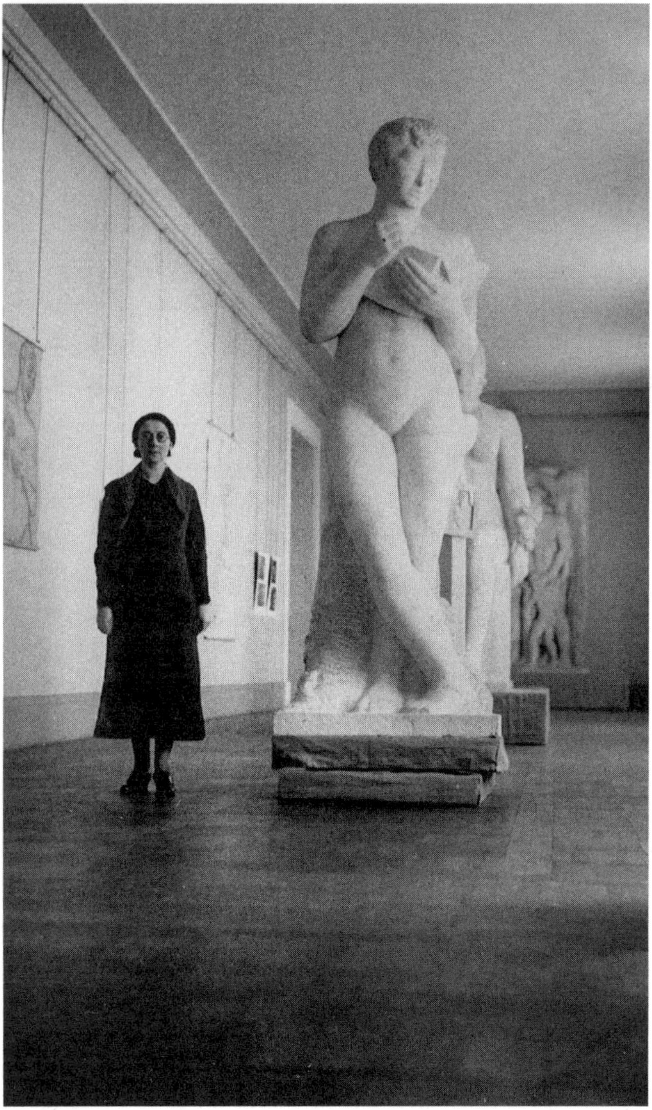

Rose Valland at the José Fioravanti exhibition at the Jeu de Paume, 1934.

THE ART SPY

The Extraordinary Untold Tale of WWII Resistance Hero Rose Valland

MICHELLE YOUNG

HarperOne
An Imprint of HarperCollins*Publishers*

hc.com

FIRST HARPERONE PAPERBACK EDITION PUBLISHED IN 2026

Designed by Kyle O'Brian

Ornament art © KENJIROU MORITA/Shutterstock

Library of Congress Cataloging-in-Publication Data is available upon request.

ISBN 978-0-06-329590-2

Printed in the United States of America

26 27 28 29 30 LBC 5 4 3 2 1

For my Franco-American daughters, Charlotte and Emma Rose, and for Augustin, who showed me France

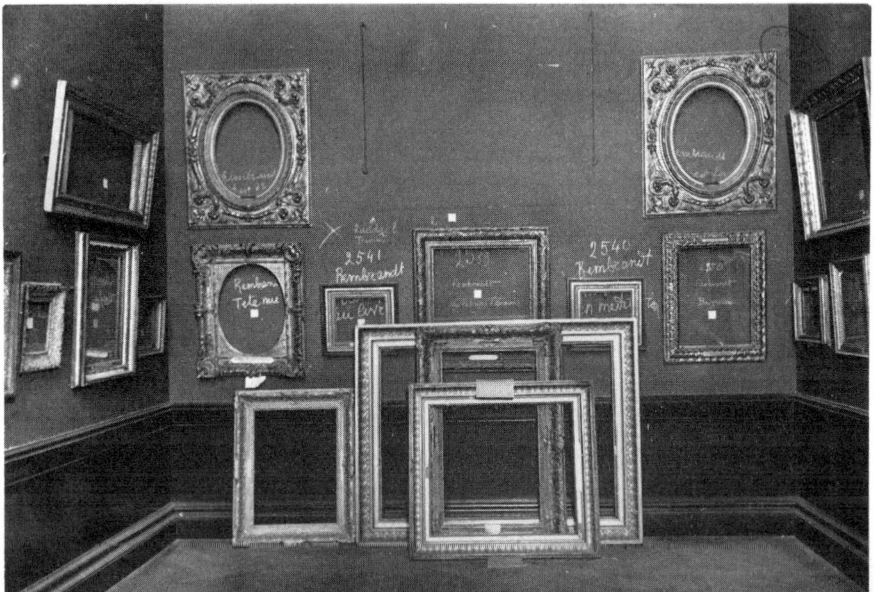

Empty frames in the Louvre, circa 1942.

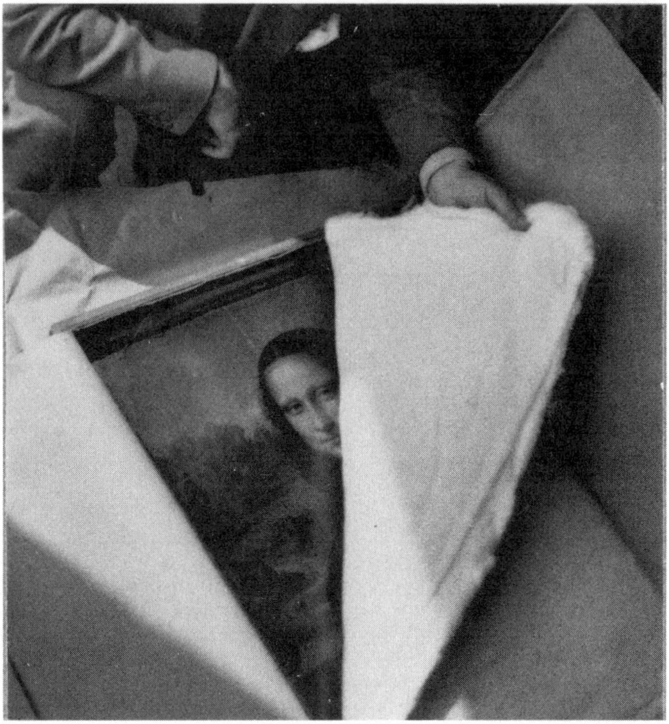

The unveiling of the *Mona Lisa* from its packing case, around June 1945.

AUTHOR'S NOTE

THEY SAY TRUTH IS STRANGER THAN FICTION. IT IS ALSO OFTEN MORE exciting. This is a work of nonfiction and nothing in this book was imagined. Anything that appears in quotation marks is based verbatim on interview quotes, notes, letters, articles, or books, or was left in unpublished manuscripts and archival material. Quoted material also comes from the many firsthand accounts of people who were present at the time of the events. A comprehensive list of notes and sources (including for each line of dialogue) appears at the end of the book.

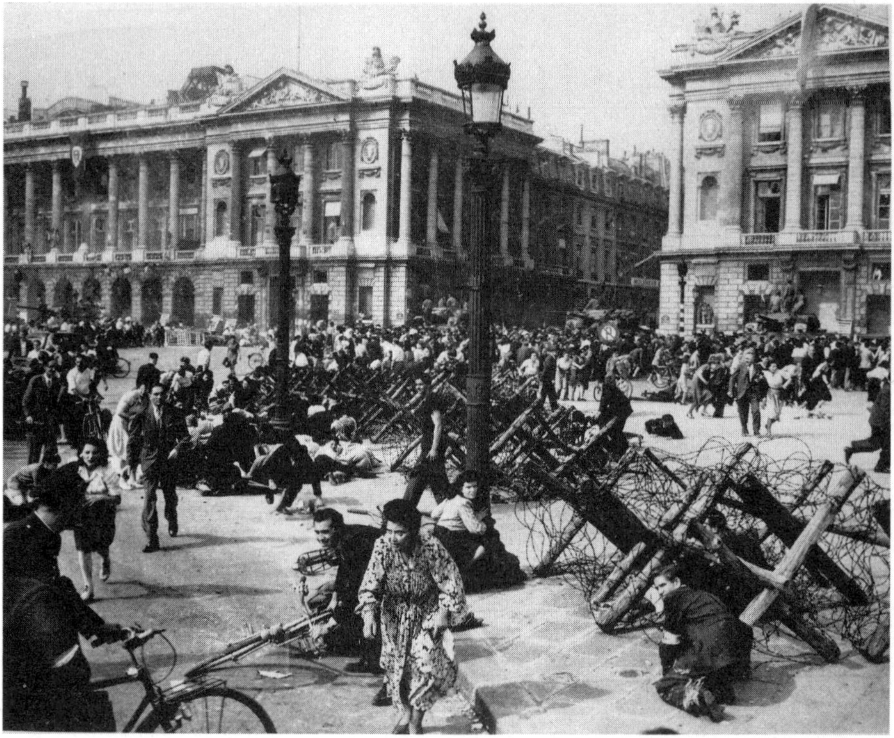

Crowds at Place de la Concorde scatter for cover as a sniper fires from a building, August 26, 1944.

PARIS

AUGUST 19–20, 1944

A TORRENTIAL STORM WAS PUMMELING PARIS, TURNING THE SKIES forebodingly dark over a city in the midst of a tense mandatory blackout. The clamor of thunder and the sounds of war rose to a crescendo as the battle for Paris began.

After four brutal years of German occupation, the City of Light was allegedly going to be liberated. Cannons boomed, and shells whistled above the Seine, just meters away from the Jeu de Paume museum. Inside that nineteenth-century building, forty-five-year-old French art historian Rose Valland peered out from a slightly open window.

The French Resistance had ordered a citywide uprising, and four thousand plainclothes police officers wearing tricolor armbands—the red, white, and blue of the French flag—invaded the police headquarters facing the Cathedral of Notre-Dame and took over Paris's city hall, flushing out the Nazi occupiers.

The Germans countered with bombs and blasts from their own armored tanks, trying to take the buildings back. Gunfire from street skirmishes rang out throughout the city. Bullets shattered windows and pierced buildings. German soldiers on foot attacked the street barricades built by Parisians out of burned-out cars, furniture, sandbags, barrels, cobblestones, pianos, and even urinals.

From the Jeu de Paume, Rose could see dark smoke rising from the Grand Palais, the glorious palace of iron, steel, and glass on the

Champs-Élysées that was used throughout the occupation for propaganda exhibitions. The Germans had sent a remote-controlled tank barreling into the building to kill the French Resistance fighters who had barricaded themselves inside.

At just under five-and-a-half feet tall, Rose was dwarfed by the scale of the Jeu de Paume's colossal arched windows, but there was nothing timid about her. Four years earlier, the Nazis had seized the museum to make it a headquarters for its art looting force, the Einsatzstab Reichsleiter Rosenberg, to process the Jewish-owned art they had begun to plunder en masse in France. Her boss, Jacques Jaujard, the director of the Musées Nationaux—the French national museums—immediately ordered her to "remain at all costs at the Jeu de Paume museum" and covertly spy on the Germans. Iron-willed Rose was determined to see her orders through, but she did not know that she would risk her life for the next four years to achieve her mission.

Rose had a reputation for being overly serious and too blunt for her own good, but her unflappability had proven useful in the war. She had learned to play the role of a nobody to the Nazis—not important enough to notice, not congenial enough to be flirted with, and too grave to be easily friends with.

Unlike the other women who worked in the French museums, she didn't bother much with her looks. Her most defining accessory was her round spectacles, which gave her an air of erudition. Although it was in vogue to wear one's tresses in soft waves just above the shoulder, Rose simply brushed her brunette locks to the side and pulled them back in a neat bun. She left her eyebrows natural and mildly unkempt, unlike those popularized by cinema stars like Arletty and Danielle Darrieux, who wore them razor thin and drawn in darkly with pencil. Sartorially, Rose did her best to fit in. Though she would have much preferred to wear pants, she donned feminine, ankle-length dresses and blended in with the rest of the women in Paris—modest, traditional, and discreet.

Still, the Germans had accused Rose of everything in their arsenal:

sabotage, theft, and signaling to the enemy. They subjected her to invasive interrogations and searches, and even expelled her from the museum on several occasions. But she talked her way back in every time, explaining calmly that she was just a lowly employee of the French national museums who oversaw the building's maintenance and the remaining art collection. In reality, she was one of the most well-educated art historians in France—and nearly every one of the German accusations had been true.

Rose was also concealing another dangerous secret: she had been living for almost a decade with the love of her life, Joyce Heer, a British citizen who worked for the US embassy. Not only was her partner considered an enemy alien by the Nazis, but homosexuality was codified under Vichy French law as an "unnatural act." Any misstep could lead to imprisonment, deportation, or worse for both Rose and Joyce.

The Jeu de Paume was Rose's first curatorial job after a decade of studies that took her all the way from her small countryside village in eastern France to Paris, the nation's epicenter of fine art, and she felt personally responsible for the museum's fate. Although it was not as prestigious as the Louvre, the Jeu de Paume had become a highly respected museum in the seven years Rose had worked there, in no small part due to her industriousness. It was renowned for its exhibitions on international and modern art, as well as for its fine permanent collection. It sat proudly on an elevated terrace in the Tuileries Garden in the heart of Paris at the corner of the Place de la Concorde and rue de Rivoli. The long rectangular building, designed like a Grecian temple, was built originally for court tennis during the reign of Napoleon III. Across the Tuileries was the Louvre. Now, the Jeu de Paume faced potential destruction, unwittingly situated at the center of the climactic final battle for Paris.

The last of the German staffers in the Einsatzstab Reichsleiter Rosenberg—the Reichsleiter Rosenberg Taskforce—had abandoned the museum in recent days as the formidable Allied forces advanced toward Paris. Rose and two French guards were the only people left inside the museum.

Rose was ready to sacrifice her life to protect what was left of the museum's permanent collection: paintings and sculptures by the likes of Salvador Dalí, Frida Kahlo, Wassily Kandinsky, Max Beckmann, Giorgio de Chirico, and many others. She and the guards would sleep on straw mattresses in the makeshift bomb shelter of the museum until it was all over, one way or another.

But sleep was the last thing on Rose's mind. She watched from the tiny opening in the window as German soldiers on the rue de Rivoli, the grand street that runs alongside the Jeu de Paume, shouted orders into an abyss of chaos. As night fell, tanks and military vehicles raced back and forth, readying for their last stand. Machine-gun fire popped all around the museum. Resistance fighters attacked the German dugouts and fortifications along the Place de la Concorde and rue de Rivoli. Sniper shots reverberated from the rooftops of nearby buildings. "A sort of frenzy of shouting and commands came to us," Rose later recounted.

The Jeu de Paume was just two blocks down the street from the luxurious Hôtel Meurice, where General Dietrich von Choltitz, the German commander in chief of Paris, was holed up. If he surrendered, Paris would be back in the hands of the French. The offices and apartments of the German Army, Navy, and Air Force stretched from the Place de la Concorde all the way to the Louvre. What had been a sumptuous playground for the German top brass was now their last line of defense.

In the middle of the night, Rose looked on with dread as some fifty German soldiers arrived on the Jeu de Paume's terrace. Through the downpour and lightning, the men installed rows and rows of crisscrossed wooden spikes wrapped in barbed wire, blocking the monumental doorway that once welcomed the likes of Hermann Göring, Adolf Hitler's cruel right-hand man, and Alfred Rosenberg, the mastermind behind the Nazi Party's most ruthless ideologies. "We were in an entrenched camp!" Rose later described with uncharacteristic emotion.

Concrete blocks lay embedded in the ground just a few feet from the museum's main entrance. A German armed sentry was posted in a new watchtower just twenty steps away, and to Rose's dismay, he trained his sights on them. The Jeu de Paume's complete isolation was clear. Rose fretted about what was to become of her beloved museum.

Did the Germans think she and the guards were armed Resistance fighters? So many other government buildings around Paris were now occupied by the Resistance, and it would be logical to assume that the Jeu de Paume was too, since it belonged to the French state. But in fact, the museum's French guards only had one pistol between them.

Rose also knew that Colonel Kurt von Behr, the cunning former head of the Einsatzstab Reichsleiter Rosenberg, was still in Paris, busy trying to send one last train of art to Germany. There were nearly one thousand paintings and fifty sculptures on that transport, made by artists like Pablo Picasso, Georges Braque, Henri Matisse, Paul Cézanne, and Claude Monet. Rose knew more than practically anyone about the crimes that von Behr and the Nazis had perpetrated to loot artwork from France, particularly from Jewish families. A large portion of the art on the train belonged to the family of Alexandre Rosenberg, a young Free French soldier who was fighting his way to Paris.

Unbeknownst to Rose, a special directive had also come in from Berlin commanding that the Jeu de Paume be used for defense and, if required, "neutralized." And Colonel von Behr had given an order to make Rose, in particular, "disappear."

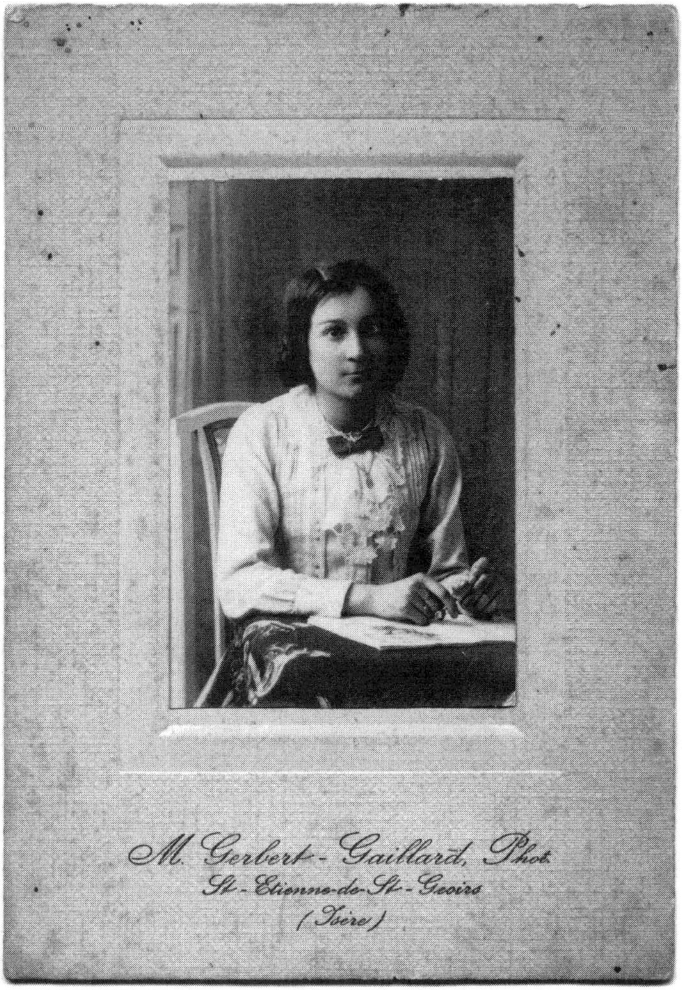

Rose Valland, around sixteen or seventeen years old.

PARIS

1939

THE ONE THING ROSE VALLAND LOVED MOST IN THE WORLD WAS ART. For as long as she could remember, she lived and breathed it. Life, as she painted it, was awash with bright pinks, reds, purples, and yellows. It was colorful and hopeful—a stark contrast to her somber childhood. This search for beauty, in all its forms, drove Rose in a singular, obsessive fashion. It was also her ticket out of Saint-Étienne-de-Saint-Geoirs, the isolated village she was born in, fifty miles southeast of Lyon.

Since the early days of the Holy Roman Empire, this area of eastern France was renowned for its religious martyrs and the piety of its people. The many fortified stone castles and citadels in town were a stark reminder of the religious wars that dominated this region during the Middle Ages.

There was an immutable harshness to the landscape and the climate, with cold, cloudy winters and hot, rainless summers. Locals toiled in the fields of the treeless open plain and worked in textile factories producing silk and other woven fabrics. In the distance stood the snowcapped Chartreuse Mountains, where silent Carthusian monks had produced a potent green liqueur—an "elixir of long life"—for nearly a thousand years.

Rose's early years were not particularly joyful or beautiful. She came from a simple, working-class family of mechanics, wheelwrights, and blacksmiths, and her father worked the smithery attached to their modest stone house. From birth, Rose was surrounded by the harsh clanging of iron and a dark soot that hung in the air and stuck to everything.

She was surrounded by deep sorrow. Her older brother died as a toddler, rendering Rose an only child. Life at home was dominated by the hardy matriarchs of the family, while Rose's father was mostly uninvolved in her life. When Rose wrote home as a young adult, she usually only addressed her mother. "*Ma chère Maman*," the letters opened.

Rose was a sickly child and started school late, but she caught up quickly. Her mother was determined and formidable. She nurtured Rose's early talents in academics and the arts and diligently applied for local scholarships. Rose's own aptitude and persistence put her consistently at the top of every school she attended. As a precocious teenager, Rose was shipped off to an all-girls boarding school, and then, after placing first in a regional academic competition, she spent all of World War I on a scholarship studying at the Teachers College in Grenoble, an industrial city thirty miles from home. While writing a thesis on the pedagogy of drawing, Rose witnessed the transformation of Grenoble from a center of glove manufacturing into an armament hub where explosives, shells, and chemical weapons were fabricated for the war.

At twenty, considered a prime age to get married, Rose was accepted to the École des Beaux-Arts in Lyon, France's third-largest city at the time with over half a million residents, where she won regional and national awards in art history and in the fine arts for painting, drawing, and decorative arts. She was then one of only a handful of women admitted to the École des Beaux-Arts in Paris, the prestigious art school where Eugène Delacroix, Edgar Degas, Pierre-Auguste Renoir, and Jean-Honoré Fragonard had all studied. The entrance exam took nearly forty hours and included live drawings of the human figure, anatomy, perspective, and architecture, as well as a test in art history. Out of three hundred candidates, Rose finished sixth, ensuring her a spot.

However, Rose soon learned that the school barred all the female students from the drawing workshop because of the use of nude male models. The women's only class was full, and the school director refused to open another one, but Rose found a way into the drawing teacher's studio anyway.

Rose's degree from the École des Beaux-Arts in Paris would qualify her to be an art teacher, but her interests soon expanded. She enrolled at the École du Louvre, a school that trained future curators, museum administrators, and art historians. These careers were traditionally only open to men, but the Great War had wrought dramatic changes in French society. Women like Rose came to Paris to attend university and to find work. The low cost of living and the collapsing franc attracted artists from all over the world who relocated to be amid the explosion in modernity.

Since the start of the twentieth century, women in France had gradually gained more rights, including the right to have their own salary, to maternity leave (albeit unpaid), to join a union without a husband's consent, and to an equal education between the sexes in middle school and high school. But as Rose discovered, sexism still prevented women from getting hired for jobs they were more than qualified for.

In addition to her degree at the École des Beaux-Arts in Paris, Rose also obtained a diploma in art history at the Sorbonne, combining certificates in Greek archaeology, medieval archaeology, and the history of modern art, and took supplementary courses in Byzantine archaeology at the École Pratique des Hautes Études, one of the best universities in France. She also took English language classes and went abroad for several months in England to improve her language skills. In all, Rose dedicated nine years of her life pursuing degrees in higher education.

But no matter how well Rose did academically or how far she was from home, she could never quite shed the severity of the world she had come from. It showed in the way she carried herself, her reserved demeanor, and her direct, masculine manner. She never quite fit in. Though she adopted a way of speaking in the lilting manner of the educated upper classes that belied her working-class origins, she lacked the social ease of the elite.

While Rose's female classmates were chummy and physically affectionate with one other, Rose was an awkward loner. Her closeted attraction to women led her to treat them particularly harshly. Love evaded her.

Her internal life, however, was one of exuberance and full of modern ideas. "Isn't movement the very expression of life?" she wrote in the opening of her dissertation at the École du Louvre. The introvert in Rose wanted to show that joy and life could emanate through art without words needing to be spoken. She wrote that when art closely imitates real human movement, it could make someone feel something close to the sublime, "an enjoyment that no words can make us feel, that music itself cannot give us." Through the making and study of art, she could express a vivacity she dared not show in her personal life. She was a woman yearning to break free and to make her mark somehow.

The 1920s, when Rose first came to Paris, were known as *les années folles*: the crazy years. An exuberant raucousness pervaded the streets day and night. The cafés were brimming, and nightlife buzzed. Paris was the epicenter of it all—art, cinema, dance, theater, and music. The entertainer Josephine Baker found refuge in Paris from discrimination in America and shocked even the French with her nearly nude performances, stunning at the Folies Bergère in a surrealist-inspired skirt made of faux bananas.

Technology was celebrated and admired. The city of Paris expanded the metro, connecting the once-distant suburbs with the city center. Architects like Le Corbusier, his cousin Pierre Jeanneret, and Walter Gropius introduced a new style focused on formal simplicity and pure architectural lines, producing gleaming white structures that seemed to land from another planet.

All the notable artists, like Henri Matisse and the cubists—Georges Braque, Pablo Picasso, and Juan Gris—designed sets and costumes for the new Ballets Russes premieres. The first of the Paris school of painters to sign up was Picasso. For "Parade," Picasso dressed the dancers in colorful cardboard manifestations of his cubist still lifes, trapping the performers stiffly as they held exaggerated paper smoking pipes, walking sticks, and megaphones. French poet Guillaume Apollinaire described "Parade" as "surrealism," coining the use of the term for the very first time. But not everyone was ready for it. "Parade" so outraged the audience at the premiere that Picasso bolted out of his box seat to escape the booing. In 1924, two years after Rose arrived in Paris, Coco Chanel joined the party, designing the costumes for "*Le Train Bleu*," with Picasso doing the sets.

Social norms were changing, too. In the cinema and in fashion, women like Greta Garbo and Marlene Dietrich wore pantsuits and cut their hair short. Rose followed suit, pushing the boundaries even further by dressing *à la garçonne*, with a gender-bending boy cut and a chic blue suit she particularly loved.

Paris, the lesbian capital of Europe in the Roaring Twenties, would have been a place for Rose to start exploring her emerging sexual orientation. She was in an open-minded city far from the conservative religious milieu she grew up in. Gay women from around the world, including *New Yorker* columnist Janet Flanner, Polish painter Tamara de Lempicka, and British poet Renée Vivien, fled to Paris in search of sexual freedom. Bars like Le Monocle, Le Hanneton, and La Souris—hidden in plain sight in Montmartre—and the salons of Gertrude Stein and her lover Alice B. Toklas, as well as those of American heiress Natalie Clifford Barney, were a haven for women from all walks of the sexuality spectrum. Inside, lipstick lesbians, tuxedo-clad women, and the bi-curious mingled. Dressing *à la garçonne* was rebellious but also potentially dangerous for Rose and other women like her, who were sometimes violently attacked. Their nonconformity was seen by some as a threat to traditional values.

In her student years, Rose lived beneath the angled low ceiling of a *chambre de bonnes*, once the tiny attic residence of maids and household staff, converted throughout Paris into cheap housing. Her apartment was sparsely decorated, but she kept a religious shrine with an image of Jesus on her wall. In a rare photograph from this time, Rose stands engrossed in a book as the light floods in from the window, like a composition from a Jan Vermeer painting.

Major cultural events came and went. Paris hosted the 1924 Summer Olympics, where the United States was the most medaled country by far, winning ninety-nine. The dashing Johnny Weissmuller, an American swimmer and future Hollywood actor, nabbed three gold medals and one bronze. Rose had longed to shout "*Vive Uruguay!*" to celebrate the country's first-ever appearance at the Olympics and its gold medal win against Switzerland in soccer, but she could not afford the tickets. "One needs time and money," she wrote to her cousin Adrien, "the two things I am always missing!"

By the 1930s, art deco evolved into art moderne, a cleaner, more streamlined architectural style. Rose, who unsuccessfully applied for a job at the 1937 International Exposition of Art and Technology in Modern Life, would have seen Picasso's *Guernica*, the artist's heart-wrenching interpretation of the civil war in Spain, adorn the Pavilion of the Spanish Republic.

Rose dreamed of getting a job as a curator at the Louvre, but her chances were slim. France's long-established institutions were slow to change. There were no female curators on staff, and the only positions available to women in the curatorial departments were as unpaid volunteers—as an *attaché bénévole*. It was equivalent to an unpaid internship. In the 1920s, there was only one female *attaché bénévole* at the Louvre, Jacqueline Bouchot-Saupique, who had advantages Rose didn't have—she was the daughter of a famous art historian and wife of the sculptor George Saupique, who made the bas-relief works on the largest ocean liner in the world, the *Normandie*. Family background made all the difference in France.

Rose's personal demeanor did not help matters, either. A male curator at the Louvre described her as "utterly serious" with no sense of humor that he could detect. She was not afraid to speak frankly or

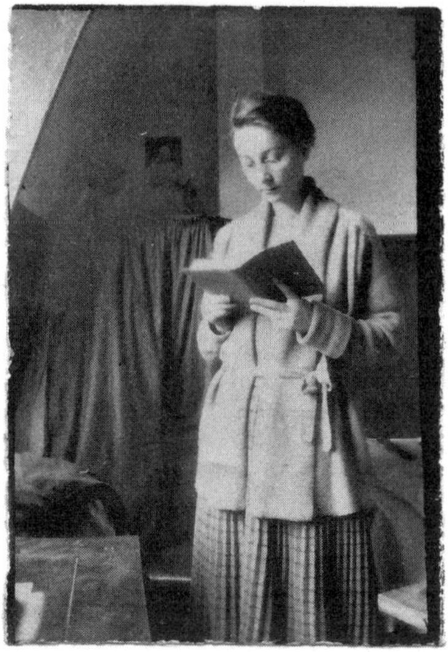

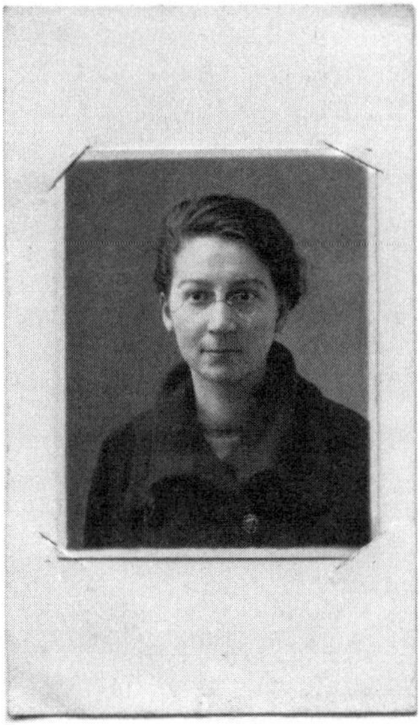

Portraits of Rose Valland in her twenties.

confront people in positions of power. She would size people up with a long, unflinching stare while she assessed if they could be trusted. She could be distant and cold, even with family.

But beneath the surface, Rose actually had a keen sense of humor and could be charming when she wanted to be. The more she felt at ease, the more she revealed her true personality. While she kept women at arm's length, she enjoyed close relationships with men, particularly those with whom she could have intellectual conversations. Letters to her closest cousins, Marguerite and Adrien, were peppered with exclamation marks and concern for their well-being. On occasion, she allowed herself to delight in catty gossip from home. She signed letters to intimate friends and family with her nickname, Rosette, which only her nearest and dearest called her. To those she loved and respected, she was unfailingly loyal. One colleague praised her for having a "big heart," and another noted that she preferred to work with "worthy people, truly consumed with the same desire for truth and decency as she was herself."

Rose's greatest difficulty professionally was Henri Verne, the chauvinistic and classist director of the French Musées Nationaux, who was determined to thwart her career.

HENRI VERNE OVERSAW ALL THE national museums in France and the École du Louvre, where Rose first encountered him as a twenty-five-year-old student. Inside the Louvre, Verne presided over a court full of political intrigue. He was charming with the ladies he liked and protected the men and women who flattered him, even if they were frivolous or insipid. To those outside his circle, he could be vicious and uncompromising.

Verne looked like a man who wanted people to know he had made it. He wore bow ties to set himself apart from the other cravat-donning curators and sported a carefully trimmed beard and mustache. He peered out from behind round eyeglasses with piercing eyes. For his formal portrait, Verne made sure to wear an elaborate eighteenth-century embroidered frock coat and his Légion d'Honneur medal, a five-armed cross pendant made of enamel and gold. Exhibited at the 1938 Paris salon, the painting showed the Parisian social set that Verne had not only obtained France's highest order of merit, established by Napoleon, but that he also held the level of Commander, the third-highest level of distinction for the award, which required three decades of exceptional merit.

However, Verne did not have a degree from a prestigious art school like the École des Beaux-Arts. He had been a paralegal in the Ministry of Commerce and then an administrator in the Ministry of Foreign Affairs, the Ministry of Labor, and finally, the Musées Nationaux. Promoted to director of the Musées Nationaux in 1926, Verne was celebrated for modernizing every aspect of the Louvre, from its layout to the installation of electricity and the use of X-rays and photography to document art. He radically changed how art was curated and displayed, choosing to isolate and showcase the works of art in clean, minimalist galleries instead of cramming them inside excessively decorated rooms, which had been the prevailing practice.

The museum directorship was an administrative position that did not require an art history degree, but Verne was eager to prove his knowledge. Using the scientific method, Verne reorganized the departments of the Louvre, the basis of the museum's organization today.

Verne had spent his career searching for respectability in the art world and, by all accounts, achieved it. He was not only a notable writer on the arts but also a teacher at the École du Louvre. A year before his retirement in 1939, Verne still taught an astounding nineteen courses at the school, including the history of the Louvre collections, architecture, decorative arts, antiquities, and Asian art.

Verne's lack of official artistic training may have led him to express his opinions on art forcefully and inflexibly, especially as he got older. As such, Verne was caught off guard by the attention Rose's thesis topic received from the students and faculty at the École du Louvre. She used an avant-garde theoretical approach to look at how movement was expressed in Italian art over the course of many centuries. The idea that movement could exist within a fixed image was already subversive—works of art were conventionally thought of as static, like a moment captured in time—but to compare art formalistically across time periods was doubly so.

Rose was building off concepts promulgated by the eminent art historian Henri Focillon, her mentor from the École des Beaux-Arts in Lyon, who became the chair of the art history department at the Sorbonne, a rival of the École du Louvre. Focillon was considered one of the most brilliant theorists and orators in the field of art history, and Verne likely compared himself to him. But Focillon was unmistakably avant-garde while Verne was firmly traditionalist, as if desperately holding on to a world he saw slipping away.

Rose's thesis defense at the École du Louvre was so well-attended that people were turned away because of the crowding. It would have taken hours for Rose to present her 109-page typewritten dissertation. Rose's staunchest supporter, her mother, came for the momentous occasion. She proudly recounted to her sister that Rose maintained her composure and "showed no emotion" despite the large number of spectators. She also reported on the high level of fascination with the topic in the room. Who could have imagined that the daughter of a blacksmith would successfully distinguish herself among not only men but also the intellectual elite of France? Rose had done it with no family connections to recommend her nor any generational wealth to sustain her. She had come so far, literally and figuratively.

Unfortunately, Verne was one of the three jurors on Rose's thesis defense, along with Gabriel Rouchès, the Louvre's curator of paintings, and Jean Charbonneaux, professor of Greek and Roman archaeology at the École du Louvre. Verne was reluctant to pass Rose at all, contending that the study of movement did not fall within the scope of what was considered art history. As a result, she received a grade of only "*assez bien*," an average mark, which would hamper her job prospects at the Louvre. Rose was a Roaring Twenties overachiever, but Verne took issue with her unconventional ideas. She was certainly different from the other women in the Musées Nationaux, who knew better than to shake up the establishment. It would have been a painful blow for Rose, whose ascent into the fine arts world from her small village in France had been met with approbation and acclaim until then.

When Verne's boss, the director general of the Beaux-Arts, inquired about Rose's application for an *attaché bénévole* position at the Louvre a year later, Verne even penned a rancorous response. He wrote that although he could confirm that she successfully defended a thesis at the École du Louvre, she only passed with the "extreme indulgence of the jury." He added that hiring her "would not appear desirable." This was not the last nasty letter Verne would write about Rose.

Despite all of Rose's degrees and awards, Verne repeatedly sank her candidacy for jobs at the Louvre. Blocked from that avenue, Rose greatly expanded her search. One door she tried was that of André Dezarrois, the curator at the new Jeu de Paume museum, which had just opened in February 1932. It was focused on "foreign schools" of modern art, which was still disdained by institutionalists as inconsequential. Even other graduates looking for jobs saw the museum as too avant-garde to be prestigious. Dezarrois thus had few other candidates besides Rose to serve as his assistant, so she got the job, even though the Jeu de Paume was under the jurisdiction of the Musées Nationaux, where Verne held court. Dezarrois also desperately needed someone who knew how to type, a skill that Rose had.

Rose took the job at the Jeu de Paume as a last resort. While almost all art curators started as unpaid *attachés*, worse, Rose was forced to start as an unpaid secretary—a *secrétaire bénévole*. In the French public service, there was almost no path for a secretary to become a curator. By the time Rose was hired in February 1932 as a *secrétaire bénévole* she was already thirty-three years old and felt dejected, lamenting that it was "too late for a brilliant career."

By 1939, with a new European war on the horizon, Rose had been toiling away at the Jeu de Paume, unpaid, for the previous seven years. As time passed, the only thing that changed was her age and her dwindling funds. On the side, she made ends meet by teaching art history at an art school and French at a finishing school for wealthy foreigners, working for an art magazine, giving tours of other museums in Paris, moonlighting as a freelance art critic for French newspapers, and acting as an art broker. Even though the art business was dominated by men, Rose's contacts with art museums around the world and with Parisian gallery owners would have been attractive to collectors who bought into the modern art movement early. She enabled the sale of *L'homme dans la ville* by Albert Gleizes, a colorful abstract painting of a man surrounded by skyscrapers, from a private collector to the Guggenheim Museum in New York. She also facilitated the sales of *La Gare*, an energetic synthetic cubist painting by Fernand Léger that celebrated the modernity of the train station, and *Le Moulin à Café*, an oil painting of a coffee grinder by Juan Gris.

Dezarrois, Rose's boss at the Jeu de Paume, was a World War I aviation hero and respected art historian. He did his best to buoy her career, paying her to work on his illustrated art magazine, *La Revue de l'Art*, and allowing her to take on responsibilities far beyond what a secretary would ordinarily have been doing, even while Verne denied numerous requests to pay or promote her.

It took four years just to transform Rose's unpaid secretarial position into one as an unpaid *attaché*, and that was only after repeated requests, along with letters of recommendation from some of the art world's leading figures including Henri Focillon, renowned professor Gabriel Millet, and a senator in the French government. In one of Verne's multiple denials to promote her, he went as far as to say that not only was her job at the Jeu de Paume unnecessary, but "when the need arises to provide the Jeu de Paume with the assistance of a *chargé de mission*, I would like to see someone assigned to this position who, by their previous studies and their future potential, is more particularly qualified." Ironically, Rose had many more relevant degrees than Verne had. Even so, in 1939, after three years of working as an *attaché bénévole,* she still had one more year before she could be promoted to a paid employee, if it happened at all with Verne holding the reins.

AT THE JEU DE PAUME, even though Rose was desperately poor and overburdened, she found it exhilarating to organize exhibitions at the forefront of the avant-garde art movement and see the creations arriving from all over the world. In Rose's own words, they were "the most explosive international artistic events." The building, dilapidated by the end of the 1920s, had been completely renovated and modernized in a three-year undertaking led by Dezarrois. The French art magazine *L'Art et les Artistes* lauded the Jeu de Paume as one of France's "most modern museums." The *Bulletin de Musées de France* hailed the official inauguration of the museum in 1932 as a "brilliant event," noting that all of artistic and literary Paris was present.

The Jeu de Paume boasted eighteen exhibition rooms across two floors and two sculpture halls. Double-height arched windows ran the length of the museum on both sides, along with new glass skylights. The most dazzling innovation was electric lighting, which was only partially installed in the Louvre when the Jeu de Paume opened.

In the short seven years since it was inaugurated, the Jeu de Paume had hosted exhibitions featuring art from over a dozen countries. The curation was daring and diverse, from surrealism to folk art. Photography of New York City skyscrapers and Fallingwater, the celebrated home that modernist architect Frank Lloyd Wright built over a Pennsylvania waterfall, adorned the walls in 1938, part of an extensive overview of American art over three centuries—an exhibition that Rose organized in partnership with the Museum of Modern Art in New York. This tour de force of an exhibition included daily screenings of Hollywood films, from *The Execution of Mary, Queen of Scots* from 1895, produced by Thomas Edison, to *A Day at the Races* with the Marx Brothers from 1937.

Much like Dezarrois, Alfred H. Barr Jr., the director of the Museum of Modern Art, delegated the administrative work to a capable female assistant, the art historian Margaret Scolari Barr, who was also his wife. Over long, indulgent French luncheons and meetings inside the Jeu de Paume, Rose and Margaret plotted how the exhibition would come together and fit in some gossip about the ongoing succession rivalry between Dezarrois and the Louvre's suave deputy director, Jacques Jaujard.

Politicians, art connoisseurs, art historians, and artists like Picasso, Braque, and Marc Chagall attended the exhibition openings at the Jeu de Paume. Lectures and musical programming from the featured countries added an experiential dimension. Dezarrois basked in critical success with Rose as his unsung second in command.

Dezarrois had a history of severe angina that would take him out of commission for extended periods. When not ill he also traveled extensively to procure new works of art and plan for future exhibitions. Dezarrois found Rose indispensable. She was his only assistant, and she confessed to her cousin Marguerite that she barely slept and was "overworked."

Among the fifteen exhibits Rose helped organize was a 1937 show called *The Women Artists of Europe*, for which she personally worked on the loans needed and likely influenced its very existence. Rose also worked on the curation of the museum's permanent collection, wrote exhibition catalogs, and gave talks and tours on behalf of the Jeu de Paume in English and French. When she curated exhibitions, her favorite thing to do was to lay all the paintings flat on the ground and see them all at once, then decide how they would be displayed in the various rooms of the museum. For over two years, she also worked on the official Jeu de Paume catalog, which detailed the museum's increasingly large and impressive permanent collection. When the proofs were ready, Dezarrois wrote to Verne that Rose had provided "the most zealous assistance" and that he wanted to "pay a very sincere tribute" to her work on it, but Verne refused and ensured the book would never be published. Was the museum still too nascent and unimportant for the Musées Nationaux to publish an official catalog, despite all the positive reviews from the press and the public? Was the collection too avant-garde for Verne's taste? Or did the mere mention of Rose's name cause him to cancel the multiyear project? Verne gave no recorded reason.

Under Dezarrois's leadership and Rose's loyal assistance, the Jeu de Paume relentlessly pursued international cooperation for exhibitions during challenging political times. The Italian art exhibition in 1935 was celebrated for the breadth and quality of its works, as well as for the political rapprochement it attempted with Italy, already Fascist but wary of the rise of Nazi Germany. During the height of the Spanish Civil War, the Jeu de Paume hosted an exhibition that reframed the art of Catalonia, an autonomous region in Spain oppressed by Francisco

Franco's forces, separating it stylistically from the art of the Spanish peninsula. An Austrian art exhibition opened at the Jeu de Paume in May 1937 as Germany and Italy pressured Austria to capitulate. Ultimately, Germany annexed Austria anyway in March 1938, but Rose reacted adroitly to the state of affairs. By October 1, 1938, only two days after the Munich Agreement was signed, she reorganized the museum's permanent holdings to showcase the art of Czechoslovakia and Poland, each in their own dedicated rooms, in an act of protest. Featuring the art of the contested countries was bold and timely. It demonstrated how nimble the Jeu de Paume was curatorially and how geographically broad its collection was.

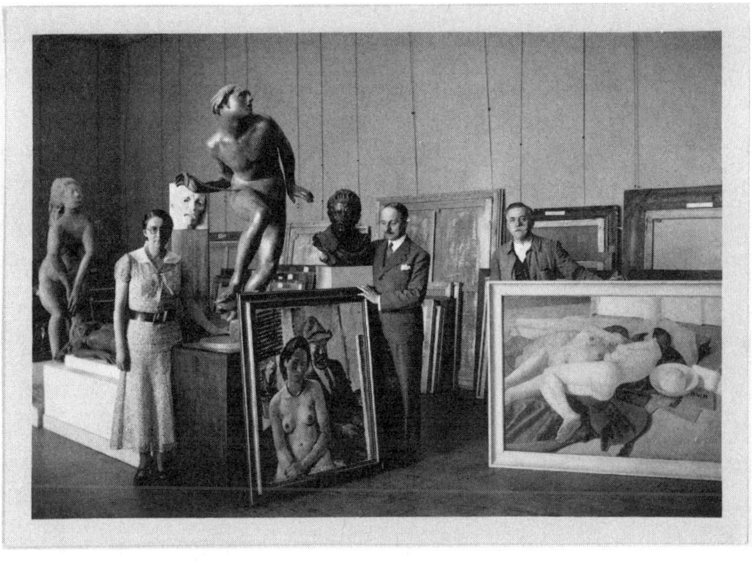

Rose Valland, André Dezarrois, and a guard preparing for the Italian art exhibition at the Jeu de Paume, 1935.

In an uncertain political climate, art was a reminder of the beauty in the world and humanity's capacity for creation. The making and consumption of art was a way to cope with the apprehension people felt, both individually and societally. It was also an opportunity for cross-cultural exchange as borders were threatened or trespassed by unwelcome interlopers. The Jeu de Paume was settling into its role as both an arbiter of international art and as a diplomatic instrument for France. Each exhibition dedicated to a foreign country or foreign artist was an opportunity to strengthen ties between nations, particularly against a backdrop of growing unrest in Europe.

War in France, meanwhile, was still a distant prospect, and Rose remained optimistic, writing to her cousin Marguerite in the spring of 1939, "The events are not very brilliant from an international point of view! But I don't believe in war yet."

Germany invaded Czechoslovakia in mid-March, declaring it the "Protectorate of Bohemia and Moravia." The front page of the French newspapers put the news in large capital letters: "THE GERMAN ARMY OCCUPIED PRAGUE" and "CZECHO-SLOVAKIA is dismembered by Germany." Rose wrote to Marguerite in reaction, "We are on the edge with these international events! What a life! This Hitler turns out to be very tiring."

Uncertainty about war was also bad for Rose's side job as an art dealer, and she elaborated to Marguerite, "I too hope that we will not have war, but these perpetual threats are a real obstacle to business, especially in the luxury trade and I will unfortunately be one of the first to feel it." Although she usually tried to console her anxious cousin, Rose admitted that she would be "very worried" if the ambiguous political situation persisted. Rose lamented the political events unfolding in Europe: "This disrupts everything and thwarts all the business we could have hoped for."

It may have come as a relief to Rose and Marguerite when André Tardieu, the former French prime minister three times over and somewhat affectionately known as the "Shark of French politics," made a reassuring statement about the prospect of war. "I haven't changed my mind as to the chances of a war," he said. "A war is not probable. It will be relatively short. And we will win it." Unfortunately, he would only be correct on one of those counts.

PARIS

SUMMER 1939

THE SUMMER OF 1939 WAS LIVELY AND GAY, EVEN WITH THE SPECTER of war hanging over the populace. The terraces of the cafés near the Paris Opera were packed with men and women of many nationalities discussing the latest goings-on. Fashion magazine *Marie-Claire* reported that the vacationing men in the Côte d'Azur had ditched their somber city attire for bright green, red, and yellow outfits with bold patterning. There was burgeoning interest in the new sport of water skiing, with some trying it at night, which required the extra athleticism of keeping one arm raised to carry a flaming torch. Josephine Baker returned from a South American tour, posing at the train station with a lion, a kangaroo, six monkeys, two chickens, and a fox as new additions to her entourage. She whispered to a reporter that she had returned to one of her true loves—Paris.

A June edition of the *L'Illustration*, one of the definitive cultural magazines in France, was dedicated entirely to the New York World's Fair, the international event in Queens that Rose and Dezarrois had both worked on. He worked on-site in the United States and she in Paris, securing sculptures and other works of art he requested for the exhibition. As an administrator, Henri Verne remained in Paris, and Rose had to deal with him directly on any issues that came up in the museum with Dezarrois out of the office.

Rose had settled into something of a life in Paris. She loved her bright, sun-drenched apartment at 1ter rue de Navarre, just a few blocks from the Jardin des Plantes, the botanical garden of Paris. It was a more muted side of the Latin Quarter, away from the intellectual raucousness of the Boulevard Saint-Michel and its environs. Rose's street was particularly secluded at the top of a long hill behind the ruins of an ancient Roman amphitheater. It suited her naturally discreet personality but was still a close bicycle ride from all her old haunts at the Sorbonne and the École des Beaux-Arts.

Life was exciting amid the winding, medieval streets of old Paris. Hobnobbing on the Left Bank were the likes of Sylvia Beach, who founded the bookstore Shakespeare and Company, and the writer James Joyce. They followed in the footsteps of the expatriate writers of the "Lost Generation," like Ernest Hemingway and F. Scott Fitzgerald, who drank and smoked their way through an outpouring of prolific creativity in the 1920s and '30s

On the Left Bank, one might find Picasso holding court at the Café de Flore, free-flowing with his thoughts and ideas. Gertrude Stein and her lover Alice B. Toklas were still hosting their famous Saturday evening salons at 27 rue de Fleurus, just a block from Rose's first apartment in Paris. "Les Stein," as Gertrude and her brothers Leo and Michael were collectively known, launched the careers of Matisse and Picasso in the early part of the century and remained avid collectors and social connectors within the Parisian art and literary scene.

The studio of surrealist artist Marcel Duchamp at 11 rue Larrey was just a few streets away. Picasso also had a studio nearby. Here, from his cavernous, loft-like atelier on the top floor of 7 rue des Grands-Augustins, Picasso had created his masterpiece of the Spanish Civil War, *Guernica*, beneath the building's immense exposed wooden beams.

Rose lived with her partner, twenty-eight-year-old Joyce Heer. The stunning blue-eyed blond woman, described as a "very bubbly, happy-go-lucky sort of person" by Joyce's niece Auriel, was the perfect foil for Rose. Joyce was a natural beauty with delicate facial features. When she laughed, which was often, her heart-shaped lips would part, and dimples would appear in her cheeks. In photographs taken for identification cards and passports, she looked like a model with ivory skin, arched brow, and flaxen wavy hair, which hung in ringlets at the nape of her neck. She liked to wear fashionable dresses and elegant tailored coats, even when traveling, and never went anywhere without her high-heeled sandals. Whether she was walking around Paris, taking long country walks, or even fetching potatoes from a garden, she always had her sandals on.

Joyce had been raised in style. Born in Liverpool to a British mother and German father, Joyce spent her formative years in England and then attended an all-girls high school in Leipzig. At eighteen years old, she arrived in Paris to study at the Collège Féminin de Bouffémont, a finishing school for high society women. An advertisement for the school proclaimed it trained its students to be "capable of truly becoming intelligent and pleasant wives, mothers of diligent families, or where applicable, women capable of getting by on their own in life." Girls like Joyce were taught how to dress and entertain, encouraged to shop in Paris, attended concerts and museum exhibitions, and took courses to improve their moral and cultural understanding of the world.

Joyce and Rose met at the Collège Féminin de Bouffémont, where Rose had been the French-language teacher since 1924. They also attended the Sorbonne at the same time. Joyce studied the classics and Romantic literature, as well as advanced French, and graduated in 1931 with a diploma in French civilization, while Rose studied modern art and archaeology. They knew each other well enough that when Joyce returned to Paris in 1934 after two and a half years of working as a secretary and stenographer in Chicago, she listed Rose as a reference for her French national identification card. Joyce moved into an apartment on rue Linné, a three-minute walk away from Rose, and by the fall of 1936, the two were living together in Rose's apartment at 1ter rue de Navarre.

Joyce called Rose "Rosette"—a nickname used only by the closest of friends and family—but also had her own affectionate nicknames for her, "Rosie" and "Pouchka." The latter was a Francization of the Russian word *pushka*, meaning a gun or a cannon, which summed Rose up rather perfectly. Rose helped Joyce perfect her French and Joyce helped Rose learn German. Rose was finally in love and in a committed relationship.

Homosexuality was decriminalized in France in 1791 during the French Revolution, but much prejudice still existed against same-sex couples, especially in the traditional setting Rose grew up in and in the ranks of the civil service. As such, Rose and Joyce never publicly acknowledged their relationship.

In Paris, Joyce worked as a secretary and stenographer, first for United Artists reporting to the company's European president, Lacy Kastner. She prepared film contracts in English and German and answered international correspondence. After two years, she joined an American dry goods company as secretary to the president. In January 1937, she began working in the office of the Commercial Attaché at the US embassy in Paris, where she acted as translator, receptionist, and secretary.

Rose's hard work at the Jeu de Paume was starting to reap some benefits. Although still unpaid, she had been essentially an unofficial curator with her *attaché* title since 1936. Her name began to appear in news reports about the museum's exhibition openings. On occasion, she would be listed in the exhibition catalogs. She was communicating directly with such esteemed personages as Alfred H. Barr Jr., the director of the Museum of Modern Art, on the curation of upcoming exhibitions, and her address book was a who's who of the Paris art world including Picasso, Dalí, Kandinsky, Max Ernst, Joseph Stella, and many more. Rose also won a journalism competition organized by the prestigious newspaper *Le Figaro*. Her award-winning article was an art historical analysis of an exhibition on Italian art jointly hosted by the Jeu de Paume and the Petit Palais.

In addition, Rose was instrumental in devising the plan to evacuate the Jeu de Paume's art collection from harm's way if war mobilization ever began, as part of a coordinated effort by the Musées Nationaux. The last thing anyone wanted was a repeat of World War I when France's renowned cultural treasures—the *Mona Lisa*, the Venus de Milo, and around a thousand other artworks—were moved out of Paris only after the Germans invaded France. At that time, curators were told just to send away as many paintings and works of art as possible. The top floor of the Louvre was transformed into a hospital with a Red Cross flag visible through the glass ceiling in the hope it would deter bombings. All of this was done too late for comfort.

In 1932, as a new imperialist order was emerging in Germany, the Musées Nationaux began proactively planning for another war. Rose and the museum curators made priority list after priority list of works to be evacuated and those to be sheltered on-site, as well as lists of materials needed to protect the art, the museum, and the staff.

Maybe this was what Rose had been waiting for—what all her struggles so far were for—to save the art of France. If so, she was ready.

THE BERGHOF, GERMAN ALPS

JUNE 20, 1939

DR. HANS POSSE, A STERN-FACED SIXTY-YEAR-OLD GERMAN ART CURATOR, was being driven up the steep, winding road to the Berghof, Adolf Hitler's mountainside home in the heart of the Alps. As the car—designated officially by a red silk swastika flag—rounded another bend in the road, a breathtaking vista of the lush Bavarian mountains emerged in the early evening summer light.

Posse had received an intriguing telephone call two days earlier. "The Führer would like to see you," Hitler's architect Albert Speer told Posse, phoning directly from the Berghof. The summons, with all its implication of honor and recognition, was a sharp turn of events for the art historian, who had been forced to retire early from his longtime position as director of Dresden's Old Masters Picture Gallery the previous year.

The Picture Gallery was one of the most renowned museums in Europe. It had a collection of over three thousand paintings, predominantly from the thirteenth to eighteenth centuries, by the so-called Old Masters, including Raphael, Giotto, Titian, Rembrandt, and Vermeer. One of the Picture Gallery's most famous works was Raphael's *Sistine Madonna*, which features two cherubic angels at its bottom edge, blissfully unaware that they would later become one of the most reproduced visages in the world. While German, Italian, and Dutch paintings historically predominated the collection, by 1939, the museum also had a growing group of modern works from the nineteenth and twentieth centuries.

The reason for Posse's ouster: he had purchased and displayed modern "degenerate" paintings in the museum and was known to have a soft spot for German expressionists. Posse had also created a modern art division in the museum, curated three major modern art exhibitions—twice at the Venice Biennale and once at the International Art Exhibition in Dresden—and published a catalog in 1930 focused purely on the museum's modern paintings. In the catalog preface, Posse urgently campaigned for a new building dedicated specifically to modern art. He went as far as to reproach previous directors of having "an art policy that looks back to the past as if spellbound that hinders the continuation of the collection into modern times."

Unfortunately for Posse, Hitler's hatred of avant-garde art—now given the catchy label "*Entartete Kunst*" ("degenerate art")—had increased in virility. His disdain was likely rooted in his own failures as an artist. In his late teens, Hitler had been rejected twice from the Academy of Fine Arts in Vienna. The first rejection in 1907 struck him like a lightning "bolt from the skies," as he later recounted in his book *Mein Kampf*. He had been utterly confident he would be accepted, convinced it would be "child's play to pass the examination." In his own estimation, he was the best art student "by far" in his high school (although his report card showed more mixed results). In a state of shock, Hitler sought feedback from the school's director. He was told that the drawings he submitted showed that, without a doubt, he was "unfit" for painting. Perhaps he might find some success studying architecture instead, suggested the director. After all, his portfolio was full of paintings of buildings.

That, too, was a dead end. Entrance to the School of Architecture required attending the Building School at the Vienna Technik, and entrance to the Technik was only open to high school graduates. But Hitler never graduated from high school. He had deliberately neglected his studies to spite his father, who had pronounced that Hitler would never become a professional artist. "Artist, no, never as long as I live!" his father had yelled derisively.

By the age of twenty, Hitler had lost both his parents, and his artistic dreams were dashed. He misspent the small inheritance left to him and lived in abject poverty in Vienna, working as a day laborer and churning out derivative paintings for tourists—copies of postcards showing the city's famous landmarks. He slept on park benches and in homeless shelters. But it couldn't be his own fault, he reasoned. His rejection from the arts and cultural world in Vienna must have been due to forces beyond his control.

"Wherever I now went I saw Jews," he wrote in *Mein Kampf*, adding, "was there any form of filth or profligacy, particularly in cultural life, without at least one Jew involved in it? . . . What had to be reckoned heavily against the Jews in my eyes was when I became acquainted with their activity in the press, art, literature, and the theater." Jews, Hitler claimed, were "a people who, even in outer appearance, bore no similarity to the Germans," and if so, his logic followed, why should they be the gatekeepers of Germanic culture? Hitler became more and more appalled by what he deemed Jewish creations of "unclean products in public cultural life . . . literary filth, artistic trash and theatrical idiocy." The answer was painfully obvious to Hitler: all the art that he could not comprehend was created by those he considered "non-German"—Jews, Bolsheviks, and urban "cosmopolitan" types—who were deliberately keeping him out. It was all a conspiracy, of which he was the victim.

Even if Hitler simplified his own anti-Semitic origin story in *Mein*

Kampf for propaganda reasons, the rise of two nationalist politicians—Georg Ritter von Schönerer and Karl Lueger—had greatly influenced Hitler's beliefs. Lueger, an early demagogue and the mayor of Vienna from 1897 to 1910, demonstrated how anti-Semitism could be used to energize a base of voters. Hitler described Lueger as "the greatest German mayor of all times." Meanwhile, von Schönerer was even more of a spiritual inspiration to Hitler. Schönerer called himself "Führer" and began the use of "Heil" in greeting. He advocated for the incorporation of the German-speaking areas of Austria and Hungary into a greater Germany. In addition, he demanded "the removal of Jewish people from all sections of public life," contending that the Jewish people in Germany should not be full citizens. Jewish, Slavic, or non-German citizens were not allowed to be members of his political movement, and each member had to prove they were of Aryan descent—those of pure German or European ancestry—and pass a health examination to show they had no genetic or physical defects.

In 1931, as Hitler was leading the Nazi Party to unprecedented success in German parliamentary elections, he announced that he would "release a tornado" against modern art. Two years later, he unleashed that storm. Upon his appointment as chancellor of Germany in 1933, Hitler officially announced a new art policy specifying that "all artistic productions with cosmopolitan or Bolshevik tendencies must be thrown out of German museums and collections." At Hitler's order, degenerate art was to be taken from museums, shown to the public with a price tag calling out the museum official who bought it, and then burned. Hitler gave the German people four years to rid the country of degenerate art.

In a 1935 speech in Nuremberg, Hitler increased his threats, stating, "One will no longer discuss or deal with these corruptors of art. They are fools, liars, or criminals who belong in insane asylums or prisons." In 1937, under the direction of Reich Minister of Propaganda Joseph Goebbels, the Nazis removed over sixteen thousand modern artworks by fourteen hundred artists from German museums in two waves of seizures.

The same year, in a speech to inaugurate the House of German Art—a new museum in Munich created to showcase all the acceptable forms of German art—Hitler clarified what styles of art were to be eradicated. "Cubism, dadaism, futurism, impressionism, and so on, have nothing to do with our German people," Hitler announced vociferously inside the light-filled atrium of the House of German Art in front of a two-stories-tall swastika banner. "For all of these terms are neither old nor modern, but are simply the stilted stammering of people to whom God has denied real artistic talent and has given instead the gift of blather and deception." In his curse-laden and increasingly hysterical speech, Hitler foamed at the mouth, convulsed, banged on the podium, and waved his hands in the air.

One day after the inauguration of the House of German Art, the *Entartete Kunst* ("*Degenerate Art*") exhibition opened in Munich and was so popular it went on a multiyear tour to a dozen German cities. Some 650 of the degenerate artworks seized from German museums were put on display in the exhibition. All were shown as examples of how the country was going through a "cultural decline." "German *Volk*, come judge for yourselves," entreated Adolf Ziegler, the president of the Reich Chamber of Fine Arts, at the opening. Painted in black above a doorway were the words "*Sie hatten vier Jahre Zeit*" ("They had four years' time"), goading the artists who still refused to change their art style as directed by the Nazi regime.

Visitors perused the multiple rooms of degenerate art with grave faces, taking in the deliberately haphazard hanging of artworks, reading the didactic information cards, and crying, "Blasphemy!" "The artists are making fun of us," people were heard to say, calling the works displayed "*dumm*" ("stupid"). But some seemed to appreciate the art covertly. On the lower level of the exhibition, in front of a curation of graphic art, a woman whispered, "Aren't they lovely?" before darting away.

Emblazoned on the wall were jarring statements censuring the art like "*Deutsche ßauern, jüdisch gesehen*" ("German farmers, a Yiddish view"), "*Ideal: Krein und Hure*" ("Ideal: Cretin and Whore"), "*Verhöh-*

nung des Gotteslebens" ("Insolent Mockery of the Divine"), and "*Beleidigung deutscher Frauen*" ("An Insult to German Women"). In some cases, modern drawings and paintings were exhibited side by side with those done by so-called "inmate[s] of a lunatic asylum," in an attempt to associate the two. Red price tags were displayed alongside the art that read, "Paid for with the hard-earned wages of German working *Volk*." Among the artworks were paintings by Kandinsky, Beckmann, Piet Mondrian, Paul Klee, Edvard Munch, and many by the Nazi Party member Emil Nolde. One room was dedicated to Jewish painters, including Marc Chagall, with the title "*Offenbarung der jüdischen Rassenseele*" ("Revelation of the Jewish racial soul"). A color lithograph by Pablo Picasso was also on display.

Over one million people visited the *Degenerate Art* exhibition in its first six weeks, more than three times the number of people who saw the *Great German Art Exhibition* at the House of German Art.

Posse heard Hitler's speech at the House of German Art on the radio at home and quickly removed the remaining "degenerate" paintings on view in the Old Masters Picture Gallery. He assiduously implemented Hitler's new rules, shutting down the museum's modern art division and refocusing his efforts on a new building for German painting right in line with Third Reich ideology. Posse also cleverly rewrote his past, detaching himself where possible from the modern art collection at the museum, which included paintings by Paul Gauguin, Vincent van Gogh, Gustav Klimt, Chagall, Kandinsky, and others.

Despite Posse's rebranding efforts, he had been targeted by eager local politicians looking to please the new Nazi regime, as well as art historians who hoped to usurp his position. In March 1938, Posse was pressured by the Saxon Ministry for Public Education to resign. As a compromise, he was allowed to take an early retirement but was technically still on the job until he turned sixty.

Hitler himself then intervened on Posse's behalf, showing up at the Old Masters Picture Gallery as a "birthday gift" to his favorite art dealer, Karl Haberstock, who was a friend of Posse's. "Put Posse back as director," Haberstock had told Hitler. "He's considered to be the greatest museum expert in Germany, but just lost his position through some trifling difference with a local party official."

"You are said to have purchased such horrible pictures," Hitler had challenged Posse in the museum, but the art director explained that he had only added thirty-three avant-garde paintings to the gallery, and most were donated or on loan to the museum. A mere nine paintings were purchased directly by him using state funds. After reviewing the museum's acquisition documents, Hitler decided that Posse should be reinstated as director.

On the same day, Hitler had secretly authorized the confiscation of property belonging to people "hostile to the state," citing, in particular, Jewish property in Austria. He gave himself authority to decide how the stolen goods would be used, which meant he needed an efficient operator to allocate it all. Hitler was also looking for someone to lead his greatest cultural vision, the Führermuseum, to be built in Linz, Austria, where he was raised. Posse had all the right skills for the job and the kind of ambition Hitler liked to see—a "*Führerpersönlichkeit*" (a leader type of personality). He had been impressed by Posse's wit, his deep art knowledge, and his self-assuredness. Posse was a lavish sycophant prone to superlatives and exclamation marks and experienced at giving tours to important people. Hitler was easily flattered by educated experts, especially when their tastes aligned with his own.

Posse was certainly not against cultural plunder either. He was a favorite pupil of the famous art historian Wilhelm von Bode, who had transformed Germany's state art collection into a tribute to the nation's imperial prowess under King Frederick II. In fact, during World War I, Posse wrote to von Bode: "I myself would be delighted to be present at the dissolution of the Louvre." He might soon get that chance. According to Albert Speer, Hitler was seeking Posse's advice on the "Linz museum matter."

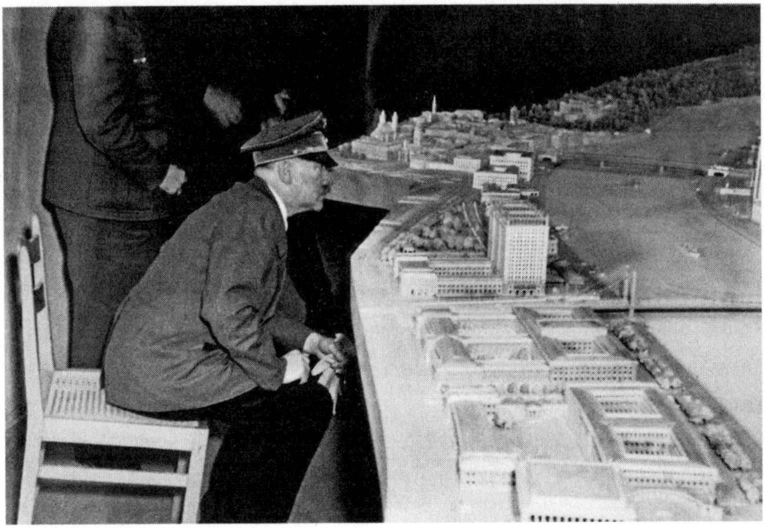

Hitler looks at the model for the redesign of Linz in the basement of the New Reich Chancellery, Berlin, on the evening of February 9, 1945.

THE DRIVER CAREFULLY MANEUVERED A precipitous, thirteen-hundred-foot ascent along a narrow, twisting road up the Obersalzberg mountain. As the car passed through multiple armed gates, Posse readied himself for the momentous meeting. He was a workaholic, and this would be the assignment of his career if everything went well. Like Hitler, Posse believed fundamentally in Germany's greatness, particularly in the superiority of Germanic culture. If the Third Reich was the means by which Germany could claim its rightful place in cultural history, so be it. Posse also owed Hitler a favor for restoring his position at the Picture Gallery. After passing the final guardhouse, Posse's car rounded a last curve and pulled up to the steps of the large chalet-inspired complex. It was the night before the summer solstice, and still bright out. The white stucco structure gleamed in contrast with the surrounding deep green firs.

The Berghof was designed to impress and had robust security measures, as Hitler used the property as both a personal country estate and a headquarters for meetings and official state visits. In addition to the numerous guard posts, the *Schutzstaffel* (the SS), the Nazi Party's paramilitary security force, also had its base of operations on the mountain. Following his lead, Hitler's top officials, including Hermann Göring, Albert Speer, and Martin Bormann, Hitler's private secretary and head of the Nazi Party Chancellery, had homes on Obersalzberg as well.

Upon exiting the car, Posse was greeted by Hitler's aide-de-camp and took the grand stairs up from the driveway. At the top of the staircase, built into a grassy slope, he was ushered through an open-air colonnade to the front door, which gave way to a Romanesque-vaulted hallway decorated with large potted cactuses. Immediately to the right was a door that led into the Berghof's Grand Hall, where Posse's meeting with Hitler and Albert Speer would take place.

The most stunning feature of the Grand Hall was a thirty-foot-wide, twelve-foot-tall window. Made of ninety leaded glass panels, the window could be retracted entirely through a mechanism that lowered all the panels and frames into the floor below, creating a picture-perfect open-air postcard view of the mountains. "From my window, I can see my father's homeland at all times," Hitler once said, referring to his view of Salzburg from there.

Posse made a mental note of the works of art displayed: *Venus and Amor* by Paris Bordone, a François Boucher, a Moritz von Schwind, and *Madonna and Child* by Giuliano Bugiardini above the red marble fireplace. Hitler had personally hung them on the walls.

It took Hitler forty-five minutes to describe his plans for the Führermuseum. Hitler wanted his new museum in Linz to have the best art from all epochs of Germanic history and to outshine the collections in the Austrian capital. The ground floor would contain prehistoric art and older periods, while the second floor would start from the nineteenth century. The art was to come from the existing German state collection, new acquisitions, and confiscated property, like that already amassed from Jewish-owned collections seized in Austria.

When Hitler showed off his art, Posse did not hesitate to offer his unadulterated opinion. "Barely useful," he said, dismissing one painting. "Not in keeping with the stature of the gallery as I conceive it," he said of another. Despite the frankness of the feedback, Hitler accepted Posse's assessments. As Speer later noted about Hitler's interactions with Posse, "As was so often the case when Hitler was dealing with a specialist, he accepted the criticisms without demur."

Hitler bestowed on Posse an immense amount of responsibility and power. "I will give you all the necessary instructions and powers of attorney. Apart from that, you only deal with me. I will decide." Hitler wanted Linz to be a showcase for a new type of city, an industrial and cultural capital in one. Never letting go of his vendetta against Vienna, Hitler called the city culturally "overfed," receiving more than its fair share of artistic capital, leaving the provincial towns of Austria to be forgotten and "left to degenerate."

Hitler told Posse he was gratified that he had won him over for this project and emphasized that the museum was not only important culturally, but politically as well. The Führermuseum would be the linchpin in his war to save Germany's culture from its supposed precipitous decline. The Third Reich would last a thousand years, with art and architecture—the right kind—as a major pillar. With his superior aesthetic taste, Hitler himself would define what pure Germanic art and architecture should be.

Six days later, on June 26, 1939, Posse was officially appointed the head of the Führermuseum project, known as the "*Sonderauftrag Linz*" ("Special Commission Linz"). Hitler wrote in the decree, "All party and state offices are obliged to Mr. Posse in fulfilling his task." Posse was given a new title, "Special Representative of the Führer," to append to his existing title as "Director of the Dresden Picture Gallery." He was also given an additional 1,000 Reichsmarks per month, on top of his salary at Dresden's Old Picture Gallery, and 10,000 Reichsmarks for travel and expenses related to his work on the Führermuseum.

The game was on. Posse was about to create a collection that would surpass even Hitler's imagination, and Rose Valland would soon be in the middle of it all.

LUCERNE, SWITZERLAND

JUNE 30, 1939

THREE HUNDRED AND FIFTY PEOPLE CROWDED INTO THE ESCOFFIER salon of the Grand Hotel in Lucerne, a bustling and fashionable city in central Switzerland. The atmosphere inside the room was raucous. Cigarette smoke and chatter filled the air. An auction of the most unusual nature was about to unfold.

Most of the attendees were Swiss spectators seated in tightly packed rows—the men in suits, the women in stylish hats and elegant summer dresses. Scattered amid the gawkers was a smattering of art dealers, private buyers, and art museum directors who came mostly from Belgium and the Netherlands. There were only a few buyers from the United States, and the French were conspicuously absent.

Some of the world's most famous modern masterpieces were up for sale. Among the 125 works of art on the block were Picasso's *Absinthe Drinker* (one of four of his works to be auctioned), Van Gogh's *Self-Portrait: Dedicated to Paul Gauguin*, Gauguin's *Landscape of Tahiti with Three Female Tigers*, Chagall's *La Maison Bleue*, and Matisse's *Bathers with a Turtle*. A rumor spread through the audience that an offer of 1 million Swiss francs was already made for the self-portrait of Van Gogh. In it, the artist depicted himself in 1888 with a shaved head and gaunt face against a swirling teal background, his eyes looking listlessly to the side. Van Gogh was inspired by techniques he saw in Japanese prints.

There were also paintings by artists who had all been presented at the Jeu de Paume, including Georges Braque, James Ensor, and Paul Klee. Eighteen paintings and one sculpture came from the infamous 1937 *Degenerate Art* exhibition in Munich. The rest was a small but notable portion of the more than sixteen thousand modern artworks seized from the museums in Germany.

Switzerland was open for business to everyone, including the

Nazis. Even as geopolitical tensions rose feverishly in Europe, the country steadfastly maintained its neutrality, as it had in World War I. Theodor Fischer, a bushy-eye-browed, sixty-one-year-old Swiss art dealer and auctioneer with the right Aryan pedigree, was selected by the Nazis to manage the sale. He was also a close friend of Karl Haberstock, Hitler's personal art dealer. Fischer eagerly put himself forward for the job with the Commission for the Disposal of Products of Degenerate Art at the Ministry of Propaganda, run by Joseph Goebbels. As it turned out, there were no other dealers with the requisite expertise in Switzerland who were not Jewish, so Fischer was the only candidate. He knew for months that the auction proceeds would go to the Third Reich and had no issue with it.

Fischer took out newspaper advertisements announcing the event as one of the "major auctions" of his gallery in 1939 with "paintings and sculptures, by modern masters, from museums in Germany" and a long list of artists' names. He sent auction catalogs directly to art collectors, museum directors, and gallery owners all around the world. A month-long exhibition of the artworks ran at the famed Zunfthaus zur Meisen in Zurich in advance of the auction.

The quality of the art was indisputably high. But it was widely known by art collectors and journalists that the proceeds from the sale would go to the war coffers of the Nazi Party. By that point, Hermann Göring had a reputation as a ruthless Nazi operator with an insatiable appetite for art and luxury goods. "Behind the Fischer Gallery there is Mr. Göring," wrote the French journalist and art critic Raymond Escholier in *Le Journal* eleven days before the auction. Without irony, he stated that Göring was the gallery's best client.

Paul Rosenberg, one of the most renowned art dealers in France, took a courageous public stand to boycott the auction. Staunchly anti-Nazi, he and his compatriots favored a rallying cry: "Not a cent to the German Reich." Rosenberg admonished buyers that the money made from this sale "would fall back on our heads in the form of bombs," and the Nazis blacklisted him in retaliation.

The Americans worried about the sale, too. The banker and art collector Maurice Wertheim pressured Fischer on the actual ownership of the paintings and asked him to confirm if the money would go to Germany. Fischer countered, "Rumors originate from Paris by big dealer endeavoring trust using political arguments." He claimed to be the victim of "Jewish propaganda" and wrote to Haberstock, "You do not realize how the Jews are plotting everywhere."

Fischer also sent a letter to all his clients calling out the "vehement propaganda" in America to "boycott this sensational public sale, pretending that the proceeds will go to Germany for the purposes of armament. The argument is ridiculous and wrong." He clarified that the funds from the sale "will be distributed in favour of the German museums so as to enable them to buy other works of art." To counter the bad press, Hitler himself announced, "I decided to sell these paintings quickly in Switzerland. If democratic amateurs find them to their taste, let them pay for them. This will give us money to buy good German paintings."

The stakes that day were high. By bringing out the crème de la crème of the degenerate crop, the Germans were hoping for a large financial haul. "We hope to at least make some money from this garbage," Goebbels wrote in his diary about the sale of degenerate art on the international art market. For potential buyers, it was not only an opportunity to acquire some of the best art in the world, but the purchase might also save the works from a terrible fate. There was no telling if another purge of art might take place, like one that occurred on March 20 earlier that year, five days after Hitler invaded Czechoslovakia. Four thousand and eight hundred of the degenerate paintings and drawings were taken from German museums and burned in a conflagration in the courtyard of Berlin's central fire department on Köpernickerstrasse.

At the auction in Lucerne, a stage had been set up. A large curtain hung in front of the mirrored side doors to keep the focus purely on the art. A floodlight at the edge of the front row illuminated the works. In the adjoining salon, over one hundred paintings were stacked upright, dozens deep, awaiting their turn on the stage.

At three o'clock, Theodor Fischer walked up to the front of the room to begin the auction. Up until now, the artistic elite in Switzerland had shunned him, preferring to buy from one of his rivals, a Jewish refugee art dealer. The Swiss-German newspaper of record, the *Neue Zürcher Zeitung*, had also largely ignored his event. Like Hitler, Fischer imagined that a Jewish conspiracy was hindering his career, and he wrote to Haberstock, "These gentlemen use such means and I have to fight against such people, just because I'm not Jewish."

Fischer surveyed the crowd. The serious buyers sat along the front. Paul Rosenberg's public declaration against the event appeared to have had an impact; little or no French buyers were seen at the auction. But some major dealers and museum directors from other countries were present. Alfred Frankfurter, the editor of *ArtNews* and a member of the 1939 New York World's Fair committee, came to bid on behalf of investment banker Maurice Wertheim. Italian art historian Lionello Venturi, known to travel long distances just to window shop, was there, too. So was Emil Bührle, the Swiss arms manufacturer. Making a big splash at the auction was handsome twenty-six-year-old Joseph Pulitzer Jr., son of the newspaper magnate, in Europe on his honeymoon with his stylish new wife, Louise Vauclain.

Pierre Matisse, a successful art dealer in New York and the son of Henri Matisse, was also in attendance and would be bidding on Pulitzer's behalf that day. To Pierre, *Bathers with a Turtle* was his father's masterpiece, and its survival could not be left to chance. Pulitzer was the right man to save the work, as the *St. Louis Post-Dispatch* journalist and arts philanthropist had the means and was already an avid collector of modern art, especially Picassos.

In May, Curt Valentin, another dealer friend of Pulitzer's, had sent him the auction catalog. Valentin was Jewish but had been allowed by the German government to emigrate to the United States in 1937. He established the New York branch of his former gallery, the Buchholz

Gallery, with stock of degenerate art seized from Germany in his luggage and the understanding that he would send proceeds back to fund the war effort.

Valentin also represented at least one secret client: Alfred H. Barr Jr., the founding director of the Museum of Modern Art in New York City, who would be using funds from the museum trustees. He was working on a retrospective exhibition of Picasso for the fall with his friend Paul Rosenberg. For Barr, the art up for grabs apparently was worth disregarding Rosenberg's warnings about provenance.

Fischer took a seat at the table on the elevated platform alongside two female staffers from his gallery who would record the bids and purchases. He was now ready with the gavel.

A shout came from the front, summoning the editor of *ArtNews:* "Herr Dr. Frankfurter, come to the telephone!" An important phone call had come in for Frankfurter.

Proceedings were put on hold until he was done. When he returned, the auction commenced.

A man in a white lab coat pointed to the sculpture of *Mrs. Kamenev* by Alexander Archipenko. Bidding started at 200 Swiss francs and it sold for 370 francs—less than half its estimate. The rest of the sculptures, apart from the Lehmbrucks, did not fare much better. A bust of Nietzsche did not meet the reserve price and was left unsold.

The most notable aspect of the auction, though, was the utter contempt displayed by Fischer. The art dealer, at the beginning of a long campaign of ingratiation into Nazi dealings, eagerly showed his loyalties. "Nobody wants that," he said with malicious relish when a painting of a woman failed to meet the minimum, adding, "this lady does not please the public."

As the painting was taken away, he announced triumphantly, "Withdrawn!" Although none of the Nazi bigwigs were in attendance, Fischer's desire to send a signal to leadership clearly trumped his desire for his commission.

The audience became particularly animated when the star painting, Van Gogh's *Self-Portrait,* appeared. Would it go for the rumored 1 million francs? Flashbulbs went off as the press documented the moment. Fischer announced an order bid from an absentee buyer for 145,000 francs. He repeated this in English, French, and German. Someone countered with a bid for 150,000 francs. It was announced that the bidding increment would be 5,000 francs going forward. The price rose to 165,000.

"Going once, twice, three times—sold!" Fischer bellowed and banged the gavel.

The audience members talked excitedly back and forth with each other. What a deal! But it was not over yet.

A man piped up that his bid had been missed.

Remarkably, Fischer acquiesced. "Place your bets!" the audience was told as bidding reopened.

One of the Belgian coalitions, led by Auguste Buisseret, the Liège alderman of fine arts, went in at 170,000. Frankfurter countered with an offer for 175,000.

The Belgians could not go any higher.

Fischer said again, "Going once, going twice . . . three times . . . sold!" The painting was Frankfurter's for 175,000 Swiss francs plus a 70,000-franc commission for Fischer. It sold at 80,000 francs below the pre-auction estimate.

As soon as the painting was taken down, Frankfurter slid it into his car trunk and sped away while spectators looked on, engrossed by the drama. The urgent phone call he had received earlier was a warning about unrest in the free city of Danzig, a contested port town on the border of Poland and Germany. Frankfurter was not going to stay in Europe any longer than necessary. Maurice Wertheim, the painting's new owner, would bequeath it to the Fogg Museum at Harvard University in 1951, where it still remains.

The three-hour auction brought in only 660,000 francs, two-thirds of what was anticipated. Two of the four Matisse paintings went for half their estimates. A few paintings sold above expectation, including a moody Amedeo Modigliani portrait of a woman with a characteristically elongated neck. Forty works of art, including two by Picasso—*The Absinthe Drinker* and *Head of a Woman*—did not sell at all because their reserve prices were not met.

"'Decadent' Sale Fails," proclaimed the London *Daily Herald*, whose reporter added a personal opinion that the paintings were not degenerate "either in subject or treatment, which lends colour to the view that the Nazis' object was not so much the purification of German art as 'real money.'" A correspondent from the London *Daily News* reported that the auction "must have been disappointing to the Nazi authorities if the object was to secure foreign currency."

The Belgians were crushed about losing the Van Gogh self-portrait but still made out very well, winning sixteen bids, including two Picassos and works by Gauguin, Chagall, Max Liebermann, Emil Nolde, Franz Marc, and others.

Curt Valentin's clandestine mission for the Museum of Modern Art was also fruitful. He purchased five paintings on Barr's behalf: Matisse's *The Blue Window*, Paul Klee's *Around the Fish*, Ernst Ludwig Kirchner's *Street Scene*, Wilhelm Lehmbruck's sculpture *Kneeling Woman*, and André Derain's *Valley of the Lost at Vers.*

Barr was in Paris while the auction unfolded but was duly updated and wrote the next day to the Museum of Modern Art's executive director Thomas Mabry, "I am just as glad not to have the museum's name or my own associated with the auction." He added that it was very important that the press releases from the museum state that the works of art were purchased from the Buchholz Gallery in New York.

No such secrecy was necessary for the Pulitzers. Pierre Matisse successfully netted three works for Pulitzer—the much-desired *Bathers with a Turtle*, a sculpture of a seated girl by Lehmbruck, and a painting of three women by Otto Mueller. The newspaper publisher told a reporter, "To safeguard the art for posterity, I bought—defiantly!"

The art purchased at the auction in Lucerne went out all over the world into museums and private collections, but *Nietzsche* and many of the other unsold works would never be seen again. Even more "degenerate art" would soon pass by Rose Valland's watchful eye.

JEU DE PAUME

JULY 24, 1939

IN A NEAT SCRIPT, ROSE MARKED THE JEU DE PAUME'S LATEST ACQUISITION in the museum's inventory register. Entry number 929 was a self-portrait by the Mexican painter Frida Kahlo. Rose wrote "*Portrait de l'Artiste*" ("Portrait of the Artist") in her proud and erect penmanship. Colloquially, the painting was being referred to as "The Frame." On the inventory, it ended up sandwiched between a painting of Don Quixote by the American artist Richard Florsheim and an oil painting of a Mexican market in Tehuantepec by the Italian artist Luigi Settanni—all entered by Rose on the same day. In "The Frame," Frida painted herself on a sheet of aluminum, with her hair pulled back and a yellow flower atop her head. With pursed lips, she gazes out below her signature heavy brow.

Rose had no idea these works would be the last she would add to the register for nearly eight months. After all, the Jeu de Paume was on a buying spree that year. Sixty paintings and eight sculptures had been added within the previous year. It was easy to imagine that the pace would simply continue in tandem with the museum's growing renown.

Rose had overseen this record book since the museum's opening in 1932. Yet, the inventory had no room for female artists in its nomenclature. "*Nom du maître*"—"Name of master"—was printed atop the second column with no feminine version of the French word. More women artists had been added to the museum's permanent collection since Rose started working there, and she made it a point to add "*Mme*," short for *Madame*, in the register next to the women's names.

Frida was presented in Europe and the United States as the wife of Diego Rivera, and Rose duly named her here as Frida de Rivera. Kahlo, Frida's real last name and the one she preferred, was missing.

Rose was also operating in the shadows behind a more powerful male figure, her boss, André Dezarrois. She was essentially running the museum now, curating and installing exhibitions, managing the custodial staff, and maintaining the building. She was also intimately familiar with, if not influential in the decision to purchase "The Frame," but in the end, it was up to Dezarrois to formally request its acquisition.

With characteristically self-derogatory flair, Frida derided "The Frame" as an "idiotic photo in a frame decorated with parrots, the most horrible piece of shit I've painted." But Dezarrois was delighted. The Jeu de Paume did not have anything of note from Mexico in the collection, and he was eager to rectify that. He thought Kahlo was "curious and gifted," on top of being the wife of Diego Rivera, whom he called "the greatest living painter in the Americas." Dezarrois wanted to host an exhibition of Mexican art at the Jeu de Paume and calculated that buying a work by Frida might connect him to Rivera. The painting was exhibited in Paris as part of an exhibition about Mexican art at the gallery Renou et Colle. After visiting the exhibition, artist Wassily Kandinsky and gallery owner Maurice Renou both selected "The Frame" as their favorite. Frida herself attended the opening but was having a hard time, physically and mentally, in Paris, with a long hospitalization for an infection.

Dezarrois told Frida with childlike excitement when they met aboard the SS *Normandie* on his way to the New York World's Fair at the end of March that year, "You don't know it, but I went to the gallery three times, from before the opening until we decided which of your paintings to buy." "We love it," he said of "The Frame."

The Jeu de Paume paid one thousand francs for what would turn out to be the only purchase of Frida's work from the Mexico exhibition at Renou et Colle. Frida blamed the poor sales on the impending war, proclaiming that "the rich bitches don't want to buy anything." But all in all, it was a real coup for Rose, Dezarrois, and the Jeu de Paume, which became the first major museum anywhere in the world to acquire a work by Frida Kahlo. Even Frida could be pleased: "The Frame" went for a price higher than any other painting she sold before. More importantly, she could finally leave France and the French. "Let them eat shit," she griped, "I'm going home."

ÉVIAN, FRANCE

AUGUST 1939

EIGHTEEN-YEAR-OLD ALEXANDRE ROSENBERG WAS SPENDING THE summer holiday with his family at the luxurious Hôtel Royal—the upscale Belle Époque resort sprawled across a hilltop in Évian, the spa town famous for its mineral springs. The hotel, built by the Évian Mineral Water Company, was originally planned as a retreat for King Edward VII of England, who vowed to be one of its first patrons. He died before that could come to pass, but the hotel kept the "Royal" in its name, nonetheless. On the Hôtel Royal's outdoor terraces and inside its ornate vaulted rotundas, one could still find royalty from Europe, the United Kingdom, or even the Middle East and Japan.

All of Évian was dedicated to leisure. Holiday trippers could take the wood and steel funicular from the quayside at Lake Geneva, stopping at the thermal baths, the hotels, and the *buvette cachat*, a magnificent art nouveau pavilion of wood and stained glass. There, at this temple to water, a global gathering of chic clientele mingled and imbibed under a spectacular wooden dome. Apart from some talk of impending war, the summer of 1939 felt merry and blithe, just like any other holiday season in Évian.

Alexandre, a serious young man with a shy half-smile, did not consider the society scene his cup of tea. Everyone close to him called him Kiki, a nickname his parents gave him shortly after he was born. With a mop of brown hair, high cheekbones, and round tortoiseshell glasses, Alexandre had the youthful intensity of a boy in search of where he could make his mark. He had a fascination for rare books, and was interested in philosophy, math, and literature. He was studying at the Sorbonne and about to start his second year of university, but war had put that all in flux.

Alexandre's father, the preeminent Parisian art dealer Paul Rosenberg, who had boycotted the recent degenerate art auction in Lucerne, was preoccupied with his work as usual. Paul represented Picasso, Braque, Matisse, Fernand Léger, and Marie Laurencin, and had the right of first refusal for all their creations. His clientele included some of the most famous art collectors and museums around the world. He had devoted much of his time that year planning the Picasso retrospective at the Museum of Modern Art in New York.

The Rosenberg family had come to Évian for Paul's health, which had been fragile for decades. The fresh air and therapeutic water offered a possible cure for his stomach ulcer and other ailments, and they had summered there for years.

Among the illustrious guests checking into the hotel the same week as the Rosenbergs were Charles Corbin, the French ambassador to Great Britain; Count Charles de Chambrun, the former French ambassador to Italy; the Maharaja and Maharani of India; the Princess Bishnu of Nepal; the count and countess of Zagreb; and two Rosenberg relations, Yvon Helft, Paul's brother-in-law, and Marguerite Loévi, Paul's mother-in-law.

Artists loved the place, too: Marcel Proust wrote parts of *In Search of Lost Time* at the resort, and the French actor Sacha Guitry brought many of his wives and lovers there. (Incidentally, Guitry would soon undertake a far more dangerous mission than a love affair: he and his latest actress wife were about to smuggle two replica Enigma machines—cipher devices used by Nazi Germany—within their proliferation of suitcases to London's Victoria Station. The machines were bound for Bletchley Park, a secret war station for British codebreaking and intelligence in England, and would soon land in the hands of cryptographer Alan Turing.)

While on vacation, Paul continued to run his business, the Galerie Rosenberg, in Paris, but he was preparing for war to come. He wrote to Picasso from the hotel that he was "conscious of the dark events ahead." Naturally apprehensive, with the additional weight of having been mobilized in World War I, Paul followed the developments in Europe closely and with growing trepidation.

The previous year, at the urging of US President Franklin Delano Roosevelt, thirty-two countries had convened at the Hôtel Royal with the goal of finding a multinational agreement to increase amnesty acceptance quotas for the growing number of Jewish refugees fleeing Nazi Germany. Almost all the countries refused, except for Australia, the United Kingdom, and the Dominican Republic, which agreed to take one hundred thousand refugees. The United States backpedaled and did not increase its own quota of thirty thousand per year. The bungled opportunity had direct consequences, trapping the Jewish population—already stripped of their citizenship and rights—in Germany and, subsequently, Czechoslovakia. Kristallnacht, a murderous and devastating pogrom against Jews in the Third Reich, took place in November 1938, just four months after the failed Évian Conference.

Paul's parents were Jewish immigrants from Bratislava, a city on the border of Hungary and Slovakia. Paul was not worried about having his citizenship revoked in France but was focused on keeping his family and his art collection out of the path of the German army. Six of his paintings—two Picassos, two Braques, one by Camille Corot, and one by Gustave Courbet—were in Buenos Aires for a French-government-sponsored exhibition called *French Painting from David to Today*. Thirty-two of his Picasso paintings had just arrived in New York to be included in the Museum of Modern Art retrospective on the artist, with eight more arriving shortly. Another, *The Violinist*, was already on loan to the museum.

Paul was now thinking of moving his entire art collection to the Museum of Modern Art, where the director, Alfred H. Barr Jr., eagerly offered to provide a safe harbor for it "in the event of war," something he also offered to Picasso, who personally loaned ninety-five pieces for the retrospective exhibition. Barr was more opportunistic than altruistic—after all, storing the art would provide the director with easy access to some of the most coveted works for future exhibitions.

Meanwhile, the Évian cure was doing wonders for Paul, who told Picasso by letter, "I'm feeling like a charm . . . I have . . . the agility of a cat!" and encouraged his friend to visit him.

When not on summer holiday, the Rosenbergs lived together in Paris in a large house at 21 rue la Boétie, a few streets north of the Élysée Palace, the residence of the president of France. The six-story ashlar stone building was designed to impress and doubled as an art gallery—one of many in the neighborhood. Carved pinecones, symbols of regeneration and enlightenment, decorated the entranceway. There were several arched shop windows on the ground floor, perfect for displaying art—although sometimes Parisians mocked the avant-garde art as they walked by. French Jews, like their German counterparts, had long been appreciators and patrons of avant-garde culture, and Paul's father had been a passionate, early collector and dealer of impressionist art.

Visitors to the Galerie Rosenberg were first welcomed into a stone rotunda and ushered across a geometrically patterned yellow and onyx marble floor. A sweeping cantilevered marble staircase with a cast-iron railing spiraled between the first and second floor. Larger-than-life statues by Auguste Rodin and other artists loomed in the circular foyer.

A long, sunken, wood-paneled exhibition hall on the ground floor, which extended into the back courtyard, housed the modern paintings. The room was filled with natural light, filtered through an art deco glass ceiling cut into geometric diamond- and square-shaped patterns.

Leather Chesterfield couches and velvet armchairs in the center of the room offered a place to rest while studying the artwork or negotiating a price. Electric light bulbs added extra luminosity. If a potential buyer seemed hesitant about the Picassos, Braques, or Légers, Paul would whisk them up the gallery staircase to see the nineteenth-century works, which were the firm's mainstays.

Paul curated group exhibitions to link modern art to its past. "In my view," he once wrote, "the shortcoming of contemporary exhibitions is that they show an artist's work in isolation." Paul believed one could be a collector of both Corots and Picassos, and his approach was known throughout the art world in France as "the Rosenberg method." Entry to the exhibitions, which took place all year round, was free. Each event was a news sensation. Ever the perfectionist, Paul personally hung all the artwork.

The Rosenberg family lived on the upper floors of 21 rue la Boétie. A winding staircase, decorated with paintings by Picasso and André Masson, among others, connected the levels. Georges Braque, who began his career as a talented decorator, custom-designed the family dining room on the third floor. Four marble mosaics, cut into cubist compositions with lemons, pitchers, and other still life stalwarts, were inlaid in the black and white marble tiles. On the walls, five still life paintings by Picasso complemented the mosaics.

Alexandre was born in this art-filled home on March 8, 1921, four years after his sister, Micheline. Picasso, who lived next door at 23 rue la Boétie, witnessed Alexandre's birth and was named the godfather. A few days later, Picasso accompanied Paul to the town hall to register the birth, countersigning with his famous autograph. So did Gabriel Picard, the Rosenberg's concierge at 21 rue la Boétie.

Paul was a true aesthete and looked it. He was thin and elegant, sporting an English-style mustache and dark, straight hair, which he combed over tidily. A cigarette could almost always be found perched between the slender fingers of his right hand. His wide-set eyes took in his clients and the art he obsessed over. Often, he seemed more comfortable with his paintings and his artist friends than with his own family, and in fact, asked his children to call him by his first name. He could talk long into the night with his friends, clients, and colleagues on any number of subjects. His nonchalant sophistication belied a tough, astute mind for business.

Paul saw his first Van Gogh painting at ten years old, which caused him to "shriek with horror," but he came to embrace the avant-garde and bet big on modern artists. Paul went in early enough to nurture the next generation of talent, thereby securing a future in the art business for Alexandre. "It is for his son that, as the good father, the merchant Rosenberg buys paintings by Picasso, André Lhote, and Marie Laurencin," a friend of Paul's observed when Alexandre was just five months old. "He lives on the Cézannes and Renoirs, the Corots and the Lautrecs." Alexandre, on the other hand, did not feel ready to join the family business yet and was a little wary of its commercialism.

To set himself apart, Paul only bought and sold paintings he truly believed in—works of art that would be known for posterity. That meant acquiring the best quality works that would command the highest prices. He was known for his unerring eye and claimed he could tell if a painting was authentic or a forgery by just touching the canvas. Some criticized his pricing, which he liked to set above market value, but he responded logically, "This doesn't hurt anyone. And it helps all painters."

Paul was devoted to his clients and artist friends, and wrote long, warmhearted letters to them during periods when he did not see them in person. He made sure to lift the self-esteem of his often-mercurial artists, especially Henri Matisse, who was plagued regularly with self-doubt. A few years earlier, when sales were slow for Matisse, the artist told his son in a letter, "Only Rosenberg has shown any warmth and offered me an exhibition," and shortly after, in another letter, "I saw Rosenberg, who galvanized me, told me I was wrong to allow myself to be forgotten."

The relationship between Paul and Picasso was even closer. In 1918, Paul had convinced the artist to move next door to an apartment at 23 rue la Boétie. Picasso brought his new wife, Olga Khokhlova, who was a ballet dancer he met on the set of "Parade."

It was a real upgrade for Picasso, who had previously lived in Montrouge, an industrial suburb south of Paris. This new home signaled a newfound wealth for Picasso, who discarded his bohemian life and embraced the bourgeois, wearing suits and smoking cigars.

Picasso called Paul "Rosi," and Paul nicknamed the artist "Pic." The two would converse through their kitchen windows, which both faced an enclosed shaft behind their buildings. Sometimes, Picasso would show a painting in progress through the window. Even more often, Picasso would be over at the Rosenberg house. Alexandre's older sister, Micheline, affectionately called the artist "Casso," and Alexandre was close to his godfather as well. Paul saw Picasso as his "spiritual brother," and the two were much more than just business partners. They were "inseparable," said Paul's granddaughter Anne Sinclair. Paul would send a note next door: "Can we come up and see you after dinner? Please reply through the window." Or even more jovially: "I dropped in at yours, you weren't there. I hereby summon you to my house."

Picasso would sketch on his visits to 21 rue la Boétie, gifting the Rosenbergs with charcoal drawings such as *Micheline Dressed as a Nurse* and *Micheline with a Rabbit.* A portrait of Paul shows him seated casually at home in a dapper double-breasted suit holding a cigarette. Picasso also made more formal paintings of the Rosenbergs, including one of Paul's wife, Margot, with Micheline on her lap, the child looking "*rondiste*" rather than cubist, according to Paul.

Though Picasso and Olga married for love, it was an ill-fated match. When things began deteriorating, Paul helped the artist get another apartment one floor up at 23 rue la Boétie, which Picasso also used as his studio. In 1935, the couple separated, and Paul assisted in the inventory related to the split, much like he was doing for Henri Matisse in the summer of 1939. In a letter from Évian encouraging Picasso to visit him, Paul wrote, "Olga does not dare come here. Isn't that an added attraction for you?"

THE LOUVRE, PARIS

AUGUST 1939

LUCKILY FOR ROSE, MUSÉES NATIONAUX DIRECTOR HENRI VERNE WAS being forced to retire early. He was beset by scandals and drained, both physically and intellectually. A museum accountant had embezzled 540,000 francs. A Watteau painting was stolen in broad daylight, and a fire had broken out in the Louvre, with Verne nowhere to be found. Then there was the harbor sinking of the *Paris*, the boat carrying France's invaluable artworks to the World's Fair in New York City.

In the midst of all this drama, Verne continued to treat Rose bitterly. Although he agreed to put her fully in charge of the Jeu de Paume at one point in the previous year, during one of André Dezarrois's absences, he was unwilling to pay her.

The good news was that Jacques Jaujard, the deputy director of the Musées Nationaux, would be the acting director by the end of August, and he saw Rose's potential to be a great curator. Jaujard was tall and thin, with a long nose that downturned slightly at the tip. He had an intense, focused demeanor with dark creases in his cheeks and half-moon eyes that revealed a life with its fair share of darkness, an aspect reminiscent of Humphrey Bogart, the American cinema star. He had a full head of wavy brown hair that he combed back neatly and a penchant for double-breasted suits and cigarettes. A male colleague at the Louvre described him as "seduction itself." But despite his appearance, Jaujard was the opposite of a matinee idol—he was the ultimate civil servant, humble and discreet.

Jaujard came from a blue-collar background and knew how to talk to people from all walks of life. While Verne entertained his grudges, Jaujard proved to be the consummate operator with a politician's powers of persuasion. He was also an inspirational leader with a natural charisma who listened with "sensitivity, courtesy, and kindness." As a colleague described admiringly, Jaujard could take "a discussion of confused words" and summarize it in a way that was "dazzlingly clear and obvious." He prided himself on acting only on reason and was known for being candid and direct.

In June 1932, Hitler led the Nazi Party to become Germany's largest political party. The continuing economic crisis, kicked off by the stock market crash of 1929, became the perfect rallying cry for Hitler's rhetoric of fear, anti-Semitism, and national pride. A fire in the Berlin Reichstag, the national parliament of Germany, in 1933, allegedly the handiwork of a Dutch communist, became the basis for a military state. The Nazis suppressed civil rights, used a paramilitary force to intimidate voters and political opponents, opened the first concentration camps for political prisoners, and passed the "Enabling Act," which gave Hitler dictatorial power. In tandem came a general "cleansing" of anything "un-German," which included art, literature, and scientific ideas that did not align with Nazi ideals.

In response to the new imperialist order emerging in Germany, the Musées Nationaux began proactively planning for another war. In October 1932, Verne directed his curators to make priority lists of important artworks to be evacuated, which he called an "eventuality that must be anticipated," and gave instructions on how to evacuate them.

The Musées Nationaux had a large purview. Should war come, the national institution would oversee the evacuation of art from not only the Louvre but also from numerous affiliated museums and cultural organizations in Paris such as the Jeu de Paume, Musée de l'Orangerie, Musée Rodin, the Paris Opera, the Comédie Française, the national theater company, and many museums in the French provinces.

In 1933, Verne completed the first draft of the plan. It involved evacuating the most important works first and sheltering the rest in place.

The same year, Jaujard was named deputy director of the Musées Nationaux and took on the complex task of preparing the French national museums for war. By 1934, a new plan was in place to store the most significant works of art in various castles in the Loire Valley, including the Château de Chambord, which would serve as a central hub. Dispersal of the collections would minimize the risk of fire or bombings.

In March 1936, in a direct violation of the Treaty of Versailles, Germany reoccupied the Rhineland, a demilitarized zone on the border of Belgium, Luxembourg, the Netherlands, and Germany that Allied troops had administered since the end of World War I. A month later, Verne finally got a budget (albeit limited) to prepare the museums for war. He sent out letters to all his curators asking them to send updated priority lists of art. He also asked for a list of purchases needed for packing the art, such as crates and boxes, as well as items required for protection on-site. Due to the small amount of funds available, he asked each department to create a plan that was "limited to the essentials."

Dezarrois, with Rose's meticulous help, sent Verne a detailed report of the Jeu de Paume's needs. The permanent holdings, as inventoried by Rose, were impressive for such a young museum: over 3,000 works of art, which included 810 paintings, 112 sculptures, 364 drawings, 1,500 engravings and lithographs, and 220 commemorative medals. Heeding Verne's directive, only fifty-seven objects were selected for evacuation, with an additional hundred or so drawings and engravings to be added "if necessary."

Rose compiled the list of art on four pages of Musées Nationaux letterhead. In an indication of her level of anxiety, she initially wrote "*Tableaux à sauver en cas de guerre*" ("Paintings to save in case of war"). She later crossed out "save" and "war" and wrote "*évacuer*" ("evacuate") and "*d'alerte*" ("alert"). The museums were not calling it war yet, but Rose was already assuming a worst-case scenario.

Dezarrois gave credit to the Jeu de Paume's employees, saying, "Our caretakers, very experienced in this kind of work thanks to the exhibitions we organize at the Museum, would carry out this task, I am certain, in the minimum amount of time and with the maximum amount of care." He did not mention Rose by name, but she was the only other curatorial staffer and had helped him devise the museum's evacuation plan.

The basement was set up to hold two hundred paintings in case they needed to be protected urgently before any large-scale evacuation could occur. Dezarrois and Rose noted: "The Museum's storerooms are clearly insufficient to preserve the very important lot that will remain. The basements are dug very superficially. . . . The building with its large bay windows is extremely vulnerable and naturally offers no resistance to any bombardment."

Rose, Jaujard, and the Musées Nationaux staff put their evacuation plans to the test in September 1938, when it seemed that Hitler would soon invade the Sudetenland, a German-speaking region of Czechoslovakia, and likely trigger a new European war. For four days, the museums prepared the artworks for shipment, packed them, and put them on truck convoys headed to the Château de Chambord in the Loire Valley. With Dezarrois recalled to the French Air Force, Rose was officially given full command of the Jeu de Paume. With her no-nonsense attitude and unparalleled work ethic, Rose was just the kind of person Jaujard needed for this unprecedented effort.

The political crisis ended on September 30, 1938, but not without a catastrophic concession. Czechoslovakia was forced to give up the Sudetenland as a result of the Munich Agreement, signed between French prime minister Édouard Daladier, British prime minister Neville Chamberlain, Italian prime minister Benito Mussolini, and Hitler.

When news of the accord came through, packing stopped abruptly at the Louvre and the Jeu de Paume. The unloading of a third convoy at Chambord was paused, and all the art was moved back to Paris in a week.

Chamberlain flew back to England and declared triumphantly in front of 10 Downing Street that he had secured "peace for our time," encouraging the people of the United Kingdom to "go home and get a nice quiet sleep."

Daladier was welcomed home to France as a hero as well. "Long live Daladier! Long live peace!" people shouted, waving their hats as his motorcade traveled from Le Bourget airport into central Paris. French President Albert Lebrun stood up in his convertible, basking in the glory. Small pieces of paper flew down from building windows like in a New York City ticker-tape parade.

From the Jeu de Paume, Rose witnessed the triumphant arrival of France's leaders to the Place de la Concorde. The museum seemed to open its doors, as Rose described later, "onto a world whose anxiety had miraculously disappeared." The German expatriate writer Rodolphe Manasse-Morris observed, "France has abandoned itself, and the French are in a delirium of joy."

"But it was only a truce, we all felt it," reflected Rose's colleague, Lucie Mazauric, who worked in the Louvre archives. "I feel torn between a cowardly relief and shame," wrote Léon Blum, the former French prime minister. Winston Churchill, who had been warning about Hitler since 1933, did not mince his words while criticizing Chamberlain: "You were given the choice between war and dishonour. You chose dishonour and you will have war."

Rose felt the Jeu de Paume had proven itself poor in the defense of the artistic heritage they were charged to protect. The packing and evacuation felt "hasty," and she could see a lot of room for improvement. Rose and Dezarrois also worried about the basement shelter, which had been retrofitted but not designed to sustain a bombardment. "Any bomb falling on the Museum would create the greatest devastation in this basement," Dezarrois wrote in a report to Henri Verne, adding, "For the same reasons, the basement is insufficient to serve as a shelter for the personnel who would remain at the Museum, and would even be dangerous." In addition, the first of their seventeen crates to be used for packing arrived late, six days after the alert began. Their first aid supplies never made it, and they deemed the nearest aid station—a fifteen-minute walk away at the Ministry of Finance on rue de Rivoli—too far. The Jeu de Paume also had many heavy sculptures that would require special equipment to move but lacked a team specialized in art transportation.

Pierre Schommer, a nervous forty-five-year-old arts administrator in charge of operations at Chambord, had long been concerned about the potential bottleneck along the road to the vast castle where the art would be stored, and called it one of the "thorniest aspects" of the evacuation plan.

He also worried about the fire hazards inside, describing with great eloquence and animation that all of Chambord was in a "state of complete degradation." He described shutters affixed where there were no windows, along with broken and lockless doors. When a lock was missing a key, he had to locate the appropriate one from the four hundred rusty keys delivered to him in a wheelbarrow. There was only one bathroom in the entire 440-room, 300,000-square-foot castle, no kitchen, and only one spot with potable drinking water. No royal or noble had lived in it since the onset of World War I, and it had no heating.

Schommer was also alarmed by the castle's many half-floor apartments, secret cabinets, and hidden staircases, of which he reported there were seventy-four in all. There would be many labyrinth-like places for raiders to hide. The castle's sheer size would make it an easy target for German bombers, and he implored the Musées Nationaux to consider *schadenfreude*, the joy for the misfortune of others, which he felt was at the root of Germany's war doctrine.

Five months later, in February 1939, Jaujard participated in an even more dangerous art evacuation during the Spanish Civil War just before the fall of Catalonia to Nationalist forces. The artistic treasures from the Museo del Prado and other cultural sites, stashed in the Castell de Sant Ferran in Figueras and deep inside old talc mines in the Pyrenees, were in danger from both enemy fire and the clutches of Generalissimo Francisco Franco and his allies, Hitler and Mussolini.

Between bombings at the Castell de Sant Ferran, using only the lights of an Opel car for illumination, Jaujard and the Republic of Spain's foreign minister signed an agreement to evacuate the art. Seventy-one trucks of art, protected by French security forces, left for Switzerland. Schommer and another arts administrator, Albert Henraux, assisted in the perilous operation and watched hordes of fleeing Spaniards try to navigate around piles of abandoned trucks, artillery, animal corpses, and falling bombs. In total, 1,845 crates holding 364 paintings and 180 drawings were moved to the League of Nations headquarters in Geneva over five days under Jaujard's direction. The Spanish masterpieces were now on display at the Musée d'Art et d'Histoire in Geneva in an exhibition that Paul Rosenberg and Matisse traveled to see despite the turbulence afoot in Europe.

AT THE LOUVRE, INTENSE PLANNING and preparation commenced following the signing of the Munich Agreement. The museum's architect designed a series of bomb shelters for the Louvre and commenced an extensive excavation beneath the museum. Study after study investigated how to protect buildings and the art inside from bombings, gas attacks, and fire. The museum administration hired specialized workers and procured more packing supplies. Jacques Jaujard also took feedback from the curators regarding the 1938 evacuation and crafted new, meticulously detailed plans.

Schommer and Henraux spent the intervening months speeding around the country evaluating châteaux to use for additional depots, which would further disperse the risk from Chambord. They needed castles within a certain distance from Paris, with large enough doors for oversized paintings and sculptures, close to a supply center and a water source (but away from military or industrial targets), with basements that were large but also dry, and with enough buildings on the estate to house six to eight households.

Many of the country's nobles were eager to offer up their estates, preferring to house inanimate works of art than nosy government employees. Even ludicrous locations were offered up, such as a family burial vault too flooded even for the dead. In the end, eighty properties were requisitioned, including many grand Loire Valley castles.

Jaujard also had to deal with an unexpected shortage of trucks and drivers. The museums of Paris needed thirty trucks, but only twelve were promised. Jaujard worried that even fewer might be available when the time came due to further military requisitions, protestations from truck owners, or military mobilization of the drivers. He called this a "serious risk" and "the most worrying situation." But, ever the problem solver, he went directly to the truck owners and signed contracts with them, thereby bypassing the military. Meanwhile, he stashed 7,500 liters of petrol in the Tuileries Garden and at Versailles with additional stock at Chambord.

He also studied alternate transportation methods. After many years of investigating the plausibility of transporting art by river, it was determined that a *péniche*, a flat-bottomed self-propelled boat, could be used for moving works of art that could survive humid conditions and submersion if sunk.

For months, Rose had worried about war. The elation following the Munich Agreement eleven months earlier was now a distant memory and the situation with Germany had escalated again. In March 1939, Germany appropriated what was left of Czechoslovakia and annexed part of Lithuania. In April, Hitler withdrew from both the German-Polish Non-Aggression Pact, and the Anglo-German Naval Pact, and declared that the free city of Danzig was "a German city" that "wishes to belong to Germany." In June, Reich Minister of Propaganda Joseph Goebbels told a rabid crowd in Danzig that they would "Come home to the Reich!" Regarding Poland, Hitler told his generals that, "There is therefore no question of sparing Poland, and the decision remains to attack Poland at the first opportunity. We cannot expect a repetition of Czechoslovakia. There will be fighting."

In early August, in anticipation of conflict, the French national museums recalled all staff from summer holidays or from work abroad. Rose, meanwhile, was back in charge. Her boss, curator André Dezarrois, was called up to the Air Force again on August 7.

Rose's partner, Joyce, had just started a new position at the US embassy as a clerk and stenographer. Her fluency in German, French, and English, as well as her ability to write in long- and shorthand in those languages, was a strong asset. She was industrious and knowledgeable, and able to produce a large quantity of work. She had larger aspirations, but like Rose, Joyce needed to take the job opportunities available to her. As a British citizen, she could easily have left France with the uncertainty afoot in Europe, but she insisted that she wanted to stay in the country, no doubt to be with Rose. Together, they lived a simple but secret life that was about to be dramatically disrupted by war.

On August 22, Hitler gathered his top military commanders to inform them that he had prepared orders "to kill without pity or mercy all men, women, and children of Polish descent or language."

"Our strength lies in our speed and our ruthlessness," he told them, adding that "the object of war is, not to reach some given line, but physically to destroy the enemy."

Heinrich Himmler, the head of the SS, announced just as brutally, "All Poles will disappear from this world," and that "the great German nation considers the elimination of all Polish people as its chief task." The German military war machine was primed for an imminent invasion of Poland.

That night, German foreign minister Joachim von Ribbentrop boarded his custom four-engine Focke-Wolf airplane, the Condor *Grenzmark*, at Tempelhof airfield in Berlin. A giant black swastika gleamed on the rudder. From the top of the stairs, von Ribbentrop smiled and waved to the crowd as camera flashbulbs popped in the evening darkness. He was headed to Moscow for a meeting that would have grave consequences for the world.

CINQ-MARS-LA-PILE, FRANCE

END OF AUGUST 1939

AS ROSE READIED THE JEU DE PAUME AGAIN FOR POTENTIAL WAR, PAUL Rosenberg was finalizing an escape plan for his family and his art collection. They had only been in Évian for four weeks, but war had bloomed quickly. The Rosenberg clan headed from their chic vacation to Cinq-Mars-la-Pile, a countryside town about twelve miles west of Tours along the Loire River. The region, dotted with the country's most famous châteaux, could be reached easily from Paris by train.

Paul rented a stately house called Le Grand Porteau, planning to sit out the war there with his family. There was plenty of room for art in the house—in the cellar, which was dug into the rock behind the house, in the attic, and, of course, on the walls.

Le Grand Porteau was an important enough landmark to be featured on tourism postcards but was still sufficiently concealed for the tight-knit Rosenberg family to live discreetly. It was set back behind high stone walls, with tall, old-growth trees and a large garden. It also came equipped with a luxury item found only in upper-class homes: a telephone.

As war approached, Paul continued to communicate regularly with his artists. He advised an overwrought Matisse to stash his paintings and valuables in a safe place. Braque told Paul he planned to escape to Geneva before the borders closed. The Museum of Modern Art staff was still working out the details of the Picasso exhibition, with a potential five more works to be shipped from Paul's London gallery, if war could wait and some finicky details could be worked out.

Ever cautious, Paul prepared to close the Galerie Rosenberg in Paris in fear that it could be damaged or destroyed by enemy bombs. Inside, he left his business documents, an art library of 1,200 books, and photographic plates of all the art he had bought and sold, along with a portion of his art collection. Much to the frustration of Alfred H. Barr Jr., who had hoped the Museum of Modern Art would safeguard the Rosenberg collection, Paul decided to ship his nineteenth-century paintings to the London gallery on Bruton Street that he ran with his brother-in-law, Jacques Helft. He sent his twentieth-century works to a warehouse in Tours under the name of his chauffeur Louis Le Gall—a decision that would prove providential.

MOSCOW

END OF AUGUST 1939

BY NIGHTFALL ON AUGUST 21, A NONAGGRESSION PACT BETWEEN GERmany and the Soviet Union was more or less finalized, and a new trade deal between the two countries had been signed. The terrifying military alliance would have borders on fourteen countries. It also meant that the Soviet Union had actively rejected peace with Western Europe. Ongoing negotiations in Moscow for a triple military alliance between the Soviet Union, France, and England—reported as a done deal by the French newspapers—had obviously failed. The next morning, the people of France read the ominous tidings in *Le Petit Journal*, which rushed the news to print overnight. That evening, German foreign minister Joachim von Ribbentrop arrived in Moscow to complete the agreement.

It was a win-win for Germany and the Soviet Union. For the Soviets, the treaty would stave off Nazi belligerence. It would also keep the door open for future Soviet incursions into Eastern Europe, a region the country had long coveted. Meanwhile, Germany—cut off from imports from Western Europe—could get crucial raw materials from the Soviet Union and invade Poland with impunity.

The nations of Western Europe scrambled to formulate an action plan. The French ministers cut short their holidays to return to Paris, and the British Cabinet convened, as did the Oslo Powers—the consortium of Holland, Belgium, Luxemburg, Denmark, Norway, Finland, and Sweden. Leopold III, the King of Belgium, pleaded with the Oslo Powers to declare neutrality and warned, "Is our continent going to commit suicide in a terrible war that would know neither winner nor loser, but in which the spiritual and material values created by centuries of civilization would sink?"

The British ambassador to Germany, Sir Nevile Henderson, secretly delivered a note to Hitler in the Berghof. It stated that France and Great Britain would aid any efforts to restore trust with Germany if it backed away from Poland but that they would respond with force to the use of force. In a short ten-minute conversation, Hitler made it clear to Henderson that he had no intention of conceding and that any attack on Poland was in defense of Germany's vital interests.

Germany and the Soviet Union signed the Treaty of Nonaggression at one in the morning on August 24. Ribbentrop, Vyacheslav Molotov, Soviet Minister of Foreign Affairs, and Joseph Stalin, secretary-general of the Soviet Communist Party, were present. Hitler was notified right away by telephone. Germany could now invade Poland and the free city of Danzig without interference from the Soviet Union.

In response, France and the United Kingdom activated their war machines. The British called up infantrymen, made room in London's hospitals by moving patients to the countryside, sandbagged buildings, and prepared for an "instant blackout" in case of an air raid.

In France, the Council of Ministers approved "exceptional security measures." On August 24, Parisians woke up to cloudy skies and newly pasted white posters all over the city, summoning reserve soldiers. Factories were requisitioned for the country's national defense needs. So were Paris's buses, followed by the taxis. Trains out of Paris were free of charge to anyone who could leave the capital. Over sixteen thousand children were evacuated from schools. The Jeu de Paume museum was closed by end of day.

Journalists went out in search of a panicked populace but could only praise Parisians for their sangfroid. According to reporters, they sat, calm and collected, at the cafés, reading the latest from the newspapers. They waited patiently to pick up their government-allocated gas masks. Reservists queued up in an orderly fashion for the trains and buses that would take them to war.

Pierre Schommer, the arts administrator assigned to the main art depot at Chambord, was on a short seven-day vacation in the Loire Valley. On August 24, Schommer heard the news of the nonaggression pact while crossing the city of Tours and hopped on the last bus heading toward Chambord. The next day, French prime minister Édouard Daladier gave a radio speech explaining the grave situation and implored his people, "Frenchmen, French women, I have no need to tell you your duty. I know you are ready to assure every sacrifice for the safety of our country."

Great Britain and Poland announced a Mutual Assistance Agreement. France announced it would stand with England and uphold its own treaties with Poland.

If Hitler was bluffing, he would need to back down soon. He firmly believed that neither France nor England would defend Poland, given how he had been permitted to annex Austria, the Sudetenland, and Czechoslovakia without consequence. But the visceral reaction from France and the United Kingdom this time momentarily unsettled him, and Hitler countered that he had no desire to have war with either country. He told the French ambassador in Berlin several times that it was painful for him to think about going to war with France. "I will not attack France, but if she joins in the conflict, I will see it through to the bitter end," he pledged. "I believe I shall win, and you believe you will win: what is certain is that above all French and German blood will flow, the blood of two equally courageous peoples."

For months, the German press had been pushing Nazi propaganda about alleged Polish atrocities, which included claims of forced labor camps and ethnic cleansing of people of German descent in Poland. Meanwhile, the Nazis were planting false flag operations all along the Polish border and in Danzig to make it seem like the Poles were instigating a war. "I will provide a propagandistic casus belli. Its credibility does not matter," Hitler told his generals.

Only US President Franklin Delano Roosevelt remained optimistic that war could be avoided, as he reiterated in a press conference and in a message to Hitler: "Countless human lives can yet be saved and hope may still be restored that the nations of the modern world may even now construct the foundation of a peaceful and a happier relationship." The German Foreign Office responded harshly that Roosevelt "appears devoted to the illusion that his person or his government is fit for suitable mediation."

The European countries were now simply waiting to see how far Hitler would go. So was Rose, and the rest of the French museum staff.

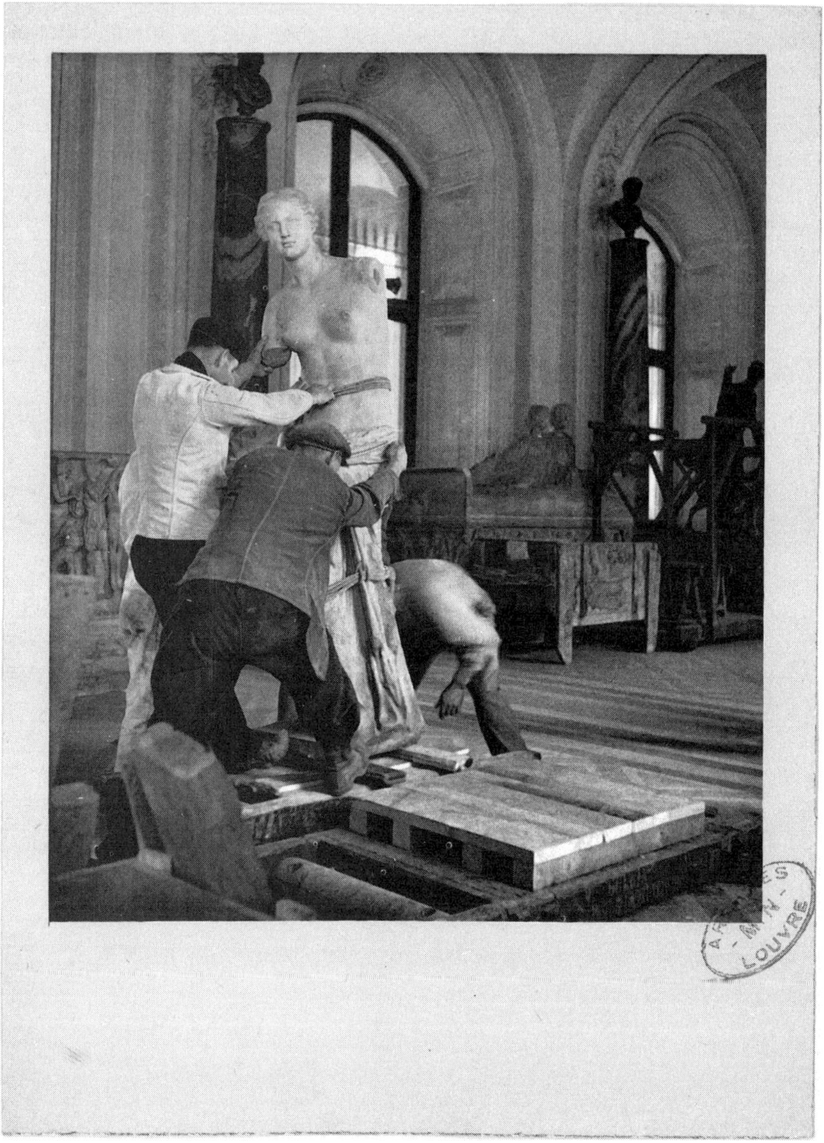

Preparing the evacuation of the Venus de Milo from the Galerie Denon in the Louvre, September 1939.

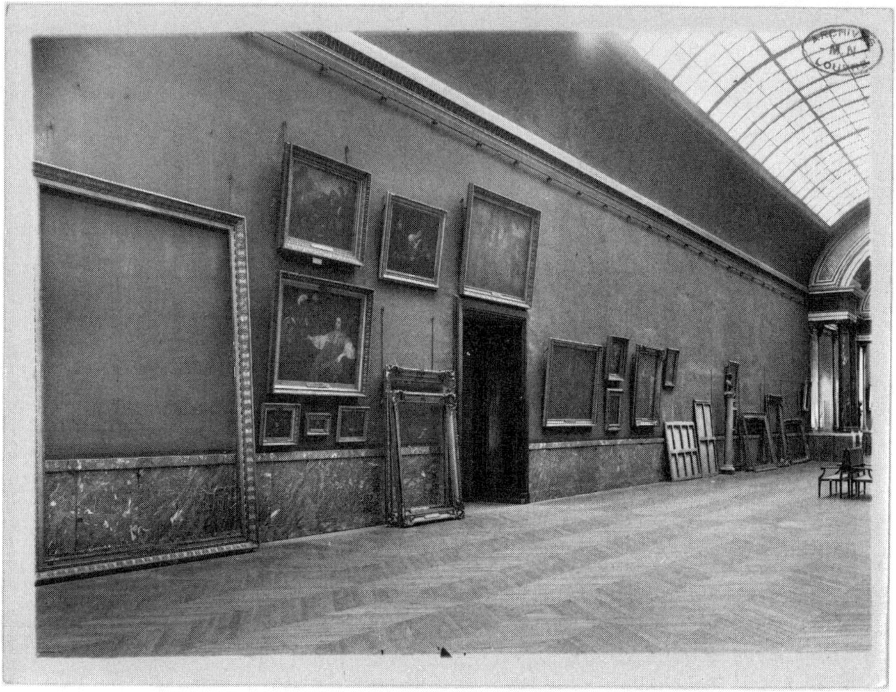

Evacuation of the Louvre during the crisis over Sudetenland, September 1938.

JEU DE PAUME

AUGUST 25, 1939

AT 8 A.M. ON AUGUST 25, TWO MONTHS AFTER REICH PROPAGANDA Minister Joseph Goebbels roused the people of Danzig to "come home to the Reich," the German warship *Schleswig-Holstein* entered the port of the city with over two hundred naval shock troop soldiers. Hitler was starting to make good on his threats.

At 5 p.m., the French museums received a message they knew would come: start packing.

To Rose, the previous year felt in hindsight like "one long and continuous slide to the inevitable." She was used to operating solo but there was a new sense of gravity. Packing materials overflowed from the Jeu de Paume's basement and storage rooms onto the exhibition floors. It would also be a long time before her boss, André Dezarrois—attached to the French Air Force—might return, if at all. The responsibility of the Jeu de Paume—the art collection, the building, and the staff—rested entirely on her shoulders.

As Rose reflected later, "Whatever the threats weighing on its inhabitants, France had above all to save the spiritual values that it held as an integral part of its soul and its culture. Sheltering its works of art, its archives, its libraries was indeed one of the first reflexes of defense of our country."

Rose was incredibly efficient, as usual. By evening on August 25, only hours after the green light, the packaging of the most precious paintings was done. Unlike the Louvre, the Jeu de Paume did not get extra packing volunteers from Parisian department stores like the Samaritaine, the Grands Magasins du Louvre, or the Bazar de l'Hôtel de Ville. But under Rose's direction, the handful of guards at the museum did the job, most of whom were tough, independent-minded Corsicans. They knew Rose well and trusted her, as she trusted them.

They packed a total of 119 paintings from the Jeu de Paume into eighteen crates, ready to be trucked to Chambord. The crates could fit between two and twenty-six paintings, depending on the artwork size. Among the boxes were works of art by Picasso, Klee, Kandinsky, Chagall, Modigliani, Juan Gris, John Singer Sargent, and Mary Cassatt. All the smaller paintings would have been wrapped in fiber quilt batting for cushioning and a special oiled moisture-wicking paper to protect them from humidity, then placed flat into wood packing cases.

As per the instructions, each crate was stenciled with "JP" for Jeu de Paume and the words "MUSEES NATIONAUX," "FRAGILE," and "MN." Each crate also had a unique number. Rose wrote out inventories on Jeu de Paume letterhead as the hired typists did not make their way out to her museum.

At the Louvre, the largest evacuation ever attempted was underway. Immediately after the museum was closed, the workers and volunteers took the fifty most notable paintings off the walls, gingerly detached them from their frames, and brought them down to the Louvre basement on trolleys to be prepped for departure. They even unhooked the largest history paintings in the Grande Galerie, including Eugène Delacroix's *Liberty Leading the People*, Théodore Géricault's *Raft of the Medusa*, Jacques-Louis David's *The Coronation of Napoleon*, and Paolo Veronese's *The Wedding Feast at Cana*, which measured 33 feet wide and 22 feet tall.

The workers wrote the names of the paintings in chalk on the walls to aid their future return, and placed the empty frames on the ground or left them in place. Where the face of the *Mona Lisa* once peered inscrutably at visitors, a worker scribbled her French name: La Joconde. He smudged out his first try and rewrote it more neatly just above, perhaps in deference to her iconic status. There was little chatter, just the rustling sounds of paraffin paper and the sound of hammering as the masterpieces were shut in their temporary wooden tombs.

The Venus de Milo was also slated for removal, taken off her pedestal and put onto a hand truck. Four men moved her carefully onto a wood platform and tied her waist with rope for additional stability. A custom crate would soon be built around her.

The French Beaux-Arts ministry was working furiously to protect Paris's monuments, too. Specialist workers led by Georges Husman, the director general of the Beaux-Arts last seen in charge of the World's Fair in New York, unsealed and removed the ancient and priceless stained-glass windows in the cathedrals of Notre-Dame, Saint-Chapelle, and Chartres, piece by piece. Each piece was numbered and placed into wooden crates, then trucked away to storage locations, which included the vaults of the Bank of France and the basement of Saint-Chapelle. At Chartres, it would take just four days for one hundred artisans to remove the 5,803 pieces of glass—a task that took over five months at the onset of World War I.

Overnight, the famous lights of Paris were darkened as a practice run for air raids. Workers climbed up long, precariously perched ladders to put safety caps atop the city's Belle Époque lanterns. New blue lights popped up indicating the location of air-raid shelters. The packers at the Louvre, who worked nearly all through the night, could only use the small lamps provided to them for emergency lighting.

Over the next few days, Rose and the staff packed up the next batch of important paintings in the Jeu de Paume, 165 in total. The greatest challenge lay ahead—securing the art to be sheltered on-site. Approximately two-thirds of the entire collection still needed to be safeguarded, but the Jeu de Paume's basement was too small, consisting only of a few rooms immediately surrounding the central staircase. Of those, only one room was intended for storage; the rest were functional: a boiler room, a former coal storage area, a breakroom for the museum guards and caretakers, and bathrooms. Furthermore, the basement storage room was not large enough to accommodate everything that remained, so Rose had the boiler room converted into an additional storeroom.

Between the two rooms, they fit 524 paintings, nearly a hundred sculptures, and the museum's archives. The doors were then padlocked closed.

The museum guards moved twenty sculptures, too large to be lowered into the basement, into the walled garden and piled sandbags to their highest features. The electric torches and lighting apparatuses in the museum were stored and secured.

The Louvre staff sent the first artworks, including the *Mona Lisa*—gingerly ensconced in a red velvet-lined custom crate—to Chambord at 6 a.m. on August 28. Jacques Jaujard calmly directed the whole evacuation from ground zero in the Cour Carrée, the enclosed open-air courtyard of the Louvre. It was a hundred-mile journey on a carefully plotted route. Armored guards rode in each truck, and Musées Nationaux staff bookended the convoys in private cars. The energetic Albert Henraux, who valiantly guided the 1938 art evacuation at top speed in his Hotchkiss car, led the first convoy of eight trucks.

The French crown jewels and 225 other crates from the Louvre were also on board the first trucks. Another convoy with six trucks left at 2 p.m. From then on, two convoys departed daily from the Louvre. The first seventy paintings from the Jeu de Paume, packed into fifteen crates, left for Chambord on the morning of August 30.

Outside of the museum world, the English, French, and Americans were still having meetings with Hitler and his ministers, trying last-ditch efforts to stop a major conflict. But privately, the diplomats doubted that war could be avoided. The Western European nations continued to mobilize. The border between France and Germany was closed, and telephone and telegraph communications were shut down. Restrictions on the French populace began, with cafés and restaurants to be closed by 11 p.m. daily. The French military took control of the radio.

On August 31 and September 1, a subsequent shipment of 163 paintings from the Jeu de Paume, mostly placed uncrated in padded trucks, left for Chambord. Rose was working so rapidly, she grabbed two tickets to the opening of a Tibetan painting exhibition at the Musée Guimet as scrap paper, noted the convoy number, date of departure, and number of paintings on the back, and pinned it to her inventory lists. These paintings ended up stacked dozens deep in the chapel of Chambord castle.

With all the important artwork now at Chambord and the final preparations at the Jeu de Paume fully in process, Rose could take a small breath. But any sense of relief was short-lived. On one hand, Hitler was making assurances that he would meet directly with Poland, a sign that perhaps the conflict could be de-escalated at the eleventh hour. But his follow-up demands became more and more unreasonable and contradictory. In addition to Danzig and the Polish Corridor, he suddenly added Silesia and Gdynia to his territorial wish list and stated that he no longer envisioned that Poland could stay independent. He told the British ambassador that he would only meet and negotiate with Poland if they agreed in advance to all his demands.

During the night on August 31, German SS officers disguised in Polish military uniforms, under direct orders from Gestapo director Reinhard Heydrich, attacked the Sender Gleiwitz radio station in Germany and broadcast an anti-German message in Polish to make it seem like Polish anti-German factions were behind it. Dozens of similar incidents took place the same night. Polish men, as well as prisoners from concentration camps, were executed, then dressed as Polish saboteurs and left at the sites of the attack as further "evidence."

In the early hours of September 1, Hitler issued a proclamation to the Wehrmacht, the German Army, that clearly showed his formal resolve to attack Poland, stating that "the time has come to oppose force with force." At the port of Danzig, the *Schleswig-Holstein* fired its cannons on a military depot. As the last cases of art from the Jeu de Paume were loaded up onto trucks, German troops crossed the Polish border at multiple entry points and began their assault. Danzig was officially declared part of the Third Reich. Nazi agents within Poland took over the railways, arrested officials, requisitioned trains, and occupied stations. In a mass attack, German planes dropped bombs on Warsaw and 150 towns all over Poland.

Hitler also made a speech at the Reichstag, laying out the basis for his actions and proclaiming the superiority of the German military. He pledged to protect women and children but swore that "whoever departs from the rules of human warfare can only expect that we shall do the same." He would fight "until victory is secured" or "not survive the outcome." He also appointed his second in command. "If anything should happen to me in the struggle, then my first successor is Party Comrade Göring," his portly *Generalfeldmarschall* in charge of the Luftwaffe, the German Air Force.

On September 2, French president Albert Lebrun addressed the French Parliament. To loud applause, he confirmed that "with great calmness, with cool resolve, and in perfect order, France had taken the steps required by her own safety and her faithfulness to her obligations." "*Vive la France!*" he concluded to even more thunderous clapping.

Then French prime minister Daladier followed with an even longer speech, stating, "France rises with such impetuous impulses only when she feels in her heart that she is fighting for her life and for her independence. Gentlemen, today France is in command." The deputies rose to their feet and applauded loudly and at length.

Both England and France demanded that Germany announce a withdrawal from Poland by the next day, September 3.

Over at the Louvre, around midday, a large group of museum workers gathered atop the grand staircase where the Winged Victory of Samothrace still stood triumphantly. The sculpture was originally intended to be sheltered in place at the museum, but a new study showed that the vaulted ceiling above her would not survive a bombing. The Louvre's Asian Arts department curator, George Salles, came to tell everyone, on behalf of Jacques Jaujard, that war was about to be declared. The sober news meant that Victory needed to be moved out urgently.

Made up of 118 fragile pieces of white Parian marble, the winged sculpture was encased in an open scaffolding and attached to a complex rope and pulley system. At 3 p.m., Victory was lifted off of her prow pedestal. Two groups of men held up the sculpture as it rolled inch by inch down a wooden ramp, shaking perilously. "The rope is cracking!" one of the men yelled. When the sculpture made it miraculously down the grand staircase without a scratch, the elderly curator nearly collapsed from stress on the stone steps. "I will not see her return," he said ruefully, while wiping away a tear.

By nightfall, the Louvre was nearly empty. Over the prior week, ninety-five trucks had whisked away most of the museum's most precious objects—more than twelve hundred crates, thousands of paintings, and tens of thousands of sculptures.

At half past noon on September 3, Robert Coulondre, the French ambassador in Berlin, met with German foreign minister von Ribbentrop, who informed him that Germany did not agree to the ultimatum. Coulondre responded, "I have the painful duty to notify you that as from today, September 3, at 5 p.m., the French Government will find itself obliged to fulfill the obligations that France has contracted towards Poland, and which are known to the German Government."

"Well," von Ribbentrop replied, "it will be France who is the aggressor."

"History will judge of that," Coulondre replied.

And with that, war had come to Europe once again.

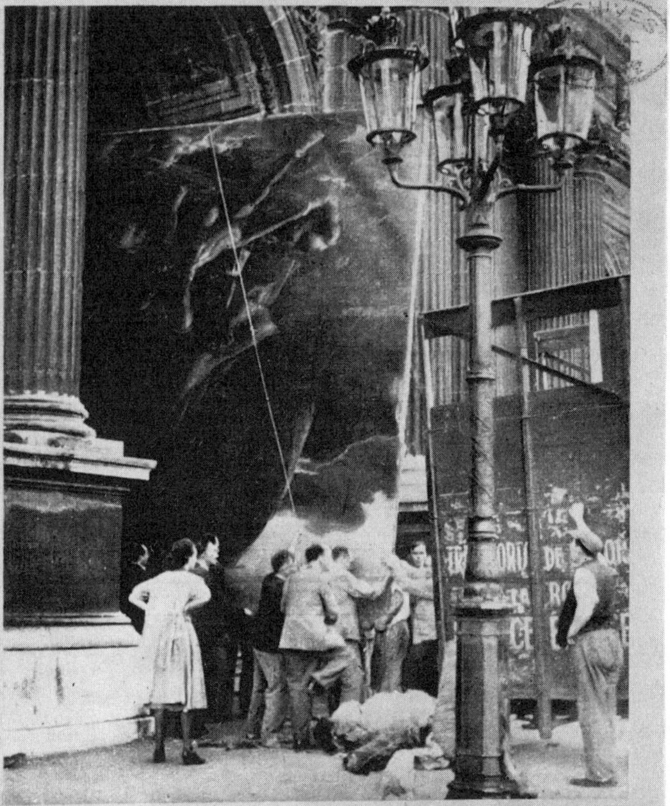

Le Radeau de la « Méduse » *est chargé dans une remorque à décors de théâtre.*

The Raft of the Medusa by Théodore Géricault at the Louvre about to be loaded onto a scenery truck, 1939.

PARIS

SEPTEMBER 3, 1939

ON THE DAY WAR WAS DECLARED, ROSE WAS STILL AT THE JEU DE Paume, although the two floors of exhibition rooms were now completely empty—an eerie scene for a place that once welcomed so many curious visitors.

So much still needed to be done. Rose had to protect the building from air raids as German bombs could fall any minute. The seventeen-foot double-story arched windows needed to be sandbagged and boarded up to prevent them from shattering into deadly shrapnel. Rose was retrofitting the former coal storage room as a temporary bomb shelter for the Jeu de Paume staff. The room conveniently had an iron door and a hatch that led up to the walled garden. In the meantime, she was waiting for a trench to be dug in the garden for the construction of a more robust shelter.

Rose also needed to organize her paperwork on the art evacuation. She wisely created different ways to inventory the artwork that allowed for redundancies should anything get lost. First was the standard list of paintings by crate as ordered by the French museums. Then she made a separate register with columns that showed the date of shipment, truck and convoy numbers, destination, and the crates on each vehicle. Another set of documents listed all the art shipped from the Jeu de Paume and the works protected on-site.

ON THE EVENING OF SEPTEMBER 3, King George VI, French prime minister Édouard Daladier, and British Prime Minister Neville Chamberlain made speeches over the radio. "Consequently, this country is at war with Germany. . . . I am certain that the right will prevail," Chamberlain intoned. Daladier meanwhile pulled at the moral heartstrings of the French people and ended with "*Vive la France!*" "There may be dark days ahead," warned King George VI.

The first days of the war in France were terrifying. Would Germany bomb France immediately? It certainly had the requisite air force power and was already unleashing destruction over Poland. Wasting no time, within a day after the declaration of war, the Third Reich torpedoed the English passenger boat *Athenia*, killing 117 people.

Rose was sleeping in the Jeu de Paume museum on a straw mattress, determined to protect the museum and the remaining artwork despite the obvious risk to her life.

The first real air-raid alarm in Paris happened in the early hours of September 5. German airplanes crossed France's eastern borders, and at 3:45 a.m., a droning glissando woke Parisians from their slumber. They grabbed their gas masks, knocked on their neighbors' doors, and headed calmly to basement shelters and subway stations. Policemen reminded distracted drivers to turn their automobile lights off. Under a bright moon, the city went completely dark. In the museum, Rose braced herself as the air-raid siren continued to blare. Around 4:30 a.m., the flak of anti-aircraft guns thundered in the distance as clouds rolled in. Joyce was much more delicate than Rose and prone to worry, so she would have been fearful about Rose's safety, as well as her own, while alone at night in their apartment.

But nothing happened. It was just a reconnaissance mission, and no bombs were dropped. The all-clear signal came at 7 a.m.—a sustained G-note that lasted three minutes—by which time Paris's bars and cafés began to open as usual. Air-raid sirens continued to ring the next two nights as enemy planes approached closer and closer to Paris.

On the third day, Rose heard anti-aircraft guns go off at Place de la Concorde and airplanes giving chase above her.

Rose found the whole experience rather exciting. "What an incredible adventure! And above all, a lamentable adventure," she wrote later that day to her cousin Marguerite. "I'm sure you're worried," she told her. "I hope you . . . take the situation calmly. Because there is nothing we can do, we must accept it calmly, as we will need our nerves." She also divulged that she was already getting used to the air-raid alerts. "It's true that they weren't too bad, but that could change," she said. Then, to reassure her, Rose wrote, "Don't worry, my morale is high and I am not doing badly."

Over the next few months, truck convoy after convoy continued to take art from the Louvre, from more minor museums, and from private collections. Most of the Louvre was evacuated within the first week, but the country's nobles, as well as art-collecting families like the Rothschilds, the Lévys, and the Bernheims, opted to put their carefully curated cultural possessions in the hands of the national museums as well. Fernand Léger, one of Paul Rosenberg's artists, deposited sixty-nine paintings. The family of Claude Monet stored seven of his paintings. The embassies of Great Britain, Argentina, Norway, and Switzerland also called in favors. So did Queen Amélie of Portugal, Princess Radziwill, and other foreign royals. Some Louvre staff, like Albert Henraux, Pierre Schommer, and Jacqueline Bouchot-Saupique, sent their humble art collections to the Loire Valley castles. By the beginning of November, over five thousand crates of art had left Paris from the national museums. Jacques Jaujard managed it all with aplomb. Rose felt he had given everyone, from guards to curators, a united purpose. They worked as a single soul, so to speak.

WHEN THE WAR STARTED, PAUL ROSENBERG and his family were safe at Le Grand Porteau, their newly rented home in Cinq-Mars-la-Pile.

His art was secure too, for now, but Paul's artists were in a state of flux. Matisse stowed his belongings in the vaults at the National Bank of Commerce and Industry, heeding Paul's advice, and left Paris. He said he would stay with Paul for one or two days en route south in search of good weather.

Picasso, meanwhile, was confused and frantic. He had spent most of August in Antibes, a resort town on the Côte d'Azur, with his second mistress, Dora Maar. He returned to Paris to protect his belongings—scattered across multiple studios and homes—but it was impossible. He was a hoarder, so every location was overfilled with items he had collected over the years. There were times when he picked things up off the street in such quantity that his jacket pockets tore. He also had dozens of paintings by Cézanne, Renoir, Matisse, and Braque in his personal collection. Hoarding gave him comfort and was a tangible reminder of the past for a man breaking convention in all things.

Dismayed with war, Picasso began painting a dark and apocalyptic scene of the local fishermen in Antibes. It was a metaphorical *Guernica*-like creation amid an explosion of deep blues, violets, and magenta. His presence in France, as a refugee from Spain, had always been precarious. The government had been keeping a file on him since 1901, when he was branded an anarchist, and became subject to annual renewals of his foreign residence permit. With a new occupier, his life in France could become even more uncertain.

Picasso decided to drive out of Paris without having accomplished much. He headed to Royan, a seaside town on the Bay of Biscay, with Dora, his dog Kazbek, and his close friend, the Spanish artist Jaime Sabartés. There, he had already set up his first mistress, Marie-Thérèse Walter, and their daughter, Maya. (His long-suffering wife, Olga, was not there but loomed in his thoughts as they were technically still married.)

He cut off contact with virtually everyone else, including Alfred H. Barr Jr. at the Museum of Modern Art, who desperately wanted Picasso to send his most recent sculptures to the exhibition in New York and to attend the opening. Barr enlisted everyone who could influence Picasso to help, including Paul Rosenberg, the artist's former dealer Daniel-Henry Kahnweiler, Dora Maar, and even Standard Oil heir Nelson Rockefeller, a board member of the museum. It would all be futile. "Picasso has disappeared," the artist Mary Callery informed Barr. "Nobody has heard from him," art historian Christian Zervos, the author of Picasso's catalogue raisonné, wrote in a letter to Barr. The bronze sculptures, which included the head of a rooster, languished in a foundry in Paris.

DESPITE THE INITIAL ANXIETY AT the outbreak of war, life in France quickly resumed a semblance of normalcy. The battles were a thousand miles away in Eastern Europe for the time being. In mid-September, Rose received an exciting letter from the Latvian legation in Paris, informing her she had been made a Knight of the Order of the Three Stars, the country's highest honorary decoration for civilians. It was a tribute to her work on the Latvian exhibition at the Jeu de Paume, and Rose was overjoyed. She felt especially moved since the exhibition was one of the last she had mounted before the war.

Rose's boss, André Dezarrois, had not forgotten her either. He was sleeping on a linoleum floor and scrounging for sheets and blankets while in the Air Force, but he managed to write to Henri Verne—who would nominally retain his title as director of the Musées Nationaux until the end of November—requesting to have Rose paid. "She has been working for the honor of the museums for ten years and the war has just dried up her meager resources," he appealed, asking if money from Verne's "secret fund" could be allocated to Rose, still an unpaid volunteer in the books, in these "times of misfortunes." But even during a war, Verne would not budge, let alone pull from his illicit slush fund for her.

Gallery owner Paul Rosenberg, meanwhile, felt shiftless. "I am desperate with nothing to do," he wrote to Alfred H. Barr Jr. He would not be able to attend the opening of the Picasso exhibition in New York, fearful that his son Alexandre might get called up for war. Business was also slow amid the uncertainty. He asked Matisse whether it was time to renegotiate their contract. The last version, signed as recently as July, had a clause that nullified it in times of war. He also encouraged Matisse to come to Tours to remind him of the "good old days." "The idleness does not suit my character," he told the artist while remaining determined. "I want to do something, and I will do it," he swore.

But something more personal nagged him—Paul was worried about Alexandre's future. Due to the war, Alexandre would have to postpone his second year at the Sorbonne, and with no university in Tours, Paul feared that his son would become too indolent. Paul hoped to relocate his family to Bordeaux, a city in southwest France, and enroll Alexandre in university there. "I still don't know when I'll come back to Paris," he wrote to Matisse, echoing others who had fled the French capital.

PARIS

FALL 1939

THE DAYS STRETCHED INTO MONTHS. POLAND HAD FALLEN BUT MUCH of Paris was living like the war would never come. Air-raid alerts were social events, particularly in the hotels where you could procure a cup of coffee, soup, or even a Hermès sleeping bag in the Ritz's basement shelter. The theaters and the opera reopened, and the denizens of Paris got their joie de vivre and their snark back. There was also no shortage of the thing most important to French people—food—with rock lobsters, oysters, and game in abundance. But with no action on French soil, a major bout of ennui had set in. People started referring to it as the "*drôle de guerre*," the "funny war." The British called it the "phoney war." The war seemed to barely touch their lives. Sporadic battles and air attacks all took place in distant locales, far outside their borders. Secretly, however, Hitler was planning a major offensive to invade France, as well as the neutral countries of Holland, Belgium, and Luxembourg, as early as November 12.

ROSE'S LIFE, MEANWHILE, WAS FILLED with a new daily routine: checking on the stored artwork and making sure everything in the Jeu de Paume—fire protection system, electrical circuitry, locks, and so forth—functioned. As cooler temperatures arrived, the art stashed in the boiler room became an issue. It was an obvious fire hazard, so turning on the heat would not be possible. Leaving it off was also not a solution—humidity from the cold temperatures could damage the paintings, and Rose and the staff would freeze in the winter.

Curatorial work at the Jeu de Paume also normalized to some extent, albeit at a much slower pace. Rose helped coordinate the loans of nine paintings from the museum's collection for an exhibition at the Polish embassy, which also served as the seat of the Polish government in exile. She also made the Jeu de Paume's first new acquisition since the outbreak of war, a drawing of Gandhi by Lou Albert-Lasard, an Austrian woman living in Paris who studied with Fernand Léger. In her small way, Rose found it possible to support working female artists.

The most exciting news was that she was finally being paid. Due to a new emergency war budget, she, along with several other unpaid *attachés* and volunteers, would temporarily be getting 1,250 francs a month. It was not a lot—only about a quarter of Dezarrois's salary, whose job she was doing—but it was something. It was all thanks to Jacques Jaujard, who was managing the wartime personnel issues and signing off on matters on behalf of Verne, who was scarcely to be found given his impending forced retirement. According to Pierre Schommer, Verne was like a "king confined," waiting out the time left of his disgraced tenure while Jaujard, his heir-apparent, ran the show expertly.

In November, the Rosenberg family moved into a small neo-Gothic castle, Le Castel, in Floirac, a small village right across the river from Bordeaux. Alexandre enrolled at the University of Bordeaux and began training to be an officer. Paul poured his energy into curating an exhibition at the Musée des Beaux-Arts de Bordeaux. He also signed new wartime contracts with Matisse and Braque and returned to his work as an art dealer with renewed vitality.

As Matisse's confidant, Paul encouraged the artist through his latest period of despair and reminded him that he was a great talent. With his usual pessimism, Matisse felt that any greatness ascribed to him was merely an illusion. Thrust into another war at seventy years old, he wrote to Paul, "I need to remind myself that my days are now numbered and try to overcome my torment." Paul also went to see Picasso in Royan and brought back five paintings. They were not to Paul's wife Margot's liking, but Alexandre hung a portrait of a woman with a coiled nose in his bedroom to the merriment of the family and staff. "Howls from his mother and the housekeeper," Paul wrote to Picasso.

While the Rosenbergs settled into their new place in Floirac, the *Mona Lisa* was strapped onto a gurney and covertly moved in a hermetically sealed, airtight truck from Chambord to the Château de Louvigny, about thirty miles north of Le Mans. The usual suspects for such a high-risk art maneuver were present: Pierre Schommer was inside the vehicle during the roughly hundred-mile trip, practically gasping for air while vigilantly checking the straps of the stretcher, and Albert Henraux was once again driving the lead car. The *Mona Lisa* would spend the winter hibernating inside an armoire.

The Louvre's large history paintings made their way to various castles across France. The Winged Victory of Samothrace, the Venus de Milo, the Code of Hammurabi, and Michelangelo's *Slaves*, along with the French crown jewels and the scepter of Charlemagne, arrived at Valençay, a magnificent Renaissance château. There, the quixotic Prince of Talleyrand kept a chattering parrot collection and allowed kangaroos, llamas, peacocks, and zebras to roam free in the castle gardens.

At Chambord, Schommer obsessively patrolled the castle grounds with two dogs and a gun in hand and surveilled the terraces of the castle overnight. Schommer was right to be vigilant. Unbeknownst to anyone in France, there were many close calls that first winter. Hitler called off the November 12 invasion at the last minute but readied the troops thirteen more times, only to cancel the attacks again. German airplanes occasionally flew overhead, a roaring reminder to the French of their enemy's imperialist might.

Behind the scenes, Hans Posse, the director of Dresden's Old Masters Picture Gallery, was working diligently on the acquisitions for the Führermuseum. He sorted through the looted artwork gathered in Vienna—most of it from the Rothschilds—and took 122 Old Master paintings by Rembrandt, Hans Holbein the Younger, Anthony van Dyck, Lucas Cranach the Elder, and others. He then moved on to Czechoslovakia, where everything, Jewish-owned or not, was up for pillaging.

All the art for Hitler's consideration was brought to Munich and hung in the air-raid shelter of the Führerbau, a building used for major diplomatic events. However, the pace of collecting was already causing storage space concerns. Hitler believed that only a large castle would be sizeable enough to contain all the art that would eventually be in the Führermuseum, and he tasked his underlings with finding somewhere suitable.

Hitler spent hours staring at the wood models of Linz and the

Führermuseum in the basement of the Reich Chancellery in Berlin. He would regularly grab a pencil and make a sketch and could draw buildings, cross-sections, and renderings quickly. Although he ran political matters in a combative and domineering fashion, Hitler was deferential and polite when discussing art and architecture and often acceded to the designer's opinion in the end. As architect Albert Speer later wrote, "He asked for changes amiably and without any note of protest."

Hitler envisioned Linz as a bustling metropolis with imposing public buildings on both banks of the Danube River and a suspension bridge that would connect the two parts of the city. The Gau House, the district headquarters of the Nazi Party, would contain a large event hall, under which Hitler planned to put a crypt for his final burial place. There would also be a stadium, a train station, a town hall, a library that could hold 250,000 books, a military headquarters, and multiple monuments and museums.

The future Führermuseum would sit on one end of a large plaza, from which a long line of imperial-style buildings would extend. Designed in the neoclassically inspired style preferred by Hitler, the Führermuseum would feature an almost five-hundred-foot-long colonnaded front facade topped by a central sculpture. It would be larger than any art museum that had come before it, with over twenty-two miles of galleries, curated by Posse with the highest possible discretion.

Hitler kept track of building plans in over thirty cities, but Linz was his favorite, and he dedicated the most time to it. The Führermuseum, in particular, was a frequent topic of Hitler's social gatherings, where all subjects related to the museum would be discussed, from the lighting to the furnishings to the hanging of the paintings in the galleries.

With the fall of Poland came more art to sort, but Posse dismissed most of what he found there. He took only three Old Masters and thirty Dürer drawings, but Hitler loved them so much that he brought them to his military headquarters. As a well-trained art historian, Posse knew that the Führermuseum collection would be incomplete with only the new acquisitions from Eastern Europe and what Hitler had collected himself. There were so many masterpieces in France if he could only get his hands on them. Luckily for Posse, the floodgates of art would open soon, giving Hitler and his henchman unbelievable riches to fight over—and maybe die over.

FLOIRAC, FRANCE

SPRING 1940

PAUL ROSENBERG SPENT THE SPRING TRAVELING ALL OVER FRANCE, visiting his artists. In March, he hand-carried two new paintings from Matisse's studio in Nice on the train. He even planned to reopen his gallery in Paris. "What a fine reopening that will be!" he predicted optimistically, envisioning an exhibition with five new paintings each from Matisse, Braque, and Picasso. He was instrumental in two Picasso exhibitions that opened in Belgium and the Netherlands, and he was still working on the exhibition for the Musée des Beaux-Arts de Bordeaux. He also had a speaking tour through America with the Art Institute of Chicago on the books.

Le Castel was starting to feel like home as well. Paul's wife, Margot, was pleased that the house was finally decorated. There were new paintings and comforting old ones moved from 21 rue la Boétie in Paris and from the warehouse in Tours. New works by Matisse—the very best that the artist had ever done, in Paul's opinion—were hung in the living room, while new Picasso paintings went up in the dining room. The art even improved their social lives. To Picasso, Paul wrote, "Thanks to you, our meals are less monotonous, your canvases provoke both appreciation and hilarity."

Both Matisse and Braque came to visit Le Castel. Paul also saw Picasso, who just had his French naturalization rejected again. Allegedly, he had been overheard at the Café de Flore in Paris making anti-French statements. The perpetual suspicion of communist and anarchist sympathies had not gone away either. Whether it was the two wars on his mind—the Spanish Civil War and the war with Germany—or his complicated love life, Picasso was going through a dark phase creatively.

PARIS

SPRING 1940

BY SPRING, THINGS WERE STARTING TO HEAT UP ON ALL FRONTS. Hitler told Hans Posse in person that the invasion of Western Europe was finally about to begin. "Wonderful mood," the art historian wrote in his diary—invasion meant more loot. With frightening speed using a new strategy called blitzkrieg, the Nazis conquered Denmark in one day and the Netherlands in less than a week. The looting of Jewish property began immediately, and the Dutch art market was flooded with a sudden influx of inventory. Posse would soon present Hitler with his first annual acquisition list for the Führermuseum. The new bounty would undoubtedly make the report even more impressive.

In Paris, Rose was dealing with a whole new situation. Crude military men had replaced the paintings and sculptures at the Jeu de Paume. The *aérostiers*, the French Air Force's hot air balloon corps, had been billeted in her museum for months and did their ballooning day and night in the Tuileries Garden.

A detachment of anti-aircraft forces (the *défense contre les aéronefs*, or the DCA) had also been recently added into the mix. They were using up the museum's gas and electricity and monopolizing the telephone to communicate with their command posts, driving up utility costs. Rose was determined not to let that happen.

First, she reported their behavior—by letter and in person—to Jacques Jaujard to establish on the record that the spike in utility usage was not due to the regular operations of the Jeu de Paume. Jaujard was in a tricky spot since he had warmly welcomed the DCA free of charge due to the security benefits their presence could have for the museums. He punted the issue back to Rose, who charged over to the battalion commanders and demanded that they not only share the costs but also warned them not to waste precious resources. By the time the *aérostiers* drama was concluded, Germany was nearly done tearing through Belgium, and Winston Churchill was the new prime minister of the United Kingdom.

In the southwest of France, Paul Rosenberg was taking some additional precautions surrounding his art, given the latest war developments. He put 162 artworks in a bank vault in Libourne, a town twenty miles northeast of his home in Floirac. The breadth of just this subsect of Rosenberg's collection was astonishing—works by Monet, Cézanne, Van Gogh, Renoir, Gauguin, and Picasso, among many others. When Braque visited the Rosenbergs at Floirac at the end of May, Paul convinced him to get a vault in the same bank.

All of these decisions were timely. On May 10, 1940, in a brilliant tactical move, the Germans invaded France through the Ardennes, a densely forested mountain region on the border of Belgium, which the French thought impenetrable from their experience in World War I and had primarily left undefended. The assault was fast and unexpected, and the French were vastly outnumbered, particularly by the Luftwaffe. The French were left in shock by the kind of war the Germans were waging, just as the Belgians, the Dutch, the Luxembourgians, and the Norwegians had been. "Ah these Bosches!" Rose stressed in a letter to Marguerite, in response to the latest events, using a pejorative French term for the Germans. "The morale of Paris is admirable," she also maintained.

Shortly after the Germans crossed into France, Picasso ran into Matisse on the street in Paris. "Where are you going!?" Picasso asked Matisse anxiously, who replied that he was headed to the tailor. Picasso exclaimed, "How?! Don't you know that the front is completely broken, the army has tumbled, there's a stampede, the Germans are approaching Soissons. Tomorrow they may be in Paris?"

Matisse answered, "I know, but then, what are our generals doing?"

"Our generals are equivalent to the École des Beaux-Arts!" Picasso retorted, referencing their mutual hatred of the school, which Rose Valland had attended. Like the school, the French generals were stuck in a different century.

In a snap, Germany had invaded France. Then, instead of going inland to Paris, the Germans headed northwest toward the English Channel, trapping the Allied forces at Dunkirk. Next, they set their sights on Paris. Suddenly, the funny war was not so funny anymore.

PARIS

JUNE 13, 1940

AT THE CRACK OF DAWN, THE PHONE RANG AT THE JEU DE PAUME. IT was Jacques Jaujard. "Leave the museum," he told Rose. It was an order: the Germans would breach the city by the next morning. But Rose was disappointed. Everyone was fleeing Paris, and all she wanted was to stay behind to protect what was left of the art in the Jeu de Paume.

She had been campaigning to remain for weeks. She pointed out to both Jaujard and his boss, Georges Huisman, the director general of the Beaux-Arts, that she was the only curator left—the sole person who knew the art and how to take care of it. The staff at the museum was already reduced to a skeleton crew, with just Rose, two guards, and a fire brigadier. Most of the guards had been reassigned to depots in the Loire Valley the previous fall. She also reminded Huisman that he had been supportive of letting her stay, and that not having someone familiar with the art on-site would be "contrary to the interests of the Jeu de Paume." She was not afraid to talk this way, even to the boss of her boss.

From the museum, Rose would have seen smoke rising and bits of paper floating down all over the first arrondissement, carried by a swirling wind. The French government and British embassy were tossing documents—classified and not—out the window and into wheelbarrows, then burning them in huge bonfires. Was there anything more definitive than a nation burning its archives?

A dark-gray veil fell over the city, and the air was impregnated with soot. Paris was looking apocalyptic. The Standard Oil Company had set its petroleum stock ablaze in the French capital to keep it out of German hands. Thick black smoke from the vast gas refineries in Normandy, also set on fire, wafted all the way north to England and south to Paris, causing temperatures to drop by eighteen degrees in the north of France. An American diplomat thought Paris looked like a scene from Dante's Inferno.

Events were indeed dire. The Germans bombed Paris and its environs on June 3, flying in 240 planes and dropping 1,087 bombs. Two hundred and fifty-four people were killed, including twenty children, and 652 people were injured. The US ambassador, William Bullitt, nearly lost his life while having biscuits and sherry at lunch with the French Minister of Air, Laurent Eynac, when a bomb crashed through the ceiling and landed just feet from where they were. Miraculously, it was a dud. After that attack, Paris had only hours to assess the damage. Air-raid sirens rang out again in the early morning three days later.

Two million Parisians were now on an exodus, joining other war refugees trying to make it anywhere farther south. In all, somewhere between eight and ten million refugees went on this journey with no set destination, most of whom were French citizens, with the rest predominantly from Belgium and the Netherlands. "Somewhere in the north of France a boot had scattered an ant hill, and the ants were on the march," wrote Antoine de Saint-Exupéry, author of *Le Petit Prince*, who observed the exodus from high above in his French Air Force plane. The roads were in complete chaos, jammed with people attempting to flee by car, bus, bicycle, and on foot. Vehicles were filled with bicycles, furniture, pets, and livestock, and topped with mattresses to protect them from bullets. Stuck in an interminable traffic jam and out of gas, people abandoned their cars and belongings, now deemed useless. Out of desperation, great-grandparents, the elderly, and the young were dumped into horse-drawn carriages, handcarts, strollers, and wheelbarrows. The streaming masses battled for space along roads occupied by a confused French military in retreat from the north of France.

It was a trail of blood, sweat, and tears. Italy had joined the war on June 10, 1940, and they, along with the Germans, strafed the refugees by plane, knowing that the French would not risk responding with so many civilians on the ground. Anytime a plane flew over, the panicked hordes dove into the ditches along the road. German troops arrived on foot as well and waged deadly ground battles, resulting in civilian casualties by friendly fire and otherwise. A French army truck fleeing south from the enemy ran over a sixteen-year-old girl at Chambord. Two art curators, Jean Cassou and Agnès Humbert, tried to save her but she bled out, surrounded by helpless museum administrators. Thousands of children were separated from their families. At Valençay, a mother was out of her mind screaming, unable to find her two young daughters.

In Paris, the French government took stock of the military situation as the enemy barreled down on the gates of the city. On June 10, a message labeled "Very Secret" arrived from General Maxime Weygand, commander of the French Army, stating the terrible truth: "The final rupture of our lines of defense may happen at any moment." The French government fled Paris that day and put the city in the hands of US Ambassador William Bullitt, who was refusing to leave. He cabled a defiant message to US Secretary of State Cordell Hull that stated, "Since the age of four I have never run away from anything however painful or dangerous when I thought it was my duty to take a stand. If I should leave Paris now I would no longer be myself." He was the only diplomat left in Paris and had been made the provisional mayor by French prime minister Paul Reynaud and interior minister George Mandel. It would be up to him and him alone to negotiate with the Germans and persuade them not to obliterate the city as they had done to Warsaw and Rotterdam.

Like Bullitt, Rose would have preferred to stay in Paris despite the turmoil. But Jaujard had made his decision. He signed her mission order, directing her to the depots in the Loire Valley. She folded this paper up and kept it with her. She would need it to pass military checkpoints. A second order from the Beaux-Arts was even more specific. It permitted her to move freely and requested that all civil and military authorities assist her in the protection of the national collections of art.

Jaujard was incredibly busy leading up to this critical juncture. He did not have time for hesitancy or arguments. He led a final evacuation of art from the Louvre and moved what was stored too close to Paris farther south. It was a dangerous mission, done under machine-gun fire from an Italian fighter plane squadron. When a curator refused to go close to the front to retrieve a series of pastels by La Tour, Jaujard told him, "Since the noise of the cannons frightens you so much, I will go myself." Curator Jean Cassou volunteered instead. Jaujard then personally accompanied the *Mona Lisa* from Louvigny back to Chambord, where she would continue on to her new home in the abbey of Loc-Dieu in the south of France.

The last art convoy crossed the Loire River just before the bridges were blown up to thwart the German advance. Louvre curator Germain Bazin, who was wearing a military uniform, used his authority as an army captain to delay the explosion. They were lucky. On another bridge, the detonation went off while a man was still biking across, killing some French soldiers as well.

Jaujard also helped the Belgians move their prized possession, *The Adoration of the Mystic Lamb*, a seventeen-panel altarpiece from Ghent. Jaujard was testing out a tactic he would employ many times in the future: shroud a high-profile piece of art in bureaucratic paperwork. Officially, it was going to the city of Pau, in the southwest of France, for an upcoming exhibition, but unofficially, it was all part of a carefully coordinated art protection plan and would never go on display.

During all this, Jaujard remained warm and reassuring with his staff. Gathering his frightened employees in his Louvre office, he smiled as he handed out evacuation orders and directed everyone to the trucks that would take them, hopefully, to safety. "I would like my Jewish colleagues to leave first," he said, knowing what fate might befall them in the hands of the Germans. There was no detail that Jaujard would overlook.

Jaujard, too, was loath to leave Paris, but he could not fulfill his duties to protect the country's artwork if he was trapped in the Louvre, waiting for the Germans to arrive. Gabriel Rouchès, Rose's thesis adviser from the École du Louvre and the head curator of the Department of Drawings, volunteered to take Jaujard's place in Paris, with only one guard to protect him. Rouchès was a good choice—he was fluent in

German, cool under pressure, and very experienced. It was especially brave considering that he was within months of his retirement at nearly sixty years of age. Most of the museum staff assumed they would never see him alive again and tearfully watched him leave Chambord. But if there was anyone who could keep the marauding Germans at bay while keeping his head on and the Louvre intact, it was Rouchès.

The women of the Louvre pitched in wherever they could. Jacqueline Bouchot-Saupique braved the roads of France again, leading art convoys repeatedly between Chambord and Paris. The staff at Chambord feared for her safety every time she drove away, and Louvre archivist Lucie Mazauric described Bouchot-Saupique's car tires as "thin as sheets of paper."

Meanwhile, Rose was entrusted with evacuating the very last of the Louvre guards and their families. At this late stage in the exodus, the roads were unnavigable. The only viable way out of Paris would be by *péniche*, the flat-bottomed boats on the Seine. Rose thought it was a harebrained decision by Jaujard, who was usually so level-headed, to send so many people in such an unprepared, unprotected, and disorganized fashion. But she would follow his orders.

In the afternoon, the loading of the last group of employees began along the banks of the Seine. Rose immediately realized that this final evacuation from the Louvre would not go as planned. The workers had brought too many belongings. "As always, in a departure of this importance, there are latecomers," Rose later described, irritated. She blamed the wives of the museum guards, who must have been trying to take too much with them, she thought. In the end, 120 men, women, and children squashed onto the boat together, with mountains of luggage piled up.

On board, Rose found one of her Louvre colleagues, Madeleine Bernheim, who worked for Pierre Schommer. The young woman had proven her mettle during the art evacuations in September 1939 as a *convoyeur*, driving a car that accompanied one of the first fleets of trucks to Chambord. Claude Ferraton, a publications editor from the Louvre, was put in charge of navigating the boat.

Between the panicked people and the toppling luggage, Rose was unsure if she could keep everything under control, including the stability of the boat. It was hot and drizzling, and amid the agitated evacuees, Rose, Madeleine, and Claude were the only ones who managed to remain calm. Hopefully the weather would hold—a torrential downpour had deluged Paris just the night before.

Not surprisingly, the *péniche* did not depart until 6 p.m. By then, the quays were deserted. A few abandoned dogs wandered about the Place de la Concorde and sheep brayed, deserted by their refugee owners in the gardens of Les Invalides. A British woman who stayed behind in Paris that day described it as a

> dead city; hardly anyone walked abroad. Every shop and house door was closed and barred. The seemingly endless stream of vehicles had come to an end. The exodus had spent itself and the town appeared to be completely empty. If any Parisians were left, they took good care not to show themselves . . . Paris, the *Ville Lumière* became the city of gloom, emptied of all its inhabitants, purged of its traffic, the theaters, cafés and hotels closed . . . No vestige of authority was to be seen . . . yet the streets were quiet, with an ominous hush, as before a storm.

The ordinarily busy river, the lifeblood of the ancient city, was devoid of boats. Artillery fire just outside Paris brought the clamoring of nearby danger, but Rose's *péniche*, carrying some of the very last people to leave the city, slid peacefully under the bridges of the Seine. High voltage electric lines, cut for the blackout, hung limply over the water. Occasionally, an abandoned boat floated by. Somewhere ahead of them were two boats carrying the archives of the Ministry of the Interior, including sensitive information about foreigners in France.

As dusk fell, Rose's *péniche* approached Charenton, five miles east of the Louvre, where the Seine and the Marne rivers meet. There was a complete traffic jam. Boats and barges bumped into one another as they merged at this confluence in Paris's industrial zone and waited their turn to go through the Port l'Anglais river lock, one-and-a-half miles south. Inside the lock, the boats would need to wait for upstream water to fill the chamber and raise them to the upper level of the river.

Claude assessed that it would take another day before their *péniche* could get through, which was confirmed by information passed back by boat from the lock operators. By that time, it would be too late. Everyone onboard would be at risk, potentially getting rounded up by the Germans or, worse, getting killed in an aerial attack. Rose later described their predicament at Charenton as one of "catastrophic disorder." With the sun going down, Rose felt the anxiety of the group rise amid the din from the bottleneck.

One thing was clear: they could not wait immobile and defenseless. A war council of three was formed. Rose and Madeleine would return to the Louvre to report what happened and request trucks to pick the group up. Claude would stay to navigate the ship and take care of the passengers. It was insanity for Rose to head back into Paris now, hours before the Germans were expected to enter the city, but the group was in a desperate situation.

ON FOOT, ROSE AND MADELEINE made their way back. The Métro was closed, but on some stretches, they were able to flag down an accommodating car. At ten o'clock in the evening, after several hours of travel, they arrived back at the Louvre and immediately apprised Rouchès of the situation. Although the French army had cut the telegraph lines, telephones were still operational, so Rouchès was able to reach the police—the few officers still working—and receive approval to send trucks to Charenton.

With their mission accomplished, Rose and Madeleine set off again to bring the good news back to their colleagues stuck on the river.

In the meantime, there was a brief, positive development on the diplomatic front. Thanks to Paul Reynaud and Ambassador Bullitt's last-ditch efforts, Paris was officially declared an open city. The French would put up no more resistance, the Germans could take it over peacefully in the morning, and bloodshed could hopefully be avoided on both sides. But that agreement was soon in a precarious position after German truce officers were shot near the Porte Saint-Denis, the triumphant arch about a mile northeast of the Louvre. In retaliation, German General Georg von Küchler ordered an all-out air and artillery destruction of Paris at eight in the morning.

All this was unknown to Rose and Madeleine as they made their way back to the *péniche* over the next few hours. The city gates would be closed at midnight, so they needed to move quickly. Rose could hear the cannonade exploding incessantly and getting ever closer. She could not tell exactly where the shells were falling, but knew they were not far. Then there were the sharp tapping sounds of French engineers mining the bridges of the Seine with explosives. Rose thought of how absurd it was to cross the bridges at this time, but she would not shy away from danger. "It was, however, necessary to arrive at all costs," she later recounted with conviction.

At 2 a.m., Rose and Madeleine finally arrived back at Charenton. They couldn't believe their eyes. The whole museum entourage had disappeared into thin air! The guards, their families, the luggage, Claude, and the boat—all gone. Not only had all their efforts to rescue their colleagues by truck come to naught, but they had also lost their transportation down to the Loire Valley. In the intervening hours, their *péniche* headed south without them.

The two women decided to walk an additional mile and a half south along the Seine to the Port l'Anglais lock and cross it on foot to avoid the traffic jam leading up to it. They then hitched a ride on a boat on the other side of the lock. It was a smart move, but now they were utterly exhausted.

Rose lay down to rest on the deck, but as they floated south, German *Stuka* planes—the sleek dive bombers leading the blitzkrieg—flew over. The sky lit up, and the smell of petroleum pervaded the air. Rose listened closely to the sound of the explosions and heard with relief that the bombs were hitting dry land and not the boats on the river. The planes were aiming for Orly airfield, just inland to their right. The fuel reserves along the river were also set ablaze, and the agglomeration of boats packed hull to hull and side to side glowed against this fiery industrial backdrop.

While the Luftwaffe was on the warpath, diplomatic negotiations between Ambassador Bullitt and the Germans continued. General Küchler had agreed to a conference with the French before bombing Paris but the French commander of the Paris region was now refusing to negotiate on the grounds that he did not have the authority to discuss such matters with the enemy. At 2:25 a.m., the Germans sent an ultimatum: send delegates by 6 a.m., or the attack on Paris would commence. The French commander acquiesced this time.

Shortly after, Rose and Madeleine hit their next obstacle. A new bottleneck had appeared at the river lock at Evry, about thirteen miles south of Charenton. Rose's pluck was being tested. A few hours earlier, Rose was able to look back at the exploding cityscape behind her—a city whose sounds were replaced by those of war—and find the will to push forward. Now, all she could see was total disaster. She had also left Joyce behind, along with the art she desperately wanted to protect, in a city on the brink of invasion, and the realization was almost too tangible. "No matter how much you run away from defeat, no matter how much you don't want to believe it, there always comes a time when it catches up to you," she would later reflect on this moment.

Then the fateful news came: evacuation by boat was no longer possible. More German columns were en route to Paris and the river flotilla could easily become a target. Forward movement through the lock would be unlikely. The two women would have to walk the hundred miles left to Chambord, if they could find roads open to them.

Rose quickly formulated a plan. To start, they would disembark at Corbeil, a town just on the other bank of the Seine. The intractable flotilla would finally serve one purpose at least: as a bridge. The boats, rubbing up against one another, filled the entire width of the Seine.

A nearby *péniche* carrying 150 Parisian factory workers and their families, several rabbits, and four meowing cats in cages was stuck in the lock itself. Those evacuees were making the best of the situation, drinking a bottle of Mumm champagne cooled down in the river while tied to a string. They subsisted off the last of their crackers, pâté, rum, jam, and bread. The boat with the Louvre employees had unloaded here earlier as well, whereupon most of the passengers had decided to abandon the group. Under a half-moon, Rose and Madeleine leaped from one barge to another to reach the opposite shore, bypassing the lock entirely.

Corbeil, usually buzzing with foundries, printing presses, and paper mills, was deserted apart from a few French soldiers. They were the last of the bridge miners from farther north, waiting for the order to blow up the bridges, and were now hoping to catch up with what remained of the French army. The soldiers gave the two famished women a loaf of bread and offered them a ride on their mule-drawn cart filled with explosives. As dangerous as that sounded, this was the mode of transport they needed—the highways to the Loire Valley might still be open to the military if they moved fast enough.

The only problem was that the soldiers were fatigued and kept falling asleep, letting the mules navigate on their own. Reinvigorated by the change in fortune, Rose took the reins and drove the men and their explosives through the night until dawn. Chambord was now twelve miles closer. Eventually she felt they could make it faster on their own without the beleaguered mules and parted ways with the soldiers.

Shortly after 5:30 a.m., Germany and France agreed on a peaceful handover of Paris. The City of Light, with its historic monuments and grand avenues, would survive another day but was forced to submit to a tyrannical regime to save itself. The German invasion elsewhere in France would not be so gentle, however. In fact, the most dangerous part of Rose's journey lay just ahead.

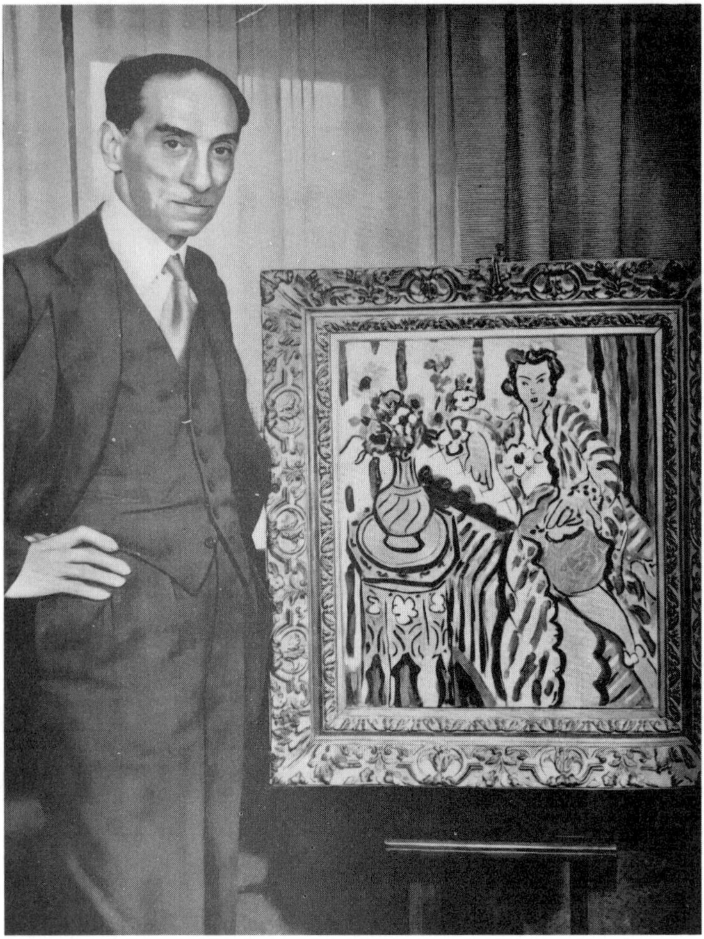

Paul Rosenberg with a painting by Matisse, 1930.

FLOIRAC

JUNE 13, 1940

WHILE ROSE WAS MAKING HER TREACHEROUS JOURNEY DOWN TO THE Loire Valley, Alexandre Rosenberg listened to a fervent debate taking place in the living room of Le Castel, the house outside Bordeaux he had been living in since the previous fall. To leave or not to leave France—the pros and cons had been weighed for several days now.

Fifteen family members crammed in the house, along with Monsieur and Madame Ledoux, the owners of Le Castel who lived in the fourth-floor apartment. Alexandre's aunts, uncles, and cousins—the two Helft families—had come from Paris, along with other relatives.

Paul Rosenberg had also invited his artists to come, out of concern for their safety. Georges Braque and his wife planned to stay for a few nights after a bombing in Corrèze, where they were staying. However, Le Castel was full by the time they arrived, and there was not a single couch to sleep on. The hotels in Bordeaux were completely booked. Thousands of people were sleeping outdoors, camping out in the city's parks. For one night, Henri Matisse and his assistant, Lydia stayed with Paul's brother-in-law, Jacques Helft, with thirty-three other people. Then, Matisse and Lydia ended up accidentally staying in a brothel. Matisse joked with Paul about the public health sign for prostitutes hanging in his room—"Discreetly examine the genitals of the client…"— it read. "I've never laughed so much and it had been so long since something made me happy," Matisse wrote.

At Le Castel, however, the conversation was heated. The Rosenberg family gathered to discuss their options. Jacques was resolute. "We have to leave, this is going to be terrible," he announced. Alexandre's mother, Margot, was hesitant. They were French and had been for generations. Why should they have to leave? Paul suggested that Jacques was overly agitated and that a potential armistice meant that the French government would find a way of working with Hitler. Paul was optimistic about staying—his business was strong, and he had many exciting projects in progress.

Jacques exploded. He shouted that he had read *Mein Kampf* twice and he could vouch that all Jews would be exterminated. Finally, he said, "I'm not going to put this up to a vote. My lot is leaving tomorrow. You can stay if you want." The force of the pronouncement was enough—the whole family decided to leave together and go to Portugal. From there, they could take a ship across the Atlantic since the Portuguese ports were still open.

A few critical administrative challenges would have to be conquered before they left, which would be no small feat given the ongoing disintegration of France. The government had fled chaotically from Paris along with all its civil servants. Many members of the Rosenberg family did not have passports. Fortunately, Jacques's wife, Marianne, knew the wife of French president Albert Lebrun's secretary from elementary school and found out that the president was holed up in the Hôtel Splendide in Bordeaux. She showed up there and managed to procure all the passports needed within a few hours.

Next was the problem of securing Portuguese visas. Fascist dictator Francisco Franco was temporarily allowing refugees to cross through Spain as long as they did not settle there, but visas were needed to leave France and enter Portugal. There were rumors that thousands of people were lining up outside the Portuguese consulate in Bordeaux, and the family anticipated a multiday wait with no guarantee. Thanks to a letter of introduction from the president's secretary, however, Marianne was allowed inside the consulate. She returned ecstatically an hour later saying, "It's unbelievable! . . . I don't know who attended us but he stamped our seventeen passports in a question of ten minutes! They're all signed, and I couldn't believe it!"

The Portuguese consul in Bordeaux, Aristides de Sousa Mendes, was issuing last-minute visas against the orders of his government. A Portuguese directive known as "Circular 14," in place from November 1939, barred visas for war refugees deemed "inconvenient or dangerous," particularly Jews expelled from their country, foreigners of "indefinite or contested nationality," and Russians. Portugal was officially neutral but allied with Franco's Spain and was trading with Nazi Germany.

Opting for a humanitarian approach, de Sousa Mendes avowed, "I would rather stand with God against Man than with Man against God." At the risk of criminal and political prosecution, the consul and his secretary provided thousands of visas to European Jews and political refugees as Belgium and France fell. Salvador Dalí fled this way, as did Margret and Hans Rey, who escaped with the manuscript for their children's book *Curious George* in their bicycle basket. At the consulate, about eight people at a long wooden table processed the transit visas as fast as possible, often for free for those who could not afford the cost. It would be more than fifty years before the Rosenbergs learned just how lucky they were to cross paths with de Sousa Mendes in Bordeaux.

While all these clerical activities were underway, Alexandre was busy assisting his father. There were seventy-seven paintings and drawings at Le Castel, either hung on the walls or stored in the greenhouse, by the likes of Renoir, Delacroix, Courbet, and Paul's modern artists. They included the largest paintings in Paul's collection (which did not fit into the bank safe at Libourne), and several Picasso portraits of the family of great sentimental value. On one wall was a

Degas pastel, the *Portrait of Gabrielle Diot.* On another was a 1904 *Waterlilies* painting by Monet.

On three pages of paper, Alexandre handwrote an inventory in rapid script, listing the painter and the French title of the painting. Each artist was given a symbol—some permutation of dashes, X's, circles, or squares—to make it easier to count how many works of each artist there were. It was an informal inventory, but it would have to do. Paul asked the house staff to pack the paintings into cases and left the art in their custody until he could decide what to do with it. He hid a few paintings inside Le Castel and above the garage. With the passports and visas acquired and their bags packed, the family was ready to embark on a journey that would take them across countries, seas, and continents.

LOIRE VALLEY

JUNE 17, 1940

AS ALEXANDRE ROSENBERG AND HIS FAMILY BEGAN THEIR GREAT ESCAPE, Rose Valland was about to reach the Loire River, over forty miles from Chambord, her intended destination. It had been a treacherous two days since she and Madeleine had left the mule and ammunition cart. Low-flying German airplane squadrons patrolled the main roads. In unseasonably hot weather, the two women ran from bombing to bombing while searching for a route to Chambord. Rose and Madeleine managed to make it safely to the banks of the Loire River at the town of Châteauneuf-sur-Loire, about fifteen miles east of Orléans. Unlike many other Loire River crossings, the bridge there was still standing—but perhaps not for long.

Night fell, and Rose was at an impasse among a sea of refugees swarming on the grassy banks of the river. The Germans were close. On the bridge, French soldiers calmly and heroically directed as many military trucks as possible to cross as enemy planes flew overhead.

Jumping onto one of the trucks, Rose and Madeleine hid for hours in the back, waiting in a long line of vehicles that moved slowly forward. With an unbearable sluggishness, a hydraulic lift elevated Rose's truck. The vehicle crossed the bridge as if in a slow procession of ants, and Rose wondered if it would ever end or if she would survive it. Her sensations were heightened to the dangers immediately around her, and she thought that the river, lit white by a nearly full moon, looked like it flowed far below her as if "into another world."

As Rose's truck moved cautiously over the bridge, the battle on the banks of the river and overhead began. The Germans fired cannons at soldiers and refugees alike, while the French returned with machine-gun fire in a last stand to keep control of the bridge. Shells exploded among the refugees. Rose could hear people screaming, but whether it was a last cry before death or before going mad, she could not tell. The sound of all those human voices distorted by fear was much more terrifying to Rose than the sharp, menacing crack of explosions. "It is a sound of war that you cannot forget," she would later recount.

Finally, the truck traveled the last few feet of the bridge and touched ground on the other side. Rose felt what she described as an "inexpressible sense of deliverance." Shortly after, the Germans bombed the bridge, shattering the cut stone piers and sending the deck into the sandy depths of the river. The soldiers on the bridge who had just guided Rose over it must have died—a final sacrifice for their nation.

Despite the carnage and the palpable tragedy before her, Rose was beyond hopeful. After the bridge, the road seemed to open up infinitely to the future. She would later maintain that she felt like she was given "a new lease on life." Rose now had a real chance of making it to Chambord to find the rest of her colleagues from the Louvre.

HENDAYE, FRANCE

JUNE 17, 1940

THREE HUNDRED MILES SOUTHWEST OF CHÂTEAUNEUF-SUR-LOIRE, the Rosenbergs and the Helfts piled into the family cars and drove 140 miles south to Hendaye, a seaside town on France's border with Spain. They had food and their most important belongings. Alexandre Rosenberg's mother, Margot, managed to bring one painting with her.

Hendaye lies on a small bay at the foothills of the Spanish Pyrenees and at the opening of the Bidassoa River where multiple bridges, including the aptly named International Bridge, cross a narrow body of water. Hendaye was now at the razor's edge between oppression and freedom, just as it had been for the fifteen to twenty thousand people who had fled in the opposite direction from Franco's Spain just four years prior.

Traffic was at a standstill for two miles before the French checkpoint. From there, it was just 367 feet to the Spanish checkpoint, but not everyone would be allowed to make that crossing. French customs officials checked all the refugees and their documents carefully. Every ten minutes, the queue would move up only one car length. On the other side, Spanish officers examined the documents just as assiduously before raising the boom gate or sending people back into France.

Alexandre's uncle, Jacques Helft, and his family were in the lead car of the family convoy, with Alexandre's family and Yvon Helft's family behind. The children, who were shielded from the worst by their parents, found it to be a fun family adventure. While waiting, Alexandre and his cousins visited friends in nearby cars. They could also leave the vehicles to buy things from shops close by.

They were living off *petit beurre*—small French butter cookies—and sardines in easy-to-open tin cans. They slept in their cars that first night.

The first of the Helft and Rosenberg family cars eventually passed through both the French and Spanish checkpoints without issue and drove on to Portugal. But disaster struck when the other families tried to cross. A brand-new decree barred Frenchmen between the ages of seventeen and forty-eight from leaving the country. That meant Alexandre, and his two cousins, François and Jean Helft, would not be permitted to cross into Spain. A sixteen-year-old cousin barely made it out of France—his birthday was less than a week away.

It was an emotional separation. "We stay with our sons. We don't care about the war," cried the mothers, Margot Rosenberg and Madeleine Helft. But the boys insisted that the family, including their mothers, needed to leave. "Get out while you can, and we will find you," they told them. Alexandre and his cousins said their goodbyes and set off on foot along the coast. There was almost no time left before the Germans would fully occupy France, but if the boys were lucky, they just might be able to sneak out through the last open port left: the Basque town of Saint-Jean-de-Luz.

LOIRE VALLEY

JUNE 17–19, 1940

AFTER THE BRIDGE AT CHÂTEAUNEUF-SUR-LOIRE, ROSE AND MADEleine walked for two days. The heat followed them southward as

German planes strafed the roads. A short sojourn to cool down under the thick forest canopy in Sologne nearly got them killed when three waves of Stuka planes suddenly swooped down and sprayed bullets intended for an ammunition depot.

Rose and Madeleine ran out from under the trees, passing an amiable-looking woman with an overturned carriage and two dead children beside her. She had gone mad with grief and was gesticulating to no one in particular, as if serving imaginary customers in a shop. It was a face Rose would never forget, encapsulating the terror and despair France had fallen into. "It taught me war, and made me hate it," she later declared. On this godforsaken road in the middle of the vast French forests, Rose vowed to fight the enemy in whatever way possible.

WHILE ROSE WAS ON THIS dangerous final leg of her journey, a forty-nine-year-old French brigadier general named Charles de Gaulle boarded a British twin-engine biplane bound for London from Bordeaux. At six foot five, de Gaulle towered over everyone around him. The career military man had distinguished himself in the trenches of World War I, was wounded in the battlefield at Verdun, and captured by German forces. In the previous few weeks, as the Germans routed France, de Gaulle had proven his military prowess once again, leading his tank division in several battles against the Germans. In rapid succession, he was promoted to brigadier general and then to Undersecretary of State for National Defense and War, pushing a message of continued resistance against the enemy.

De Gaulle was level-headed and calm, known for his blunt demeanor and intelligence, and now, in the last hours of the Third Republic, he still believed France could and should be saved. "I will never sign an armistice," de Gaulle told a friend. "It would be against French honor, and interests." He had been crisscrossing France and flying to England, working multiple defense plans at the same time, including a possible, unprecedented union between England and France and a plan to retake France back from North Africa via the Mediterranean Sea. He had also impressed Winston Churchill, who said on a return from France in mid-June that he thought highly of de Gaulle. All of this put de Gaulle at odds with eighty-four-year-old Maréchal Philippe Pétain, a World War I hero who had been brought in as deputy prime minister of France in May. Pétain believed in the inevitability of France's defeat.

The plan to create an alliance between France and the United Kingdom failed on the evening of June 16, with Pétain declaring it "a marriage with a corpse!" Those who supported appeasement spread the notion that it was a British conspiracy to take over the French Empire, making it subservient to England, proclaiming, "We do not want to be a British dominion!" and "Better to be a Nazi province. At least we know what that means." On June 17, Pétain was appointed prime minister and took to the radio waves to announce that he had contacted Nazi Germany to begin peace negotiations: "In these painful hours, I think of the unfortunate refugees who roam our roads in the greatest deprivation. I express to them my compassion and concern. It is with a heavy heart that I tell you today that we must stop fighting."

Under the terms of the armistice, the new French state, led by Pétain and headquartered in Vichy, would retain nominal authority over all of France, but the country would be divided into two zones by a demarcation line. The northern three-fifths, which included the Atlantic Coast, would be administered by the German military and called the Occupied Zone. An Unoccupied Zone, south of the demarcation line, would be governed by the new French puppet administration based in Vichy. Paris, situated within the Occupied Zone, would remain the de jure capital of France.

Only people who carried an *Ausweis*—a German-issued identity card—or a *Passerschein*—a free movement card—could cross the demarcation line.

The new Vichy French State was required to pay a heavy indemnity to Germany in the form of raw materials, supplies, food, and currency, with occupation payments of 400 million francs per day. In practice, Paris and the Occupied Zone would be run as a dictatorship by the occupying German forces, who would be forced to negligibly accommodate the requests of the new French government and its civil servants. It would be a clash between the process-oriented German administrators in Paris and their wily French counterparts, a cultural difference that Jacques Jaujard and Rose Valland would exploit in the years to come.

With the surrender of France imminent, de Gaulle was stripped of his position in the Ministry of War and was about to be arrested for his vociferously anti-German, anti-armistice stance—one that would be tantamount to treason under the new collaborationist government. He needed to escape the country right away.

De Gaulle departed in such a rush that he had almost nothing in his suitcase—just one pair of pants, four shirts, and a photograph. He left his family behind in France as well, including a disabled teenage daughter and a dying mother. "France must go on fighting," he proclaimed at military headquarters just before he got on the plane. On the flight, de Gaulle was filled with torment. He knew that, to many of his former comrades, his escape would be seen as sedition, but deep down he was sure that the fight for France and its honor could no longer be done from within the country.

In the Loire Valley, Rose and Madeleine continued their push to Chambord, the central hiding place for the treasures of Paris's museums. It was about a half day's walk from where the Stuka planes had unleashed their barrage. Their arrival, at the end of an Odyssean journey, went essentially unnoted.

Pierre Schommer was too busy dealing with innumerable pressing issues. The Château de Chambord was crowded with museum employees and their families, with very little suitable accommodation left for the two women. Others, including the Louvre's deputy director Jacques Jaujard, were housed in the local hotel, just steps from the castle in the small village on the Chambord estate. When Jaujard attempted to leave the hotel one day, German planes came careening down low. Amid explosions, everyone dove for cover except for Jaujard, who stayed coolly on the doorstep and did not move.

Hundreds of thousands of starving refugees also arrived at Chambord. No one knew how they would be fed, so Schommer considered holding a deer hunt. Adding to the bedlam was the inexplicable release of the region's prisoners and mental asylum patients, who infiltrated the surrounding forests. A tiger and an elephant broke out of their circus cages near Chambord and would soon fight valiantly against the Germans. As Schommer later described, the circus animals "put up unexpected resistance to the invading troops" and "sowed justified terror in the ranks of the Wehrmacht for a long time." A tank had to be used to drag the remains of the elephant.

Rose and Madeleine needed to seek other lodgings. With a main castle and outbuildings, the Château de Valençay, about thirty-five miles away, had enough accommodations for the museum staff and their families. In fact, it was housing more than two thousand other refugees, not to mention the duke's exotic animals who still frolicked freely in the gardens. The depot was being run competently by curators Carle Dreyfus and Jean Cassou, but it was hard to ignore how wretched and weary the refugees were. The indoor equestrian riding hall, normally used for training horses, was transformed into a reception concourse for refugees and museum employees alike.

Here, below the majestic towers of the castle, Rose, along with Jean Cassou, heard Charles de Gaulle's halting but powerful speech from London broadcast by the BBC, later dubbed the "Appeal of June 18." Speaking of the imminent armistice, he beseeched:

> But has the last word been said? Has all hope disappeared? Is the defeat final? No!
>
> Believe me, I speak with knowledge and I tell you that France is not lost. The same methods which have brought about our defeat can quite well one day bring victory. For France is not alone. She is not alone! She is not alone! She can unite with the British Empire, which holds the sea and is continuing the struggle. She can, as England is doing, utilize to the full, the vast resources of the United States.
>
> This war is not limited to the territory of our unhappy country. This war has not been decided by the Battle of France. This war is a world war. In spite of all our mistakes, all our deficiencies, all our sufferings, there are in the universe sufficient means to enable us one day to crush our enemies. Shattered today by mechanical force, we shall be able to conquer in the future by stronger mechanical force. The fate of the world depends on it.

He called on the French people to join him, and to fight with him:

> I, General de Gaulle, now in London, I invite the French officers and soldiers who are on British soil, or who may arrive here, with or without their arms, I invite the engineers and the skilled workmen of the armament industries, who are now on British soil, or who may arrive here, to get in touch with me.
>
> Whatever happens, the flame of French Resistance must not and shall not be extinguished.

His words resonated with Rose. Regardless of what fate had in store for her, she knew that everything protected inside the walls of Valençay and Chambord—the art and the culture of France—was irreplaceable. Her role, even if small, would be to save what might remain of the beauty left in the world.

SAINT-JEAN-DE-LUZ, FRANCE

JUNE 20, 1940

BY THE TIME ALEXANDRE ROSENBERG ARRIVED IN SAINT-JEAN-DE-Luz, a French Basque port town about eight miles from where he had separated from his family, it was teeming with refugees, along with thousands of stranded British, Polish, and Czech soldiers. After Dunkirk, 140,000 soldiers in the British Expeditionary Force and 50,000 Polish troops still remained in France. One by one, the ports along the west coast of France fell to German forces. The armistice with Germany would come any day now, and a staggeringly monumental evacuation effort was underway.

It was only a matter of time before the Germans would take over this last embarkation point. Non-French Allied soldiers left behind would then be considered enemy combatants. For the many expatriates trapped in France, it was also their last chance to return home. Alexandre and his cousins decided they wanted to escape France and continue the fight from England or North Africa, but they needed to get on one of the ships in the harbor quickly. Guy Lévy, a family friend of Alexandre's, was also here trying to get on a boat. But as the boys were neither British nor Polish, it would not be easy for them to sneak on.

Before the war, Saint-Jean-de-Luz was mostly known as a lively resort destination, popular with well-to-do British and continental Europeans as well as Atlantic-crossing Americans like F. Scott Fitzgerald, who set his short story "The Swimmers" there. The timber-framed houses were covered in bright white stucco and topped with rust-colored Spanish tiles, a style unique to the region. Villas with brightly painted window shutters dotted the hillside, rising from the bay.

Before the war, the wealthy residents of Saint-Jean-de-Luz filled their days with social calls and bridge games, picnics on the seashore, films at the local cinema, hiking, and golf tournaments. Yet, the working-class history of the town remained ever present. The fishing industry was thriving in both Saint-Jean-de-Luz and Ciboure, the municipality along the south side of the bay. Just beyond was fertile farmland that stretched all the way into the lower hills of the Pyrenees, tended by Basque men and women who would soon become the backbone of a robust resistance network.

In the fall of 1939, the year-round locals organized to receive the first five hundred refugees. They transformed hotels, *pensionnés*, and even a summer camp. As such, they were already set up to assist the far larger number of evacuees that came their way in June 1940.

Now, there were anti-aircraft guns perched on the church tower and atop the train station. Just a short distance from the port, an unofficial emergency center helped explain to soldiers how to board the boats. "Are you looking for something?" a French cavalry lieutenant would ask. "Do you want to go to England?" People were wary of him, concerned about possible French government spies in their midst.

Alexandre and his cousins found the harbor pilot and asked how they could leave France illegally. "Well, I have a lot of people asking me that," the pilot answered. "There's a Polish freighter out there in the bay. It can't come into the harbor because it's not deep enough, but you can row out there."

Forty wooden fishing boats helmed by local fishermen were shepherding the masses of refugees and soldiers from the protected port to the large ships that would take them to England. Alexandre and his cousins mixed among the Polish soldiers who collegially offered the French boys their uniforms. Alexandre was able to get hold of a Polish military cap. Other Frenchmen pinned the white eagle of the Polish military onto their berets or put on a Polish raincoat. The soldiers also taught the French how to pronounce words like "Third Company" in Polish in case they were asked by the police which military unit they belonged to.

Alexandre joined the throng of soldiers and civilians getting screened for embarkation. The crowd was surprisingly calm. Some men looked resolute; most looked tense, tired, or worried. It was eerily silent, apart from the breaking of the waves, the hum of the boat engines, and the sound of footsteps. One of the few voices was that of a French man who paced back and forth on the quay pleading with his countrymen, "Don't leave, don't leave, you must stay in your country."

The line slowly moved forward. Would Alexandre and his cousins be caught? Would their journey end here in this Basque fishing village? They managed to pass the inspection and board one of the fishing boats. More than thirty men were loaded along with them, each stepping over the nets hanging off the sides of the boats. There was little room for luggage, which was being thrown overboard into the sea. More baggage, newly ownerless, piled up on the quay alongside abandoned cars. The commander of arms at the port witnessed this chaotic scene and thought it looked like a "monstrous mess, this total absence of a single person responsible for understanding the abyss into which we had fallen."

Their destination was the MS *Batory*, a Polish transatlantic ocean liner painted in camouflage green and gray. Until recently, it was assisting in the evacuations at Dunkirk. Intense swells and heavy rainfall made for a choppy approach to the *Batory*, but Alexandre would have still seen the French flag, planted at the end of one of the colossal stone jetties at Saint-Jean-de-Luz, flapping in the wind. It was a fitting last sight for the French men and women—some of whom would never see their homeland again.

THE *BATORY* WAS NOW PACKED almost four times its usual capacity with some three-thousand soldiers, refugees, and Frenchmen looking for a fight. Among their ranks were forty brave high school students from a nearby lycée. The storm had cleared by the time the *Batory* pulled away and the ship plied north toward Plymouth, England, in dead calm waters. Two funnels pumped smoke into a sky flooded with stars. Onboard was Maurice Schumann, who would be appointed the spokesperson for Free France, the French government in exile led by General Charles de Gaulle, in just a few weeks, and François Jacob, a Jewish medical student and future Nobel Prize winner.

All together, they waited for the new future to unfold before them.

At 8:45 p.m. two days later, the *Batory* joined the host of ships anchored in Plymouth. For Alexandre, passing through Customs and Immigration proved more difficult than expected. He and his fellow French compatriots were classified as illegal aliens and were subjected to investigations. The customs officer asked him if he had any contacts in England. Alexandre responded quite seriously, "Winston Churchill."

The officer thought the young Frenchman was being impertinent, but Alexandre explained that the British prime minister, an amateur artist, was a regular visitor to his father's gallery in Paris at 21 rue la Boétie. Churchill often borrowed paintings, replicated them, and returned the originals to Paul.

To the surprise of the customs officers, Alexandre's story checked out. He was now among the first few hundred volunteer French fighters to arrive in England. Next stop: London.

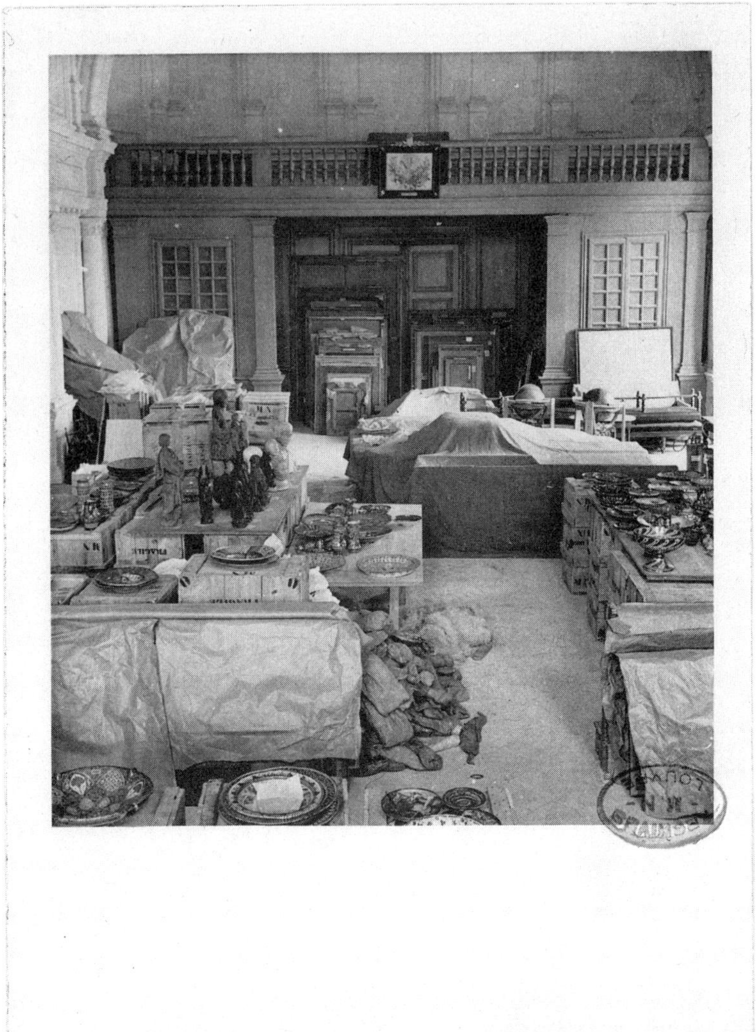

Artwork from the Jeu de Paume and other French museums inside the chapel of the Château de Chambord, 1941. The Jeu de Paume paintings are upright in the back of the chapel.

LOIRE VALLEY, FRANCE

JUNE 20, 1940

ROSE WAS STILL AT VALENÇAY WHEN FRANCE'S LEADERS CAPITULATED to Germany. Hitler and Pétain signed the armistice in the Forest of Compiègne, in the same train car and at the same location where the armistice was signed to end World War I.

Conditions at the Château de Valençay had deteriorated rapidly. The escaped patients from the psychiatric hospital had wandered to the castle, and they, along with other refugees, were hunting the duke's exotic animals for food. Fortunately, Rose would soon return to Paris to resume her post at the Jeu de Paume.

At Chambord, Pierre Schommer watched in disgust as curator Louis Hautecœur, last seen driving convoys of art to Loc-Dieu, gleefully accepted a high-paying position as superintendent of the Beaux-Arts administration with the new collaborationist government in Vichy. Hautecœur promised a great future to his old colleagues: he would reform the museums, the theaters, and the education system. As for the Jewish question? No need to overreact, Hautecœur told them. His secretary, Suzanne Kahn, was Jewish, and he claimed he could protect her. The museum curators were dubious about Hautecœur's overly optimistic promises.

Jacques Jaujard was on hand at Chambord to receive the first of the German dignitaries, who arrived in a black car and by motorcycle. Jaujard, Schommer, and art historian Marcel Aubert ran through the courtyard toward the main gate as their wives looked out anxiously from behind the château windows. The Germans wore wide green britches, tunics, tall black boots, gray gloves, and high-peaked hats affixed with a Nazi eagle. A loquacious German art historian translated for the group of officers and, to everyone's surprise, he already knew of Aubert by reputation.

Schommer subsequently received a parade of visits from German officials, who all had varying levels of interest in the priceless art stored in the castle. First, there were the men demanding inventory lists, whom Schommer fended off easily, followed by the Army commander in chief in Paris, Walther von Brauchitsch, who spoke French elegantly, and then Count Franz von Wolff-Metternich, the head of the *Kunstschutz*, the German Service for the Protection of Works in France, who was most apologetic for disturbing them. The Kunstschutz was a special division of the German army and Wolff-Metternich was only serving in a civilian capacity as an art historian. He asked the French curators if they could treat him as an old friend of Aubert's and a great appreciator and connoisseur of French art and architecture, rather than as an enemy. He never imagined he would see this romantic castle under such circumstances.

The Duke (and former Prince) of Mecklenburg, now a basic infantry soldier, also visited Chambord and spoke with the curators in perfect French. With a smirk, he said of Hitler, "Don't forget that his genius extends to architecture; may our gracious lord judge him as an artist. Don't argue in front of him that a perfect column can be anything but curved, he'll be pissed off."

The Germans soon decided not to occupy the castle and provided Jaujard with an automobile circulation permit and gas coupons, which he could use to check the art depots throughout France and to return to Paris. The curators and administrators would remain at the depots to keep watch on the art.

On his way back to Paris, Jaujard stopped in Dourdan, about forty miles south of the Louvre, to check on a truck that broke down on the way to Chambord. Two German officers had inspected the crates and took gold watches for themselves. They also sent sculptures and rare books to the *Kommandantur* of Paris. From the Louvre later that day, Jaujard sent off a missive to the Kunstschutz, demanding the return of the objects. It was the first official report of art looting on French soil.

LOUVRE ARCHIVIST LUCIE MAZAURIC WAS now installed at Loc-Dieu, a dreamy religious abbey in the southwest of France far from the Germans, watching over her beloved archives as well as the *Mona Lisa*. From there, she heard de Gaulle's speech, which gave the museum employees in Loc-Dieu a wave of hope.

Louvre curator Germain Bazin also arrived at Loc-Dieu by using his army uniform to deliberately misdirect anyone, civilian and military, going his way so he could get to the abbey unencumbered. It was not the most magnanimous gesture. He sent everyone heading south, including refugees, in other directions, and he got the police to block a road to be used only by him. "I continued my buffoonery," he later wrote in his memoir about his actions en route to Loc-Dieu, "because it was useful to me." With the armistice concluded, Bazin was also letting his anti-Semitism loose. He wanted to name a pig at Loc-Dieu after Beaux-Arts director general Georges Huisman, recently fired by the new Vichy government because he was Jewish. Bazin wrote to René Huyghe, his boss and the Louvre's curator of paintings, that he no longer knew which side—the Allies or the Nazis—he wanted to triumph, as the Allies would bring back "triumphantly and arrogantly all the *youtrerie* who fled," using a derogatory French term for Jews. "It has taken the defeat of France to get rid of them," he added.

Rose was eager to get back to Paris. Her old friends in the Jeu de Paume—the more than five hundred paintings and approximately one hundred sculptures still stored at the museum—needed her. So did Joyce. With the end of hostilities, many of Rose's male colleagues at the Louvre would be returning to their former jobs, forced to admit military defeat. All Rose needed now was a car, an *Ausweis*, and Jacques Jaujard's go-ahead.

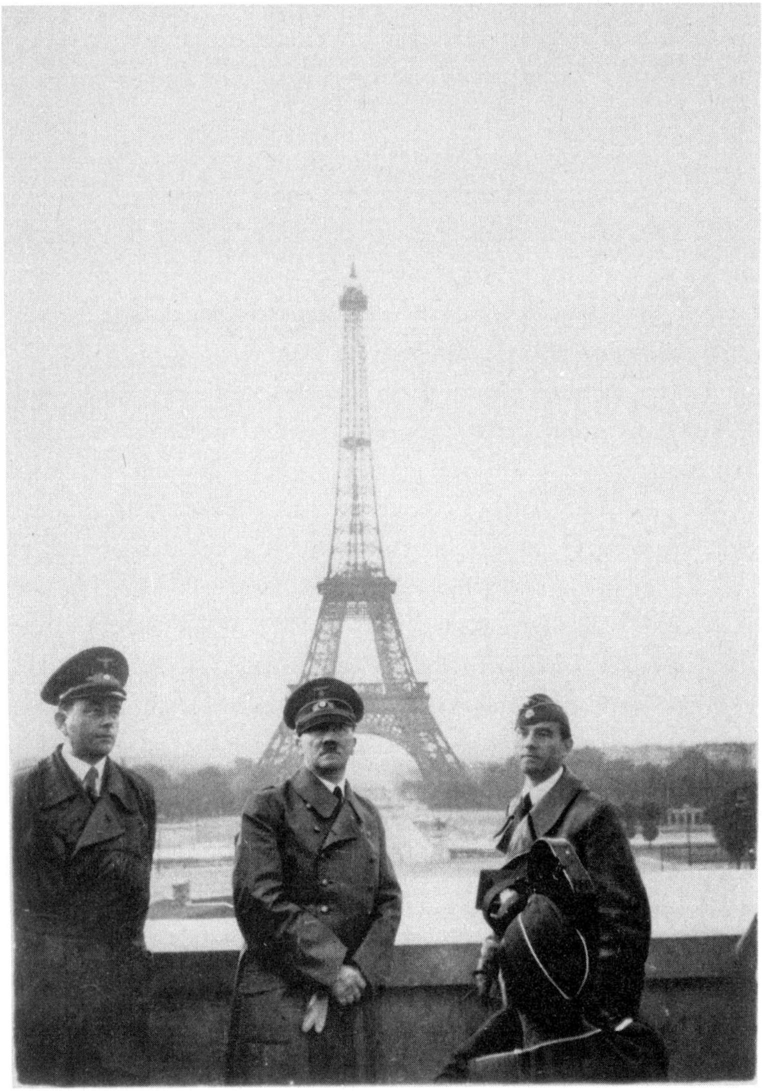

Hitler on his tour of Paris posing in front of the Eiffel Tower, June 1940.

PARIS

JUNE 23, 1940

THE DAY AFTER THE ARMISTICE WAS SIGNED, HITLER CELEBRATED HIS triumph with an outing to Paris. The visit was not for military purposes—he left that to his generals—but for his one true love: art. "I want to see Paris with my artists," Hitler told Hermann Giesler, one of the architects he invited, along with Albert Speer, who served as the General Building Inspector for the Reich Capital, and his favorite sculptor, Arno Breker. "A visit has been my passionate wish for years. Now the gates are open to me," Hitler confided to Breker.

Hitler's first and only tour would be extensive. He had been fascinated with the City of Light since childhood and believed he would be able to navigate it purely based on the maps he had long pored over. He intended to study the city's urban planning, gather architectural inspiration for Linz and Berlin, and learn from the city's mistakes.

Landing before dawn at Le Bourget airport, the entourage went directly to the Paris Opera house, Hitler's favorite building. Even at this early hour, everything was prepared just for the Führer. The lights glowed from inside; the curtain was raised as if in a performance. "Wonderful, uniquely beautiful proportions, and what a celebration!" Hitler marveled. The building's aesthetic qualities were equally as impressive as its inspiring backstory. Charles Garnier was an unknown thirty-five-year-old architect in 1860 when he won Napoleon III's open competition to design the opera house, beating out nearly 170 others including the famous architect and engineer of the time, Eugène Viollet-le-Duc. The facts and myths of the Opera house, including a deadly accident with the chandelier in 1896, inspired the Gothic novel *The Phantom of the Opera*.

Despite Hitler's professed abhorrence of decoration, he loved the interior with its explosion of gilded embellishment. In the architect Garnier, Hitler could imagine an alternative origin story for himself, as a talented yet undiscovered designer plucked from obscurity by an emperor to create the country's most important building—an edifice that would strike awe and inspiration for centuries to come.

Hitler knew the floorplan of the opera house from memory and gave the group a tour, pointing out the architectural elements and layout. They walked up the grand split marble staircase, passed through the many reception rooms, and entered the horseshoe-shaped auditorium where the seven-ton crystal and bronze chandelier hung from the ceiling. Hitler deemed it the most beautiful building in the world.

He knew the building so well that he was bewildered not to find one specific detail. "I would like to see the reception room, the President's salon, behind the left proscenium boxes," he told the taciturn gray-haired opera house attendant. "According to Garnier's plan, this is where it should be." The group went back and forth perplexed until the attendant remembered that the salon had been removed during a renovation. "The democratic republic does not even allow its President his own reception room!" Hitler said jubilantly, adding, "There, you see how well I know my way about."

When the visit was over, the group descended the exterior staircase to take in the facade, now shown to better advantage in the early daylight. The contingent entered their Mercedes sedans and began a tour of the city's most renowned plazas and streets, with all the artists in Hitler's car. The first stop was La Madeleine, where a Greek temple-like church sat at the intersection of three grand avenues. Hitler was unimpressed.

With the streets of Paris nearly empty the group had a clear sight line down rue Royale to the Place de la Concorde, where the car went in a big leisurely loop around the Egyptian obelisk at the center, passing the Jeu de Paume, the Tuileries, and the Hôtel de Crillon, where the German military government was setting up. Hitler slowly took it all in and found La Concorde rather beautiful. Then, with a hand gesture, he signaled that he was ready to drive up the Champs-Élysées, Paris's most grand avenue, to the Arc de Triomphe, still clad with scaffolding and mounds of spilled sand and sandbags. He ordered the motorcade to drive slowly.

He pointed out the sculptural effect of the arch and its opulent ornamentation and commented about the radial city planning that emanated from it. It was hard for Hitler to say goodbye to the Arc de Triomphe, so symbolic of his long-held dreams and now finally experienced in real life.

The tour then continued to Trocadero, where Hitler and the artists, all clad in military uniforms, were filmed close-up, looking onto the Eiffel Tower from an elevated terrace. Hitler looked around contentedly, observantly, and analytically. For the first time during the tour, he became rather loquacious. To Hitler, the Eiffel Tower was not only representative of Paris but also of a whole new future he wanted to shepherd in, in which technology, engineering, and architecture would come together to produce inspiring structures out of the most modern materials.

Surprisingly, Hitler spent the most time at Les Invalides. He stood solemnly with head bowed and cap in hand for a long while in front of Napoleon's sarcophagus. Was he thinking it was all fair retribution for Napoleon's plunder of Prussia? Or was he comparing himself to the belligerent former French emperor and thinking of his own legacy?

It seems it was more of the latter, as he pulled Giesler over to him and murmured, "You will build my tomb, Giesler." And then, in an unexpected decision, he ordered for Napoleon's son to be exhumed from

Vienna and buried next to his father. Hitler also found a World War I statue and its inscription offensive and told his military escort, "Let it be blown up!"

Next was a speedy visit to Notre-Dame, the Panthéon, and Paris's Left Bank so that Hitler could see the landmarks and the bohemian haunts sculptor Arno Breker had once frequented. Back on the Right Bank, in the full morning sun, a newspaper man hawking *Le Matin* papers caught sight of Hitler. With mouth agape and eyes widening in horror, he threw all the newspapers into the air and ran in search of safety. Just nearby, a group of market women pointed and shouted excitedly, "It's him! Oh, it's him!" Then, as the Louvre came into view, Hitler noted spontaneously, "I have no hesitation in describing this grandiose building as one of the most brilliant ideas in architecture." The group marveled at how the over-half-mile-long facade along the rue de Rivoli came off as one architectural gesture yet avoided any sense of monotony. Hitler immediately ordered a reassessment of Berlin's street-frontage design.

The last stop was Sacré-Cœur, where Hitler could get a panoramic overview of Paris's urban planning. After a time seemingly lost in thought, he called the city below a "wonder of Western culture" and emphasized how important it was to preserve it "intact, for posterity." He turned to his artists and said, "Now begins a time of hard work and strain—the formation of the cities and monuments entrusted in your care. As far as I can, as far as I find the time, I want to make your work easier!"

And in the blink of an eye, the whirlwind tour was over. Hitler spared only three hours to visit the city that had long captured his imagination. On the way back to Berlin, he asked the pilot to circle over Paris a few more times from the air. "It was the dream of my life to be permitted to see Paris," Hitler told Speer. "I cannot say how happy I am to have that dream fulfilled today!" He directed Speer to resume a full-scale building plan in Berlin and mused, "Wasn't Paris beautiful? But Berlin must be made far more beautiful. In the past I often considered whether we would not have to destroy Paris but when we are finished in Berlin, Paris will only be a shadow. So why should we destroy it?"

And with that, Paris was spared a second time in this nascent war.

But down below, the vultures had descended and were about to take it apart from within.

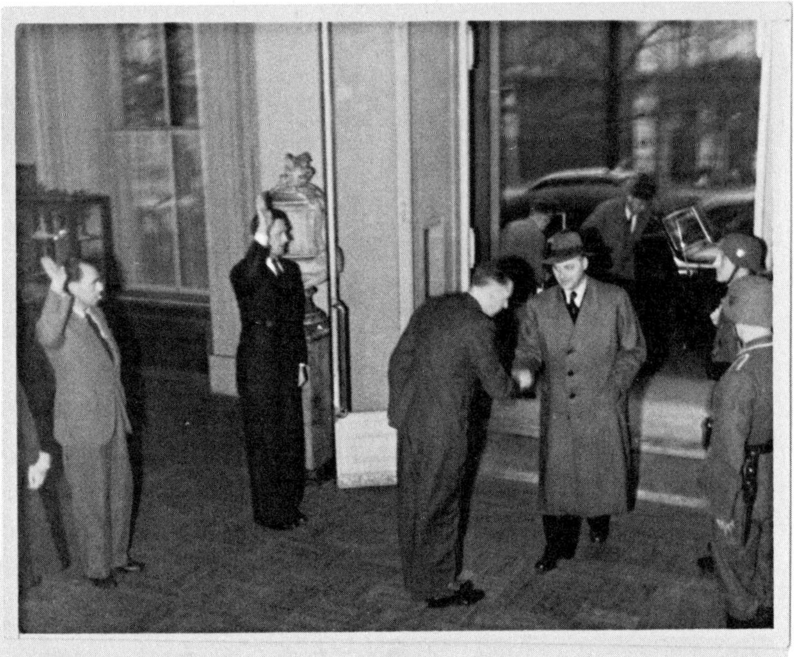

Alfred Rosenberg visiting the Jeu de Paume, November 1943.

PARIS

EARLY JULY 1940

ROSE WAS BACK AT THE JEU DE PAUME BY THE BEGINNING OF JULY. IN A reverse exodus, albeit far less dangerous, most of the Musées Nationaux workers were ordered back to their posts in Paris. A car nicknamed the "*Ausweis*" transported staff back to the capital. Only a handful of guards and curators remained at each of the depots to care for the art stored within them.

The city that Rose found on arrival was nothing like the one she left. Nazi flags emblazoned with swastikas flew from the facades of the grand buildings nearby the Jeu de Paume, all along the Place de la Concorde and rue de Rivoli, as well as the Eiffel Tower and the Arc de Triomphe. It made sense that the Germans would want to set up their new world order atop the hegemonic axis of avenues laid out by Napoleon III. The Hôtel de Crillon, the palace where Benjamin Franklin, in his role as American commissioner, once signed a treaty with France, was now the heavily guarded headquarters of the German High Command.

The city was oppressively silent, frozen in time as if in a pandemic. The enemy, however, was not an invisible disease but a barbaric invader who was about to snap the city to life against its will. Even the birds had almost completely disappeared in Paris, either killed by heavy smoke from the burning of the oil refineries in June or migrated away. The author and journalist Jean Guéhenno wrote in his diary, "What is certain is that nothing is moving or singing in the trees."

Rose wrote to her cousin Marguerite about her harrowing escape from Paris in June, and Marguerite replied anxiously, "I still shudder at the thought that you were part of this lamentable exodus, where you could have been killed. I cannot thank providence enough for having so miraculously preserved you. We have known days of immense sadness."

On her way to work, Rose bicycled past the base of the German naval forces in the Hôtel Talleyrand, just across the street from the Jeu de Paume, and the famed Louis XVI–style Hôtel Meurice, which was requisitioned by the German military command, the *Kommandantur*. At all times, armed guards in crisp uniforms flanked the entrance to the hotel, holding rifles. It was all a far cry from the prewar scene at the Meurice, when guests like Franklin Delano Roosevelt, Salvador Dalí, and Coco Chanel mingled under the stunning art nouveau glass dome in the hotel's Winter Garden. For thirty years, Dalí had booked a suite there. He caroused through the hallways on a bicycle, brought in his pet leopards, and had flocks of sheep sent up, which he promptly shot with blank bullets. Chanel also hosted many fashion shows in the hotel.

At the Place de la Concorde, right in front of the Jeu de Paume, a uniformed German conductor led a military brass band of trombones, trumpets, French horns, and a shockingly large number of tubas in celebration of major victories. All day and through the night, German planes flew overhead relentlessly, diving down low over the Champs-Élysées and rising back into the sky with a deafening roar. Below, trucks and cars filled with German soldiers paraded their might noisily around the Arc de Triomphe and down the Champs-Élysées without reprieve.

The Germans quickly transformed the quintessential French streetscape into something more familiar to them. German signs replaced French ones at the cafés and brasseries, advertising local German food at affordable prices in *pfennings*—German pennies. German-language newspapers filled newsstands. The Rex Cinema, one of the largest venues in Paris, admitted only German soldiers. Restaurants sported new signs, "For Aryans Only."

Statues deemed offensive to Germany or its culture were removed, sometimes violently. Heads were decapitated and taken as trophies, and horses were used to pull down large monuments, while anything bronze or copper was melted down for ammunition. Off went Rodin's *Balzac*, and the statues of Victor Hugo, Thomas Paine, and a slew of World War I heroes. Even French inventors and scientists were no longer acceptable.

Streets and theaters commemorating anyone Jewish were rechristened, including the Sarah Bernhardt Theater, named for the internationally renowned actress who staged many productions there. It became the generically-named Théâtre de la Cité. Streets like rue Erlanger, rue Jacques Offenbach, rue Alphand, and rue Camille Pissarro, named after

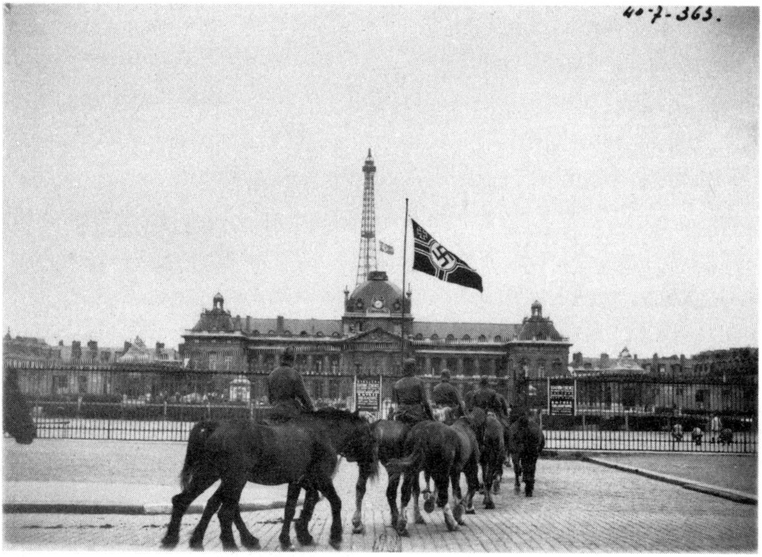

École Militaire in Paris at the beginning of the German occupation, July 1940.

the impressionist painter, became an issue. Léon Gambetta, one of the founders of the Third Republic, had the distinction of being both half-Jewish and affiliated with democratic values, so his statue was taken down from in front of the Louvre.

At the Jeu de Paume, Rose felt stalled. She wondered what to do inside a museum that had lost its main purpose—showcasing exhibitions. She checked on the collection in the basement and focused on the paperwork she typically never had enough time for. Rose was keeping her head down.

But other curators were looking for ways to undermine the Germans. Musée des Arts et Traditions Populaires curator Agnès Humbert told Jean Cassou, curator of the Musée National d'Art Moderne, who was back in Paris, "I feel I will go mad, literally, if I don't do something, if I don't react somehow." Her museum and its library had been purged by the Germans of questionable political content.

Cassou, whose hair was turning white with the stress of the previous few weeks, agreed, and they arranged to meet weekly with a small group of "like-minded comrades" to exchange information, write and distribute pamphlets, and recap the French broadcasts coming from London. Cassou called it their "secret society" and was reenergized by the activity. Humbert even thought he was standing straighter than before. The Louvre's Egyptian Art archaeologist, Christiane Desroches, joined as well, and they soon learned that other resistance groups were forming in France. Meanwhile, their boss, Jacques Jaujard, asked Desroches to make photographic records of Vichy orders sent by the likes of Abel Bonnard, the Minister of National Education, and carry them to the Unoccupied Zone to be sent to London through the resistance network. Couriers and escapees smuggled the documents over the Spanish border and on to Barcelona to the British consul there.

The nascent resistance within the museums was timely. The spoils in France were too enticing, and on June 30, Hitler issued the first directive regarding privately owned art in France with specific details for Jewish-owned property: "The Führer, following the report of the Minister of Foreign Affairs, gave orders to safeguard—in addition to objects of art belonging to the French State—artwork and historical documents, notably those belonging to Jews. This measure should not constitute an expropriation, but a transfer into our custody to serve as collateral for peace negotiations."

Using euphemistic language within an official order, the Germans could henceforth be by the book regarding any questionable activities. This was not looting, seizure, or expropriation, but merely a "transfer." They were not stealing but simply "safeguarding" the art. Rose later described the directives as a "camouflage of intentions."

Then, as Hitler was wont to do, he gave few details on how his directives should be implemented and left it to his underlings to battle it out. Since he did not specify which ministries would be responsible, many high-level Nazis came to France to try to get a share of the loot. However, none of the clever wordplay mattered to Jewish collectors and gallery owners like Paul Rosenberg. What was clear was that their art would be taken.

Without wasting any time, Otto Abetz, the new German ambassador to France and an ardent Francophile, took it upon himself to begin the looting the very next day. The tall, blond, cleft-chinned diplomat sent a letter to the military commander of Paris, stating that von Ribbentrop had tasked him with the art seizure. He also sent a list of the fifteen most esteemed Parisian art galleries—most of which were Jewish-owned—and asked the German secret police to search their premises and seize the collections. The German Army, the Gestapo, and the French police provided transportation. A commando leader, Baron von Kunsberg from the Geheime Feldpolizei (the army's secret field police), was dispatched to give his expertise in surprise seizures.

On July 4, Abetz ordered the confiscation of Paul Rosenberg's gallery at 21 rue la Boétie. The artwork inside included several heavy, life-size sculptures by Rodin and Maillol, but most of the collection was elsewhere. The Germans lamented that the proprietor was not home waiting to simply hand over his artwork. He was in Portugal.

Within a few days, Abetz cleared out the fifteen galleries on his initial list, including the Wildenstein, Seligmann, Kann, and Bernheim-Jeune galleries. He had his eye on the Rothschild collections next. The "most valuable objects" were delivered to the German embassy on rue de Lille. Paintings, sculptures, furniture, jewelry, and other priceless items filled the building to capacity.

Abetz then decided to order the seizure of not only Jewish-owned art but also the collections of all the museums in Paris and the provinces. Jacques Jaujard was obliged to give tours of the national museum depots in the Unoccupied Zone to German officials, who made wish lists of what they wanted to be sent to the embassy. At some depots, curators were held at gunpoint and forced to open crates of art. Abetz's team also made an ambitious list of *all* the works of art in France. Everything was fair game, according to the wording of Hitler's decree.

In mid-July, a new decree from the German Army in France banned any movement of art or modification of artwork by their rightful owners "in any way whatsoever without the written authorization of a commander of the military administration." In addition, all works of art with a value of over 100,000 francs now had to be declared by their owners by August 15. Bank vaults could be searched in the presence of their owners, who dutifully registered their most valuable items. More and more artwork flowed to the German embassy, with no place seemingly safe from Abetz's reach.

Picasso made sure he was present at the search of his two bank vaults in Paris, which were full with his art and those of his friends. The vault next door belonged to Matisse, who could not be there due to a major abdominal surgery. Thanks to Picasso's chicanery, the art in the vaults of France's two most famous modern artists never made it into Abetz's hands. Picasso noticed that the soldiers from the *Devisenschutzkommando*, the German Foreign Exchange Protection Commando unit, knew nothing about art and were not the sharpest. He took them around in circles, hurrying them from one room to the next and making wrong turns around the vault floor. He haphazardly took out canvases, jammed them back in, and did his best to confuse the inspectors. When they got to Matisse's vault, he told them, "Oh, we've seen these." They took nothing with them and only managed to inventory one-third of his art, for which Picasso offered extremely low valuations.

Several new decrees concerning Jews were passed in rapid succession, which increased the amount of available loot. Both the French government in Vichy and the Germans stripped any Jews who had fled France between May 10 and June 30 of their citizenship, their property now "ownerless" and thus able to be seized. This was the main legal founding on which Jewish-owned art collections, like Paul Rosenberg's, were sequestered for "safekeeping." Strangely, Vichy continued to authorize Paul's international money transfers from his frozen French bank accounts, as long he submitted monthly receipts, a classic example of the inherent contradictions afoot in the country. Jews, later defined as anyone with three Jewish grandparents, or two if married to someone Jewish, were barred from civil service, education, and leadership positions in the media, and cinema, or any companies with state funding. Jewish-owned firms, including art galleries, were taken over by "Aryan" government-appointed administrators.

The cornucopia of riches emboldened Abetz and he proposed several innovative ideas to formalize the looting process. Certain works of art, to be hung on the walls of the embassy, at the foreign ministry, or at von Ribbentrop's home, would go directly into the property of the Reich as a "prepayment and advance for war reparations." Modern paintings, described by Abetz as "savage expressionism," would be sold or used for exchange at the Paris auction houses.

Soon, more German agencies arrived in France, and the decrees kept coming. The Gestapo, with the assistance of the archivists of the Einsatzstab Reichsleiter Rosenberg (ERR), was put in charge of searching libraries and archives for "objects valuable to Germany," as well as bookstores and Masonic lodges for evidence of anti-German political activity. The ERR was a special task force led by Alfred Rosenberg, the mastermind behind the racial creeds of the Nazi Party and its position against "degenerate art." He was also the leader of the German Foreign Policy Office and Amt Rosenberg, an agency that dealt with "intellectual and ideological education" in the Third Reich.

Rosenberg was very much the spiritual and ideological leader of the Nazi Party, and his 1930 book *The Myth of the Twentieth Century* promulgated a mystical, pseudo-scientific origin story of the Germanic people, whose innate racial superiority and purity should be preserved. He had deduced that Germans were the "master race" and innately racially superior. Everyone else, especially Jews, Blacks, and homosexuals, were "*Untermenschen*"—subhuman. "Germany will regard the Jewish question solved only after the very last Jew has left the greater German living space. . . . Europe will have its Jewish question solved only after the very last Jew has left the continent," Rosenberg proclaimed.

The ERR opened its Western European office in early July at the Hôtel Commodore in Paris. In a twisted, theoretical way, Rosenberg was interested in "researching" and collecting materials from all groups of people who were anti-Nazi, especially Jews and Freemasons. The idea was to amass political evidence to use in the "struggle" against Germany's enemies. Rosenberg had very little interest in art, but Reichsmarschall Hermann Göring, Hitler's handpicked successor and a voracious art collector, did.

While searching a Rothschild palace, the ERR found sixty-two crates of books, documents, and porcelain behind false doors and inside secret cellars. It was a huge bounty, but Rosenberg was worried about the legality of seizing abandoned property from Jews stripped of their nationality. The Germans were occupiers not in their native land and ostensibly bound by the laws of the armistice. This technically gave Vichy France, which was conspicuously absent during the initial looting, jurisdiction over Paris and the Unoccupied Zone. Rosenberg was more cautious than Abetz and Göring, and the French arts administrators, including Jacques Jaujard, had yet to formulate a plan to combat the thefts.

Hitler told Rosenberg not to worry about that little legal wrinkle and that everything should be seized as soon as possible. To make it all official, Hitler expanded the ERR's mandate to include any "objects which seem valuable," not just "objects of art," as he had specified before. In 1939 as the war broke out, many private citizens, foreign embassies, and foreign organizations temporarily transferred or donated their high-value art and other objects to French museums for safekeeping. The Germans now wanted access to those treasures, too. As such, Hitler also decreed that any "transfer" of possessions to the French state or elsewhere that occurred after September 1, 1939, which included, specifically, the possessions from the Rothschild palace, "ownerless" Jewish collections, and the Polish Library in Paris, were now invalidated. The order meant that much of the art stored by Jewish collectors at the national museums was no longer safe.

Undaunted, Jaujard made fake contracts using old paper and stamps to conceal the Jewish-owned collections as donations given to the Louvre before September 1, 1939, a stratagem that would only temporarily protect the artwork until the Germans discovered the ruse. Meanwhile, the French police obligingly verified the Jewish ownership status of the collections, providing the Germans with the necessary legal cover for their looting.

Joseph Goebbels, the Reich Minister of Propaganda, was also involved in the plunder of France's artistic heritage. He directed a vast inventory project to identify all the art looted from Germany since the year 1500 by France and other enemy nations. The scope of the inventory soon expanded and included all works of Germanic origin. German foreign minister Joachim von Ribbentrop was also circling, obsessively focused on acquiring the Boucher masterpiece *Diana Coming Out of the Bath*, which belonged to the Louvre. He did not think it too bold to ask Jaujard if he could just have it.

Finally, there was the Kunstschutz, the Wehrmacht agency led by the civilian art historian Count Wolff-Metternich, and the only player taking its mandate to protect the art and monuments in France seriously. Wolff-Metternich was assiduously following the protocols of the Hague Convention regarding pillaging of civilian property and was horrified at Abetz's looting, feeling that it besmirched the honor of the German Army.

Jaujard saw a potential ally in Wolff-Metternich and welcomed him to his office at the Louvre. "I am happy to greet a senior official at his post," Wolff-Metternich told Jaujard, commending him for not abandoning his job in the face of the German occupation. Thus began a rare wartime relationship built on mutual respect and a shared common goal between two men from adversarial nations. Both were at the top of their fields in their respective countries and equally dedicated to the protection of cultural heritage. They would remain out of the political fray, as best they could.

Wolff-Metternich persuaded the German Army commander in chief, Walther von Brauchitsch, that Abetz's actions—particularly the ambassador's avowed intention to move the art out of France—were in violation of Hitler's orders, which had specified to only "safeguard" the art for future peace negotiations. Without the army's support, Abetz would not have the transportation required to remove such vast quantities of artwork from all over the country. This did not protect the Jewish-owned art collections in Paris, however—those were fair game and a far easier catch.

Still, Abetz was no longer the only one benefiting from the riches in France. He was now the target of some very powerfully placed Nazi operatives, but he had no intention of backing down.

In Berlin, the Führermuseum director, Hans Posse, was elated over Germany's military success in France and what that meant for Hitler's dream project. Berlin and Linz would be enriched not only by the urban planning lessons of Paris but also by its artistic treasures. The holes in the Linz collection—the Rubenses, the Rembrandts, and the Vermeers—could now be filled easily with the paintings from the Jewish-owned art collections in France. When that loot was exhausted, the wealth of art in the French national museums could yield so much bounty that even Hitler would not know what to do with it all.

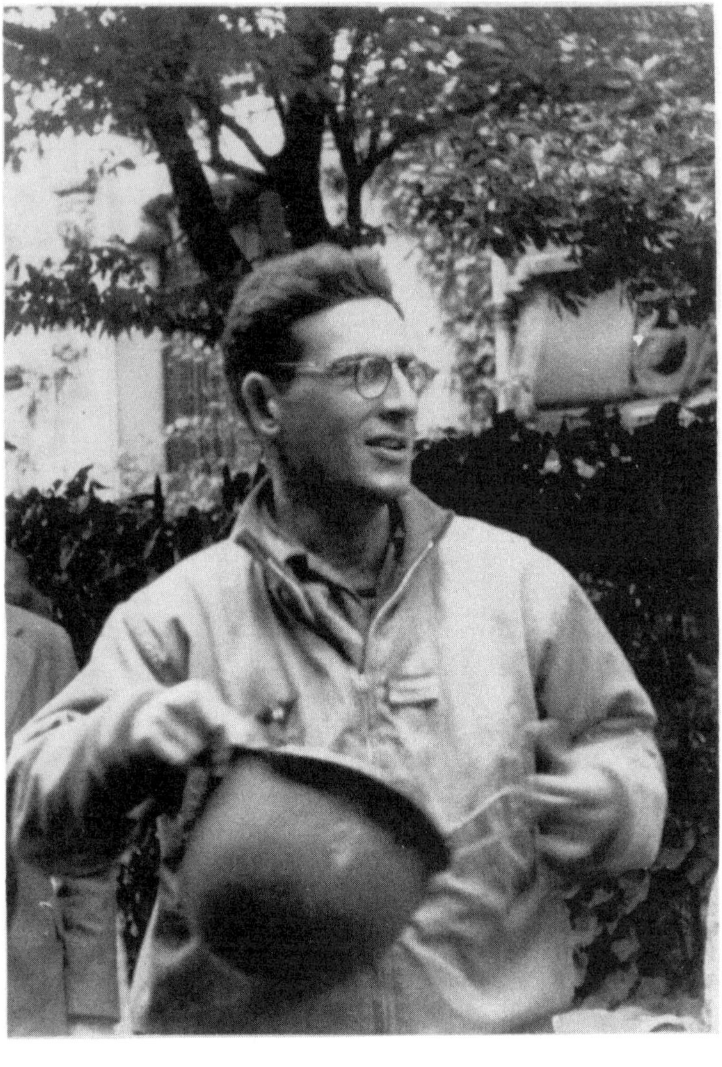

Alexandre Rosenberg at the Liberation of Paris, August 1944.

ENGLAND

SEPTEMBER 1940

JUST FOUR DAYS AFTER ARRIVING IN PLYMOUTH, ENGLAND, ALEXANDRE Rosenberg enlisted for military service in London with Charles de Gaulle's Free France. He was increasingly worried about his exiled family in Portugal, however. They hoped he would join them in Sintra, a seaside town on a cliff just outside Lisbon, where they had arrived in June after a multiple-day car journey dotted with intrigue. While crossing Spain, a sympathetic hotel receptionist warned them to stay in their rooms because Gestapo officers were hunting Jewish refugees.

Alexandre's father, Paul, threw all his efforts into obtaining visas to the United States for his extended family, but it was difficult. The United States was only accepting refugees who could prove they could earn a living and would be an added benefit to the country. Plus, his flock had grown again. Twenty-one visas were now needed, a tall order at a time when America had essentially closed its borders.

Paul was also looking for all possible angles to keep Alexandre from going to war, including questioning the validity of his enlistment. With de Gaulle in London maneuvering to take France back, were the Free French soldiers part of France or England? Paul initially hoped that he might have some say over Alexandre's decision as his parent and guardian since, under British law, parents had the right to claim a son back to civilian life if he enlisted while underage.

Unfortunately for his parents, Alexandre was of age in both France and England, and he could not be stopped from making this pledge to his country. Soon, he would take his first officer exam, and if he did not declare his readiness to serve, he would be permanently kicked out of the officers' class. Still, he was keenly aware of the pain his decision would cause his parents and wrote to them, "It is with the greatest regret that I have to tell you that I have signed my engagement."

Alexandre was in artillery training in the London countryside with his cousins Jean and François Helft and some friends from back home, including Guy Lévy, who had been on the *Batory* with him.

At the end of August, Alexandre and his fellow artillery cadets stood in front of General Charles de Gaulle, General Edward Spears, and King George VI during a drill inspection at their temporary camp in Delville. In September, they were moved from Delville to Old Dean Camp in Camberley, which was an upgrade all around. There was a gym, a theater, showers with hot water, and laundry. Alexandre reported proudly that they felt "just like real British soldiers" and relished living in the same camp as them. "What a pleasure to breathe in the middle of nature when we get up," wrote a fellow trainee in his journal. Alexandre was upbeat and optimistic about following his ideals and all that was to come. He distinguished himself quickly and was named "brigadier of the week" at the end of September.

Because Alexandre was naturally shy and sensitive, he did not dare put his more personal thoughts in the letters he sent directly from camp, as they were censored and read by his superiors and fellow officers in training. His camp location was kept secret, because Vichy France considered the Free French rebels as traitors, while Germany deemed them "*franc-tireurs*," or unlawful combatants, who could be executed upon capture. Instead, he relied on his father's secretary, Winnifred Easton, from the Rosenberg & Helft gallery in London, to serve as a faithful go-between.

Alexandre and his cousins considered Winnifred and Alfred, another employee of the firm, their "war-time parents." Winnifred brought them letters, money, gifts, and succor. She hosted the boys when they had leave. She even brought over the French delicacy *bou-*

din, or blood sausage, from the same maker General de Gaulle bought from. "What is good enough for the Generalissimo is good enough for the mere brigadiers!" she told Alexandre jokingly.

EMOTIONALLY, IT WAS A DIFFICULT time for Paul. He had lost nearly everything—his business, his fortune, his friends, and now his son to de Gaulle—but he did his best to remain optimistic. He had written to all his old art contacts in the United States for letters of recommendation, and the most influential turned out to be Alfred H. Barr Jr., the director of the Museum of Modern Art. Barr convinced the American immigration authorities that Paul had great artistic value for the United States—namely, his relationships with Picasso and Matisse. Plus, the Picasso exhibition at the Museum of Modern Art was a bona fide hit. Thanks to Barr's recommendation, visas came through for the Rosenbergs, the Helfts, and all the cousins.

Paul also communicated with his loyal chauffeur Louis Le Gall and asked him to send all the paintings from the villa in Floirac, France, to Lisbon. Le Gall got to work immediately, but the moving company was taking a long time, strangely.

As for Paul's artists, rumor had it that both Picasso and Matisse had escaped from France. In fact, they were safe and sound in the country. After his accidental brothel stay, Matisse moved into a house in Ciboure, with a sweeping view of the bay of Saint-Jean-de-Luz. As Alexandre was jockeying to get on the *Batory*, Matisse and his assistant, Lydia, managed to procure a taxi and fled the Basque Country with the artist's prized pet birds in tow. They eventually made it to Nice where they rented rooms at the Hôtel Regina. Despondent with the war and feeling like he was aging rapidly, Matisse focused his attention on a painting called *The Dream*, featuring a curled-up, sleeping woman who perhaps embodied the peace he sought in his life and for the world.

Picasso finally left Royan for good and returned to Paris with his chauffeur, his dog Kazbek, and all his belongings. He ruminated about the Germans, telling his friend, the artist Jaime Sabartés, in a letter,

> This is a race apart. They think they are very wise and perhaps they are. They have made much progress—and so, what? . . . Anyhow one thing is certain and that is that we paint better. Fundamentally, if you notice carefully, they are very stupid. . . . So many troops, so many machines, so much power, so much noise to get here! We arrive more quietly. . . . What nonsense! Why can't they do what we did? They probably even think they have conquered Paris! But we, without moving from here, took Berlin a long time ago and I believe they will not be able to dislodge us.

He was referring to the quiet domination of French art, the modernism Hitler so desperately wanted to expunge. Picasso could not yet foresee the brutal attack Hitler was about to wage on modern art in France.

ULTIMATELY, PAUL DID NOT MAKE it to England to see Alexandre. As the Rosenbergs prepared to emigrate to America, the German blitzkrieg began, destroying swaths of London. For most of September, the German Luftwaffe incessantly bombarded the city. A large bomb fell across the street from the Rosenberg & Helft gallery. The force of the shell blew in all the remaining windows that had survived an earlier attack, destroying the woodwork on the doorways and shattering the glass inside.

Communication with England was cut off, and Alexandre became increasingly concerned about whether his family had left for the United States or not. Through Winnifred, he wired to his parents, "Terribly anxious and desperate cannot do anything, cable news immediately, love," but the message was rejected. The family had already left on the

SS *Exeter* bound for New York, and telegrams could no longer be sent to sea from England. Alexandre could only hope for a safe wartime crossing for his entire extended family.

FLOIRAC

SEPTEMBER 15, 1940

AT EIGHT IN THE MORNING, FOUR DAYS AFTER THE ROSENBERGS' DEparture to New York City, five vans descended on Le Castel, the Rosenbergs' rented villa in Floirac. Within minutes, the house was surrounded by eight Gestapo officers and German soldiers, along with a Frenchman and an Italian. *Where is Louis Le Gall?* they demanded, asking for Paul Rosenberg's loyal chauffeur.

Le Gall was shocked to learn that not only did the Germans know him by name but that they were also well-informed about his relationship with Paul. They had surveilled him for three weeks and knew, given that the Rosenbergs fled Europe together, that Le Gall had been given control of what was left of the art collection. They would arrest him if he did not let them into Le Castel.

Two shady Parisian antiques dealers had tipped off the Gestapo. One was Yves Perdoux, a friend of Jacques Helft, Paul's brother-in-law. Le Gall now understood why the moving company had delayed the shipping of the paintings in Le Castel so many times. He was given the run-around while the Germans and the two French conspirators plotted to take the Rosenberg family's art collection.

The intruders made a thorough search of Le Castel and the outbuildings of the property, including Le Gall's house, and interrogated him and his wife. Then, the Germans carried off seventy-six paintings and delivered them to the German embassy in Paris. One painting remained hidden in the villa. Le Gall also suspected that Monsieur and Madame Ledoux, the owners of Le Castel, had cooperated with the Germans. He heard them making derogatory comments about "Israelites." "I couldn't save anything," Le Gall told Paul's friend, Jean-Gabriel Lemoine, the curator at the Musée des Beaux-Arts de Bordeaux, speaking of his grief at losing the paintings.

Eleven days later, Göring's art dealer, Walter Andreas Hofer, took his pick of the Rosenberg loot—thirty-three paintings and drawings by the likes of Degas, Monet, Pissarro, Renoir, Van Gogh, and Henri de Toulouse-Lautrec. It was a painful loss of a deeply personal collection of art for the Rosenbergs, including numerous family portraits, but neither Paul, en route to New York, nor Alexandre, in officer training in England, had any inkling of what had happened in Bordeaux.

JEU DE PAUME

END OF OCTOBER 1940

GERMAN SENTRIES WATCHED AS A SEEMINGLY UNFLAPPABLE, DARK-haired woman walked up to the entrance of the Jeu de Paume. Rose's heart may have fluttered, but she revealed nothing in her expression. SS soldiers, rifles in hand, stood guard outside, wearing helmets and knee-high black boots. For identification, she showed her *Ausweis* and was let through. Her name was typewritten on the card, her last name with an extra space between all the letters as if for impact: Rose V a l l a n d.

The Germans took little notice of this woman.

"Remain at all costs at the Jeu de Paume museum." That was what

Louvre director Jacques Jaujard ordered her to do. Jaujard knew he could trust Rose to keep watch.

For months, Ambassador Abetz had been undermined by those within the Nazi political machine who wanted to get in on the looting game. Alfred Rosenberg's Einsatzstab Reichsleiter Rosenberg (ERR) and the German Army, which had administrative powers in France, aligned themselves against von Ribbentrop, Abetz, and the Foreign Ministry. In mid-September, Hitler unambiguously pronounced that he had given "the right of confiscation" to the more ideologically driven ERR and gave Rosenberg authority to remove items to Germany for "safekeeping."

This was the first directive that allowed for the extradition of cultural objects and a decisive win for the ERR, which turned around and immediately liquidated the Parisian mansions of the Rothschild family, their châteaux all across France, their bank vaults, and even the warehouses of shipping companies where their art was already packed and ready for shipment to the United States. This process was repeated for collections belonging to the Seligmann family, Alphonse Kann, David David-Weill, and Moïse Lévy de Benzion.

Another directive ordered that all the looted objects stored at the Germany embassy be relocated to the Louvre, to remove it from Abetz's jurisdiction. From the German Army's point of view, this would be more proper since the Kunstschutz, charged with protecting art and architecture in occupied countries, was under its purview.

Kunstschutz head Wolff-Metternich approached Jacques Jaujard with the scheme, convincing the museum director that it would be better to keep the stolen art in the Louvre instead of with Abetz, who was already in the process of shipping art to Germany. Nearly all of Abetz's plunder—a profusion of paintings, statues, furniture, and carpets mostly from the Édouard de Rothschild and Alphonse Kann collections—disappeared through his front gate.

The ERR also seized two hundred of Abetz's crates of stolen art, which were sitting in the warehouse of the Schenker transport company, the preferred shipper of the Nazi regime. The shipment was about to depart for Germany. Three rooms on the ground floor of the Louvre, usually occupied by Near Eastern antiquities, were allocated for the works of art coming in from the German embassy but were quickly filled.

Baron Kurt von Behr, the director of the ERR in Paris, then asked to requisition the Jeu de Paume museum, hoping for more space and autonomy to do business away from prying eyes. The stand-alone museum was a perfect fit, with convenient truck access, but its use required Jaujard's approval since the French national museums were under Vichy rule.

Jaujard met with von Behr and Wolff-Metternich, and the Germans verbally agreed that if the Jeu de Paume was to be used for ERR art storage, the French could make a parallel inventory of everything transferred there. Conveniently, Jaujard had someone perfectly positioned to do it: Rose.

Now, Rose crossed the threshold of the Jeu de Paume to find a chaotic scene. The ordinarily quiet museum was a hub of activity. Soldiers paced back and forth in confusion, blocking the way to the white marble staircase that led to her office.

From a window, she watched as truck after truck loaded with art arrived from the Louvre and the German embassy. Military escorts from the Luftwaffe accompanied each convoy. They marched through the museum, moving hundreds of boxes into the offices and exhibition rooms. The clap of their boots on the parquet floors and the clatter of the wooden crates made jarring new sounds, which echoed, as Rose later ruminated, "without restraint between these walls accustomed to other echoes." The Germans were taking over the museum—*her* museum.

The remaining paintings and sculptures from the Jeu de Paume collection were still piled up in the basement for Rose to watch over. She thought a lot about how she could possibly fulfill Jaujard's command and stay on at the museum. Protecting the artwork might not be enough of a cover. Her unofficial role as curator of the museum seemed ludicrous, given that the art collection was in the basement. Perhaps she could emphasize her managerial role, coordinating the guards and staff, and continue the work she already did handling building maintenance. Five museum guards remained, assigned to manage the boilers, cleaning, and other upkeep. The Germans might need to keep someone around who knew how everything worked and could speak French with the staff. She could pass herself off as a lowly but indispensable employee.

That evening, as Rose prepared to leave the museum, she looked around at the disarray. For all the rumors of German orderliness, the rooms were a mess. She was under orders to return, no matter what, and see what would unfold. The information she reported to Jaujard would be sent to the Resistance and de Gaulle in London. She was so devoted to the art that she had agreed to Jaujard's request without thinking much about her own safety. It was certainly more exciting than the documentation work she had been doing, but also far more dangerous. If she was discovered spying on what the Germans were doing, she could be arrested or even shot.

THE NEXT DAY, NOVEMBER 1, Rose was seized with trepidation as she approached the sentries. *Ausweis bitte*, demanded a guard in front of the museum. She showed her identification card and, to her relief, the soldiers let her pass. Would she ever get used to this? Her forty-second birthday was starting out ominously.

Twenty soldiers were in the process of opening all four hundred cases of art that arrived. Canvases of the Old Masters—Vermeer, Rembrandt, David Teniers the Younger—passed from soldier to soldier down a long line. "The Luftwaffe wasted no time!" Rose noted. She cringed as a few paintings were dropped and stepped on. A magnificent portrait of a woman holding a scepter by Jean-Baptiste Santerre suffered a long tear. Nobody was writing anything down or checking the paintings, which were now piling up against the walls of the museum.

There were new Germans, too. Soldiers with brown uniforms and red swastika armbands walked back and forth inside the rooms like merciless policemen looking for misconduct, particularly on the part of the French workers. Packers accompanied the cases of art that arrived from the German embassy on rue de Lille, just across the Seine. The Kunstschutz, the German Service for the Protection of Works in France, sent three art historians to help.

"A real agitation permeated the atmosphere," Rose observed. "Go quickly!" the Luftwaffe soldiers were instructed. Everyone seemed to be panicking, but why? German art experts in white coats chatted quietly in hushed tones, looking smugly at the quality of the artwork they were setting up for display.

Nobody in the museum knew this, but Rose understood German, thanks to Joyce. She could read German, too.

Rose pieced together that the Reichsmarschall Hermann Göring himself was coming to the Jeu de Paume. There was no man closer to Hitler than Göring. No wonder the boxes were being opened so hastily and sorted through. Speed was of the essence—an entire exhibition needed to be curated and hung by the next day.

The legality of the ERR's takeover of the Jeu de Paume was contingent on the creation of the duplicate inventory, which would allow the French the opportunity to document the art that was looted. Rose simply settled down where she could, scribbling in a notebook anything she could glimpse. Moving around the canvases to get all the information was like an acrobatics act. It was strange, but she could swear the German soldiers were purposely increasing their speed now that she had started working.

Rose was surprised that no other expert had started the German inventory—was this diplomatic task only important to her? Nobody around her seemed to care. So, amid the hustle and bustle, she did what she was trained to do: make lists as complete and precise as possible. She feistily wanted to "show these Germans that a French woman also knows how to obey orders."

At noon, a uniformed ERR officer arrived. He cut a long figure, his countenance severe and tight. He looked on edge, and Rose felt sure that not a single drop of kindness could emanate from the man. He brusquely grabbed her notebook and shut it closed in an authoritative gesture. "We cannot proceed with the request of the French civil servants to make inventories," he said. "Moreover, our German scholars are capable of doing them perfectly themselves." This chilly man was Dr. Hermann Bunjes, a Harvard-educated art historian and SS officer. It would not be the last time Rose would encounter Dr. Bunjes at the Jeu de Paume.

Several colleagues from the Musées Nationaux also showed up to help Rose with the inventory, but Bunjes commanded them to leave. Rose then made a calculated decision. Bunjes's order did not affect her since she worked explicitly for the Jeu de Paume. "My intention was fixed, I would endeavor to stay," she professed later. "I did not yet understand very clearly the reasons that were pushing me to this decision, nor in what way I could be useful and justify my presence since there was no longer any question of a French inventory. Only my determination not to leave the place was clear." It was as if some greater force was pushing her to remain at the museum, propelling her into action before her rational self could process the reasons. Jaujard's support removed any last doubts in her mind.

Since she could no longer write anything down in her notebook, she would have to keep track in her head. It was a good thing she had an almost photographic memory. "Everything had to be surveilled and remembered because you never know in the moment the detail that will matter later," she recalled.

Adding to the confusion that day was the dramatic, unwelcome return of Rose's boss, André Dezarrois, who believed he had a right to verify the status of the works entrusted to his care as the curator of the Jeu de Paume. His timing, on the very day the Germans took over the museum, was particularly unfortunate. Dezarrois lost his temper at the sight of the Nazis invading the museum and tried to force his way into his old office and the storage rooms, where the locks were broken, undoubtedly by German soldiers. He also loudly protested the fact that the artworks on the walls of the museum consisted of stolen, Jewish-owned art. German soldiers forcibly removed him from the museum, searched his apartment, and interrogated him. He was prohibited from setting foot inside the museum again at the risk of arrest.

Jaujard recommended that Dezarrois leave Paris for his own safety. But Jaujard had another motivation: an unruly curator would disrupt the delicate political maneuvering he had already set in motion.

If that was not enough turmoil, ERR director Kurt von Behr also swept into the museum, his dark green wool military coat adorned with a collar of wolf's hair. Rose thought he looked very much the part of a triumphant German warrior. For extra gravitas, he insisted on wearing his World War I German Red Cross uniform, affixed with two medals and a long row of military decorations. He also donned a visored Red Cross officers' cap, which had the great advantage of shading his glass eye.

The French spy service had known about von Behr since at least 1936, when he was already working for the Gestapo in Spain in support of the Fascists in Mallorca.

"Tall, handsome . . . not lacking in charm and spoke French well," Rose noted of her first impression. She was also wary of him. Rose knew right away that von Behr knew nothing about art. He liked only the expensive and flashy.

Rose, the unassuming employee at the Jeu de Paume, found herself having a mundane conversation with von Behr. It was a social conversation, and he was attentive to what she was saying. "As they were still in the euphoria of their victory, the conquerors were friendly, to convince us that they were not savages," she later wrote of this encounter. If all went well, maybe von Behr would let her stay on at the museum. When she looked back decades later, she seemed to criticize her somewhat lackluster resistance to such obvious evil that first day. She explained, we "kept many illusions to try to control the conqueror. Our efforts, already ill-suited to the whole situation, were even less in tune with the concerns of the moment. We French could only cut a sorry figure in the celebration which was being prepared."

The German art historians, meanwhile, were almost ready with the last-minute exhibition for Göring. The sheer caliber of the artwork hurriedly put on display was astounding. Some of the most famous paintings in the world hung on wire from tracks on the ceiling. *The Astronomer* by Vermeer, owned by the Rothschild family since 1886, was on one wall. A Rembrandt painting was on another. Tapestries, sculptures, and precious furniture were in each room. Gothic and Renaissance paintings with thick, heavy wood frames were hung together. Dutch and Flemish Master painters were given special attention. Rococo paintings were in one room, and British portraiture in another. Neoclassical paintings and French history paintings were placed side by side.

Rose saw works by Gauguin and Renoir carried past her. On the second floor, in a room in the far back of the museum hidden behind a curtain, Rose found paintings by Dalí, Picasso, Braque, Léger, Van Gogh, Matisse, and others. It was a room just for "degenerate" art.

At the end of his visit, von Behr made it clear that Rose was allowed to remain at the museum. Jaujard planned to address the question of the inventory with Wolff-Metternich the next day.

That evening, the Jeu de Paume closed its doors to anyone—French, German, or otherwise—who did not have an *Ausweis* from von Behr himself. Rose was now one of the only French eyewitnesses to what would become the greatest art theft in history.

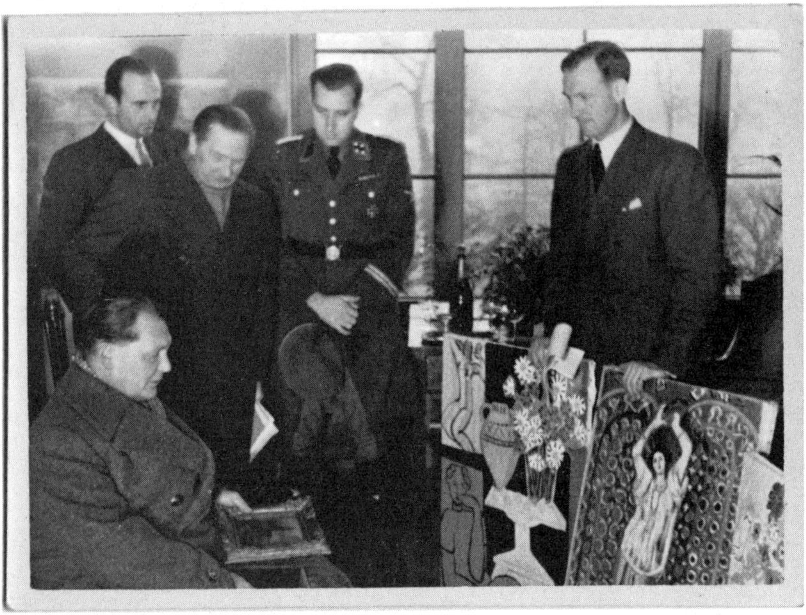

Bruno Lohse *(far right)* presenting Hermann Göring *(far left, seated)* two Henri Matisse paintings from the stock of the ERR.

JEU DE PAUME

NOVEMBER 2, 1940

THE JEU DE PAUME WAS READY FOR A SPECIAL VISITOR. IN ADDITION to the careful curation of art and furniture in each room, the museum was enhanced with potted palm trees and beautiful carpets, taken from the stash of valuables looted from Jewish collectors and placed over the parquet wood floors. Some of the world's finest artworks were on the walls. Champagne was served, and all the German officers wore ceremonial dress uniforms to impress Reichsmarschall Hermann Göring on his first visit.

Göring was the second most powerful man in the Third Reich. He held a long list of titles and accolades, having proved his loyalty to the Nazi Party starting with the Beer Hall Putsch, a failed coup d'état led by Hitler in 1923. He rose through the ranks, becoming Reichsminister of aviation, prime minister of Prussia, president of the Reichstag, commander in chief of the Luftwaffe, and was now Hitler's designated successor. In 1936, he was given full powers to execute the "Four Year Plan" to rearm Germany and prepare its economy for war. He also created the Gestapo, the official secret police of Nazi Germany, which continued to operate in occupied Europe. The title of Reichsmarschall of the Greater German Reich, created just for him after the successful invasion of France, granted him authority over all officers in the armed forces, not just the Luftwaffe.

Göring was a cunning, manipulative, and ruthless man who knew how to use his intelligence and charm to outwit his enemies and competitors. He also had no qualms about eliminating them, as he had done in response to an alleged coup against Hitler in 1934. Göring laughed gleefully through the killings, deriding one man as a "homosexual pig" and informing him that he was going to be shot. In general, Göring was intently focused on attaining glory and power for the Third Reich, while also enriching himself along the way.

Göring had been coming to Paris for shopping trips all summer, popping down from the Luftwaffe headquarters in northern France on the coast of the English Channel. His hotel of choice was the Ritz, where a bathtub large enough for his portly figure was custom-installed for him in the imperial suite. His bubble baths would be hours long, interspersed with injections of drugs, part of a water-based cure his doctors were implementing for the morphine addiction he had picked up during World War I. Hotel staff constantly delivered an abundance of towels, champagne, and caviar.

At 2:30 p.m., Göring made a dramatic entrance into the Jeu de Paume with his art dealer, Walter Andreas Hofer, along with ERR and Luftwaffe officials. His civilian dress—a long coat and a fedora hat torn in the front—surprised everyone, and Rose found Göring's heavy silhouette mediocre-looking and bourgeois compared to the spit and shine of the officers.

The works of art were shown to him one after another, with the paintings, jewelry, and furniture from the Édouard de Rothschild collection taking center stage. Göring was dazzled and looked at each object so carefully that the viewing took all day. The collection at the Jeu de Paume far surpassed anything he had access to in Holland and the Netherlands, and when he learned much more was in storage, he decided to extend his trip.

He returned to the Jeu de Paume two days later to see all the treasures. He was garrulous and excited, talking with the art experts around him and making loud declarations about the wonders of his favorite paintings. Rose watched as he took the smaller paintings into his hands and examined them closely, trying to look like a true connoisseur. At times, he smoked a cigar. Göring evaluated each work of art for its suitability at Carinhall, his extravagant hunting estate known as the "Petit Versailles," about forty miles north of Berlin. He had long believed himself to be "the last Renaissance man," and he finally had a stockpile worthy of his discrimination.

Göring had even more reason to be enthusiastic. He had written an executive order that would benefit him enormously while also pleasing the Führer. He was in such a rush to get his hands on the loot, fearing that the treasures might slip through his fingertips, that he decided to issue the order without getting Hitler's approval. He was confident the Führer would agree.

Hitler would have priority on the stolen art, the second choice would go to Göring, the third to Foreign Policy Office leader and ERR mastermind Alfred Rosenberg, and the fourth to German museums. A fifth category, thrown in for good measure to appease the French, allocated everything else to French museums or to be auctioned off to benefit French "widows and war orphans."

Göring cajoled Rosenberg to agree to the new order by offering continued use of the Luftwaffe to transport all of Rosenberg's newfound "research" materials—German valuables the Nazis were collecting from the French libraries and archives. Göring also gave Rosenberg access to his personal network of collaborationist French detectives and criminal agents to track down Jewish-owned collections and told him that he would always be willing to share intelligence reports. For his part, Rosenberg needed Göring's political clout to keep his position. Göring told Rosenberg that he would pay for the art he took from the ERR to a trustee appointed by the German state to be used for some future purpose. In reality, Göring had no intention of paying for any of it.

There would also be no competition from Hans Posse, the director of the Führermuseum, who was more interested in quality than quantity. Although Hitler originally wanted Posse to manage all the pillaged art in the Reich, the art historian already had an unlimited budget and did not need to waste his time sorting through hundreds of thousands of artworks for hidden gems. He had no motivation to take on the additional responsibility of handling stolen art from all over Europe. Having top priority on the art at the Jeu de Paume on Hitler's behalf would serve Posse just fine.

Posse had just left Paris four days earlier, after more than a week in the Ritz Hotel. He met with high-ranking Nazi officials in town and learned that the seized Jewish-owned art was being moved from the German embassy to the Louvre. He spent his time with various Parisian art dealers, like Yves Perdoux, who had revealed the location of Paul Rosenberg's collection in Le Castel. He also had his eye on paintings owned by the Louvre, now scattered in various châteaux throughout France. He did not need to battle things out with Göring in the Jeu de Paume.

To make things appear proper on paper, Göring had a French artist, Jacques Beltrand, act as an appraiser and provide valuations that would be favorable to him. From the initial bounty at the Jeu de Paume, Göring selected twenty-seven paintings, including a Rembrandt and a van Dyck that belonged to Georges Wildenstein. He considered this first selection a very small kickback in return for his assistance in locating Jewish-owned art. "I have brought to light, out of their hiding places, a very large part of the artistic treasures," he wrote to Rosenberg, bragging that he had done it through bribery and use of his criminal network. He was being disingenuous, as most of his first selection came from Abetz's loot.

To complete his visit to Paris, Göring made a secret stop at the Louvre at 2 p.m., where the museum's opening was delayed just for him. Dr. Bunjes made advance arrangements with the museum staff to ensure that the visit would be "incognito." The Reichsmarschall and his automobile entourage arrived through the gates of the Cour Lefuel, a grand inner courtyard with a horseshoe-shaped staircase and bronze statues of screaming wolves and wild boars. Göring strolled into the museum through a pillared portico.

The viewing took place in the curators' meeting room. The Louvre staff closed all the shutters and covered the windows with thick beige velvet curtains, which had the added benefit of serving as the backdrop for the main piece of art Göring wanted to see, the sculpture of Saint Marie-Madeleine (Mary Magdalene) by Gregor Erhart. The fifteenth-century nude sculpture, made from the wood of a linden tree, depicts Marie-Madeleine with hip-length, wavy blond tresses that flow around and over her exposed breasts. Nicknamed the *Belle Allemande*, the "Beautiful German," the sculpture was once suspended high in the church of a Dominican convent in Germany and had taken on an almost mythical reputation.

Göring gazed at Marie-Madeleine for a long time. He divulged that he was interested because he already owned a sculpture of the Virgin Mary by the same artist. He then asked to visit the sculpture department, where he stopped in front of the *Virgin of Olivet* and the *Diana of Anet* and asked if French sculptors could make copies for his own personal collection. He also wanted to acquire a bronze cast of the *Diana of Fontainebleau*. The French curators politely promised to convey his wishes to Louvre director Jacques Jaujard.

Four days later, Göring asked Germany Army commander in chief Walther von Brauchitsch to remove selected artworks from the Jeu de Paume to Germany. Even Bunjes, who had executed all of Göring's requests thus far, was concerned by the overreach and sent a letter to Dr. Harald Turner, chief of the SS military administration. "In addition to this absolutely irregular state of affairs from a legal point of view," Bunjes wrote forcefully, "the prices are so low that I ask you to have them checked and rectified by another expert." But not much could be done. Göring had achieved a major coup, deftly circumventing Ambassador Abetz, the German army in France, and even the ERR's Alfred Rosenberg. His first shopping trip to Paris under his newly declared rules of acquisition surpassed even his own expectations, and nobody could stop him now—except Hitler.

PARIS

FALL TO WINTER 1940

ROSE COULDN'T STOP GÖRING, BUT SHE COULD DOCUMENT EVERYTHING he did. Shortly after Göring's first visit, she went to visit Jacques Jaujard at the Louvre to report what she had seen and heard. Rose found Jaujard in his cozy office. There was a pleasant view of the Seine from the window. A long row of books and bound inventories were the main records of where France's artistic treasures had gone, from the museums and from private citizens who had entrusted their most valuable belongings to Jaujard. In there were Rose's own handwritten lists of everything she had packed up from the Jeu de Paume. Jaujard's office felt like a sanctuary to Rose, who spent her days right in the center of Nazi thieving.

She recounted to Jaujard how Göring did not hide his fervor for the works of art shown to him. She called him a "passionate amateur," something the Reichsmarschall himself probably would have bristled at. The contrast between Göring as aesthete and Göring as vicious brute was hard to square, and the indirect role Rose and the Jeu de Paume guards had to play to entertain such a dangerous, barbaric Nazi official was disturbing, to say the least. Rose despised how he seemed so untouchable. "No complaint, human or legally justified, could reach him," she later wrote. Of his presence in the Jeu de Paume and his looting of art, she asserted, "I have often thought that Göring was putting on a show and that the whole process had been dreamed up before it was carried out."

She and Jaujard could not foresee how far Göring and his henchmen would go in their personal acquisitions, but they were already concerned. The rank of the people visiting on Göring's first tour of the Jeu de Paume, and the pomp attached, was alarming. If Rose and Jaujard's worst fears were realized, the artwork would be shipped to Germany and possibly lost forever. They were determined to thwart this with everything they had. Nothing in the armistice permitted the Germans to loot French art, whether from the national museums or private citizens. The decrees from Germany were all very specific, related to "protection" and "safekeeping."

Even Göring carefully avoided words in his orders like *taking* or *seizing*. Instead, art objects that would "serve to complete the Reichsmarschall's collection" should merely be "transported" to the Jeu de Paume and the Louvre. He also made sure to make his acquisitions seem above board by having the art appraised. He claimed that he would pay, but he would never deliver the funds on anything he acquired at the Jeu de Paume.

Jaujard had been in the civil service long enough to know that there was nothing quite like paperwork to cause a delay. The Germans, who always wanted everything by the book, could not imagine that the very professional and serious museum director was doing anything other than following procedure. The French, on the other hand, were comfortable navigating in ambiguity and perfectly poised to use this cultural difference to their advantage. It was, at this point, their only weapon.

Jaujard looked for loopholes within the flurry of orders and decrees. At the moment, the so-called "abandoned" Jewish collections—art belonging to any Jewish person who had fled France—were his primary concern. Jewish-owned companies were now being transferred to Aryan "provisional administrators" in the absence of their owners, and Jaujard endeavored to have this precedent apply to the Jewish-owned art collections. If it worked, the collections could at least have administrators looking over them instead of being subject to uncontrolled looting. Jaujard also hoped that he could convince the Germans that the administrators should be a committee of museum staffers or art historians.

Progress was slow. But in a month, the Ministry of Finance stepped up and sent letters to the Nazi leaders. At the minimum, the

French wanted access to the rooms of seized art and to resume Rose's double inventory. They also wanted permission to enter the houses and apartments that the Germans were liquidating. It might be impossible to stop the looting, but any access could offer a means to spy. The evidence could be used later in war tribunals. It would have been painful for Rose to see her museum used as a laundering facility for stolen art by deceitful men with dubious intentions. Her job, her life calling, was about celebrating the beauty in art and presenting it to the public, but now she was witnessing the wholesale theft of the world's finest creations.

Jaujard was also confronted with a new, discomfiting task. The decree that barred anyone Jewish from working in the civil service would go into effect soon, and he was required to send a list of all his Jewish museum employees. There was a narrow list of possible exemptions—those who fought in World War I, distinguished themselves in the recent war, or were bestowed a Légion d'Honneur or another medal. Jaujard rushed to mail every employee of Jewish descent to see if they might fit under this loophole. It pained him, and he told them he was unfortunately "duty-bound" to report any exemptions to the minister in just a few days, after which the exemptions would no longer be accepted. He was going to do everything in his power to keep his Jewish workers employed, just as he was fighting to have museum workers who had been taken prisoner of war released from detention camps.

Meanwhile, Rose was responsible for gathering intelligence as more Jewish-owned art collections piled up in the Jeu de Paume. She duplicated the building keys and the keys to the safes. On some days she slept over in the museum, making secret copies of the inventory lists the art historians made. Every two to three days, she went to Jaujard's office to report to him or his secretary, Jacqueline Bouchot-Saupique.

Conveniently enough, Rose was relegated to the Jeu de Paume's telephone room. It was just next to a narrow winding staircase that led down to the entrance of the museum. She would listen to the German conversations happening in the office next to her, take papers that were left behind or replicate them at home, and fish carbon copies of documents out of the trashcans.

At home, Joyce could help Rose decipher the German documents. The next morning, Rose would put the crumpled pieces of paper back into the garbage. Using her impeccable memory, she made additional notes and scribbled down information she recalled: who visited, what the staff said and did, which Jewish-owned collections were delivered, and which paintings were in each room. Paperwork abounded inside the ERR, and Rose discovered it was sometimes easy to get near documents by pretending to visit the exhibits in the museum or to speak to the art historians who happened to be near the documents. This was how Rose began to glean the names and addresses of the collections that were being stolen.

The men responsible for the looting were also far from discreet. Unidentified deliverymen would arrive at the Jeu de Paume and dump a truckload of art, saying things like, "These are from Rothschild," and "These are from the Avenue du Bois," usually never to be seen again.

Baron Kurt von Behr, focused on living lavishly, managed the Jeu de Paume much like a mobster boss. He wined and dined the most important military and political figures in Paris. Meanwhile, Dr. Hermann Bunjes, the Harvard-educated art historian, oversaw the deliveries. Two intimidating Gestapo men were brought in to liquidate Jewish-owned businesses and dwellings, using intelligence and muscle provided by the French collaborationist police. The duo had absolutely no interest in any form of documentation, and most of the objects ended up labeled as "unknown" origin, despite a frantic attempt by the German art historians to rectify the chaos.

Indeed, so much art was coming in that the staff was quickly overwhelmed. In one swoop, the ERR seized 367 cases of art from Édouard de Rothschild's château in Normandy, along with additional crates from Henri de Rothschild's enormous palace in Paris, and the Rothschild vineyard and manor in Bordeaux. Even if the historians knew where the art came from, it often still took considerable research to figure out exactly what specific work they were looking at. It frustrated some of the German art historians that the Jewish owners did not leave behind detailed inventories for them—it would have made their jobs a lot easier!

The ERR was also working with the Feldpolizei, the German secret military police, which was using informants to track down more treasures. A secretary of art dealer Jean Seligmann delivered all the remaining works of art from her employer's Place Vendôme gallery to a German officer she was dating and gave Göring's agents a tour of where other Jewish collectors had stored their art.

In just six months, the Germans had stolen some of the largest private art collections in France, and they were only getting started. While the Rothschilds were a fruitful early target due to the exceptional scale of their wealth and collections, nearly eighty other Jewish family collections were on the ERR's list. At this rate, the private cultural heritage of France could be decimated in less than a year. The room at the Jeu de Paume filled with all the undesirable, "degenerate" modern paintings—dubbed ironically as the "*Salle des Martyrs*" (the Room of the Martyrs)—was filling up briskly.

Meanwhile, Jaujard's effort to regain control inside the Jeu de Paume was having minimal effect. At first, the Germans disclosed what was being moved between the Louvre and the Jeu de Paume, but that practice stopped after the first month. The Germans also banned both Jaujard and Rose from the ERR rooms in the Louvre. Armed sentries remained at the entrance of the museum, while more and more German art historians arrived to handle the increasing influx of art to be inventoried. A photographic lab was also built inside the Jeu de Paume, and each piece of artwork was documented on a preformatted index card that included a Leica photograph of it, the artist, date of creation, size, any art historical information, who owned it, and, often, precisely where it was seized. The meticulous art historians initialed their names on the cards.

As Rose and Jaujard had feared, Hitler issued a new order in mid-

November about the confiscated art in the occupied countries, specifying that Hans Posse would make the decisions on how the works of art would be used. This opened the possibility for looted art to be exported out of France, but due to the political jockeying and Göring's dominance over the ERR, no art had left yet.

To Rose, the level and type of activity in the Jeu de Paume reminded her of the major international exhibitions she used to curate, except the mood was sinister. The Germans were not interested in cultural exchange, but in a spree. All she could do was watch helplessly as her museum was transformed into a twisted version of itself and hope that her reports to Jaujard would have some use.

She tried every pretext to circulate within the museum, including surveilling the building's electrical wiring and its fire alarm system. At any given time, there were at least eight armed German sentries and dozens of ERR staff, including the German art historians, photographers, and secretaries. She decided that the only way to accomplish her spying was to appear to do whatever the Germans wanted her to do and to be as discreet as possible. If she was caught, she would pretend her love of art had led her to poke around imprudently. "This curiosity was plausible," she would later recount.

When the special wartime budget expired, Jaujard took the time to write her a particularly personal letter, commending her "dedication to the Musées Nationaux" and praising her effectiveness, particularly over the summer. He wrote that he was informing her of a reversal of payment "with regret" and that he wanted to reiterate his gratitude for her valuable assistance. But Rose was more than angry. After all she had been through—risking her life to direct the "last minute" escape of museum employees by boat, returning to Paris after the traffic jam on the Seine, and nearly getting killed multiple times on the way to Chambord—the museums again would not pay her? What more could she have done?

She started to write down her grievances, her handwriting deteriorating rapidly as she emotionally crossed out words and whole paragraphs, and ultimately gave up. She described the boat escape as one of "catastrophic disorder and unpreparedness which nearly cost us our lives." Ten days after Jaujard wrote to Rose, he managed to finally get her appointed officially as a *chargée de mission* (project manager) at the Jeu de Paume. With it came a salary.

Rose and Jaujard were an unlikely duo, brought together by unthinkable circumstance in a high-stakes game. On the surface, forty-five-year-old Jaujard was suave, assured, and inspiring. Rose appeared like an unremarkable loner and was considered a *vieille fille*, a spinster past her prime at the age of forty-two. But they were much more alike than they seemed—highly intelligent and indefatigable. And perhaps even more importantly, they had both learned how to adapt to a wide variety of circumstances and to conceal their working-class upbringing. Rose had additionally kept her sexuality private for most of her life, and in her new role as a spy, she would need to pull on that cloak of invisibility even more. With Joyce living in her apartment, Rose's risk of being deemed an enemy of the German occupiers was even higher. Even though there was no law in the Third Reich that criminalized lesbian relationships, like there was for gay men, the Nazis were known to harass lesbian communities.

Rose and Jaujard were still figuring out their own rules of engagement with the Germans when a new nemesis appeared at the Jeu de Paume just after the new year.

ENGLAND

DECEMBER 1940

THE WAR WAS NOW BEING FOUGHT ON MULTIPLE FRONTS. BY THE END of September, Japan formalized an alliance with Italy and Germany, and in November, the Axis powers expanded to include Hungary, Romania, and Slovakia. The Free French soldiers, led by General Philippe Leclerc, headed to Africa with the hope of convincing the French colonies in West and Equatorial Africa, as well as Cameroon in Central Africa, to join General Charles de Gaulle in the fight against the Axis.

The Battle of Britain, fought in the air between the British Royal Air Force (RAF) and the Luftwaffe, raged through the end of the year. In October alone, the Luftwaffe launched 783 air attacks on Britain, dropping 8,300 tons of bombs—half of which landed on London. Despite heavy military and civilian casualties—the bombing raids killed twenty-three thousand British citizens and wounded over thirty-two thousand between July and October 1940—the RAF managed to keep the Luftwaffe at bay. German military invincibility was punctured for the first time in the war, garnering a psychological win for the Allies. In December, the British launched a counteroffensive against Italian troops in East Africa and Egypt.

In the meantime, Alexandre Rosenberg was doing splendidly in England. He had just passed his brigadier examination and was made a cadet, in line to become a commissioned officer. The months of studying had paid off, and he hoped he would be promoted within a few months. He was now living outside the Camberley training camp in a small, pleasant home where he had his own bedroom, a living room, and a bathroom. He spent evenings with friends in front of the electric fireplace, listening to one of the many orchestral and symphonic records stacked next to the gramophone. It was a real upgrade from the metal Nissen barracks at camp.

It also meant that his adoptive English parents, Winnifred and Alfred, could visit him easily at "*chez lui*," as Winnifred put it. She had taken to calling herself "Snow White." Alexandre, his cousins, and the other French boys were her "dwarfs" to whom she gave all the maternal attention they desperately lacked. She put together a Christmas care package and even bothered them about their underwear, as Paul Rosenberg instructed from New York. They were embarrassed and horrified to talk to her at all about undergarments and assured her that what they had was quite sufficient.

Alexandre was relieved to hear that his family had arrived safely in New York City in late September. They moved into a hotel on East Fifty-Eighth Street and Madison Avenue known as the Madison, a residence hotel that catered to wealthy families accustomed to having house staff. An elaborate entertainment venue, the Baroque Room, offered supper and dancing with live jazz performances. The Madison had the additional appeal of an in-house French restaurant, Le Cordon Bleu, founded by a former manager of the Ritz in Paris.

Paul resumed a characteristic breakneck work schedule. He gave speeches in cities across the United States about both modern art and historic French art and worked with Winnifred to ship the paintings in his London gallery to the United States. He remained unaware of the fate of his artworks in France. He also curated and participated in numerous exhibitions all around the country.

In France however, one of Paul's artists was not doing well. In Nice, Matisse was very ill with intestinal problems; a tumor had been discovered. He could not work at his usual pace but managed to finish two pared-down still lifes with seafood themes. He wrote to a friend about his exploration into abstraction, "I can go no further," but he could easily have also been referring to his ability to paint, given his health.

Matisse had also declined two opportunities to leave France. The first was an offer to teach at Mills College in California. The second came from Varian Fry of the Emergency Rescue Committee, who was helping artists and writers escape the country. Fry would go on to help Marcel Duchamp, Marc Chagall, Max Ernst, Wanda Landowska, Jacques Lipchitz, Hannah Arendt, and over two thousand other cultural refugees cross the Pyrenees into Spain and get to the United States through Portugal.

Like Matisse, Picasso was invited overseas but he did not want to leave France either. He left his apartment on rue la Boétie, which must have been a little lonely without his friend and neighbor Paul Rosenberg. He moved into his studio on rue des Grands-Augustins in the Latin Quarter and installed a dramatic potbelly stove with a sculptural flue pipe he acquired from a collector. It was as much an art piece as a functional item, and soon he no longer had wood for it due to war shortages. He turned down special treatment from the Germans, telling them, "A Spaniard is never cold," and headed to his favorite cafés like the Brasserie Lipp and the Café de Flore to stay warm. German soldiers also visited the studio, where Picasso had hung a large photo of *Guernica*. One soldier asked Picasso, "Ah, so it was you, Monsieur Picasso, who did that?" to which Picasso replied impertinently, "No, you did it!" referring to the bombing of Guernica, the Spanish town that it depicted. Picasso also had postcards of the painting printed and would push them into the hands of his German visitors, saying, "Take it, take it! Souvenir!"

In New York, Paul was looking at properties in midtown Manhattan where he could open a new arm of his gallery. Despite everything happening in the world, it was an exciting time for the Rosenberg business, but a storm cloud was just on the horizon.

PARIS

DECEMBER 1940

IN PARIS, THE STRESS OF THE GERMAN OCCUPATION HAD TAKEN A toll on Rose's partner, Joyce, and her mental state was deteriorating rapidly. As a half-German British citizen employed by the US embassy, Joyce lived in a world of constant uncertainty. Knowing that Rose was in danger day after day at the Jeu de Paume did not help.

The more Joyce fretted, the more her performance at work suffered. Her superiors responded by putting more pressure on her, and she was about to have a breakdown. Her boss, Robert D. Murphy, the American consul, reported that he found her several times "on the verge of hysteria." But her fluency in German was indispensable to the embassy in wartime, and despite the stress on her nerves, she put in long work hours. Murphy wrote in her review at the end of September that "she has so far risen to the need."

Diplomatically, the American presence in Paris was nebulous. The United States was the only embassy left in town. But for the time being, the Germans were willing "to indulge in a little make believe" and treat members of the American Foreign Service still in Paris as if they had diplomatic status. A new US embassy was also set up in Vichy to service the new French state in the Unoccupied Zone.

While Murphy commended Joyce's dedication and translation abilities, as well as her appearance and the way she interacted with the public, he was completely unempathetic about what she was going through personally. He wrote in her annual review that she was "inclined to magnify dangers and trivialities." Even more disparagingly, and seemingly out of spite and frustration, he wrote, "Her intelligence and general capacity do not qualify her for more than ordinary clerical work."

But Joyce was rightfully worried. The Germans now required her and the roughly four thousand British subjects still in France to register as "enemy aliens" with the Germans at their local *Kommandantur*. They had to provide their home address and sign in at the office six days a week. The Germans warned they were considered "prisoners on parole."

The British embassy and its staff had fled Paris the day before the Germans arrived, leaving its citizens in Occupied France adrift virtually without diplomatic support. A note left on the door advised anyone British to seek help at the US embassy.

The British found themselves suddenly treated like the enemy, even by non-Germans. They lived in perpetual terror that they might be overheard speaking English or spied on, something Joyce would have been even more concerned about as a clerk for the US embassy. The American Hospital in Paris dismissed their British employees and volunteers fearing German retribution. Anti-British propaganda posters went up all around the city, with one showing Churchill as an octopus with his tentacles wrapped around France and the rest of the world. Some café owners distanced themselves from their British patrons. But other French men and women took in British refugees and sheltered injured soldiers at significant personal risk.

In early September, 1,648 British men between the ages of sixteen and sixty-five were rounded up and interned. Not even the deputy British consul, in charge of the British Interests Section at the US embassy, was spared. Would they take British women next?

On October 16, the Germans issued a new decree: anyone sheltering a British citizen must declare them or be sentenced to death by firing squad if caught. Joyce was an enemy alien in an occupied country, cut off from her family in England, and in an illicit relationship with a woman spying on the Nazis. Rose was sheltering a British citizen and could be shot. No wonder Joyce was struggling to keep things together.

For Joyce, the dreaded knock on the door came early on the wintry morning of December 5, with Paris in a total blackout. All over the city, British women like Joyce opened the door to find a bright torchlight in their faces. It was the French police. Orders had come down at 5 a.m., and they were systematically going to all the addresses listed by British women who registered with the *Kommandantur* and escorting them to the *mairie*, the local town hall. The same thing was happening all over the country. They all said some version of the same thing: "I have come to fetch you," or "I must ask you to come with me," or "We would like you to accompany us to the *mairie*." In some cases, German military policemen showed up as well, far less polite, banging on the doors roughly and storming into the apartments. Joyce would have been terrified.

Some women were advised to take something warm or to pack a

bag, while others were told not to bring anything. "Just a formality," the policemen told them. A check on their paperwork, and then they would be home within twenty-four hours.

Some women quickly grasped what was really going on. "*Maman*, they've come to arrest me," one told her mother. But many others thought it was just another administrative procedure, as the Germans were wont to do. The French policemen were apologetic, embarrassed even to be following German orders. "*Ayez courage*," they told the women as they left them at the town hall, knowing full well what was in store for them. "Today it's you; tomorrow it will be us," one officer said.

The town halls were chaotic and crowded. Mothers with sick children and babies, nuns, pregnant women, widows, prostitutes, nannies, dancers from the Folies Bergère, elderly and infirm women—including some who were bedridden—and a few elderly men. There were bags everywhere. On paper, everyone had a British passport, but the diversity was astounding. There were widowed French women who married British men in World War I; Russian and Armenian refugees who had British passports; Jews from Palestine, which was a British territory; Black women from Nigeria; Afrikaners; a Russian princess; and the daughter of an Indian maharajah. A rumor went around that they would be taken to a camp in Germany.

In the afternoon, German soldiers flooded the town halls all over Paris and corralled all the detainees into black police vans and open trucks. "*Los! Los! Raus!*" ("Move! Move! Out!") they shouted. Packed inside the vans, the women could barely see above the windows. They were offloaded at the Gare de l'Est train station to an alarming scene. Thousands of British subjects clamored and objected, now confronted with the serious predicament they were in. The Germans struggled to remain in control and hastily herded everyone onto a very long train. When each carriage was full, the soldiers locked the doors and affixed barbed wire around the handles for good measure.

Joyce and the other women waited for hours in the freezing train cars. There was no heating, no lighting, no toilets, or water. Food was delivered—soup, black bread, and raw, pungent, unidentifiable, inedible meat in tins that the women dubbed "monkey" meat and promptly tossed out the window. Starving and sick babies screamed relentlessly; adults whimpered, wailed, and wept; the ill and the elderly suffered. Frantic rumors flew around: they might be deported to Germany and used as slave labor, or more optimistically, they might get repatriated or sent to the Unoccupied Zone.

Finally, after nightfall, the train departed the station. Black coal exhaust blew from the locomotive. The women rushed to the windows of the train cars, and French railway workers on the tracks waved them off, calling, "*Bonne chance, bonne chance!*" The women still did not know where they were going.

For two days, the train traveled from station to station, siding to siding. The smell inside the cars from all the women relieving themselves was unbearable. Several women gave birth. A three-day-old baby, taken from his mother in Paris, died.

There was a long stop in Belfort, close to Alsace near the border of Germany. It would be hopeless if they crossed into Germany, but suddenly, the train changed direction and headed south.

At last, the train reached its final destination—Besançon, France. They were less than fifty miles to Switzerland, close to the Jura mountain range. Looking out, the women saw a row of German soldiers and a lot of snow. A young girl screamed at the sight in fear of the uniformed men and their dogs that barked menacingly. Everyone on the train shivered, their lips almost frozen. The disembarkation was even more chaotic than the scene at Gare de l'Est. The German guards were unprepared and disorganized. They shouted out names and marched everyone through town to an enormous complex of Napoleon-era barracks. Foreboding-looking sentries in full military uniform holding rifles guarded the premises.

Joyce's worst nightmare had come to fruition. She was a prisoner of the Germans. Abruptly, her relatively peaceful life living with Rose was over. Gone was the fun, happy-go-lucky woman who loved to laugh.

Did anybody even know she was here? Not even Rose knew at this point. Joyce would need to muster the little strength she had left to survive.

JEU DE PAUME

EARLY 1941

A CHARMING YOUNG GERMAN ART HISTORIAN ARRIVED AT THE JEU DE Paume, but something about him made Rose nervous. On the surface, he had all the right credentials. He had a PhD in art history and had been a small-time art dealer before the war. He spoke excellent French after studying the language in Paris in the 1930s. He came from an artistically inclined, well-to-do and well-connected family. His father was a respected art collector. But the blond, thirty-five-year-old man had a sinister side.

At six feet and four inches, the handsome and athletic Bruno Lohse towered over everyone. Rose thought him "deceptively amiable," as she was good at spotting fakes. He had been a member of the Nazi Party since 1937. For his sports prowess, he was awarded the SS Sports Award, medaled in the pentathlon and javelin, and won a national title in handball. When Germany went to war, he was drafted into the army as a truck driver and took part in Hitler's campaign for Poland. He was hospitalized in the summer of 1940 with a stomach ulcer, the beginning of many decades of health complaints, and was transferred into an anti-tank unit. Due to his art history expertise, he was assigned temporarily to Paris to assist the overwhelmed ERR.

He was only scheduled to be in Paris for four weeks, but he was getting used to the lifestyle. The Germans brought Paris back to life to convince Parisians that there could be a semblance of normalcy despite the occupation and to entertain the many officers, soldiers, and civil servants sent there from Germany. There was dining, dancing, and women at establishments like Maxim's and the trendy Shéhérazade cabaret. Lohse was staying in luxury accommodations at the Hôtel Commodore, a short walk to the Opera and Paris's *grands magasins* department stores. Despite the rationing in Paris, Lohse could still get niceties like silk stockings to gift to his increasingly large number of French paramours. He was determined to ingratiate himself with Nazi leadership to stay in Paris.

ERR director Kurt von Behr, occupied with entertaining and amassing his expensive wine collection, made time to greet Lohse on his arrival to the city. Behr regularly stole wine and other luxuries from the Jewish-owned collections that came into the Jeu de Paume for himself and to give as gifts to his friends. He told Lohse that the ERR was tasked with confiscating "ownerless" Jewish collections and that Hitler had declared the whole art operation at the Jeu de Paume a secret. Although the confiscations had been a spectacular success, his boss, Foreign Policy Office leader Alfred Rosenberg, wanted to shut it all down. Behr told Lohse, "You have been brought here to make an inventory so that we can close," meaning Rosenberg intended to shut down the Jeu de Paume and cease the looting operations. Lohse's first assignment was an inventory of the Alphonse Kann collection. Composed of over twelve hundred pieces, it was the second-largest art collection seized so far, after the Rothschild theft.

Baron von Behr, of course, had little interest in shuttering an activity so lucrative to himself and telephoned Berlin, asserting that it would be impossible to close so quickly given the work left. When he got off the phone, he told Lohse that they had "gone mad in Berlin," wanting the ERR to finish much sooner than possible.

During the inventory mayhem, Reichsmarschall Hermann Göring announced that he would return in a few days. All inventory work was paused to curate a new exhibition with artwork the Reichsmarschall had not yet seen. It was a last-minute trip, which would become Göring's standard operating procedure, at great inconvenience to the ERR staff each time.

Inside the Jeu de Paume, Rose noticed that the Germans were more agitated than usual and whispering a lot among themselves. Soon, the arrival of the Gestapo heralded the impending appearance of the Reichsmarschall.

In the intervening months, Rose had fine-tuned her spying strategies. She asked the guards, who had all worked with her for a long time, to tell her of anything suspicious. Rose particularly trusted a brigadier named Paul Moïse, who accompanied her like a bodyguard to investigate whenever there was an unexpected arrival at the Jeu de Paume. Louis Deforges, frequently assigned to help the art historians with the handling of the paintings, reported on the activity in the ERR's three rooms at the Louvre, which Rose was not allowed to enter. Gaston Petit, the head of the Louvre's security staff, kept her apprised of the degenerate paintings still in the Louvre. She also befriended the head packer at the Jeu de Paume—a man named Alexandre who liked to gossip—and the truck drivers employed by the Germans, who informed her where the art was coming from and where it was going.

In addition to stealing and copying German documents, Rose smuggled out photographic negatives of the stolen artwork overnight. She had them developed and carefully returned the negatives in the correct files the next morning.

She was afraid, of course, but fear was now a normal state for her. There was also no news from or about Joyce, and Rose would have been very anxious about her partner's whereabouts. The old Rose, with her head full of the study of art, had died on that bridge over the Loire in June 1940. There was no time to panic or get overwhelmed while under the close watch of the enemy. "When you're the weakest, you have to be the cleverest," she believed. Chain-smoking cigarettes helped. It was a new vice, but when she smoked, nothing else seemed to matter except her work. It was all a dangerous game—any small misstep or misreading of an informant could blow Rose's cover. Other Resistance operatives were learning that the hard way. Across town, members of Jean Cassou and Agnès Humbert's Resistance network were arrested.

On the evening of February 4, Göring met with von Behr and Bunjes. The latter worked for the German Army but had recently switched his alliance to the ERR and von Behr. German Kunstschutz head Wolff-Metternich and Jacques Jaujard had lodged protests regarding the legality of the ERR's activities in France. Despite Göring's claims to the contrary, the ERR appeared to be systematically looting Jewish-owned art without any compensation.

Bunjes was concerned as well and felt obligated to tell Göring about the potential issues. Göring refused to entertain any challenge to his authority but promised to speak to Hitler about the French complaints. "My dear Bunjes, leave that worry to me. I am the highest legal authority in the country," he replied.

When Bunjes mentioned the Hague Convention and how the Germans would be judged in the court of international justice, Göring answered, "Thank God it is we who will decide." Pillaging and violence against civilians was against the code of the Hague Convention but the Germans had taken over the Netherlands, where The Hague was located.

Göring then gave von Behr an album of photographs of the works of art both he and Hitler wanted, as well as the ones he desired. Göring also wanted to commission a copy of the Winged Victory of Samothrace. How wondrous it would look at Carinhall!

At 3 p.m. on February 5, Göring arrived at the Jeu de Paume with art dealer Walter Andreas Hofer, newly appointed as director of his art collection, to tour the new treasures. Göring was irritated to find Wolff-Metternich and Baron Bernhard von Tieschowitz, deputy chief of the Kunstschutz, at the entrance. That would mean unwelcome oversight since Wolff-Metternich and the rest of the Kunstschutz did not look favorably on the ERR's art confiscations. Göring thanked Wolff-Metternich for coming but said that his presence was unnecessary for the visit. He wanted to settle the matter with Harald Turner, the

German chief of military administration staff in France, and did not want new authorities around to mix things up.

The Reichsmarschall was then let into the Jeu de Paume. Conveniently, Lohse had ingratiated himself with von Behr so effectively that he was given the honor of touring Göring through the exhibition. Lohse was only too aware of the opportunity and came exceptionally prepared. He was an expert on seventeenth-century Dutch paintings and organized the tour to showcase his knowledge. He brazenly debated Hofer about a few paintings of disputed provenance, impressing Göring with his art expertise and confidence.

After the tour, Bunjes reminded the Reichsmarschall about the note of protest from the French government against the activity of the ERR, based on the Hague Convention. Bunjes also added that Otto von Stülpnagel, the new military commander of France, had a "visibly opposite" position about the treatment of Jewish-owned art treasures than that of Göring. "My orders are the rules. You will act immediately according to my orders," Göring responded.

Göring ordered the art at the Jeu de Paume be shipped to Germany without delay. Everything Hitler and Göring wanted, along with the Rothschild collection, was loaded onto two railcars attached to the Reichsmarschall's private train. The French appraiser Jacques Beltrand, whom Rose believed was "terrified," provided a laughingly low valuation of 5,000 francs for a Cranach painting of Venus. Göring promised that payment for the art would be forthcoming, but once again the funds would never appear.

Fifteen crates were earmarked for Hitler. They contained fifty-three paintings, including the highly coveted *Astronomer* by Vermeer and Boucher's *Madame de Pompadour*, as well as works by Rembrandt, Francisco Goya, and Franz Hals, coming entirely from the Rothschild, Seligmann, and Wildenstein collections. Göring also sent two of his staffers to Bordeaux to seize the collection of Édouard Jonas, a former member of the French Parliament and art dealer, now stripped of his citizenship for fleeing the country and for being Jewish.

The next day, Göring summoned Lohse to his office at Quai d'Orsay and gave him a special mission to survey the Paris art market for objects to purchase. The two formed a quick bond: Göring was awed by Lohse's knowledge of art history and his youthful self-assurance, while Lohse may have found the father figure he had long been looking for. Lohse and his father, an anti-Nazi, were not particularly close. Göring and Lohse found much to talk about.

The next month, Lohse received a document that authorized his work on behalf of Göring and requested all military, state, and Nazi Party organizations to facilitate his efforts. Lohse treasured it. He folded it and always kept it in the breast pocket of his suit. Göring also provided Lohse with a private car and an expense account at the Banque de France, and permitted him to wear civilian clothes. Lohse would soon be officially transferred to the Luftwaffe, tying him even more closely to Göring, who gave him a personal phone line through which he could be reached, day or night. Lohse was about to have a very good war.

Rose continued to be wary of Lohse. Thefts were happening at the Jeu de Paume, and she observed that they only occurred when Lohse was there and the straitlaced art historian Günther Schiedlausky was not around. One happened in the middle of March 1941 when Lohse's brother, Siegfried, was visiting. A safe with money and jewelry was forced open with a hammer while the guards and packers stayed overnight to prepare a shipment. The night watchman, Basson, saw an SS driver try on a ring. The next day, one of the German secretaries tried on a ring. Two days later, both rings were missing.

The ERR itself was at a crossroads. On the one hand, it had professionalized the looting operation. Its art historians, focused on the inventory, believed they were doing a good job from a preservation standpoint. Bunjes, however, was alarmed at the transportation of the art to Germany and believed that moving the art over international borders contradicted the terms of the armistice. Bunjes was fine with the taking of Jewish-owned art but believed it should be kept safe at the Louvre until the signing of a peace agreement, whenever Britain lost the war and a permanent treaty was agreed on. Bunjes took his complaints to the German military authorities in France, who listened but were constrained from taking action.

In the meantime, another thirty train cars containing four hundred crates of art, mostly from the Rothschild collection, departed for Germany. Rose overheard phone conversations about the last-minute preparations and notified Jaujard immediately, but there was not enough time to intervene.

On the other hand, von Behr and Lohse saw what riches could be gained by keeping Göring happy. They were among the lucky few who could live out the war in Paris in luxury, far from the military front. But they had a major problem: Göring was an insatiable predator. Now that the most notable Jewish-owned collections had been seized, von Behr and Lohse would need to devise much more sinister methods to locate and loot art. Inside the Jeu de Paume, Rose was ready.

BESANÇON, FRANCE

END OF JANUARY 1941

JOYCE WAS ABOUT TO ENTER HER THIRD MONTH AS A PRISONER IN Besançon. The conditions were appalling.

The women were crammed in the dozens into tiny rooms and cellars. When they first arrived, they found all the rooms and straw mattresses soaked in water, the aftermath of an attempt to wash away the grime and disease from the most recent occupants. Large holes in the ceilings let in the freezing cold air. Dirt was everywhere; lice, fleas, and other bugs crawled over everything, as did rabbit-sized rats. Everything smelled like urine. Each floor had a hole intended as a toilet, but it was almost always clogged. With characteristic British wit, the women dubbed these privies "Stand and Deliver." Sometimes, they had to relieve themselves in open latrines in the courtyard. It was not uncommon for a detainee to slip on the ice and accidentally fall into the trench of excrement. They bathed in horse troughs.

Most women lacked basic necessities like toothbrushes since they had no opportunity to pack at the time of their arrest. Soap was difficult to come by. In answer to their requests for supplies, the guards pointed to a pile of rubbish in the middle of the courtyard left behind by the previous prisoners, and the women scrambled to find what they needed in there. Heat came from wooden stoves, which often filled the rooms with black, choking smoke and barely sufficed to warm the air. The winter of 1940 was one of the coldest on record, and temperatures at Besançon reached as low as four degrees Fahrenheit. Even with stoves on, icicles built up on the inside of the windows. When firewood ran out, the women stole planks to burn.

Food was scarce—rotten vegetables, some moldy bread, or beans—and required waiting an hour in long lines in the snow. Most of the nourishment came from potatoes. The food was often sprayed with sulfur, which was used as a pesticide. At times, dinner was just one spoonful of jam and bread. If they asked for more, the German soldiers would spit into their food. Joyce's favorite sweets, licorice "allsorts," were certainly not on the menu.

Unsurprisingly, the internees were continuously sick with colds, flu, bronchitis, dysentery, and food poisoning or injured from falls on the ice. Hundreds of women died within the first months. Children froze to death in their sleep. There was at least one suicide. Many of the women, whether through shock or malnutrition, no longer menstruated. Joyce was also in fragile health, with recurring dental abscesses and an infection of the upper maxillary bone, which required "long and delicate treatment," according to one of the prison doctors.

Clashes between the internees and the German captors were not uncommon. Sometimes the women would protest about the interminable potato peeling. One time, they demanded Mendelssohn's compositions instead of what they described as the "turgid" German music that came over the loudspeakers. This confrontation did not end well, with the *Kommandant* saying, "You know perfectly well that he cannot be played. He was a Jew," and then screaming, "This is not a holiday camp!"

Nonetheless, some entertainment was still possible. There was an improvised bar in the camp dubbed La Cantine where the British women would mingle with the remaining French male prisoners, who procured alcohol from black market sources in town. At a raucous party in the middle of January, an inebriated female prisoner kissed the *Kommandant*, who promptly banned any future gatherings. The Germans even leaked photographs of a drunk detainee to a German newspaper, which included it with the headline "British Woman's Debauchery." Meanwhile, British prostitutes and their madams, who had been arrested all over occupied France, set up business bartering sex for cigarettes, money, and favors with German soldiers. Two nights in the German quarter of camp yielded a pack of cigarettes, for example.

On the flip side, detained British nuns created a school for the children and gave religious lessons to the adults. Many a lapsed churchgoer eagerly signed up to get the cakes and biscuits provided with the catechism class. Former teachers and professors gave classes to the prisoners as well.

BACK IN PARIS, ROSE MUST have been frantic with worry, but she could not let it overwhelm her. What is remarkable is that Rose, who documented every act of the art thefts in meticulous detail, appears not to have recorded a word about her fears and feelings while Joyce was imprisoned. Many others, including Paul Rosenberg, Picasso, and Resistance member Agnès Humbert, recorded their emotions and feelings of turmoil in diaries and letters after their loved ones disappeared. But this relationship, which had the strength to endure the war, in which Rose and Joyce were bold enough to live together during a time of prejudice, was so precious to Rose that she would not outwardly complain, at least in written form. She did not know if Joyce was alive or dead, escaped to England, or seized by the Nazis. Perhaps Rose reasoned that if she wrote about Joyce, the records might be discovered, putting them both at even greater risk. The long months not knowing what happened to Joyce would have been agonizing.

There was also too much happening in the Jeu de Paume, between Göring's visits and von Behr's looting, for Rose to lose her focus. Plus, she and other Parisians were preoccupied trying to survive a frigid winter and massive food shortage. The exodus in June and the military draft had caused a severe disruption to food production and supply chain. Rationing was instituted in October, and a large black market flourished. It was difficult to obtain meat, fish, and fruits without paying exorbitant prices. Coal was rationed. Meat and other foods were requisitioned and shipped to Germany. There was not enough food left in the country to provide for all of the German occupying forces and the French population. There were restrictions in place for basics like bread, milk, oil, and sugar, as well as the food so close to French identity: cheese. Same with chocolate. It must have been especially difficult for Rose, who was a bit of a gourmand. Prewar, her letters were filled with references to the hearty delicacies she shared with her cousins, Marguerite and Adrien, like pigs' feet, duck, chicken, and fish. She was known to enjoy a "palatial" work lunch.

Month after month, the grocery stores were empty in Paris. Even with ration tickets, there was nothing to buy. The writer Jean Guéhenno noted, "At home, we've lived exclusively on parcels sent by friends and cousins in Brittany for the past two weeks." Disease, particularly tuberculosis, was spreading. The death rate, amid a particularly harsh winter, was skyrocketing, especially among infants.

The US embassy, meanwhile, did not seem concerned that one of its clerks had disappeared. As part of a report to the secretary of state, the consul wrote pithily that "Heer and Nona Palmer, British employees, are no longer with the Embassy," and that it had employed two new clerks competent in German. The embassy assumed Joyce had simply returned to England like many other expatriates or was somehow marooned elsewhere in France and not returning to work. The embassy also stopped paying her.

It was not until late January that the embassy discovered that Joyce had been arrested and interned at Besançon. Internees were allowed to send and receive mail for the first time that month, delivered by the Red Cross. They were limited to fewer than twenty-five words and two letters per month, but it would have been just enough for Joyce to send her whereabouts. Maynard B. Barnes, the first secretary of the US embassy, discussed Joyce's situation directly with the German diplomat Dr. von Roeder at the Hôtel Majestic in Paris and followed up with a formal request for her release. Barnes cited Joyce's poor health, her essential work for the embassy as a German translator, that she had grown up in Germany, and that her father had been a German prisoner of war in England during World War I.

Thanks to the efforts of the US embassy, Joyce was released on February 13, 1941, and returned to Paris. Rose and Joyce would never speak publicly of this period in Joyce's life and rarely mentioned it to family. The horrors of what she experienced remained a secret between the couple. They dealt with all the pain and trauma of her arrest and internment between themselves, as they always did.

LIBOURNE, FRANCE

EARLY MARCH 1941

AT ABOUT 9 A.M. ON MARCH 10, SEVERAL MEMBERS OF THE DEVISEN-schutzkommando, the Foreign Exchange Protection Command, entered the National Bank of Commerce and Industry in Libourne, twenty miles east of Bordeaux. They had orders from the ERR to confiscate the contents of a basement vault belonging to Paul Rosenberg. This was where he had put 162 paintings, moved from the warehouse in Tours in May 1940 as an extra safekeeping measure. He likely believed that the masterpieces would stay undetected in this small, quiet town, but the Germans were leaving no stone unturned.

Paul was sent an "invitation" to be present at the bank search, but unsurprisingly, as he had fled to America, he did not get the letter. And as he did not send a response, a date was set for the opening of the safe without him. Present that morning at the bank was also the director of the bank branch, a bailiff from the town of Libourne, and a specialist locksmith from the company that built the bank vaults.

This was a momentous development for the ERR's art looting endeavor. The Rosenberg collection was one of the last large, unaccounted-for Jewish-owned collections, and it contained many high-value paintings by Paul's artists like Picasso, Matisse, Braque, and Léger. Even if Hitler despised the style of the "degenerate" paintings, they could be sold easily on the open market at exorbitant prices, with the proceeds then used to fund the German war effort.

Paul's gallery in Paris was one of the first raided by the Germans in July 1940, but it had contained disappointingly few valuable works. Paul had been more cautious about protecting his art than many other collectors and took care to divide his collection up between several locations in France and overseas, place them in banks, and, in one instance, conceal his ownership under his chauffeur Louis Le Gall's name. It took the Germans almost a year to find the last known assemblage of Paul's paintings that remained in France.

This particular type of vault required both a key and a three-digit combination code that only Paul would know. Without it, the locksmith would have to try all one thousand possible combinations. One of the German commandos stepped in to say that, given the short amount of time, he could not wait until the combination was found. The bank should take all measures to open the vault or prepare it for a break-in, he asserted.

About two hours later, the bank director had two sealed envelopes in his possession. The first had a key to Paul's safe sent from the Bordeaux branch of the bank, and the second contained a probable three-digit code, 9-2-1, written on a transparent piece of paper. The key was entered successfully into the lock, and the code was entered, but the vault would not open. The locksmith would now need to try all the combinations, which he attempted for more than four hours.

It would take more than two weeks of intermittent efforts by the locksmith, who was likely deliberately sabotaging the efforts. He went at it for two full days and said he would come back later with a colleague to assist. He did not return for another two weeks, at which point he announced that all the possible combinations had failed for some reason he could not understand.

The only thing that remained now was to get the safe ready for a break-in, as requested by the Germans. For the ERR, only one outcome was acceptable: possession of the valuables inside the bank vault—even if it had to be done by force. The locksmith drilled a hole and disabled the combination lock, allowing the vault to be opened with only the key. The vault was then closed back up with strips of calico and wax seals to await the Germans.

On April 18, a little over two weeks later, the commandos returned and unsealed the vault. They found it full to the brim with artistic riches. There were thirty-three paintings by Picasso, fifteen by Braque, twenty-one by Matisse, thirteen by Laurencin, five by Degas, ten by Renoir, eight by Corot, seven by Pierre Bonnard, five by Monet, and fifty others by Van Gogh, Cézanne, Delacroix, Jean-Auguste-Dominique Ingres, Géricault, Pissarro, and others. The most valuable were two Renoir oil paintings, both titled *Mademoiselle Grimprel*, depicting two blond sisters, each wearing a different color ribbon in her hair.

The Germans also discovered that Georges Braque had a vault next to Paul Rosenberg's. Even though Braque was considered an Aryan and his property was legally safe from seizure, the commandos decided to break into that one, too. In addition to Braque's own canvases, he had some gold, as well as a small collection of art that included a Cranach painting, *Portrait of a Girl*, that would undoubtedly interest Hitler and Göring. In fact, Göring's art dealer, Walter Andreas Hofer, would use it as leverage. Hofer told Braque that he would get his belongings released quickly if he sold him the Cranach. As Braque was neither Jewish nor an enemy of the state, he knew that his belongings were not subject to seizure. He decided to bide his time and pretend he was interested in the offer. The Nazis ultimately released Braque's possessions, but the bank would later send him a bill to cover the cost of the damage inflicted on the vault. "We would be obliged if you would repay the expenses thus accrued—" the letter stated, "namely, 1,000 francs for expert advice and 200 francs for our trouble."

The ERR carted off Paul Rosenberg's paintings after a formal valuation of each work of art by a local expert. The Germans were not finished with Paul just yet, even after the wholesale robbery of his paintings in Paris, Floirac, and Libourne. The Nazis implemented their plan to confiscate Paul's crown jewel: his six-story home and gallery at 21 rue la Boétie in Paris.

Before the Germans took over the building, Gabriel Picard, the Rosenberg's concierge, had stolen as much as he could out of the house for his own personal gain. It was a major betrayal from a man Paul had known for over two decades and thought he could trust, even having him cosign Alexandre's birth certificate. In fact, Picard had been squirreling out objects since the Paris mass exodus in June 1940.

Picard and his wife stole 140 bottles of fine wine, 150 bottles of champagne, a portrait drawing of Madame Rosenberg, bronzes including Rodin's *Thinker* that Picard took to an appraiser, a marble bust, an inlaid side table, a Regency-era barometer, and a large wood and bronze clock. He had draperies made from Paul's tapestries.

Several of Paul's loyal employees and friends tried to enter the house to rescue what they could, but the Picards resisted. Paul's Paris secretary, Léa Roisneau, hoped to save the library and the photographs of the paintings but was not allowed in. Picard told her, "If the Jew Rosenberg comes back, I will throw him out the door."

The Gestapo requisitioned 21 rue la Boétie on April 25, 1941. Two days later, they removed the contents of Paul's library. A week later, the Germans took away the remainder of the furnishings, including all the linens, curtains, and carpeting, and seized the Rosenbergs' Ford and Peugeot cars, along with 250 of the remaining bottles of wine and champagne. They sold off an archive of forty-five hundred photographs of paintings that had once passed through Paul's gallery. The house was stripped bare.

Paul had a bad feeling about his property in France. "I am rather afraid that something has gone wrong but what can I do about it?" he wrote resignedly. Then, a letter arrived from Roisneau that brought the grim news to New York: "There's nothing left, nothing, nothing, nothing."

PARIS

SPRING TO SUMMER 1941

AT THE JEU DE PAUME, ROSE OBSERVED INCREDULOUSLY THAT THE DEliveries of Jewish-owned possessions had not slowed down at all. In Rose's words, it was a "confiscation factory." The ERR had extended its net and was now widely using the Devisenschutzkommando, the Foreign Exchange Protection Command, to search bank vaults and safety deposit boxes. In one order, Göring authorized the seizure of eleven private collections, mostly held in banks, both foreign and domestic.

The ERR also decided it was finally time to start seizing privately owned art stored in the depots of the Musées Nationaux. It started with the collection of David David-Weill, president of the Council of French National Museums, whose art had long been on the radar of the Germans.

By summer, the Germans had seized more than ten thousand objects from Jewish-owned collections in France. In a tangled web, informants, collaborationist French policemen, criminals, gangsters, the Gestapo, and commando units all participated in the thefts. What had shifted over the previous year was the scope. The Germans now wanted to confiscate every Jewish-owned collection in the country. The ERR was well-positioned to satisfy both the free market and the aesthetic desires of the most important people in the Nazi Party, including Hitler.

Reichsmarschall Hermann Göring dedicated an exorbitant amount of time toward art acquisition. Göring visited the Jeu de Paume seven times between February and August. He created a network of art agents throughout the occupied countries and often upended whatever he was doing just to see one piece of art, redirecting his special train and relocating his entire entourage. In Paris, von Behr would typically receive only forty-eight-hours' notice before a Göring visit.

The Jeu de Paume had turned into a grotesque distortion of what a museum should be: a place to preserve, interpret, and display works of art for cultural education and appreciation. Instead, it was a personal art gallery for Göring.

There was now an overabundance of new stolen art. The ground floor could no longer be used for exhibitions and was now dedicated to storage. Sometimes, the museum itself was so full that new confiscated art was sent first to the ERR rooms in the Louvre, which delayed their inventory by the German art historians. This gave Kurt von Behr, Bruno Lohse, and others an opportunity to steal objects before they were ever noted in the official record.

The room at the end of the second floor, farthest from the main entrance, was known as the Salle des Martyrs. "Degenerate" paintings by Picasso, Matisse, Braque, Chagall, de Chirico, and other modern artists hung from floor to ceiling on nearly every inch of the walls and on two long display racks in the center of the room. Léger's *Woman in Red and Green*, which belonged to Paul's brother Léonce Rosenberg, was there. There were several Dalí paintings and a Degas drawing of a ballerina from Paul's collection. The room was a veritable "chamber of horrors" to the Germans, and they treated the paintings as if "they were made of an explosive or dangerous material to handle," Rose detailed.

Rose hoped the Germans' aversion to degenerate art would mean they would leave all these paintings behind in France. Just in case, she encouraged Jaujard to find a way to keep them. Jaujard planned on testing a little-known French statute called the right of preemption. This law, which had been in effect since 1921, allowed cultural institutions to halt sales or purchase items of cultural significance before they were sold to the public.

Bruno Lohse and Robert Scholz, director of Alfred Rosenberg's Office for Pictorial Arts, were the most fanatic and spoke frequently in near hysterical terms about the degenerate nature of modern French painting. From a practical perspective, they believed their role was to prevent the shipment of degenerate art to Germany, as both Göring and Hitler despised modern art. They also felt that no matter the outcome of the war, the artworks should never go back to their original owners and preferably should be burned. Scholz was undoubtedly a disciple of Hitler's virulent modern art diatribe, but Lohse was motivated more by greed. What if there was something more financially beneficial to the ERR and to his mentor, Göring, than the total destruction of the modern paintings? Lohse wondered.

Before Göring's next visit, Lohse paid a visit to Gustav Rochlitz, an art dealer who was now actively selling to Germans in Paris. His gallery at 222 rue de Rivoli was just a five-minute walk from the Jeu de Paume. Lohse asked Rochlitz if he had any exceptional paintings to sell to Göring. Even though Göring could take what he pleased from the Jeu de Paume, he could never be satiated. From a back room, Rochlitz took out a still life by Jan Weenix and *Portrait of a Man*, attributed to Titian, and Lohse took them promptly to the Jeu de Paume to be included in the forthcoming exhibition for Göring to see.

Göring turned down Rochlitz's paintings because they were too expensive. Lohse then asked Rochlitz if they could be acquired through an exchange instead. To "pay" for the Old Masters that Göring preferred, Rochlitz went to the Jeu de Paume and picked out eleven "degenerate" paintings he wanted. Five came from Paul Rosenberg's collection seized in Le Castel: three Matisse works (*Women at a Table, Sleeping Woman*, and a still life), Picasso's *Mother and Child*, and Corot's *Madame Stumpf and Her Daughter.* A still life by Braque, Degas's *Madame Camus at the Piano*, and Cézanne's *Douleur* were also traded from the Kann collection, along with an Alfred Sisley landscape from Georges Bernheim and Renoir's *Reclining Woman in Summer Dress.*

Lohse was now at the center of a new lucrative business venture.

Eight more exchanges using twenty "degenerate" paintings to "pay" for work by Old Master painters took place before the summer. The steady disappearance of paintings from the Salle des Martyrs would have distressed Rose. In July, eighteen paintings were exchanged for a single artwork. In the final exchange of 1941, Rochlitz traded four Matisse paintings from Paul Rosenberg's collection for a Jan Bruegel painting that went to Göring. As the senior member of the ERR, von Behr signed the exchange contracts but also completed at least one deal for his own benefit.

After receiving the modern paintings, Rochlitz would turn around and resell them to friendly French dealers or export them to Switzerland, which had to be done via secret diplomatic pouch or through Germany. From there, the paintings were sold to buyers all over the world. There were very few French dealers who did not participate in some way, and an enormous number of eager middlemen appeared, including Henri Verne, the former head of the Musées Nationaux and Rose's nemesis, who sold two questionable Rembrandts directly to the ERR.

It was a win, win, win. Art dealers like Rochlitz made a significant profit as did those in Switzerland, including Theodor Fischer of the infamous degenerate art auction in Lucerne in June 1939. Thanks to the art sales, the Nazi war chest ballooned with desperately needed foreign currency. The parsimonious Göring, who always bargained, could satisfy his insatiable appetite for art without paying for anything. Lohse had proven his usefulness to Göring and kept his special privileges, which had expanded to include a virtually unlimited line of credit at the Banque de France. With this, Lohse also made expensive, high-profile purchases at auctions in Paris on behalf of his benefactor. Finally, the ERR was effectively laundering away its problematic art and adding a stock of art in the style that would please Göring.

It was a wondrous loophole, and over the next few years, more and more exchanges were to come until the Germans would take a much more drastic measure. The fate of the Salle des Martyrs would come to define Rose's life in more ways than one.

THE GALERIE ROSENBERG, PARIS

APRIL 1941

IN A PERVERSE TRANSFORMATION, THE GERMANS TURNED PAUL ROSENberg's home at 21 rue la Boétie into the Institute for the Study of Jewish Questions, a dark propaganda outfit dedicated to anti-Semitic "research" and exhibitions. Behind the scenes, the organization assisted in the deportation of Jews in France.

Radio Paris, a collaborationist station, announced, "Today saw the rechristening of the building previously occupied by Rosenberg. The name alone tells you all you need to know." Under an arched alcove in the former gallery lobby, the following quote was installed, reading:

> THE JEWS ARE LIKE AN ASIAN COLONY ESTABLISHED IN FRANCE. THEY ARE WITH US AS IN A FOREIGN LAND. TRIPLY FOREIGN BECAUSE THEY ARE NEITHER FRENCH, NOR CHRISTIANS, NOR EUROPEANS.

The windows of the building, which once beckoned discerning collectors, now attracted anti-Semites eager to absorb the institute's racial theories. The gallery, with its dramatic art deco skylight, was now an events hall where a large poster of a Jewish "Bird of Prey" was shown violently tearing apart a woman representing France. A caption read, "Frenchmen, help me!" Photographs of Jews to be denounced filled Paul Rosenberg's former galleries. Another quote on the walls read, "We fight against the Jews to give France back its true face: a native face," along with an enormous portrait of French prime minister Maréchal Pétain. The on-site bookstore stocked tomes about the threat of the Jewish race. The writer Céline was offended to discover that his two recent anti-Semitic pamphlets were not in the shop.

From New York, Paul Rosenberg still did not understand the extent to which the Nazis had eviscerated him. Tragically ill-informed, he wrote to Winnifred, his secretary in London, "Up to now they have not touched what was in Bordeaux, Libourne and Tours." But in fact, they had already taken everything he owned, personally and professionally (apart from what was in Tours under Louis Le Gall's name). Referring only to the confiscation of 21 rue la Boétie, Paul told Winnifred, "Perhaps it is better that I should ignore what mischief those Nazi swines have done to me."

Some strange things happened that made the war seem close to home, even in America. A letter sent to Alexandre in England by his mother in the United States was reviewed by the German censor, even though it was sent directly between those two unoccupied countries. Paul was also convinced he had been approached by a German spy masquerading as a chambermaid in a hotel in Chicago when he was there for work.

Although business was slow, Paul, his wife, Margot, and his sister Micheline were buoyed emotionally by joining France Forever, a nonprofit organization dedicated to supporting France and its allies against the Nazis. Paul also helped old friends—including Georges Huisman, the ousted Jewish director general of the Beaux-Arts—try to escape France. Paul wrote Huisman that he had encountered "a lot of selfishness and above all, difficulties coming primarily from the State Department." He added touchingly, "My dear friend, do not believe for a single moment that I am forgetting you. Far from it."

Alexandre was still thriving in military training in England. His officers spoke highly of his character and his work ethic, and his future looked promising. But Paul was meddling in his life again. He sent an envoy to persuade Alexandre to work for the Free French forces in the United States instead, far from the front line. Alexandre was polite and thoughtful but did not seem convinced. How could he ever live down abandoning his comrades? The whole affair made Alexandre sad and even more silent than usual. To placate everyone, Alexandre said he wanted to wait for his officer's commission and then decide.

Shortly after his plea, Paul's health took a turn, and he was sent to bed rest with stomach ulcers. Paul sent a flurry of telegrams and letters to Winnifred in England. "Tell [Alexandre] that his sufferings are added to mine and do not help me to get better." But Paul knew his son only too well and wrote to Winnifred, "He does not want to tell us that he has refused and wants us to keep on hoping that he will soon be with us again. . . . You can well imagine how much calmer I would be if I knew he was coming over here." In the end, Alexandre's gut instinct would be correct. He would have a remarkable role to play in the coming battles, just not in America.

PARIS

MAY 1941

IT WAS A BANNER YEAR FOR THE ERR. AS MORE ART CAME IN, MORE staff was hired. The ERR's head photographer, trying to ingratiate himself for promotion, took official staff portraits. Everyone wore their

Sunday best, with the stolen art in the Jeu de Paume used as props. Rose purloined the negatives of the portraits, had them developed, and kept the photos neatly stacked in her apartment like a deck of most-wanted cards. She also photographed the identity papers of the S.S. officers in the museum.

She perfectly fulfilled her role as a spy, managing to stay under the radar of the Germans. She always responded to questions—whether about building maintenance or more pointed interrogations about missing artwork—in such an utterly serious, humorless demeanor that the Germans could only assume she was telling the truth. She frequently interspersed the words "*N'est-ce pas?*" ("Is it not?") as a rhetorical question to emphasize the veracity of her statements.

As for the other Resistance spies among the Musées Nationaux staff, their anti-Nazi efforts were not going so well. Agnès Humbert, who had been secretly printing the pamphlet *Résistance* with museum curators Jean Cassou and Christiane Noblecourt, was arrested. Other members in their organization were missing. They had joined forces with another Resistance group at the Musée de l'Homme, which had a mimeograph machine. They clandestinely left leaflets on the metro, under fabric in department stores, in post offices, in shopping baskets at the markets, and inside mailboxes. Humbert also got her hands on some stickers and used her museum's typewriter to type out "*Vive le général de Gaulle*" ("Long live General de Gaulle") and "*Nous sommes pour le général de Gaulle*" ("We are for General de Gaulle"). These tiny bits of resistance ended up stuck on telephone boxes, inside subway tunnels, and even on public urinals and on the back of German trucks. The group also smuggled military papers, survey maps of German installations, and other documents into the Unoccupied Zone.

In mid-April, two men approached Humbert inside a medical clinic just a few blocks south of Rose's apartment. They asked to search her house. There, they found an unfinished copy of *Résistance* she had left by accident in a small stack of papers. Written damningly atop the front page was "Copy and circulate." She admitted to copying it but told them she had given up the project after making only five copies because she was a terrible typist. Humbert figured it would only cost her a few months in jail. Fortunately, they did not find the files for *Résistance*, including its distribution list and copies of every pamphlet ever printed, hidden under her stair carpet.

She was turned over to the Gestapo. A multi-hour interrogation commenced, but Humbert did not give up any of her compatriots. She even surreptitiously chewed up and swallowed incriminating evidence that was in her bag. She was imprisoned but was spared the death sentence because of her gender. Many of the men in her network, including several from the Musées Nationaux staff, were executed by firing squad shortly thereafter. Pierre Schommer, overseeing the Chambord depot, heard about the killing of his colleagues on the radio.

Luckily, Jean Cassou had not yet been caught and was now on the run. He turned to Louvre director Jacques Jaujard for help. Jaujard took Cassou in and showed him a hidden key to his apartment in the Louvre, telling him he could come back anytime. In this new, ambiguous world where close friends were betraying each other, Jaujard remained one of the few people whom Cassou could fully trust.

By now, the Louvre itself was a den of Resistance activity. The Louvre staff clandestinely produced multiple Resistance publications, and Jaujard knew everything going on inside the labyrinthine compound. The Louvre also adapted to wartime necessities. An air-raid shelter was built underground next to Jaujard's office. Its construction revealed lost layers of fortification from the twelfth and thirteenth centuries. Watertight doors and an independent air circulation system were installed to protect against gas attacks. Stenciled arrows and the word "*abri*" ("shelter") were written on the stone foundations for wayfinding inside the tunnels. Aboveground, twenty-four hundred tomato plants in neat rows surrounded a sculpture of a rococo painter. A pumpkin patch was around the corner. These gardens were just two of the many planted at the Louvre by the National Relief Service in an attempt to offset food shortages.

Amid this backdrop, Göring visited the Jeu de Paume a total of thirteen times in 1941 and took away hundreds of works of art along with precious jewels. The Reichsmarschall had a weakness for opulent jewelry—emeralds in particular—and Rose would see him play with them in his pocket like loose change. On one of his March visits, he was presented with three hundred pieces of the most beautiful jewels in the world, including rare sixteenth-century treasures. The jewels were guarded day and night by a special guard. Göring took no less than five Rothschild jewels, including an emerald ring, two gold and emerald medallions, and two sixteenth-century baroque pearl pendants set among precious stones, enamels, carvings, and gold. Rose believed that Göring "enjoyed seeing himself dragging his victory trophies behind him."

Although the looting activity was supposed to be a secret, the doors were open to a rotating cast of art dealers. Kurt von Behr provided them with a one-time visitor's card to the Jeu de Paume. Lohse would bring dealers through to make their selection of art for the exchanges. A notable regular was Maria Almas-Dietrich, who had sold to Hitler since before the war. She and her daughter, a close friend of Hitler's paramour, Eva Braun, were regular visitors to the Berghof, Hitler's alpine residence in Bavaria. Almas-Dietrich had a dubious understanding of art history and often inadvertently peddled fakes, but she sold more paintings to Hitler than any other dealer by far. Göring would also meet dealers directly at his office at the Quai d'Orsay and, on rare occasions, took pleasure in going to the galleries in Paris.

Rose found Lohse "unscrupulous." He was taking on power so rapidly that it caused discord within an already acrimonious staff, who were jealous of his special status but fearful of his Nazi Party ties. Although he never wore his SS uniform to work, he sometimes donned a sweater with the SS insignia while socializing and had a trusted SS man at his disposal for spying and confiscations. He was also known to have denounced some colleagues to the Gestapo and had a volcanic temper when crossed.

The longer Lohse stayed at the Jeu de Paume, the bolder he became. He and von Behr now had their eye on the last remaining large Jewish-owned art collection in France—the Schloss collection—which contained over three hundred Old Master paintings. Until the occupation, the heirs of financier Adolphe Schloss kept this splendid collection hung from wall to wall in a Paris townhouse. They then secretly moved it to a château in the Unoccupied Zone. Vichy leaders like prime minister Pierre Laval were also searching for it. So were the Germans. In fact, Hans Posse had tried to buy it a year earlier. The heirs offered to sell it for 40 million francs, but the deal fell through.

To procure the Schloss collection, Lohse would have to associate himself with some distinctly shady characters, both German and French. Very soon, he would be at the center of a dangerous game for this last, highly coveted Jewish-owned art collection.

TO AFRICA

MAY 1941

ALEXANDRE ROSENBERG RECEIVED HIS OFFICER'S COMMISSION ON MAY 23 and was ordered immediately to Africa to join de Gaulle's forces. From Brazzaville in French Congo, the new capital of Free France, de Gaulle hoped to retake France and Europe from the Nazis. Alexandre's destination was kept a secret from his family and friends. They only knew he was going somewhere with a "very hot climate."

Alexandre wrote to his parents and asked them to take courage, but his words did nothing to alleviate their suffering. Margot, emotionally overwrought, told Paul, "How do you think I can live without any news from my son, and if I do receive news it will be so old anyway that I will not know if he is still living or not." Paul, whose health had improved (he had reassured Alexandre that he did not have cancer), told Winnifred by letter about their distress regarding Alexandre's deployment: "We have all broken down under this sad news and have had no courage left for anything."

On May 27, Alexandre and about a hundred other fellow Free French fighters departed for Africa. Guy Lévy and two other friends were with him. Winnifred told Paul they were cheerful and brotherly boys "with plenty of common sense and good logic." In exactly one month, they would be in Pointe-Noire in French Equatorial Africa.

PARIS

SUMMER TO FALL 1941

IT WAS A HOT SUMMER IN PARIS, WITH TEMPERATURES REGULARLY reaching over ninety degrees Fahrenheit. Rose wrote to her cousins that "apart from the few red flags which float here and there, we hardly notice them," remarking on the Nazi flags still flying in Paris and how Parisians were just getting on with their lives as best as possible.

Joyce went back to work at the US embassy and demanded pay for the time she was incarcerated. The request went up and down the diplomatic hierarchy, with some questioning the validity of her imprisonment. "I don't think we should try to pay salary unless her incarceration was for reasons connected with her employment by this

Government," one wrote. "If we find she was interned in the line of duty, I think we should entertain a salary claim from her." Another contended that it would "appear far-fetched" to consider her on duty while she was interned. Yet another concluded that even though she was likely interned on account of her nationality, she was living in Paris "presumably in the line of duty" and that they might as well entertain a salary claim.

But much more was happening at the embassy besides Joyce's pay claim. The German Foreign Office ordered the removal of all foreign diplomats, their families, and servants from Paris by June 10. Over one hundred US embassy employees evacuated at the last minute by crossing the Spanish border using the same route the Rosenbergs took to the United States. Joyce continued working for another month and a half with the remaining staffers responsible for closing the embassy, two blocks from the Jeu de Paume. Their work included burning diplomatic seals and secret codes and putting records into vaults.

In early June, Laurence W. Taylor, the American consul in charge, gathered Joyce and the other employees—a total of twelve men and three women—and told them they were entrusted with absolute confidentiality on diplomatic matters and that they "must not fail in any way." Taylor told one of the other female civil servants, "It is a great adventure we are facing; I hope you will be happy. We do not know for how long it will be." Most of the floors of the embassy were locked and the corridors darkened. With so few employees left, every footstep in the neoclassical stone building echoed.

The Department of State offered to transport Joyce back to the United Kingdom, but she chose to remain in Paris with Rose. It was a difficult period financially for Rose and Joyce, as Joyce lacked any form of formal income after the US embassy closed at the end of July. As a British citizen and an enemy alien, it was impossible for Joyce to find a job. Joyce's mother was trying to locate her, sending multiple welfare requests through the US embassy in London, but even the American diplomats in France had no record of her whereabouts after the embassy closed. They could only feebly reply that "it is assumed that she has remained at Paris."

In October, Joyce made contact with the US embassy in Berlin, stating that she was in financial distress and receiving medical treatment for an inflammation in her ears that was threatening her with partial deafness. The embassy offered to send her 1,750 francs a month in assistance from British funds. This made Joyce and Rose's challenging life in wartime Paris just a little bit easier.

JEU DE PAUME

FALL 1941

THE ERR HAD A NEW STRATEGY TO SEIZE ART NOW THAT THEY HAD exhausted almost all the Jewish apartments, castles, storage facilities, and bank vaults owned by Jews in the Occupied Zone. The homes were to be stripped down and all valuable wall decorations removed. Rose watched as the bas-reliefs from the Édouard de Rothschild mansion, across the street from the Jeu de Paume, as well as twenty wall panels from the home of the recently deceased financier Louis Louis-Dreyfus, arrived at the museum.

Lohse then curated a new exhibition of statues for Göring, but Rose was alarmed by the weight of the statues on the museum's floors. She consulted with the building architect and informed Lohse that each room should not have more than a two-ton load. He acquiesced to her demands and lowered the statues to the ground floor.

During his December visit to the Jeu de Paume, Göring took almost all the Édouard de Rothschild statues back to Germany on his special train, along with fifty impressionist paintings and drawings mostly from the Rosenberg collection. Art dealer Karl Haberstock had written to Göring about the "collection belonging to the Jew Paul Rosenberg" and reserved many of the paintings in advance. Among the spoils were five works by Monet, six from Renoir, three by Cézanne, five by Degas, four by Corot, three each by Courbet and Georges Seurat, a Van Gogh, a Pissarro, and an Honoré Daumier. They were not to Göring's taste but were selling for top dollar in Berlin and could easily be exchanged.

The Germans kicked out anyone French from the museum during Göring's visit, but Rose managed to discover where the art was going anyway. She noticed that some items were earmarked for specific people. Two of Paul Rosenberg's paintings were headed to a private collector, while a carpet was sent to a liaison officer between Göring and Hitler. A Gobelin tapestry was going to someone called "Captain Eiske."

Hans Posse, in charge of Hitler's Führermuseum, deigned to visit the Jeu de Paume for the first and only time in November. He met with Kurt von Behr at the Hôtel Commodore and then took a tour of the collections in the Jeu de Paume with Lohse. Posse picked out the artwork he wanted for Hitler and had them shipped to Germany. Alfred Rosenberg, meanwhile, was increasingly displeased with Göring's looting. "Don't ever mention the word *Einsatzstab* to me again," he barked repeatedly, referring to the ERR.

NEW YORK CITY

FALL 1941

IN NEW YORK, PAUL ROSENBERG'S BUSINESS WAS STILL SLOW, BUT HE was starting to make inroads in the American market. He traded Van

Gogh's *Starry Night* to the Museum of Modern Art for two paintings by Cézanne and Toulouse-Lautrec. Had Paul not sent *Starry Night* to London in 1938, when he bought it, it would have been looted along with the rest of his collection in France.

Art shipped from Paul's London business increased the stock for the gallery he was about to open in New York, Paul Rosenberg & Co., at 16 East Fifty-Seventh Street. Paul was optimistic about his new company and countered any criticism from competitors by reminding them he had been in business in New York nineteen years earlier with Georges Wildenstein: "I am no newcomer."

Paul was appalled, however, to hear about the boom in the French art market. Paintings were selling for ten times more than before the war. His name could still be found on labels on the back of many works of art, but dealers bought anyway, knowing full well that the paintings were his. "I was a billionaire without knowing it," he managed to joke. Léa Roisneau, his secretary in Paris, kept him apprised of the collaborationist activities of the French art dealers, many whom were exchanging art directly with the ERR, and Paul found all this news deeply disheartening.

Léa also informed Paul that everything else, including what was in Le Castel and Libourne, was gone and that some of his oldest employees in Paris had "not behaved as they should have." Much later when Paul found out that his concierge, Gabriel Picard, had betrayed him, Paul would take it very personally and sue him for theft, abuse of trust, fraud, and embezzlement.

Although Paul was unaware that French citizens who fled France had been stripped of their citizenship or that mass roundups and internments of Jewish people in France had begun, his resentment toward the Nazis was already palpable. Paul wrote to Winnifred about the seizures of his property: "I really do not believe that measures of this kind will help the invaders or will prove in their favor and I am sure that they will not be surprised if I nourish bad sentiments towards them. . . . Their behavior is atrocious and when it becomes known to the public it is certain that they will revolt against such barbaric ways."

In fact, the perpetrators were not just German. The French Commission for Jewish Affairs had led the charge on the roundups in May. More than six thousand summonses went to foreign Jews for a status review of their papers by the French police. About thirty-seven hundred people complied, believing it was just a formality, but were arrested on arrival and then transferred to internment camps in France. The writer Jean Guéhenno observed the arrest of several men and wrote the next day that "Their wives and children begged the police, shouted, wept. . . . The working people of Paris who saw these heartrending scenes were full of indignation and shame."

Paul also heard from his brother, somewhat inaccurately, that 21 rue la Boétie was to be sold. The news hurt most for sentimental reasons. "After all it is the birthplace of Kiki [his nickname for Alexandre]. Well, maybe one day I shall find myself in a position to buy it again, let us hope," he wrote to Winnifred.

Alexandre arrived safe and sound in French Congo at the end of June. From here, Free France trained its soldiers for the campaigns to take North Africa from the Axis powers. The area was a hotbed of anti-Nazi patriotism. Some of France's African colonies had looked on in disbelief as France, their alleged "protector," capitulated to the Nazis. They responded by pledging their allegiance to the French leader-in-exile, Charles de Gaulle, rather than to Maréchal Pétain and the Vichy regime.

Back in August 1940, under de Gaulle's orders, the audacious Colonel Philippe Leclerc, alongside two dozen fearless soldiers, successfully overthrew the Vichy governance at Brazzaville in French Congo and nearby in Cameroon and Chad. French Equatorial Africa, a stronghold for Free France, was geographically protected by friendly British and Belgian colonies along with deadly desert and jungle terrain and was the perfect staging zone for de Gaulle's fight to reclaim France.

All the French soldiers admired Leclerc, who had escaped German imprisonment twice in 1940 and was building an incredibly diverse, merit-based battalion. The troops included escaped Frenchmen like Alexandre, *pieds-noirs* (French settlers born in Algeria) and soldiers from the French armies across Africa. There were fighters of all religions—Catholic, Jewish, Buddhist, and Muslim—in the ranks.

Alexandre was delighted to be in a place with better amenities: it was well-lit, and he could "eat to his heart's content," unlike in England with its rationing and blackouts. The newly minted officer found military life in Africa easy and the routine almost like being on holiday. The soldiers spent some afternoons casually on the beach in Pointe-Noire—the young men dressed identically in khaki cargo shirts and shorts, waders, and wide-brimmed, felted slouch hats. Alexandre and his friends planned to send dispatches twice a month via radio to say hello to friends and family in England.

In New York, Paul still hoped he could get Alexandre over to America, even if for a short month. It was a fool's dream. But Paul mapped out a route through multiple countries. Margot was a nervous wreck and repeatedly threatened to join Alexandre in Brazzaville. "It is better to be in Africa than without news," she would say. In New York City, they were hearing about the German invasion of the Soviet Union, the indiscriminate sinking of American ships in the Atlantic Ocean and Red Sea, and the execution of dozens of French railway employees for dynamiting German trains.

Within France, there were now over a dozen labor camps and internment camps, including one predominantly for Jews in Drancy in the outskirts of Paris. In June 1941, a new law was established requiring everyone Jewish to report their names and addresses to the local authorities. Between October 1940 and September 1941, Vichy promulgated fifty-six laws, decrees, and ordinances related to

Jews in France—often without the prompting of Nazi Germany—effectively excluding Jews from owning property, from many professions, from moving about freely, and even from owning a radio. By the summer of 1941, half the Jews in France had no means of income or subsistence.

A shocking personal tragedy in the Rosenberg family overshadowed the autumn of 1941. Yvon Helft, Paul's brother-in-law and business partner, who had survived the initial exodus through Spain and Portugal, was killed in a car accident while en route to set up a new business in California. Alexandre would have to comfort his cousins François and Jean Helft when they learned their father was dead just days after they arrived in Brazzaville.

Back in Paris, Joyce finally secured a new job as a secretary at the Swiss consulate, thanks to her fluency in German, French, and English, which enabled her and Rose to regain a semblance of normalcy in the third year of the war. Joyce returned to school, studying at Rose's old haunts, including the École du Louvre for art and archaeology, the École Pratique des Hautes Études at the Sorbonne, and the Institut Catholique in Paris.

On December 7, 1941, Japan attacked the United States at Pearl Harbor, which finally brought America into the war. Jean Guéhenno wrote of the momentous occasion, "I am too full of emotion to note anything here. The world is undergoing a revolution, and all France is doing is watching, like a coward: this mistake committed in June '40 appears more enormous every day."

At the Jeu de Paume, Rose could tell that a "major offensive" was being planned for the remaining looted art. To assist with what would undoubtedly be a mass exodus of paintings, 150 unemployed people with no art experience were brought in. "I don't know anything yet about the chosen victims," she reported grimly to Jaujard. However, she learned of a major exhibition underway in Germany at the castle of King Ludwig II in Neuschwanstein under art historian Günther

Schiedlausky's direction. If there was any hope of a reprieve in the ERR's plundering after this cleanse, it was dashed when Rose got wind that around 240 homes belonging to Jewish families were about to be raided. The monster needed to be fed.

JEU DE PAUME

EARLY 1942

THE BEGINNING OF 1942 WAS FRIGID. "WE ARE SO COLD WE CAN hardly think of anything else," the writer Guéhenno noted in a one-line diary entry on January 21. The English had resumed bombing the outskirts of Paris, hitting industrial targets like the Renault car factory and Le Bourget airport, where Hitler had landed for his tour of Paris in June 1940. The sky lit up as the rockets traced through the air, bombs flashed, and fires broke out on the ground. The blasts were so powerful that windowpanes and lamps shook in central Paris. The Allied show of force rallied Parisians to fight back. Along the stretch of the Seine between the Jeu de Paume and the Louvre, someone carved big V's for victory and the cross of Lorraine into the bark of all the plane trees.

At the Jeu de Paume, there was a flurry of intrigue. A new secretary, Ilse Puetz, liked to walk around the museum in only her negligee. She and the married Kurt von Behr were having an affair. Despite her disapproval of Ilse's personal and professional behavior, Rose admitted she found the young woman very beautiful with her enormous green eyes and magnificent voice. As for von Behr, she thought him "cynical and without pity, with a haughtiness and very Prussian cruelty." He was willing to use any means necessary for his ends, including threats of denunciations and deportations to force people to comply with his demands.

Schiedlausky and Robert Scholz were also having dalliances with the secretaries. The ERR's business manager, Hermann von Ingram, was dating art historian Annemarie von Tomforde, a woman Lohse knew from university. Tomforde brazenly stole items from requisitioned Jewish-owned apartments, filling suitcases full of silver, furs, expensive home goods, and artwork. She even created her own abbreviation to mark on the shipping crates: "TOM" for Tomforde. Rose despised her and considered her the epitome of Nazi dishonesty and brutality.

Tomforde denounced and framed her colleagues for thefts. Lohse repeatedly reprimanded her for irresponsible behavior, and in response, she turned von Ingram against him. Tomforde also used von Ingram's power in the ERR to try to push out female staffers she felt threatened by, particularly Helga Eggemann, the former director of art history at the University of Berlin.

Eggemann was well-educated and elegant, and currently dating a wealthy financier and SS man who was living at the Ritz. Rose noted that she clearly had "plenty of money for her toilets and numerous purchases."

Tomforde viewed Eggemann as a rival and tried to use her only weapon—bullying. She framed Eggemann for stealing a painting, sent many anonymous letters threatening her, and convinced von Ingram to fire her. Lohse reinstated Eggemann's job, but his relationship with von Ingram soured permanently thereafter.

Two rival factions soon formed inside the ERR: von Behr and Lohse versus von Ingram and Scholz. Slanderous accusations and counteraccusations lobbed back and forth. Everyone needed to pick a side. In the madness at the Jeu de Paume, you were either trying to be a serious art historian or trying to steal the art. Rose told Jaujard that "money seems to have more importance than artistic considerations" inside the ERR.

Rose reported on the conflict to Jaujard until its dramatic culmination. "Epilogue to the struggle of the von Behr and Schiedlausky clans," she wrote, explaining that von Behr and Lohse sent Schiedlausky to the Russian front as a lowly private, likely by submitting a simple request to Göring. Ilse Puetz was sent off to Kyiv and von Behr's wife returned to Paris from Berlin. "In retaliation or simple coincidence," Rose wondered.

Baron von Behr sensed that he was falling out of favor with Berlin and proposed a new looting operation aimed at the mass liquidation of Jewish-owned apartments and their furnishings. It would be called M-Aktion (the *M* standing for *Möbel*, or furniture in German) and would be run separately from the Jeu de Paume. He bet correctly that the looting of furnishings would not be subject to the same level of intense scrutiny as artworks. He only needed to relinquish the most valuable items to the museum. Everything else was immediately relocated to Eastern Europe, where fancy antique furniture was apparently needed for the German occupational forces.

Although Rose had initially overheard that von Behr had earmarked 240 homes of Jewish inhabitants for seizure, that number would balloon to a staggering 69,619 by war's end. "Different rumors have circulated," she wrote to Jaujard. Behr ran a prison camp in Paris, where Jewish detainees were forced to repair, pack, and ship furniture and art to Germany. He also collaborated with Louis Darquier de Pellepoix, the commissioner general for Jewish affairs, a Vichy organization in charge of proposing anti-Jewish laws and regulations, and used ERR staff to track down Jews wanted by the SS intelligence agency.

Behr's career redirection was a boon for Lohse, who was named codirector of the ERR in Paris, alongside Walter Borchers. With Göring as his patron, Lohse was untouchable and began stealing whatever he wanted. Rose often saw Lohse take paintings from the museum. One time, he snatched a Matisse and a Renoir formerly owned by Paul Rosenberg, a Van Gogh landscape, and a Gauguin. "Sold? Exchanged?" Rose scribbled down in her notes for Jaujard. Another time, he took four paintings in his car. He took a trip to Switzerland, likely to launder art. Thirteen more official art exchanges took place in 1942, mostly for Göring, but also for von Ribbentrop, Hitler, and others. The "degenerate art" collection in the Salle des Martyrs continued to dwindle.

Lohse also took carpets, furniture, and silverware for his new apartment, seized from a Jewish family, and hung at least one stolen painting on his wall. For smaller items, Lohse used what they dubbed "*la valise*" ("the suitcase"), but he was not afraid to take larger objects openly from the Jeu de Paume. Once, while stealing a rug, he was stopped by the head of the German guards. Lohse simply tried again a few weeks later and succeeded.

As the weather improved in March, Rose wrote to her cousin Marguerite, "Here comes the spring and this doomed winter has passed." She was short on clothing due to wartime restrictions and asked for wool fabric to make a skirt. "You know it's not easy to get new clothing," she told her.

In May, almost four thousand foreign-born Jews were arrested in Paris, and many of their homes looted shortly thereafter. Lohse personally attended the raids, but he was not the only one. Other art historians, including Helga Eggemann and Annemarie von Tomforde, also went, allegedly to serve as the necessary qualified art historian to identify objects of value. It also enabled them to steal without any guards or police present.

In the meantime, Jacques Jaujard was still petitioning the Germans to have French officials present during the seizures and for Rose to do her inventory, citing the original agreement. Bunjes countered these requests with an official nine-page report. He feared that permitting any form of access to the Jeu de Paume would leave the door "wide open for espionage." He reiterated that the French "must not be given any insight into the workings and results" of the ERR staff. He claimed that the French would "gain material for eventual anti-German culture propaganda," "minimize German credit for the preservation of French art treasures," and "gain counterargument against German demands to return art stolen by French troops in Germany." Ironically, however, a spy was already in place. The Germans had simply forgotten about her.

Rose hated what the Germans were doing to the cultural patrimony of France and to individual families. She called them "greedy and dangerous" with "unbridled appetites." Jaujard also described the confiscations as "painful." Faced with utter silence from the Vichy regime regarding the actions of the ERR, Rose concluded solemnly that "the confiscations of Jewish property would last as long as the Hitler regime's hold on our territory." She prepared herself for a long, protracted fight in the hopes that the Allies would one day prevail and her intelligence could be used. With her inside glimpse into the operations of the ERR, she could see how, as she later stated, "the persecution against the Jews was coupled with the looting of their property."

General de Gaulle's chief of staff in London soon learned of Rose's dangerous work for the Resistance. She was also directly informing a French Resistance operative named Pierre-Louis Duchartre about where the Jeu de Paume crates were headed. His cover, working for a trade organization for arts and crafts, helped conceal his movements around France. He and his contacts at the French national rail system, the Société nationale des chemins de fer français (SNCF), kept track of the crates and checked if they were redirected somewhere at the last minute.

As both morale and morals declined within the ERR, paranoia grew. One of Göring's visits in March changed location at the last minute. The Jeu de Paume was too exposed and easily surveilled from the German headquarters along the rue de Rivoli. "Due to the possible risks and in order not to attract attention," as Rose reported to Jaujard, Göring viewed the paintings at the ERR headquarters at 54 avenue d'Iéna instead.

Rose was kicked out of the museum four times—once for a two-week stretch. In August, an exhibition for Göring at the Jeu de Paume coincided with the amphibious Allied landing at Dieppe, a test operation on the Normandy coast to assess the possibility of an amphibious invasion of France. Rose was consequently expelled from the museum for five days because she was French. When the brutal battle ended favorably for the Germans—the Allies lost 60 percent of their ground troops at Dieppe—she was allowed to return.

Each time, she talked her way back into the museum, explaining that her presence was needed to care for the art collection in the basement. She knew, however, that she was being allowed to stay out of sheer convenience for the Germans. It was easier for them to liaise with one person than all the guards individually. She also installed a telephone in her apartment to stay in touch with Jaujard when she was not allowed in the museum. A Jeu de Paume guard, Paul Moïse, called her at home when he needed to warn her of suspicious German activities in the museum. In her small apartment in the Latin Quarter, she kept warm with the heat of a small fire and a bottle of black-market cognac, smoking cigarettes to stay focused. Preternaturally calm, Rose also did not allow herself the luxury of crying or feeling sorry for herself.

To sabotage the day-to-day work of the ERR staff, Rose now made intentional mistakes—ones that sometimes made her look inept—and she instructed the French packers and other workers to do the same. She often had to decipher and assess the seriousness of some of the German intelligence she gathered. For example, when one Gestapo man claimed that his team would soon loot all the castles in multiple regions along the Seine, she wrote to Jaujard, "Should we believe it or is it just bragging?" She also tried her best to determine the titles and names of the ERR personnel and the relationships between them. They were constantly being changed or reassigned, and she often guessed the spelling of their names and sprinkled question marks over her reports about them such as "Von Behr is no longer the head of service, he has a superior (?) whose name sounds like 'Von Ingram'" and "The head of the service in Paris, Colonel (?) von Ingram is appointed to Africa?"

Life in Paris was punctuated by increasing violence. For months, the Resistance had been sabotaging infrastructure and attacking German soldiers and officers, in one case by blowing up a brothel with a bomb in the record player. The *Kommandantur* offered a reward of 15 million francs to anyone who provided information that led to the discovery of the latest string of assaults. In one notice to Parisian residents, the military commander of France, Otto von Stülpnagel, accused "hired agents of foreign countries" of perpetrating the attacks. "I no longer will tolerate that the lives of German soldiers be threatened by assassins," he wrote. "I will not waver before any measure, however severe."

The Germans took suspects hostage and executed twenty of them, predominantly railroad workers. Vichy did its part and dismissed several hundred Paris policemen for attitudes "not in accord with the national revolution." The Germans also imposed a curfew, with infractions leading to arrest.

Psychologically, the war began to feel interminable. A British woman, who had been in the same internment camp as Joyce, wrote that in Paris, "Darkness only envelops us, mute and oppressive. It would seem as if life were being slowly smothered under a pall of misery and despair." Parisians received little accurate news, as the German-controlled press, run by Reich Minister of Propaganda Joseph Goebbels, praised the *Kommandantur* and the occupiers. Jean Guéhenno, who had known the men executed in Jean Cassou and Agnès Humbert's Resistance network, wrote about the German reprisals in his diary: "How long will this last? A year, two years, ten years perhaps. We'll have to find a way to live through this horror, to settle into it, to wait. But how? We're in blood up to our bellies."

Rose's *Ausweis* now had to be renewed monthly, a change that reflected the growing fear of betrayal from within the ERR. In September, Rose cut short a trip to the Unoccupied Zone (presumably to see her family in Saint-Étienne-de-Saint-Geoirs) to return in time for the monthly *Ausweis* renewal. She could not risk losing access to the Jeu de Paume.

With the slowdown of important art coming through the Jeu de Paume, Göring's visits became less frequent and the procedures more predictable. And so, Rose used the quieter period to work on her doctoral thesis, which she had put on pause in 1932 when she started working at the Jeu de Paume. She would successfully defend this thesis on the Byzantine frescoes of Aquileia, Italy, at the École Pratique des Hautes Études in January 1943, just as activity picked up again inside the Jeu de Paume. As the war progressed poorly for the Germans, with the loss of North Africa and Stalingrad, Rose would become more and more of a target.

NEW YORK CITY & PARIS

EARLY 1942

"I STILL RETAIN MY NATIONALITY, FOR HOW LONG NO ONE CAN TELL," Paul Rosenberg had written in mid-June 1941. His skepticism was well-founded. On February 23, 1942, an order from Vichy officially "denationalized" Paul and his family for leaving France without a valid reason.

Paul vowed to fight. He sent a telegram directly to the Vichy government with the words "PROTEST STRONGLY" and followed up with a formal letter. Both went unanswered. Paul hoped he could appeal the decision with Vichy and wrote to his friend Gilbert Lévy, whose son was in Africa alongside Alexandre, asking for help to find a lawyer. It was all futile. Lévy would be deported and sent to Auschwitz, where he would be killed in the gas chambers.

From his safe harbor in America, Paul had little knowledge of how horrifying the situation for Jews in France had become. Deportations of French Jews to Auschwitz and other extermination camps had begun, with the Vichy government not only complicit but also participating in the process.

By April 1942, Paul himself would see the reality for what it was, writing, "Given recent events in France, I do not wish to communicate in any way with a government run by a man like Laval. I would rather lose all I possess." That was, of course, what had already happened.

Rose described the "cruel reality" that was confronting Paul and the many other French Jews who had abandoned everything—their country, their belongings, their businesses, and their homes—in the face of persecution, only to have that very abandonment used as the justification for taking their property and their citizenship away from them. The consequence was "direct and brutal," she concluded.

Rose had met some of the perpetrators of the deportations face-to-face, like Kurt von Behr, whose wider circle included Carltheo Zeitschel, the commissioner for Jewish affairs in the German embassy. Zeitschel had already proposed to carry out a mass "sterilization of all Jews in the occupied territories," and wrote a letter on the urgent need to round up fifty thousand Jews "as soon as possible" from France's Unoccupied Zone for deportation to the east. The Vichy government offered ten thousand Jews from the Unoccupied Zone, almost twenty-eight thousand from Paris, and more from the rest of the Occupied Zone. Over eleven thousand—3,625 of whom were children—were rounded up on just the first day of mass arrests on July 16, 1942. Some nine thousand French policemen and members of law enforcement, along with a few hundred young volunteers who signed up to assist, went in small teams from house to house where Jews had registered their addresses.

On the first day, over seven thousand Jewish men, women, and children were put into Vélodrome d'Hiver in Paris's fifteenth arrondissement, just a third of a mile from the Eiffel Tower. There were only five bathrooms and almost no food or water. The windows and doors were sealed shut to prevent escape, and the dark blue glass roof, painted for bomb protection, made the velodrome stifling hot in daytime and frigid at night. In a week, nearly thirteen thousand Jews had been arrested and crammed into the velodrome. The smell, from thousands of people urinating and defecating, was unbearable. People committed suicide by throwing themselves off the upper levels of the stands. Those who tried to escape were shot.

The Jewish detainees were held in these appalling conditions for five days, after which they were transferred to the Drancy internment camp in the suburb of Paris. At the end of July, the adults and children were separated from each other, and deportations to Auschwitz extermination camp began. Every few days, one thousand people were herded into French train cars and sent to the border of Germany, where they were transferred onto German transportation. Most would not survive the war.

IN NEW YORK CITY, PAUL opened his new gallery. In 1942 alone, he hosted exhibitions on Picasso, Max Weber, Braque, and Cézanne, along with benefit shows, including one on Van Gogh for the American Red Cross and another for US Navy relief. His first benefit show was a centennial exhibition on Renoir that saw upward of a thousand visitors daily. Still, business remained slow, which Paul attributed to uncertain consumer sentiment, anxiety about the future, and high estate taxes in the United States. Meanwhile, he heard with chagrin that the Nazis had sold his Van Gogh self-portrait featuring the artist's ear cut off for 11 million francs.

Alexandre turned twenty-one in Brazzaville in early March. Paul and Margot hoped to fly to Africa to see Alexandre but any available spots on the military planes went to officers and officials. Paul felt glum but acknowledged that his son was "pleased to do his duty." He told Winnifred that worrying about his family and his business had broken him down. He wrote despairingly, "The time approaches when it will be two years since I have last seen my son and I do not foresee when I shall be able to see him once more. What a life! What a life!"

If anything, Alexandre was hoping to see more action. Some of his comrades had already shipped off to fight the Germans and Italians in Egypt and Libya. There were painful losses, however, in the Battle of Bir Hakeim, where Roland de Silva, the youngest of Winnifred's "dwarfs," was killed. He was just sixteen when he escaped from France and enlisted. Another comrade, Robert Saunal, was taken prisoner at Bir Hakeim along with over eight hundred others. Alexandre would have to wait a bit longer for his war to truly begin.

THE LOUVRE

AUGUST 8, 1942

THE NEWS HIT ROSE "LIKE A BOMB." *THE ADORATION OF THE MYSTIC lamb*, the massive Van Eyck altarpiece entrusted to France by Belgium, had been stolen outright by the Germans from the Château de Pau.

Even worse, the collaborationist French leaders in Vichy were more than complicit.

The fifteen-foot-wide, twelve-panel altarpiece was considered a masterpiece of the Proto-Renaissance period. In the art world, it represented a significant milestone in three-dimensional representation and the use of color. For Catholics, it depicted numerous foundational moments in the Christian faith, including Adam and Eve and the birth of Christ. For the Belgians, the altarpiece was part of the cultural soul of the nation. For Rose, the polyptych held "symbolic value" of the trust Belgium had placed in France, "to our friendship and to our vigilance." For the Germans, obtaining *The Adoration of the Mystic Lamb* was their highest priority.

As part of the reparations stipulated in the Treaty of Versailles, Germany was forced to give six panels of the altarpiece to France. The Germans now wanted the whole altarpiece, not just the three panels, claiming it had Germanic origins and subject matter. After the war, a report by the Supreme Headquarters Allied Expeditionary Force would call *The Adoration of the Mystic Lamb* "the most important work of art seized by the Germans from any country during the course of the war."

The curator at the Château de Pau, Jean Molle, received instructions not to part with the altarpiece unless three authorizations were presented—the first from Jacques Jaujard, the second from the mayor of Ghent or the director of the Beaux-Arts in Belgium, and the third from the Kunstschutz. This procedure was laid out in agreement with the Kunstschutz and Vichy.

But Molle buckled when a delegation of Germans came to the Château de Pau on the morning of August 3. At half past ten, Molle opened the crates that contained the altarpiece. A little over an hour later, the priceless work of art was packed and loaded onto a truck headed to Germany. Molle had a lot of explaining to do about why he allowed the theft to occur.

Jaujard returned from vacation to the devastating news and wrote a letter to his boss, Louis Hautecœur, in Vichy, in which he could barely contain his emotion. We will be judged, he contended, "when it is known that we have relinquished it without resistance and without even raising the slightest protest." He ended with a foreboding prediction that the taking of the altarpiece "constitutes a formidable precedent for the future."

On November 20, the Musées Nationaux curatorial staff held an emergency meeting and decided to collectively protest the abduction of *The Adoration of the Mystic Lamb*. They had made a solemn commitment to Belgium that the altarpiece would be protected. Their honor, and that of the French state, was at stake. In a joint letter, they stated that they wanted it returned.

French minister of national education Abel Bonnard was enraged by the public protest. Vichy had agreed to hand the altarpiece over to Germany, and the French leaders did not appreciate the dissent, especially so publicly. "I will break you!" Bonnard told Jaujard by letter, for not restraining the protesting curators.

By telephone, Hautecœur sanctioned Jaujard for insubordination and threatened to fire him immediately. He also intimated a litany of vague but far more sinister misfortunes. Jaujard refused to stand down. As he wrote once, "It is better to risk your life than your reputation, your reputation than your conscience."

All two hundred curators and assistant curators of the Musées Nationaux (with one exception) threatened to quit simultaneously if Jaujard was fired. The ploy worked, and Jaujard kept his job. In the coming years, one of Rose's most urgent missions would be to track down the fate of the altarpiece.

Unfortunately, the Germans were not just interested in *The Adoration of the Mystic Lamb*. Their demands had widened to everything of Germanic origin and anything else they liked. They also wanted art from French museums. Ribbentrop was still keen on acquiring Boucher's *Diana Coming Out of the Bath*. Göring still wanted the

Belle Allemande and other works. Meanwhile, Himmler had his eye on the Bayeux Tapestry, an eleventh-century treasure that was dubiously deemed Germanic in origin and was hidden at the Château de Sourches.

Jaujard continued to resist repeated German demands to visit the art depots and their additional requests to "exchange" art from the French national collections. He used all the ruses he could, agreeing to requests that posed little risk, negotiating for the sake of negotiating, delaying, and pushing back when the time was right. But then Jaujard's one ally among the occupiers, Wolff-Metternich, was recalled to Germany.

In response, Jaujard became even more sly. He attempted to use the French law of preemption to buy paintings formerly owned by the Rothschilds and other Jewish families now held at the Jeu de Paume. The budget the Vichy government allocated would simply return to their own coffers in a bizarrely circular route, but at least a few works would be saved. Jaujard also diligently continued to fight for the release of his museum employees from work camps.

But he also had to make some concessions. Jaujard agreed to help put on a show dedicated to Arno Breker, Hitler's favorite sculptor. "There is only one people without fault: the Germans," Breker once said privately to his good friends. Hitler called Breker his Phidias, referring to the sculptor who designed the statues inside the Parthenon for Pericles.

The Breker exhibition—a pure propaganda vehicle—was the brainchild of architect Albert Speer, the recently appointed Reich minister of armaments and war production. The Germans wanted the exhibition to take place either in the Jeu de Paume or the Orangerie, and Hautecœur seized the opportunity to bring Rose's boss, André Dezarrois, back from curatorial purgatory to organize it. Fortunately for Rose, the exhibition went to the Orangerie, sparing her from having to deal with additional Nazi histrionics—at least for the time being.

JEU DE PAUME

WINTER 1942

ROSE WATCHED SILENTLY AS THE WINTER OF 1942 BROUGHT NEW paranoia to the Jeu de Paume. In early November, 107,000 American and British troops invaded French North Africa and took it from Vichy France, which responded by severing all diplomatic relations with the United States. A few days later, Germany decided to take over the Unoccupied Zone in France.

A terrifying-looking SS man from the Gestapo by the name of Dr. Petof now accompanied the ERR staff to empty the apartments "abandoned" by French Jews who had left the country. "Dangerous character," Rose noted. Georgian soldiers, part of a unit of émigrés who joined with the promise of Germany's assistance in their fight for independence from Russia, now joined the German sentries and special commandos doing surveillance for the ERR.

Before Göring's November 1942 visit, the Gestapo destroyed all the locks on the museum cupboards and searched the basement storage rooms for explosives and weapons. A search of the museum grounds and periphery also took place. The Feldpolizei came to investigate when the lights on the glass roof of the Jeu de Paume remained on all night during a blackout.

Rose was regularly accused of sabotage and of sending "signals to the enemy," be it the Allied forces or Resistance operators. The smallest incidents—a hole in the paint, a chip in a cup, a broken boiler, a damaged statue—were all attributed to potential "sabotage." Rose would later write, "The word sabotage was then a fashionable word that was part of the [ERR's] usual vocabulary." Rose submitted to each interrogation.

For Rose, the most painful investigations were those for theft. Art objects disappeared all the time from the Jeu de Paume under the nose of the Gestapo and the military guard. The self-interested Germans found the French easy scapegoats. "It is us, French, who were asked to account," she later said. "I never evaded these interrogations, although it was very unpleasant." Beyond interrogations, the Germans sometimes called for humiliating body searches of the French staff. Nothing was ever found but the French guards at the museum were repeatedly targets of mass firings.

Some of the German art historians began to open up to Rose. They shared information, almost as if in confession. When Hamburg, Germany, was bombed heavily by the Allies, Walter Borchers, whose mother and sister lived in the city, told Rose, "This is my punishment for what I am doing." Rose reassured him that he was not personally responsible for what was happening.

Rose's spy craft also became more nuanced. She began discreetly eyeing the shipping labels to decipher their destinations. Starting in February 1941, shipments went directly to Germany on first-class, air-conditioned train cars, separate from the items Göring took on his train.

She began surveilling ERR staffers after work, even discovering their home addresses, down to the floors and apartments they lived in. In the middle of the night, outside an apartment near Trocadero, she saw Lohse add items to a German military van filled with carpets and paintings. She could only catch portions of the name of the other man involved, which sounded Polish or Slavic. She also uncovered the locations of additional ERR offices and storage warehouses in Paris.

Some of Rose's time was allocated to mundane maintenance. After two years of war, the Jeu de Paume had decayed physically. Gutters and ceilings leaked, chimneys needed to be swept, and the windows had accumulated layers of grime. She received a barrage of complaints from the Germans about the building. "I find them fully justified," Rose admitted to Jaujard. However, Jaujard's deteriorating relationship with Vichy and a general lack of funds made repairs impossible. Conditions became so bad that the Germans decided to take care of some of the structural issues themselves.

The plotting at the Jeu de Paume took another turn. Hermann von Ingram was pushed out of the organization after he was caught stealing fabric from the Maurice de Rothschild collection. Kurt von Behr gave him an ultimatum: leave Paris or face a military tribunal. Instead, von Ingram offered to donate a large sum to the French "winter relief" fund and left for Berlin.

Göring visited the Jeu de Paume again on November 24, 1942. He arrived at 5:20 a.m. and stayed for two hours, leaving before the sun rose. He chose eighty-five items—paintings, furniture, tapestries, and carpets—to be loaded onto his train. The visit ended with a dramatic sabering of a champagne bottle in celebration, likely due to the large bounty.

Collaborationist art dealers arrived at the museum in the days following Göring's visits to buy and exchange from the remains of the spoils. Ten art exchanges took place in 1942, which primarily benefited Göring. Rose continued to note how low the valuations by appraiser Jacques Beltrand were. An important Van Gogh landscape, which should have been valued at over 1 million francs, was reduced to 500,000 by Beltrand and then cut further to 100,000 by Lohse.

A new wave of confiscated art was also on its way to the Jeu de Paume. A total of 540 cases from a Rothschild château near Rouen arrived in November. The ERR also successfully seized art collections in the Unoccupied Zone, signifying a new level of Vichy complicity. Rose beseeched Jaujard to try to stop the new seizures. "Could we not prevent these new lootings?" she wrote, perhaps hoping to encourage him to involve the Vichy government again.

Meanwhile, in Germany, death had come for Führermuseum curator Hans Posse. He died slowly and painfully of oral cancer, but worked to the bitter end for Hitler's museum, taking meetings daily in a hospital in Berlin. Hitler ordered a state funeral. Joseph Goebbels delivered the eulogy, and Arno Breker sculpted the death mask. Hitler immediately appointed German art historian Hermann Voss to replace Posse and continue the dream of building the Führermuseum.

Back in France, the search for the Schloss collection, the last massive holdings of a Jewish collector, escalated. Lucien Schloss had hidden over three hundred Old Master paintings in a friend's castle near Tulle in central France, believing it safe in the Unoccupied Zone. But everyone, French or German, was on the hunt. Louis Darquier de Pellepoix, the monocled, faux aristocratic, anti-Semitic commissioner general for Jewish affairs, and his co-conspirator Jean-François Lefranc, an art dealer, offered to let Lohse and von Behr know where it was hidden, in exchange for a 25 percent commission for Vichy. Both sides would benefit, considering that de Pellepoix and Lefranc needed help from the Germans to transport and protect the art. Lohse sent a note to Göring suggesting that they collaborate with Lefranc, writing, "After all, these French are traitors to their own country, and a traitor wants to be paid."

It was agreed that once found, the collection would be held under French control at the Dreyfus Bank in Paris so that the Germans could not confiscate it outright. The Louvre would get the first choice, exercising its legal right of first refusal to preempt the sale of any artwork deemed important to French cultural heritage. The only catch was that de Pellepoix and Lefranc had no idea where the Schloss collection was located.

CAIRO, EGYPT

MAY 1943

IT WAS FINALLY ALEXANDRE'S TURN FOR BATTLE. HE AND HIS FRIEND Guy Lévy were headed east to Egypt to join the recently victorious Allied forces. North Africa had been won back from Germany and

Italy, largely due to the wily methods of General Philippe Leclerc, who put together a rogue-like force from French Equatorial Africa, uniting the French colonies against Germany.

For more than two years, Leclerc had been personally running reconnaissance missions and deadly raids to push the Italians north toward the British in Libya. In May 1943, the Axis powers were kicked out of Africa entirely due to the joint success of the French, the Americans, and the British Imperial Forces. Nearly 270,000 Axis soldiers were taken prisoners of war. The Germans were on the defense, especially given their recent loss at Stalingrad to the Soviets.

Leclerc, now a three-star general, was turning his armored column into the 2nd Free French Armored Division (2nd Division Blindée or 2nd DB, for short). He brought in Free French recruits like Alexandre and large numbers of volunteers from the former Vichy-led Armée d'Afrique, absorbed military units wholesale, and even added women to the ranks. He told his soldiers, "I promise you, I will lead you back into France, and more than that, I promise you also that we will take Paris and Strasbourg." Fighters were literally walking across Africa to beg Leclerc to let them join him.

For once, Alexandre's father was supportive. "I can rightly say that I am proud of my two children," Paul wrote, although he and Margot were still racked with fear for Alexandre. Alexandre could not tell his parents where he was headed but they suspected it was somewhere in the "Far East." By summer, Winnifred heard from her new batch of "dwarfs" in England that Alexandre and Guy *might* be in Egypt.

Even at that distance, Paul hoped to connect his son with the art world. When Alexandre made it to Cairo, Paul wanted him to call on an art client at his home. Not surprisingly, Alexandre did not have time to hobnob, which Paul attributed to his son's shy nature. "Since my boy has never mixed himself with any business he imagines that the people I know are only casual acquaintances and that he would be imposing on them were he to see them," he wrote to Winnifred.

In truth, Alexandre may have been simply too busy keeping his soldiers in line. Free French boys were arriving by boat, train, and foot from the far corners of Africa and the Middle East to the military camp next to the Pyramids. Once settled, they encountered the usual troubles that come with youthful exuberance in wartime. On the streets and in the cafés in Alexandria, they got into brawls with French Navy sailors, accusing them of cowardice if they did not join the fight. Some were hospitalized with diseases like dysentery and blackwater fever. They would soon all need to get onto a ship to Tripoli.

Paul had always believed ultimately that the Germans would be defeated. The recent Allied success in Africa revitalized him, as did his son's new deployment. "We are rejoicing at the thought of victory which surely cannot be far away now," Paul wrote with a certainty he had not mustered thus far in the war.

JEU DE PAUME

SPRING TO SUMMER 1943

THE JEU DE PAUME WAS EMPTIED. ROSE HEARD FROM WALTER BORCHERS that the Germans wanted to curate a large exhibition in Germany "to show the world what the Jews stole." The ERR also expected a huge wave of confiscations from the Unoccupied Zone.

For the first time, the Germans shipped out a large number of impressionist paintings from the Jeu de Paume to Germany—paintings by the likes of Édouard Manet, Monet, Renoir, and Pissarro—signaling a change in philosophy. Borchers announced that Hitler now "appreciated the impressionists." Rose observed with concern that all the paintings from the Salle des Martyrs were packed up, with the exception of a few pieces by Picasso and Pierre Bonnard. Modernist paintings by Matisse, Braque, Marie Laurencin, and Picasso, which were not acceptable in Germany, would be sold in Switzerland or another country, and were labeled A for *absetzen* ("sell"). Impressionist paintings by Manet, Sisley, Courbet, Monet, and Degas, newly acceptable to Hitler for their market value, were set aside, earmarked to be transferred to Germany, and labeled T for *transfer.* But what was that last category—V? It was concerning.

The ERR had also added new depots in Paris to accommodate the loot. Rose counted at least six. She was amazed by the quality of the artwork still coming in after almost three years of incessant confiscations.

Inside the Jeu de Paume, the rival factions grew more hostile toward each other. Bruno Lohse thundered that he wanted to "screw everyone," after anonymous letters were sent to Germany denouncing him and Helga Eggemann. "Without a doubt by Mme von Ingram," Rose noted, referring to the newly married Annemarie Tomforde-von Ingram. Lohse and Tomforde-von Ingram launched into a violent screaming match. When Lohse lost his temper, he would become red with rage.

Other strange things unfolded. Scholz deliberately hid some expensive Édouard de Rothschild carpets from von Behr before shipping them directly to Germany. They were valued at 200 million francs. Rose suspected von Behr had stashed them at the Louvre for himself and had forgotten about them. The carpets, along with three Giovanni Boldini paintings, were never inventoried nor exhibited, but just reappeared at the Jeu de Paume and were quickly dispatched to Germany, accompanied by an SS soldier. "How can this hasty departure be interpreted?" Rose asked Jaujard in her report. "Is this because of the exceptional value of these rugs? Probably."

Rose also observed that Lohse regularly took paintings from the Jeu de Paume but threatened others who did the same. "Dr. Lohse (!)

warned us that he would have any art thief shot without mercy," she told Jaujard. In March, Lohse carried out five paintings by Bonnard, Sisley, and Eugène Boudin. Two were seized from Paul Rosenberg's collection in Le Castel.

Baron von Behr, on the other hand, had fallen precipitously from grace in the previous year. His day-to-day responsibilities in Paris running M-Aktion, the group created to liquidate the "abandoned" apartments of Parisian Jews, remained unchanged. However, he was clearly on very precarious footing with his superiors in Berlin. Rose reported that von Behr was criticized for "not having had sufficient control" after trucks of requisitioned Jewish-owned property were hijacked during the Vel' d'Hiv' roundup. Quite dramatically, Göring did not invite him to his fiftieth birthday party in Germany that year.

Behr must have felt the slight keenly. The birthday revelers sipped from seventy-five bottles of champagne and twenty-one bottles of cognac, all taken from the Jeu de Paume's stash of stolen valuables. Rose made note that sixteen Flemish and Dutch paintings were also sent from the museum for Göring—quite the birthday gift! The previous year, von Behr had gifted Göring an original signed copy of the Treaty of Versailles and a letter to Napoleon III from German composer Richard Wagner, both stolen from the Jeu de Paume. Now, Göring decried that he did not want to hear about von Behr anymore. There was chatter that the Reichsmarschall might return for a visit to the Jeu de Paume soon, but he had yet to appear.

In the meantime, ERR leader Alfred Rosenberg made a gross miscalculation with Hitler. Rosenberg proudly sent Hitler twenty-nine albums of photographs that showcased the amazing treasures the ERR had "protected" in France, particularly via the Jeu de Paume, from which Hitler could choose for his birthday. Instead of a grateful thank-you, Rosenberg received a terse order that everything under the jurisdiction of the ERR would now be transferred to the Special Mission for the Führermuseum. All the art at the Louvre and the Jeu de Paume would be sent to Germany and out of Rosenberg's grasp.

Rosenberg then scrambled to find administrative reasons why this request could not be fulfilled right away. He responded that the inventories were still unfinished and the ERR art historians were the only people capable of completing them. A definitive catalog of the ERR's holdings was imperative to continue the various exchanges in negotiation with the French museums, he claimed, as the stolen Jewish-owned art could be traded for artworks coveted by leaders like Göring and von Ribbentrop, like *Diana Coming Out of the Bath* or the *Belle Allemande*.

Rose noted sarcastically: "We cannot note without irony that Rosenberg's first reaction to defend himself is to hide behind French interventions . . . which he himself fought."

At the beginning of April, von Behr was formally removed as ERR director, but he continued to manage M-Aktion. He was building a bomb shelter at his office, the first inkling that he was worried about the future.

With Lohse fully in charge, the ERR staff found no reason to pause their thieving. Within just a few months, Rose saw Lohse put a four-foot-wide landscape painting by Jan van Goyen in his car and ship engravings and woodcuts to his mother in Berlin. Lohse told Borchers to hide a painting of *Leda and the Swan* behind the Jeu de Paume's main staircase, saying loud enough that Rose could hear, "This will be for us." He also befriended the museum's chief packer, who helped keep Lohse's thefts under the radar. The ERR staff had been accused of stealing, but the packer used his shipment logbook to clear them during a wrongdoing investigation after von Behr's departure. "You saved the whole gang," Lohse told the man. Then, when Lohse shipped off an important painting and tapestry to Berlin for himself, he made the packer swear to keep it a secret.

For art historian Annemarie Tomforde-von Ingram, nothing was too big or too small to steal. She snatched decor for her new Berlin apartment that she shared with von Ingram, including a bed made of lemon tree wood, display cases, linens, and even two stained mattresses, as well as suitcases of everything from sardines to chocolate.

The entire ERR staff, including von Ingram, shared a bounty of roast pork, salmon, bottles of cognac, and champagne. They also took two tons of La Vierge soap, a rare luxury in wartime. Helga Eggemann, meanwhile, was now bold enough to vocalize her anti-Semitism. When certain pieces of furniture from the home of Édouard de Rothschild were identified as copies, she announced, "With these Jews, we are always robbed," as if the Germans deserved not only everything French Jews owned but also exclusively those of the highest quality.

In contrast, the Germans were merciless with the French staff. When two landscape paintings vanished, an angry Borchers threatened to call the Gestapo, insisting that the French must have taken them to inform the Allies of what was going on inside the Jeu de Paume. When a Rembrandt drawing and a Chinese vase went missing, Rose was asked to account for the disappearances. "I was called in the morning by von Ingram," she reported to Jaujard, "to talk about the latest thefts and an altercation which occurred between a German and the guard Battini. Explanations are asked of me in front of everyone." Rose suspected that Tomforde-von Ingram was the actual thief. She had recently seen her stealing frames from the Jeu de Paume, and knew she had a box packed for Germany at a shipping company. Instead, the entire team of French guards was blamed, fired, and replaced.

Then, Tomforde-von Ingram claimed to have over a thousand francs stolen from her, so Lohse demanded that all the French employees be stripped and searched thoroughly by German soldiers. A female cleaner was completely undressed. This was the first time Rose noted that a woman at the museum was so violently checked. Helga Eggemann and two other German women also reported money stolen, ranging between eight hundred and two thousand francs.

Rose stood up for her guards and protested to Lohse about the unequal treatment between the French and German staff. She told him it would be "difficult for our guards to carry out" the thefts, given the police presence at the museum. The searches yielded nothing. Lohse promised Rose that from then on, the same measures would be applied to everyone, regardless of nationality. Shortly after, Lohse declared that German law would be applied to thefts, which meant that the Gestapo or the German Army would be called in to investigate, and the severest penalties would be inflicted.

When seventeen valuable silver coins went missing shortly after, he asked all personnel to sign a pledge to keep everything they saw or heard within the ERR a secret, during and after the war. "The slightest infraction will result in severe punishment," the declaration read. Lohse specifically accused Rose of "knowing too much" and threatened repercussions from high up if she did not comply. Lohse told Rose he would "be obliged to break off all collaboration with the Musées Nationaux" if they did not sign the oath, meaning he would no longer allow Rose or anybody else from the French museums to access the Jeu de Paume.

Rose nonetheless refused to sign or let her guards sign, arguing that as French civil servants, they were prohibited from any direct engagement with a foreign country. Given Lohse's recent threats, it was a daring and brave act on Rose's part to protect her guards, but it did not alleviate the suspicion surrounding them.

Then, a locked cupboard containing all the switches and circuit breakers was broken open a second time, leaving bayonet marks, which necessitated an investigation by the German Army. "I hope this incident will have no consequences for us," Rose told Jaujard nervously.

Rose was a convenient subject of suspicion, particularly for Lohse, when things were not going well. One time he told her irately to "Piss off!" Of the incident, she noted dryly to Jaujard, "Good to know."

But von Behr had something even more brutal in store for Rose, who remained unaware of it until after the war. He decided he would remove her from France under some work pretext and have her taken to Germany to be "eliminated" after crossing the border.

Although she was oblivious to her specific death sentence, Rose knew that her life was in danger. The Gestapo followed her home frequently. She felt waves of fear, which swelled day after day, especially when she had to show her *Ausweis* to the German guards at the museum entrance. She bottled everything up: all the secrecy, her treacherous daily routine, and the perpetual dread of being caught. She wrote later, "It went on like this, like an agonizing routine." Sometimes, she was so afraid she found it impossible to write. But she prided herself on her sangfroid, and she would not let Jaujard or herself down by faltering now. All she needed was to keep thinking faster than the Nazis and maybe she could survive. More than ever, she felt a strange kinship with the confiscated masterpieces all around her. "It was to them as well that I belonged, like a hostage," she wrote, her fate undetermined.

THE SEARCH FOR THE LAST cache of great art, the Schloss collection, persisted. De Pellepoix and Lefranc were in hot pursuit of the Schloss children and were planning to arrest them. One informant suddenly got a guilty conscience and sent an anonymous telegram to warn Henri Schloss, one of the sons of patriarch Adolphe Schloss who had amassed the collection. Lamentably, Henri ignored it and was soon arrested in Nice by the Marseille arm of de Pellepoix's Commission for Jewish Affairs. He refused to give up the collection's hiding place or reveal where his brother, Lucien, was. Nothing was found in his villa. But in a stroke of terrible luck, Lucien sent Henri a telegram that arrived during the interrogation. A return address was on the envelope revealing Lucien's location in Lamastre, seventy-five miles south of Lyon, where he was arrested and beat by German policemen.

Armed with the location of the art collection at last, a race commenced between the French and the Germans, and various factions within—who would get the Schloss collection first? On the German side, Lohse and von Behr hired the Bonny-Lafont gang, a group of lawless French ex-convicts sprung from prison by the Gestapo to do its bidding, along with a man from Himmler's powerful security service (Sicherheitsdienst, or SD) to protect the convoy. It meant that von Behr and Lohse would not mind spilling blood to control the Schloss collection.

The unlikely crew descended on the collection in a château near Tulle, pretending to be French policemen. The group pressured the guard to hand over the seven crates of art and loaded up the truck, taking the custodian hostage. The French, led by Lefranc and de Pellepoix, arrived too late.

On the way to Paris, while still in the Unoccupied Zone, local French police tried to overtake the truck. A fight broke out on the roadside. Lohse telephoned Göring in Berlin, who instructed him to give the collection to the French. Lohse would have to follow protocol on this one. It was a situation Lohse later attributed to an "apparent lack of responsibility on the part of de Pellepoix and a lamentable lack of judgment in the choice of an escort."

At this point, the Schloss collection was too contentious for even Göring to touch. The Germans had seized it illegally from the Unoccupied Zone. Göring backed off, knowing that Hitler wanted the art for the Führermuseum. As head of the Luftwaffe, which had recently suffered defeats, Göring could not risk antagonizing Hitler further.

At the Jeu de Paume, Rose watched the apportionment of the Schloss collection. All the usual suspects were there: Lohse exchanged pleasantries with de Pellepoix, while Lefranc, the new Aryan administrator of the collection, made jokes that Rose described as "off-color" and did not repeat. Lefranc was allowed to keep some paintings to sell on the open market and even boldly took a painting out of the Dreyfus Bank under his arm. Dr. Erhard Göpel, an agent for Hitler, purchased paintings for the Führer.

Hitler received 262 Old Master paintings. Vichy got its commission, and a fictitious buyer purchased twenty-two additional paintings on behalf of the Germans. The French museums, represented by Germain Bazin and René Huyghe, bought forty-nine paintings using their right of first refusal, paying the funds into a Vichy-controlled bank account. The Nazi leadership widely praised Lohse for his role in securing the collection.

Overall, almost everyone got something out of the entire affair except—of course—for the Schloss family. Dozens of paintings disappeared as if into thin air, many never to be seen again. Lohse would deny it, but he had been pilfering paintings, and Rose was on to him.

JEU DE PAUME

JULY 22–23, 1943

ROSE'S WORST FEAR WAS COMING TO FRUITION. THE GERMANS HAD decided the fate of the remaining modern paintings from the Salle des Martyrs. The last classification, V, was for *vernichten*—destroy.

For several days, the entire staff had diligently unpacked and sorted hundreds of modern paintings in the ERR rooms at the Louvre. On July 22, Gaston Petit, the head of security, saw the Germans slash a painting formerly owned by the Jewish heiress Madame Schwob d'Héricourt. Eugène Finitzer, a Jeu de Paume guard, watched as the Germans knifed and kicked the canvases with "unbridled satisfaction." Pictorial Arts director Robert Scholz sliced the paintings from top to bottom, and then Walter Borchers came over to stab them repeatedly. Any works by a Jewish artist or that depicted anything deemed Jewish, particularly family portraits, were desecrated. They slashed the women's faces and chests. "In them was a poison to be destroyed," Rose described of the rabid view the Germans took toward the chosen paintings.

The jarring sounds of canvas punctures and long knife tears echoed through the marble-floored rooms, which had historically been used to showcase art, not to attack it. Each painting held thousands of years of collective evolution in the art of representation, technique, and subject matter—thousands of years of contemplation on how the real three-dimensional world and the complexity of human nature could be embodied on a two-dimensional canvas. Art is transcendent—a visual medium that stirs emotion and helps people understand their place in a world that can never be fully comprehended. Even the earliest men and women made rudimentary art within the environment around them. This wanton destruction in the ERR rooms in the Louvre served to erase a form of expression through which humans differentiated themselves from animals. And yet, here were men of a supposedly superior race acting in the most inhuman, destructive way.

Hundreds of paintings were destroyed at the Louvre and torn from their frames. As Rose described, "the choice was sumptuous." Almost all the paintings by Dalí and Masson were lacerated into obscurity. Several family collections, including that of artist Eugene Spiro, were completely destroyed. Some Picassos, including a painting of a harlequin and a still life with musical instruments, were left in tatters. In more halcyon days, many of these artists were celebrated on the walls of the Jeu de Paume.

When the men were finished, they piled the painting scraps onto military trucks and drove everything to the Jeu de Paume. From there, Rose watched them unload the remnants of the paintings and the frames into the walled garden.

More horror unfolded the next day. In the morning, the Germans designated Paul Blondel, a French guard at the Jeu de Paume, to set the scraps and frames ablaze. An armed German sentry supervised the destruction, preventing people from approaching the scene, while his underlings tended the pyramidal funeral pyre. Rose, who saw everything from the large ground floor windows and glass doors of the museum, watched in abject horror. Over and over, she would see a flash of a painting and then watch it melt away, devoured by the inferno. The frames and canvases crackled and snapped under the flames. A column of smoke billowed into the sky. The Germans looked like witless disciples participating in a sacrificial ritual. The fire was still raging at 5 p.m., the end of Blondel's shift. "Impossible to save anything," Rose wrote despondently that day to Jaujard.

Rose estimated that five or six hundred paintings met their ghastly fate in this fiery sacrifice to Hitler's artistic creeds. She made a partial list of the artworks that were destroyed: paintings by Picasso, Léger, Klee, Ernst, Francis Picabia, and others. She told Jaujard that the works of art were "massacred." She compared the decision-making of Scholz and Borchers to that of a war tribunal, with "a verdict pronounced behind closed doors . . . applicable immediately without appeal."

At least four Jeu de Paume guards, Paul Blondel, Eugène Finitzer, C. Develay, and Rose's trusted informant, brigadier Paul Moïse, witnessed the paintings being burned firsthand. Gaston Petit, the Louvre's head of security, also confirmed that it took place. About six weeks later, in early September 1943, a short article about the burning would appear in the Resistance newspaper *Libération*, with the headline "*Flambez peintures!*"

While the Nazis would later vehemently deny that this ever happened and use all their means to discredit Rose's account, three of the Jeu de Paume guards would submit notarized testimony attesting to the veracity of the event. A fourth, Develay, would submit signed testimony.

The most valued modern and impressionist paintings miraculously escaped a death sentence—only because of their financial value—and were moved back into the Salle des Martyrs, safe for the time being, where Rose watched over them intently. Lohse, usually around for the most nefarious deeds, was on such bad terms with Scholz, Borchers, and the others that he repeatedly refused to come inside the Jeu de Paume. As such, he was fortuitously absent during the cutting and burning of the paintings. Was there a line Lohse would not cross? Maybe he was just lucky. Instead, Helga Eggemann kept him informed on what was happening inside.

Two weeks later, Rose watched as large concrete blocks, to be used for defense and as machine-gun installations, were unloaded on the terrace outside the Jeu de Paume. They were just a few feet from the museum near the main entrance in front of Place de la Concorde. With a prescience she would later remember, Rose asked Jaujard, "Are we going to become one of the last bastions?"

MOROCCO

FALL TO WINTER 1943

ALEXANDRE ROSENBERG, NOW A SECOND LIEUTENANT, AND HIS FRIEND Guy Lévy were officially members of the 3rd Colonial Artillery Regiment (3rd RAC), which was part of General Philippe Leclerc's 2nd DB. The 3rd RAC included European and African soldiers of all races, particularly Black fighters from Chad.

Leclerc relocated his division to be closer to the American military camps on Morocco's Atlantic coast. The soldiers were training for a secret invasion to take back France through Normandy, but only Leclerc and de Gaulle were in the know. Africa was the first front; France would be the second.

New tanks, jeeps, and trucks painted with the French tricolor flag arrived by ship from America's Midwest industrial belt. The American tanks were faster and far more modern than the latest German Panzers. The delivery also included an enormous cache of new American guns—Thompson submachine guns, Colt .45 automatic pistols, automatic rifles, and more. Everyone in the 2nd DB was required to wear American uniforms.

Leclerc preferred direct contact and made daily rounds to check in with Alexandre and the other officers. His pithy but clear directions always seemed to fix things up quickly. He also regularly invited small groups of officers to dine with him. Once the men were with Leclerc, they wanted to follow him to the ends of the earth. His whole being, body and soul, was imbued with one unassailable goal: to take France back and restore her honor.

Some of the hardest tasks were figuring out how to work with those the Free French forces had long disdained, like ex-Vichy soldiers, and unify the many disparate and culturally diverse fighters under one cause. Leclerc also needed to train young men with little to no military background apart from boot camp in England. But over and over, he made the impossible possible.

In December 1943, de Gaulle entrusted Leclerc with liberating Paris and appointed him "Interim Military Governor of Paris." "Tell Leclerc *always* to keep that letter with him," de Gaulle instructed his liaison officer who delivered the order. De Gaulle firmly believed that it was essential for Paris to be liberated by the French—their nation's pride and future depended on it. However, liberating Paris was not a top priority for American General Dwight D. Eisenhower, the Supreme Commander of the Allied Expeditionary Force in Europe. As such, de Gaulle's order was to be kept a secret until absolutely necessary.

At a New Year's celebration, Leclerc told his men, "The year 1944 will be the year of Liberation." Soon, the United States military inspector would visit to determine whether the 2nd DB was combat-ready. There was just one problem for Alexandre and his fellow officers in the artillery battalions: their equipment, coming from the United States, had been accidentally sent to the Allied forces in Italy.

JEU DE PAUME

NOVEMBER 1943

THE JEU DE PAUME WELCOMED SOME NOTABLE NAZIS AS 1943 CAME TO an end, even as the Axis suffered major military setbacks. First came Alfred Rosenberg, on November 4, 1943, three days after Rose's forty-fifth birthday, for his first and only visit. Rosenberg had little standing left within the Nazi hierarchy, and even less within the ERR itself, at least in Paris. Rose observed that his visit would have gone completely unnoticed had the scent of chrysanthemums not taken over the museum that day, left over from All Saints Day' on November 1. The flower symbolized death in France, placed on graves to honor the dead. The Germans were likely unfamiliar with this French tradition, but Rose noted the "smell of cemeteries" wafting through the Jeu de Paume. Here, the flowers served as a foreboding symbol of Rosenberg's political fate.

The art historians on staff curated an exhibition, nonetheless. Rosenberg arrived with a motorcade of seven cars at 4:30 p.m. Nobody was allowed to leave or enter the museum. Bruno Lohse and another man both raised their right arms in a Heil Hitler salute. But Rose held her hands crossed one over another, refusing to make such a gesture. It was not necessary for non-Germans, so Rose would have seen no reason to act like a sycophant, particularly given how atrocious she found the actions of the ERR. An official shook Rosenberg's hand.

Rosenberg climbed the museum's grand staircase to the second floor. The main attraction was an exhibition of seventeenth- to eighteenth-century paintings by French artists, coming mostly from the David-Weill collection. The rest of the museum was curated with Chinese and Egyptian art, statues, furniture, porcelain, and jewels. Overall, the caliber of the art shown was not remotely as high as what was exhibited in the early days of the ERR's reign at the Jeu de Paume. Rosenberg's visit was quick—slightly over an hour—especially compared to Göring's marathon stays.

On December 10, the ERR's true leader graced the doorstep of the Jeu de Paume again after a long hiatus. It would be Göring's final visit. His grip on power, though far from lost, was waning, and he no longer had direct access to Hitler because of the sustained German military losses. The German art historians were even more stressed than usual because nothing appropriate was in stock to show to Göring. A large export of over eight hundred cases of art had been sent from the Jeu de Paume to Germany and Austria on November 15, and the only art on hand was earmarked for Hitler.

An exhibition was cobbled together by importing some Right

Bank gallery artwork and a barely finished Arno Breker statue of a wounded soldier from the foundry. The Gestapo searched the place more thoroughly than usual, concerned that the Resistance could be hiding in cupboards, ready to kill. Resistance attacks had increased throughout Paris.

Göring arrived in a small retinue of two cars, dressed incognito in a neutral gabardine coat and an old hat. He was accompanied by von Behr, recently promoted to colonel, Walter Andreas Hofer, some SS men, and Göring's friend, Friedrich Carl Hanesse, commander general of the Luftwaffe in Paris and soon-to-be general of all of the Luftwaffe, to whom Göring entrusted the storage and transportation of his art collection. Rose quietly observed every tiny detail of the proceedings.

Göring was so disappointed by the poor quality of the art offerings that he lashed out at everyone around him. He called Hanesse an "old idiot" and other choice insults. As for the art, Göring merely grunted at the Arno Breker statue and barely looked at any of the paintings, proclaiming that they did not interest him. The Georgian surveillance guards, who pledged allegiance to whichever power was more likely to support their claims for independence from Russia, paraded on the steps of the Jeu de Paume and shouted in French "Long live Stalin!" to goad a weakened Göring.

To appease the angry Reichsmarschall, the Germans reminded him of the art exchange proposals still under negotiation for the *Belle Allemande*, *Basel Antependium*, and others. It seemed to improve Goring's mood. The next day, he sent a flurry of requests for those works of art to be sent to his office at Quai d'Orsay for inspection. Jacques Jaujard returned the requests with his usual diplomatic form—outmaneuvering the Reichsmarschall with polite language noting all the problems and potential delays.

With the Allied invasion of Italy in full swing and deadly bombardments raining down on Germany, both sides began to suspect the war might not end well for the Axis powers. In anticipation, more and more shipments of valuables were sent to the Reich to ensure they would not be lost in an Allied invasion. These included not only art but also books, furniture, and decor. The flurry of export activity gave Rose the opportunity to document the shipments leaving for Germany.

The Germans would not make it easy. The labels, written enigmatically with codes and letters, required decrypting, along with dogged research and cross-checking to figure them out. Lohse guarded these addresses as trade secrets, but Rose found them and decoded them anyway. She also wrote down which owners the crates came from, the abbreviations, and the box numbers. To diffuse the risk, the Germans no longer sent everything solely to Neuschwanstein. Art went to other castles in Germany, Austria, and Czechoslovakia. The Schloss collection went directly to Hitler's Führerbau in Munich.

Once, in a stroke of bad luck, Lohse caught Rose by surprise while she was trying to decipher an address. She had ordinarily been so careful. Rose told Jaujard of Lohse's lengthy rebuke, recounting, "He takes the opportunity to remind me that everyone here is bound to secrecy and that there would be serious risks in talking about what is happening . . . Looking into my eyes, he tells me that I could be shot."

Rose answered Lohse calmly: "No one here is stupid enough not to know the risks they are taking." She then deftly convinced him that appearances were not what they seemed. It was one of the most threatening exchanges the two had ever had, and it reflected the increasing suspicion Lohse and others in the ERR had about Rose and her activities.

Both Rose and Jaujard were indeed taking serious personal risks for the Resistance. For weeks, Jaujard hid the Resistance maquis Pierre Dalloz in his apartment in the Louvre until arrests began to occur among the French administrative corps in Paris. Jaujard told Dalloz, "It would not be good for you or me if the Germans found you here," at which point Jacqueline Bouchot-Saupique took him in. Jaujard was also discreetly hiding people wanted by the Germans in the deep recesses of the Louvre, whether they were Resistance fighters, Jews on the run, or Allied paratroopers.

In her apartment, Rose kept piles of papers scribbled with all her evidence. She saved documents like Picasso did objects. She scribbled her notes down on any paper she could find—graph paper of all sizes, lined paper, typewriter paper, index cards, and scraps of torn paper. She even saved envelopes from her mail correspondence. There were stacks of photographs printed from the negatives she stole from the Jeu de Paume. She kept the drafts of her reports to Jaujard too, peppered with her own edits and cross-outs. Her handwriting was neat and legible when she wrote formally with tall capitals and clean script loops, but it rapidly deteriorated when she wrote fast, becoming flat and indistinct. If the Germans found any of the documents she squirreled away in her apartment, she would be arrested immediately.

Rose was a genius with information, and her brain processed things like a computer. There was a method to her madness, but her papers were organized in a way that only she truly understood. She was a one-woman operation—spy, art historian, building superintendent, and archivist all at once—but how much longer could she hold on?

TEMARA, MOROCCO

GOOD FRIDAY 1944

ON A DAZZLING SUNNY AFTERNOON, ALEXANDRE ROSENBERG AND THE entire French Army in Morocco paraded in front of General Charles de Gaulle. Here, larger than life, was the leader the men of the 2nd DB had instinctively put their trust in four long years earlier. They left everything they knew behind and were the very first to stand behind him—*les Gaullistes de la première heure*—and he had not forgotten their conviction or their continued loyalty.

De Gaulle inspected the 3rd RAC and other battalions and told them that evening at the Temara casino they would sail shortly for England. Euphoria filled the air. From England, they would take back France.

Over the next few days, a massive military removal operation commenced from the port of Casablanca. Three hundred ships and aircraft carriers stretched as far as the eye could see. Grumman Hellcat fighter planes circled the air to protect the ocean convoy. A painted two-barred cross of Lorraine distinguished the tanks and vehicles of the Free French fighters from the rest—a rare distinction that Leclerc chose to allow. When the Rochambelles, the 2nd DB's all female ambulance corps, tried to board a ship, the Americans refused, but Leclerc interceded angrily, "They're not women, they're ambulance drivers!" One of Alexandre's battalion mates jotted in his diary, "It's war, nothing can stop this evolution; it is normal for women to be equal to men in all stages in life."

The journey was horrific, not because of any enemy but because of seasickness. The landing ship tanks (LSTs) were long, flat, ferry-like ships whose hulls opened wide to allow for disembarkation right on shore. Along with troops, they carried between thirty and forty tanks each, which weighed everything down and caused the boats to tip perilously. Added to this was a nearly weeklong Atlantic gale, which the British soldiers sarcastically called a "touch of wind," and the Americans dubbed a "fresh breeze." The ships creaked so unbearably in the soaring swells that the soldiers thought the whole vessel might break apart. The low supply of American food—just canned baked beans and chocolate—was also far from satisfactory. There were orders not to throw anything overboard should an enemy U-boat get hold of it, and smoking on the deck after hours would get you thrown in the ship's jail. The glow of the cigarette would make it easy to be spotted. The only upside was that everyone got to know someone new because the units were mixed deliberately inside the boats.

Alexandre's journey on the LST 199 from Casablanca to Swansea, Wales, took eleven days. On arrival, General Leclerc was right there on the quay to greet them in the drizzle—a true honor.

In New York, Paul was extremely anxious about Alexandre. He knew his son was back in England but had received no news for weeks. Margot was in a state of panic, imagining that every rocket and bomb was directed specifically at Alexandre. Business-wise, the art market was picking up, but once Paul sold a Picasso or Braque painting it was impossible to get new work from those artists, who remained stuck behind enemy lines.

In Paris, Picasso's friend group had suffered tragedies. The previous year, his Jewish friends, including the artist Max Jacob, were forced to wear a yellow star. Now, they were disappearing. The surrealist poet Robert Desnos was deported to Auschwitz. Max Jacob was sent to a concertation camp. Matisse's daughter and estranged wife, who were working in the Resistance, were arrested and imprisoned as well.

Despite the dreadful news, Picasso kept creating. He said, "It is not time for the creative man to fail, to shrink, to stop working. . . . There is nothing else to do but work seriously and devotedly, struggle for food, see friends quietly, and look forward to freedom." He was also making a stance of his own by casting sculptures using precious metals earmarked at the foundry for German military use. At night, his Resistance friends helped move the bronzes in wheelbarrows to Picasso's studio, concealing the sculptures with garbage. It was a small but symbolic gesture of defiance.

In London, the bombing resumed, reminding Winnifred of the early days of the blitz. Since then, both the British and the Germans had improved the technology and payload capacity of their rockets. She had a narrow escape when a bomb shard tore through multiple layers of window coverings and crashed into the wall above her head. She managed to duck and throw herself onto the floor just in time. She wrote to Paul, "I must tell you that if the majority of us are truthful, we are finding the experience a great deal less 'glamourous' and certainly more upsetting than in those days. The din is terrific;

so much more heavier stuff going up into the air and heavier stuff is coming down."

Everyone in England could feel that something big was coming. While Alexandre was somewhere at sea between Casablanca and Swansea, Wales, Winnifred wrote to Paul, "There is that breathless hush which precedes every storm and the hush becomes quieter and more insistent as the great day approaches."

For Alexandre, a three-hundred-mile journey through the backroads of England lay ahead once he arrived in Swansea. Despite language barriers, the British were pleased to welcome the mix of French, African, and Middle Eastern soldiers. At his division's new camp in Yorkshire, Alexandre and his fellow soldiers rigorously practiced their artillery skills. General George S. Patton Jr., the brash three-star general of the US Third Army, showed up wearing polished knee-high cavalry boots, a lacquered helmet affixed with his three gold stars, pink-hued riding breeches, and a well-fitted olive-green military jacket. An ivory-handled pistol sat snugly in his belt holster. Even the sartorially-minded French found Patton's battle dress quite elegant, albeit a little flashy. The French soldiers confused his cavalry boots for cowboy boots and the ivory gun grips for pearl, and Patton is said to have told a similarly misinformed reporter, "Only a pimp from a cheap New Orleans whorehouse would carry a pearl-handled pistol."

PARIS

SPRING 1944

ROSE HELD BRUNO LOHSE SOLELY RESPONSIBLE FOR THE SCHLOSS COLlection debacle and believed that he had organized it "against the will of Göring, who had telegraphed him to stay out this affair." Lohse would never admit full responsibility in his lifetime, but by the spring of 1944, he seemed to sense that his tenure at the Jeu de Paume might end sooner than he had hoped, either due to the war or his own political situation, and he began taking greater risks.

Lohse pilfered more than sixty modern and impressionist paintings by the likes of Picasso, Matisse, Berthe Morisot, Marie Laurencin, and Maurice Utrillo from the Jeu de Paume and was planning to sell them to the Aryan administrator of the Wildenstein gallery. Robert Scholz, Alfred Rosenberg's director of Pictorial Arts in Berlin, was initially bewildered by the theft. "How this could happen is an enigma to me," he wrote to his superior, initially believing that Lohse and Borchers had only been grossly negligent in their management of the ERR. In a seemingly unironic tone, he contended, "It can be said that it is out of the question that any worker could have taken these 71 paintings in his briefcase."

However, it became obvious to Scholz that there was "only one possibility, that the theft was committed with complicity of forces that participate in our work." There were only a couple suspects who could pull off a theft of this scale.

Rose discovered the details from Helga Eggemann, who now confided in her about Lohse's indiscretions. Scholz cancelled the deal and had the paintings shipped back to the Jeu de Paume. Lohse personally brought back seven additional paintings that were going to be part of a second deal. He was in a terrible mood. Rose reported gleefully to Jaujard, "It is Lohse who bites the dust this time."

Rose now suspected that Lohse was trying to sell directly to Hitler instead. She saw him take three paintings, including one by Rembrandt, and ship it to Hitler's home in Munich.

Lohse was also continuing to seize properties in the Unoccupied Zone. He deemed a house on the waterfront in Cannes "one of the most beautiful properties" on the Côte d'Azur and emptied it with his SS man Walter Fleischer and Hitler's representative, art historian Erhard Göpel.

Meanwhile at the Louvre, Rose examined an Antoine Coypel

painting that Germany wanted to exchange for a painting in a French museum. Rose found the inventory number R.2251 written in both ink and chalk on the back of the painting. Suspecting that it was an ERR inventory number from the Édouard de Rothschild collection, she went to consult the records at the Jeu de Paume.

She discovered that R.2251 was missing from the books, even though all the numbers preceding and following it were there. In 1942, Göring had taken R.2251, which was then removed from the inventory, and he was now "offering" it back to France as if it had belonged to Germany all along. He hoped to exchange it for the *Belle Allemande* and his other desires. Rose told Jaujard it was "very likely a new 'trick' by Lohse." Very little escaped her.

At the Jeu de Paume, Rose became better acquainted with Walter Borchers, the German art historian in charge of the staff at the Jeu de Paume, who was currently in need of allies. Lohse and the others tried to pin all the recent thefts on him. The Gestapo wanted to send him to a concentration camp for his repeated comments against the Third Reich, and Göring wanted to send him to the front. His very survival depended on getting rid of Lohse once and for all.

As summer approached, there was a collective sense that the tide of the war was about to turn. "A sort of uncertainty seems to reign," Rose told Jaujard. "Important events are expected." In New York, Paul Rosenberg was cautiously optimistic and wrote to Winnifred in London, "I hope and really believe that in the near future we shall be able to resume our conversations not by written word but verbally. What a wonderful day that will be."

All of the museum's German art historians worried about being sent to the front. Lohse loudly proclaimed his desire to serve, but Rose could see through his veneer. A conveniently timed broken ankle, allegedly suffered while skiing, temporarily kept him out of military service.

As Lohse's position at the Jeu de Paume became more and more precarious, however, Rose was increasingly seen as an inconvenient witness who had seen too much. Kurt von Behr revived his order to make Rose "disappear," which meant, in her case, deportation and execution once she was taken over the border into Germany. Would von Behr want to keep her or any other witnesses of his war crimes alive? "It was unlikely!" Rose later maintained. It was up to Lohse now to decide the timing of her demise.

YORKSHIRE, ENGLAND

JUNE 6, 1944

EVERYONE FROM THE 2ND DB WAS RIVETED BY THE RADIO, WHETHER AT camp or listening over breakfast tea in one of the Yorkshire cottages hosting them. On the morning of June 6, 1944, over 160,000 Allied soldiers made a surprise landing on the beaches of Normandy. The men and women of the 2nd DB erupted in cheers. The battle for France had begun.

As much as they wanted to, Alexandre Rosenberg and the 2nd DB were never going to be the first to land in Normandy. Assault infantrymen, paratroopers, and commandos were needed first to open the path for the two million soldiers who would later flood into France. Once the lines of battle were delineated, armored units were more effective. The goal of the 2nd DB, upon its arrival in France, was to liberate Paris.

On June 6, airborne divisions pummeled the eastern and western flanks of the beaches to allow the Allied forces to land. The nicknames of these sandy, soon-to-be bloody swaths would be seared into collective memory forever: Utah, Omaha, Gold, Juno, and Sword. To confuse the Germans, who still believed the Allies would invade at the narrowest point of the English Channel, a deception operation was underway, replete with a dummy invasion of tanks and airplanes created by

Hollywood set designers, a flurry of false communications, and a real commander—the appropriately theatrical General George Patton—in charge of the fictitious First US Army Group. The French Resistance, working with the British Special Operations Executive (SOE), sabotaged rail lines, telecommunication cables, and power stations within France, with orders delivered in an onslaught of coded radio messages, most of which were poetic but meaningless.

It became clear that, despite the capture of the Normandy beaches, the battle for France would be grueling. If the Allied soldiers survived on the beaches and successfully climbed the steep cliffs defended by German gunners and blockhouses, they would then need to navigate an endless array of small farms full of tall, thick, irregular hedges, ditches, and embankments behind which the enemy could hide.

Because of those obstacles, the 2nd DB still expected to see action. "What a great day! We are burning with impatience to get into the fight," wrote one of Alexandre's fellow soldiers in the 3rd RAC. A soldier in Guy Lévy's anti-aircraft battalion noted, "The beginning of the end. Soon it will be our turn to go. Quickly let it end!"

In New York, Alexandre's father was introduced to General Charles de Gaulle. The leader of Free France was in the United States to meet with US President Franklin Delano Roosevelt to garner American support for France's future reconstruction and encourage American leadership to help rebuild a new world oriented toward peace. De Gaulle spent four days in Washington, DC, before arriving in New York City, where he was greeted by Mayor Fiorello LaGuardia and a crowd of more than twenty thousand people at City Hall. De Gaulle then visited the France Forever office with prominent figures in his movement, including Paul Rosenberg, who had a chance to shake de Gaulle's hand, and attended a reception at the Waldorf-Astoria Hotel. "Tell Kiki that I have met his big boss," Paul wrote to Winnifred, not knowing that his son was about to deploy for France.

On July 16, 1944, forty days after D-Day, the 2nd DB received official orders to enter France. The first part of their mass relocation began the next day. Suddenly, the men were confronted with what it would mean to go back to their country, to no longer be in exile. Were they not defined by exile? So many boys had become men since they left their homeland, a place they might not recognize anymore.

General Leclerc's aide-de-camp, Christian Girard, wrote in his diary, "What will we find on the other side? . . . For four years now, we've only thought about returning to France. We've talked about it like a dream. We find ourselves in a void, thinking that this is it, that it's for tomorrow. I juggle with the idea without being able to believe it."

In a little over two weeks, Alexandre would be at Utah Beach. So would Lieutenant James Rorimer, an American art curator from the Metropolitan Museum of Art, who would soon become an important part of Rose's life.

JEU DE PAUME

BEGINNING OF AUGUST 1944

ROSE NOTICED A CONSIDERABLE MOOD SHIFT AT THE JEU DE PAUME. Panic was in the air. She had wondered when the fear would manifest. After the invasion of Normandy, it had been business as usual inside the Jeu de Paume, much to Rose's consternation. In fact, she thought it curious that the Germans seemed to *regain* their confidence. Maybe they were simply in denial. Whether in defiance or as a last desperate measure, they mounted a new exhibition in the middle of June. Who on earth would come to see it now? Certainly not Hermann Göring or Alfred Rosenberg.

About thirty paintings by Fragonard, Degas, and other artists hung on the walls; busts by Boldini, Jean-Baptiste Carpeaux, and Jean-Antoine Houdon were displayed alongside a Greek-style amphora with animal-shaped handles, as well as some eighteenth-century furniture, including a beautiful boudoir. Most were from the Weil-Picard apartment, recently vacated by a German officer who left after the Normandy landings.

But dramatically, people were disappearing, and strange things were happening. Rose learned that a German secretary married to a Frenchman had been arrested on espionage charges. Another secretary was missing and had listed a fake home address. It was incredible that Rose was still spying incognito, although she could be discovered at any minute.

It was a curious feeling to wait for your inevitable arrest when you worked in the Resistance. You lived your life normally, hoping you were still under the radar but knowing full well that at any given moment, the Gestapo or some other menacing German servicemen might show up at your door and cart you away. It was as if your identity was split in two.

Many knew it was only a matter of time. Boris Vildé, the leader of Agnès Humbert's Resistance group, told her laughingly, not long before he was arrested and executed, "Dear Agnès, we're all going to end up in prison, as you very well know." Humbert herself was currently at a forced labor camp in northern Germany, not far from the Dutch border. Her death sentence was commuted because she was a woman. But now a sadist was in charge of her prison camp, and the Germans were running eugenics experiments inside.

ART CONFISCATIONS CONTINUED THROUGH THE end of July when everyone at the Jeu de Paume began strategizing for their own survival. The first to try to save himself was the ERR's main collaborationist dealer, Gustav Rochlitz, who started using the Jeu de Paume's services to ship all of his possessions, including paintings and furniture, to Switzerland

and to an ERR depot in Bavaria. The fact that he was seeking shelter with the ERR in Germany was all the proof Rose needed of the dealer's deeply entrenched ties to the Nazi organization.

Next, Bruno Lohse made a melodramatic exit with a revolver in his belt, enthusiastically announcing his intention to fight in Normandy. "Lohse sets off with great fanfare," Rose reported to Jaujard. But true to form, he returned only two days later with a van full of chickens, butter, and a lamb to roast. The spoils supplied a grand feast at von Behr's office, a last supper of sorts.

It was indeed the beginning of the end. The last mass deportation train from Paris, with thirteen hundred Jews on board, left on July 31. In total, seventy-six thousand Jews were deported by train to concentration camps in Germany and Eastern Europe from France; eleven thousand were children. Only twenty-six hundred men, women, and children would survive. This last convoy took 986 adults and 324 children, including eighteen infants, to Auschwitz, where most would be put into gas chambers and killed directly on arrival on August 5, 1944.

For several years, clandestine newspapers and pamphlets, many published and distributed by the Resistance within the SNCF, protested the deportations. One denounced Vichy for handing over Jews "like cattle to the German authorities," but there was little knowledge of where the trains ultimately went or what happened to the people who were deported. Under Vichy law, trains could only be driven by the French and not by foreigners, so the SNCF transported more than 150,000 people to the German border where they went on, in German trains, to concentration and extermination camps. The full scope of the atrocities in the extermination camps was not well known until after the war.

As trains passed through rail stations, people on the platform would run alongside and grab scraps of paper that the deportees slipped through the open slits of the train cars with messages for the people they loved. By delivering these notes, individual French people, under the boot of the Germans, made small acts of compassion and resistance, even if they would not learn of the plight of the Jews and other detainees until much later.

The ERR was now frantically putting its affairs in order. The Allied forces that had landed in Normandy on D-Day continued their march toward Paris, making way for the imposing Third Army, led by General Patton, which arrived on French shores a month later.

A train was allocated for the departure of the ERR staff from France, who received orders to pack and ship all the artwork that was still in the Jeu de Paume, plus the museum's photography workshop. All over Paris, German soldiers emptied offices and piled archives, documents, and precious stolen art into trucks. Rose noted a frenzied rush with an added urgency that did not exist before: survival.

For good measure, Rose demanded that the Germans make an inventory of what was being packed and sent. The staff was too discombobulated to rebuff her request and gave a vague promise that it would be done, likely just to appease her. The Allies were expected to arrive in Paris in less than two weeks.

NORMANDY, FRANCE

AUGUST 1, 1944

ALEXANDRE ROSENBERG DISEMBARKED AT LOW TIDE ON UTAH Beach at 1 a.m. on the first of August, nearly two months after D-Day. The moon illuminated the misty dunes like a silvery veil. In the distance, a shell burst here and there, briefly lighting up the night sky. Bomb-laden barrage balloons, tethered by nearly invisible wire, flitted in the breeze, ready to entrap the German planes that circled overhead.

Alexandre and his fellow French soldiers streamed out of the gaping open mouth of the landing ship tank and ran ashore. Some, completely overcome, dropped to their knees, pressed their lips to the sand, and cried with joy. They raised their hands, fingers grasped around the salty soil, and gazed deeply at it through their tears. It was unseasonably cold and windy, but the weather made no difference to them. Nor did the heavy oil and diesel-laden smoke or the loud clanging coming from the beached ships. The men were home, at last.

By the time General Leclerc was allowed to disembark at around 11 a.m., the beach was nearly desolate. A makeshift flag with the Free France insignia flapped from his ship, made overnight by an American captain and his crew as a moving tribute to the Free France leader. Wearing a flat-topped kepi hat and a long raincoat, holding his lucky cane, Leclerc walked silently down the metal pontoon jetty with his aide-de-camp, Christian Girard. Leclerc murmured, "It's a funny feeling." Girard responded spiritedly, "It's very satisfying!"

Photographers and cameramen swarmed them. Leclerc brushed off the newsmen who wanted him to repeat his walk ashore, stating drily, "No, we're at war. Leave me alone." But his mood improved once he met the amiable American General Walton H. Walker on the beach. The local camembert cheese and butter at HQ worked wonders, as did his meeting with General Patton.

Soon, Leclerc was zipping back and forth in a jeep through the French countryside to size up the military situation. Bullets whizzed by his head, but being on the front line with his soldiers made him feel alive again. The closer he was to danger, the more at peace he felt. There, body and mind fused to produce a clarity that he could only find on the battlefield.

Two days later, thirty-nine-year-old Lieutenant James Rorimer, an officer in the Monuments, Fine Arts, and Archives section of the US

Army, landed on Utah Beach in a Free French ship, too. "I had an idea that I would like to land on French soil with French troops," he said. Rorimer was the art historian and curator at the Metropolitan Museum of Art in New York, acclaimed for overseeing the construction of the Cloisters. He was conversant in French, German, Spanish, and Italian in addition to his native English.

Rorimer had a vastly different mandate from his shipmates. He was tasked with preserving cultural sites by issuing warnings in advance of military offensives and protecting those monuments after battle. It was the first unit of its kind in modern warfare.

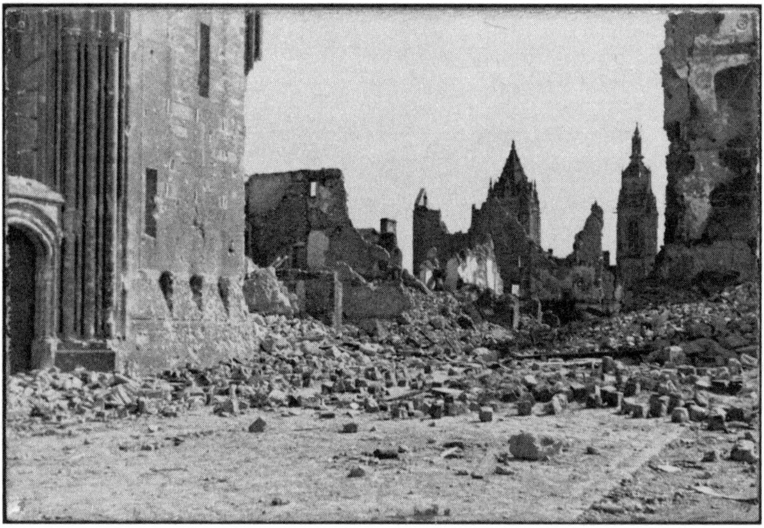

Photograph of cultural damage in Normandy taken by James Rorimer in August 1944.

The devastation left by the German retreat was sobering. Some villages were almost entirely decimated. Rubble blanketed the ground amid the jagged remains of centuries-old buildings, collapsed medieval abbeys, and churches. A heavy layer of dust carpeted everything. In a last gasp, the Germans even booby-trapped historic monuments in the most unexpected places—a church altar, a bank safe, and dead bodies. German tanks and anti-aircraft guns sat like wrecked relics. These were the final testaments to a failed last stand.

In the first week, the armored tanks and jeeps of Alexandre's battalion traversed only about ninety miles south through Normandy's ravaged villages. On August 8, they were still more than 200 miles west of Paris near Avranches but would soon pick up the pace. The French and the Americans were fighting seamlessly in tandem. Patton's Third Army stunned the Germans with its sheer force, speed, and efficiency. The 2nd DB was the perfect wingman, confident and euphoric, moving nimbly and constantly. Leclerc was pleased with the Americans, commenting, "They're a little crazy and that's what it takes to make a good soldier." Captain Thomas E. Cassidy, an American in the US 3rd Armored Division assigned to liaise with Leclerc, was equally impressed by the 2nd DB's "free-wheeling and hard-fighting attitude." The division was not simply following right in the footsteps of the Americans, but "moving with us, across us, through us, behind us, parallel with us, and generally just moving!" Captain Cassidy reported. The American 250th Field Artillerymen, attached to Alexandre's artillery battalion, learned the modus operandi quickly. When they asked the French what the route was, Leclerc told them, "We don't know! Just follow us!"

As for the art protection, the Château de Sourches was perilously close to the German airfield and military installations at Le Mans. The castle contained the large history paintings from the Louvre, including *The Raft of the Medusa* and *Liberty Leading the People*, and Boucher's *Diana Coming Out of the Bath*. Louvre director Jacques Jaujard sent a letter to the Kunstschutz, warning the Germans to stay clear of it.

Despite the destruction around them, most of the local men and women were elated to see the troops. They lined the streets, even during the night, waving and cheering, welcoming their countrymen like prodigal sons. "*De Gaulle! Vive de Gaulle!*" and "*Bravo pour le Tchad!*"

they shouted. "We were waiting for you!" The villagers ran close to the vehicles and reached up, wanting to shake hands with the soldiers, especially Leclerc's. As the tanks rolled by, they tossed up flowers, cheese, wine, brandy, and the famous local cider.

A pattern of "liberating and celebrating" set in, and the Americans lucky to be attached to the 2nd DB experienced jubilant French hospitality after every success. Leclerc planned troop movements around where he could procure a great feast and champagne—a mayor he knew here, a Resistance fighter he knew there. The lower ranks were no less fêted. The French bivouacs, spread out over the fields of Normandy, were like summer camps with roaring fires, free-flowing wine, and jovial soldiers who flowed in and out of the local houses. Not far away, the Germans must have been perplexed. The French were behaving as if they had already won. The adrenaline of the Normandy landings galvanized the Allied soldiers to fight harder and live harder than ever before.

Soon, however, Alexandre and the 2nd DB would have their first brush with danger on French soil.

JEU DE PAUME

AUGUST 1, 1944

FOR FOUR YEARS, ROSE FRETTED OVER THE MODERN PAINTINGS IN the Salle des Martyrs as if they were her children. At first, she was hopeful. Maybe Jaujard would figure out a way to save them, or the Germans would somehow forget about them—an optimistic flight of fancy. Then, as the paintings began to vanish, Rose feared what the Germans had in store for them. She tracked many of the exchanges, but even the bottomless avarice of Bruno Lohse and his art-dealing friends was not enough to make all the modern paintings disappear. There were simply too many. Then, on that summer day in 1943, her fear turned to horror as paintings were mutilated and burned in front of her eyes. Even so, around a thousand modern works of art still remained. Now, at the eleventh hour, vigilant Rose could see that something was afoot.

The modern paintings were problematic throughout the war. And now, as the Allied forces inched closer, they were also too valuable to destroy because they could be sold to fund the remainder of the war in Eastern Europe. They were also still tempting to avaricious individuals like Colonel Kurt von Behr, who had no intention of leaving such treasures behind.

As Alexandre Rosenberg and the 2nd DB landed in Normandy, Rose witnessed the final maelstrom surrounding the stash of modern art. Nearly a thousand paintings, fifty sculptures, and high-end furniture and decor were packed and placed into 148 crates. It was a masterful collection of canvases by the world's most famous living artists, as well as valuable impressionist paintings. Many of Paul Rosenberg's artworks were here as well and had escaped both the mass bonfire and the many art exchanges due to their quality and value.

Rose wrote down all the information stenciled on the crates—artist names like Picasso, Braque, Matisse, Cézanne, and Manet—along with the crate numbers, their destinations, and the abbreviations that indicated the original owners. She knew the Jewish family names so well by now, too—Kann, Lévy, Weil-Picard, Rothschild, Rosenberg, and so many more. Other crates were only labeled "Modern paintings," but Rose was able to detail what was inside them as well.

The artworks would be sent temporarily to the ERR's Nikolsburg depot in Czechoslovakia. From there, they could be sold to various Swiss art dealers to benefit the Third Reich without ever entering Germany.

On August 1, five Wehrmacht trucks arrived on the terrace of the

Jeu de Paume to whisk the modern art away. Rose watched the trucks leave but secretly got ahold of von Behr's dispatch sheets and jotted down the letters and numbers:

C.M.D.Z. 122.369
Italia 1.004.288
Kassel 18.043
Munchen 54.802
Munchen 26.331

This combination of destinations and numbers could mean only one thing: the art would leave France by train. Rose was jubilant, quite proud of her own sleuthing, and relieved at the lucky turn of events. "It was with great satisfaction," Rose later recounted, "that I learned that the convoy was headed to a train station." The SNCF was rife with Resistance operatives who could help stop the train. If the art left by truck, it would have been harder to stop because the crates would be divided into numerous vehicles, the drivers would likely be German, and they could take any number of routes to the border. The crates would now stay together, and, equally importantly, they would not leave right away due to the current bottleneck on the railway. It just might buy Rose enough time to save the art, even if that was the last thing she would ever do.

She got in touch directly with her Resistance contact Pierre-Louis Duchartre, informing him of the latest piece of intelligence. Duchartre served as a key information gatherer for the Resistance and passed the information Rose collected onto his people in the Résistance-Fer within the SNCF. Formed in 1943 with the support of the SNCF director, the Résistance-Fer merged numerous railway Resistance groups already in operation.

Rose had been in regular communication with Duchartre throughout the war, which meant that she was, in fact, working two prongs of

Resistance simultaneously: first, through her reports to Jacques Jaujard, who passed them on to Charles de Gaulle's Free France in London, and second, with Resistance networks within France itself.

In the face of the impending liberation of Paris, the Résistance-Fer was working overtime to sabotage as much train traffic as possible to prevent the Germans from escaping the country and to delay the delivery of military supplies and forces. *Of course there are ways to stall the train*, the Résistance-Fer workers told Duchartre.

SAINT-SENIER-DE-BEUVRON, FRANCE

AUGUST 8, 1944

THE 2ND DB'S FIRST CASUALTIES CAME THE NIGHT OF AUGUST 8 AS they camped at Saint-Senier-de-Beuvron, southeast of Mont Saint-Michel, an island abbey now overrun by riotously drunk American soldiers. German planes roared overhead and relentlessly bombed the command post of Alexandre's battalion for twenty-five long minutes. "We see black dots in free fall, followed by deafening explosions. . . . The bombing seems interminable, we are horrified. Where are our companions?" recounted Edith Vézy of the Rochambelles, the all-female ambulance corps of the 2nd DB.

The air smelled of burnt metal, fresh blood, and seared grass. Army vehicles were twisted up and beyond repair. The Rochambelles made repeated round trips overnight, taking the injured to the hospital. In total, twenty people were killed, and two hundred were wounded. "The arrival here was so cheerful, and here is the horrible reality," Vézy wrote. In an instant, the 2nd DB was confronted with the realities of war.

JEU DE PAUME

AUGUST 8, 1944

ALL THE MEN AT THE ERR, INCLUDING BORCHERS AND LOHSE, RECEIVED orders to report immediately for military service to defend the Reich. The most recent director of the ERR in Paris, Dr. Walter Rehbock, simply abandoned his post. He told Göring that he no longer wanted to deal with the Jeu de Paume and that Lohse, who was responsible for the mess they were in, should be the one to figure it out.

On August 5, Lohse sent a telegram to Göring, hoping to escape military duty once again. Following up by telephone, Lohse convinced Göring to exempt him from service and allow him to stay in Paris to protect the Jeu de Paume from "subversive elements" that might infiltrate it if everyone left. Instead, Lohse fled Paris hours after receiving permission to remain, leaving Borchers alone to finish liquidating the Jeu de Paume. Borchers, now the most senior person in charge, dismissed all the staff in a panic and headed to the front in Normandy.

As a last farewell, Borchers left behind the remaining large statues from the Édouard de Rothschild mansion at the Louvre, as he had promised to Rose, instead of shipping them to Germany. He also left the vitrines—the glass display cases that Rose had long admired and thought could be useful for future exhibitions at the Jeu de Paume. He wanted to leave his collection of books to Rose as well, but she warned him that they would just be taken as a war prize.

Rose was worried that Lohse or von Behr would return to Paris to ensure that the art train left for Germany. She told Jaujard ominously that they would be tempted to "suppress not only the traces of their deeds, but also the witnesses." Rose would obviously be the first on their list.

Then, the military guards at the Jeu de Paume left as well. "Ouf!" Rose wrote to Jaujard in relief. "Is this really the end?" she asked him.

ALENÇON, FRANCE

AUGUST 12, 1944

AFTER THE DEADLY AERIAL BOMBARDMENT, ALEXANDRE ROSENBERG and the 2nd DB headed rapidly south and then northeast to Alençon, crossing over 160 miles in less than twelve hours. By midday on August 12, Alexandre was defending the southern entrance to the city, 150 miles southwest of Paris, alongside the Americans.

At the same time, Alexandre's friend Lieutenant Guy Lévy left on a reconnaissance mission with three soldiers under his command toward the northwest outskirts of Alençon. Guy was known as a fighter who wanted to be "where the heat was on." They were ambushed by German forces on a small path near an airfield. In the mêlée, Guy managed to capture a prisoner but was shot near the heart while leading the charge and returning fire. His last words were simply, "I am wounded."

His men delivered Guy back to camp, where Alexandre cradled the body of his childhood friend. They had survived the last four years together and had not been separated since their exhilarating embarkation on the *Batory* from Saint-Jean-de-Luz in June 1940. It was gut-wrenching to lose Guy after they had finally made it back to France.

In New York and London, respectively, Paul and Winnifred were devastated by the news. "Gently inform Guy's brother," Paul wired to Winnifred, while fearing for Alexandre, whom he had not heard from in seven weeks. Paul was also concerned about the welfare of Guy's parents, who had been deported from France in the summer of 1943. "How terrible it will be for the parents—if they are still alive—when they find out about the death of their youngest and beloved son," Paul continued in a letter. Unknown to him or anyone else, Guy's parents had been murdered four months earlier, on April 18, 1944, in the gas chambers at Auschwitz.

Alexandre appeared to be suffering mightily from the loss. At times, when a gunshot was fired near him, he would freeze. Alexandre's condition was known to several men in the 2nd DB, including his superiors, and was undoubtedly a traumatic stress response to fighting on the front line day after day.

Alexandre's first foray into combat was not an easy one, and a perilous journey still lay ahead before Paris could be in his sights.

AUBERVILLIERS, FRANCE

AUGUST 12, 1944

AS ROSE PREDICTED, COLONEL KURT VON BEHR HAD RETURNED FOR the train. Ever greedy, he could not resist adding forty-seven railcars of seized furniture. It had taken almost two weeks for the soldiers, utterly untrained in handling fine objects, to stuff everything onto the train. "Where are we at?" von Behr asked repeatedly while at the Jeu de Paume. "Are these paintings leaving?"

At first, the Germans had been in control of the train. They sealed five railcars of art and put a special military guard on watch. But once the train was fully loaded, the Resistance rail workers knew they needed to stall. At first, they told the Germans that the rail switches were broken. Then they told them that the convoy was too heavy, which was perfectly plausible, given that there were over fifty train cars filled to maximum capacity with heavy objects. Then, a series of small mechanical issues cropped up. The art train was now waiting on a siding next to the gas tanks at Aubervilliers on the northern outskirts of Paris.

A general strike in France, initiated by the protest of a thousand railway workers, helped cause the delay. The railways were congested with both passengers and freight, as the Germans made a getaway from France. "We did it," Rose wrote prematurely to Jaujard.

With the 2nd DB still fighting in Normandy, the train could still leave France forever if the Resistance could not figure out another excuse to delay.

THE LOUVRE

AUGUST 15, 1944

JACQUES JAUJARD COULD NOT BELIEVE WHO HAD JUST APPEARED IN HIS office in the Louvre. It was Hitler's new commander in chief of Paris, General Dietrich von Choltitz. The High Command in Berlin wanted confirmation that the Bayeux Tapestry was still in the museum.

The Bayeux Tapestry had arrived at the Louvre in June, taken to

Paris by force by the SS in the middle of the night from the Château de Sourches for "safety reasons." It was now in its fourth home in five years. Jaujard would need to stop the Germans from taking the tapestry with everything he could muster.

With the Resistance rising, a general strike unfolding, and the Allied forces approaching, only Himmler, or Hitler himself, could have sent von Choltitz. Even with France slipping through their grasp, the Germans were determined to procure whatever spoils might still be left in the country.

PARIS

AUGUST 15, 1944

IN AUBERVILLIERS, THE TRAIN FULL OF ART FINALLY BEGAN TO ROLL out of the station. The railway Resistance workers had exhausted all their delay tactics at the depot. As the fifty-two-car train rumbled out of view heading northeast, von Behr must have believed his mission was complete. However, many groups of people had joined forces to try to stop the train. There were Rose, Jaujard, and the Musées Nationaux team, as well as Duchartre and his Résistance-Fer.

Rose was willing to try everything at this point. She wondered how she could convince the overwhelmed SNCF to officially intervene and stop the train once and for all. It might seem insubordinate for a lowly museum curator to ask for a train to be sabotaged. So, she went to see Jacques Jaujard and asked him to "do the impossible." She pressed him to intercede with the SNCF to prevent the train from departing France.

Less than two miles out, the train broke down—another gift from the Resistance. A worker had sabotaged the engine. The train was held at Le Bourget, the next station out, to await repairs. In the distance, Luftwaffe planes flew in and out of Le Bourget airfield. The train would sit there for the next forty-eight hours while Alexandre's battalion battered the German Seventh Army around Argentan, pounding the enemy with sustained artillery fire. General Dwight D. Eisenhower was astounded by the slaughter, calling it a scene "that could be described only by Dante. It was literally possible to walk for hundreds of yards at a time, stepping on nothing but dead and decaying flesh." But now, the Allies had just 125 miles left before they could enter the streets of Paris.

NORMANDY, FRANCE

AUGUST 19, 1944

AT THE HEADQUARTERS OF THE US ARMY'S ADVANCE SECTION IN NORmandy, Lieutenant James Rorimer expressed increasing concern about Mont Saint-Michel. The island abbey from the Middle Ages was initially spared because the rapid and high tides—anywhere between thirty to fifty feet—made its cove too dangerous as a location for the Allied invasion. It was also on a list of protected monuments, which had prevented aerial attacks so far. But now that the Americans had taken it over, the Germans might well target it.

Rorimer's new commanding officer was dismissive. "You idiot. This is twentieth-century war. Who gives a damn about medieval walls and boiling pitch?" Rorimer had heard similar dismissals from those superior to him since he had landed in Normandy. But Rorimer certainly gave quite a few damns and, with begrudging permission from the commanding officer, set off to check on Mont Saint-Michel. As no vehicle was provided to him, Rorimer alternatively hitchhiked and walked more than one hundred miles to the island.

Rorimer last saw Mont Saint-Michel as a young boy. Now, it was in a state of total chaos, but not due to the Germans. Despite several "OFF LIMITS TO TROOPS" signs, the British and Americans flowed in as fast as the tides. Thousands every day took to drinking, looting, and reveling, so much so that there was almost no food or drink left in the whole town. Electricity was cut to the island. Water was rationed. Army vehicles had torn up the cobblestones. Bars and cafés operated all night long.

Rorimer did what he could to protect the island's architecture—he posted signs, found a way to lock doors to fragile historic parapets, closed off areas, recommended a return to regular opening hours, and convinced the mayor to take away liquor licenses from any shopkeepers who continued to serve drinks to the soldiers. He went looking for someone who might be remotely in charge of what he called "indescribable bedlam" but only found Captain M. Z. Reiss of the US Air Force, who said he had no jurisdiction over ground troops.

Unfortunately Captain Reiss somehow concluded that Rorimer must be, in fact, a German spy. He was baffled by Rorimer's lack of a vehicle—what kind of officer would travel without one?—and his authority, which seemed to be higher than his rank. Reiss had no idea how little military support the Monuments, Fine Arts, and Archives officers had, or that all these curators and art historians were figuring things out as they went along in the middle of war-torn France.

Reiss hauled Rorimer to headquarters, where the bemused art curator was forced to sign various oaths and documents while his papers were examined. That was not enough, so he was then taken four miles south to Pontorson, where a Civil Affairs officer finally identified him and got him released.

Free to go, Rorimer headed to Le Mans, which was recently liberated, following at the rear of Patton and Leclerc. Top on his list was to check on the Musées Nationaux depot at Sourches. The château had survived the battle, but Rorimer found the art in bad shape. The paintings—many of the most prized artworks from the Louvre—had been stored temporarily in the humid basement for the previous few months. Open charcoal fires burned in the cellar to counteract the humidity. Rorimer feared that some of the paintings would soon be covered in a mildew that looked more like camembert cheese than art. He yelled at Louvre curator Germain Bazin, who oversaw the depot, "What! You put all your artwork in a basement? You're crazy!" Bazin would never forget the upbraiding and called Rorimer a "cow-boy" in his memoirs.

All Rorimer's work in Normandy felt like an intermission. Like Alexandre Rosenberg and the Free French forces, Rorimer had his sights set on Paris. With his qualifications, he was the perfect candidate to oversee cultural protection in the city. He spoke French fluently, had studied abroad in Paris during high school, and had connections in the French museum world, including an acquaintance with Jacques Jaujard. At HQ, Rorimer heard his name hollered out by the brigadier general.

He wondered if he might get berated again for some mysterious infraction.

Instead, he was given the news he had been waiting for: "You've got the Paris post. Get there as soon as you can. Our troops will be there sooner than you think."

PARIS

AUGUST 19, 1944

IN PARIS, THE RESISTANCE FORCES, THE FFI (FRENCH FORCES OF THE Interior), had mobilized with the police, the gendarmerie, and the

Republican Guard to help reclaim Paris. They pledged their allegiance to a new temporary government, led by Charles de Gaulle, and on August 18 the commander of the FFI ordered the Resistance to rise up and attack the police headquarters, still occupied by the Germans. Barricades went up, and guerrilla warfare took over the streets.

General von Choltitz's forces countered with tanks, bombs, and Molotov cocktails. Fighting was also rampant in the suburbs, where the art train had stalled. Meanwhile, the Allies liberated the towns and villages in Normandy one after another on the approach to Paris.

AT 11 A.M., ROSE DODGED gunshots as she crossed the Tuileries pathways to meet Jaujard at the Louvre. Firefights had broken out between German soldiers and the Resistance at both Place de la Concorde and on the Pont du Carrousel. The Louvre was caught in the crossfire, and a German tank next to the Pont des Arts kept shooting at the windows, shattering the glass.

Jaujard summoned Rose and his most trusted curators, along with the museum guards, and informed them they would need to stay at their posts twenty-four hours a day for the indefinite future. Their one objective was to guard the artistic treasures; Rose was responsible for the 524 paintings and hundreds of sculptures in the Jeu de Paume's basement and garden. There were thousands of more works of art inside the Louvre. The Louvre's head of security, Gaston Petit, coordinated the defense plan.

To prepare for combat, Jaujard asked the staff to locate the weapons that "we may have hidden in the bowels of the palace." At the Jeu de Paume, Rose had far less protection.

Now, Rose remained alone inside the museum with just two guards—with a single pistol between them—defending the works of art that had given her inspiration and spiritual guidance. She would be fighting on two fronts: one against the Nazis, still intent on stealing whatever they could, and the other against the onslaught of the battle about to commence.

The 260-foot-long museum had fifty-eight windows, almost half of which were more than seventeen feet tall, leaving Rose and the building significantly vulnerable. There were also six points of entry, plus the hatch into the former coal storage room.

While Rose was at Jaujard's office, the German museum sentries had machine-gunned the crowd outside the Jeu de Paume, which had spontaneously gathered to celebrate the impending liberation. Still, Rose felt no fear. In fact, she wished she could be with the rest of Paris, celebrating the start of their liberation. "Such outbursts of joy and enthusiasm illuminate Paris," she described of this moment, disappointed not to be part of it all.

Yet her duty was and always would be the cultural heritage of France.

The German soldiers searched the building again, only to find it completely empty apart from the art collection in the basement. The ERR had moved the last of their looted artwork to the Louvre or onto the train cars. It soon became clear that the Jeu de Paume would indeed become the German last line of defense in their desperate attempt to hold Paris. General von Choltitz identified the block of buildings across from the Jeu de Paume as one of the Germans' final support points in the war. Groups of patrols came by regularly to check the Jeu de Paume, worried there might be Resistance fighters inside. Soldiers dug bunkers inside the Tuileries Garden leading up to the museum, adding to the concrete blocks installed almost a year earlier. Then overnight, during a thunderstorm, fifty soldiers arrived at the museum. They installed rows of wooden spikes on the terrace and wrapped the defense installations with barbed wire, which gleamed with each lightning flash. The commanding officers sheltered themselves from the rain under the portico of the museum's front entrance supervising the action. Rose watched the action from inside the museum with growing trepidation.

A German soldier in a newly built watchtower now pointed his gun forebodingly at the front entrance of the Jeu de Paume—the Germans feared that all public buildings might have Resistance fighters hiding inside. Rose found this figure most unsettling, describing him as a "motionless presence that had become worrying."

The next afternoon, Rose decided it was time to examine the garden's water pipes, which would be used in case of fire. This action, part of the standard maintenance check, seemed suspicious to the guards on patrol and the Germans across the street. German soldiers promptly arrived on the scene and held Rose and her guard at gunpoint during the entire check.

The German forces that remained in Paris retreated into fortified headquarters all over the city. Ten tons of explosives protected the Senate building in the Jardin du Luxembourg. Inside the Hôtel Meurice, von Choltitz directed the German Army's last efforts. Berlin ordered him to keep the city calm. Next to the Jeu de Paume, loudspeakers blared from German vehicles, broadcasting a plea for the population to calm down and avoid unnecessary bloodshed. Choltitz sent the cars all around Paris and dropped leaflets from airplanes. He later contended that he "had to ensure that the nervous tension which was reaching its peak did not degenerate into an explosion."

From Berlin, Hitler radioed with a German order in advance of the Allied attack: "The Seine bridges will be prepared for demolition. Paris must not fall into the hands of the enemy except as a field of ruins."

Meanwhile, the Resistance finally hoisted the tricolor French flag at the police prefecture across from Notre-Dame and atop the FFI headquarters at the town hall in the nineteenth arrondissement. Rose and the curators at the Louvre yearned to raise the French flag, too, but Jaujard decided to remain cautious. "This gesture, which would have filled us with joy, could not be dared," Rose recounted.

Jaujard wanted to be sure French troops were really coming to liberate them before making such a public gesture of defiance, and his gut instinct was correct. General Eisenhower still did not plan to enter

Paris, believing it would be a waste of resources and lead to potentially high casualties. Instead, he wanted to outflank the city from the west and the east and continue the march to Germany. General Leclerc, however, had already sent a small advance detachment to Paris to ensure that the 2nd DB would be the first to enter. It was imperative for Leclerc that Paris be liberated by the French. If this riled up the American top brass, he still had those instructions from General de Gaulle in his pocket appointing him as "Interim Military Governor of Paris." If push came to shove, he would head into Paris anyway.

LE BOURGET, FRANCE

AUGUST 17–19, 1944

"VON BEHR IS BACK, AND WILL PROBABLY HAVE OUR TRAIN CARS OF modern paintings shipped," Rose noted with begrudging respect. There was a misguided courage to it, Rose thought, but in the end, Colonel von Behr was proving himself to be a tenacious, formidable foe. Everyone else, including Lohse, had already fled to Germany or reported to the front.

The colonel was clearly on edge. The engine of the art train was still malfunctioning—the work of the Resistance sabotage—and was getting repaired at the marshaling yard in Le Bourget at a sluggish pace. What was going on? The Resistance workers moved as slowly as might be believable.

Behr eventually figured out that the mechanical problems had been intentional, but he had few options left. He needed the SNCF to move the train. Surrounded by his armed guards, he petulantly walked up and down the station platform demanding the train's departure. He screamed and shouted, threatening to shoot people, but fortunately did not make good on his threats.

Finally, he had had enough. Raging, von Behr tried to take command of the train himself. He got in the cab and started tinkering with the controls.

Perhaps the Germans could pull off the theft of all time after all. "We had to act quickly!" Rose later explained. The successive dramatic events caused her to "alternate between anguish and hope." But what more could be done?

Then, Rose came up with an ingenious plan, with the agreement of the Resistance in the SNCF: they removed the locomotive all together. The long, cumbersome caravan would need to be towed to the next station from where the train was taken on a slow joy ride around the Paris outskirts. The Grande Ceinture, a railway line around Paris, was used primarily for freight. Its circular route meant the train would stay near Paris until the Allies arrived. Traffic jams on all the rail lines leading out of Paris, along with American air raids and a coal shortage, made the journey interminably slow. For days, the train circled at a snail's pace. Admitting defeat for now, von Behr retreated to his office at the avenue d'Iéna.

Finally, four days later, the train arrived at Aulnay-sous-Bois station, where it awaited a new locomotive. It was only five miles east from where it had started in Aubervilliers. It was a critical delay. After a harrowing five days, the Allies took Argentan and decimated the German Seventh Army and the Fifth Panzer Division. Alexandre Rosenberg and the artillery battalions had led that success, first by destroying enemy machine-gun installations at the outskirts of Argentan, hoping to protect the city from damage, and then by shelling the enemy when the Americans needed artillery backup. Leclerc was often at the front line, standing up in his open-air car, indicating targets with his cane. He would grab the radio to give orders directly, always ready to split the formations into smaller units to go around a challenging spot.

The Allies killed ten thousand German soldiers in their path and took fifty thousand prisoners of war. In the enemy's disorganized retreat, they lost most of their weaponry and equipment. From Argentan, Leclerc and the 2nd DB would have a direct approach east to Paris while facing a weakened enemy.

The art train, however, would not be safe until the Allies could secure it.

HÔTEL MEURICE

AUGUST 21, 1944

HITLER HAD EXPECTED GENERAL DIETRICH VON CHOLTITZ TO OBEY every command—it was, after all, what von Choltitz was known for. Earlier in the war, he destroyed Rotterdam and Sebastopol without a second thought. But in recent days, von Choltitz was doing many things contrary to Hitler's orders.

He was convinced that Hitler had gone mad. The Führer was now hunched and bloated with thinning, graying hair, high on cocaine and opioids, and bent on leaving a maximum path of destruction behind him. When angry, his entire body would shake and spasm, his face would become beaded with sweat, and his mouth would drip with saliva.

In the afternoon on August 21, von Choltitz prevented two SS commanders from taking the Bayeux Tapestry from the Louvre. He also felt with conviction that the order to blow up Paris had no military value, so he postponed the order, but soon received his own death sentence. A new order from Hitler included the following: "Paris will be transformed into a pile of rubble. The General Commander-in-Chief will defend this city to the last man, and if necessary, will be buried beneath it."

PARIS

AUGUST 22, 1944

IN PARIS, THE GERMANS MINED THE CITY'S BRIDGES AND ARCHITECTURAL landmarks. The occupying forces placed three tons of explosives on the Cathedral of Notre-Dame, two tons on the dome of Les Invalides, one ton at the Chamber of Deputies just next to the Jeu de Paume, and more on the Arc de Triomphe. The chief of staff of the Luftwaffe proposed to air bomb Paris as well.

General von Choltitz telephoned his superior, Army General-Lieutenant Hans Speidel, who was in the north of France, about the order to destroy Paris. Choltitz asked, "Wasn't it you who ordered it done?" Speidel replied angrily, "No . . . no, we did not order that. The order came from the Führer." Choltitz responded, "Excuse me, but you are the one who gave the order and you are the one who will bear the responsibility before history." Speidel agreed to spare the city.

Despite Speidel's support, von Choltitz found himself increasingly isolated. The telephone lines barely worked, and he was severely short of soldiers. Any German reserve officer left was called up, and many lacked uniforms. Seventeen-year-old boys accustomed to typing at a desk now manned anti-aircraft cannons.

Choltitz had only three hundred men—mostly from the engineering battalion—along with seventeen armored cars and four tanks, to protect the Paris headquarters of the German High Command. For him, it was a hopeless situation. The war, he told his chief of staff, was "irretrievably lost."

If he retaliated against the Resistance, it would reveal to the Allies how lightly protected he was. The only result would be damaging Paris and killing innocent bystanders, which he would not do. For the honor of the military, however, von Choltitz could not refuse the final battle with the Allied forces. In front of the officers' corps, he announced his succession plan in case he was killed.

Encouraged by news reports, the Resistance had started the insurrection too early and was now running low on ammunition as the fighting intensified by the minute. They were also convinced that the Germans would be brutal to the very end. Since the beginning of the revolt three days earlier, five hundred Parisians had been killed and two thousand more wounded. The Resistance frantically telegraphed messages to General de Gaulle and his staff to come save them.

In the evening, the 2nd DB finally got its marching orders for Paris.

At sunrise the following day, Leclerc and his loyal band pushed toward Paris. "Galloping like crazy to Paris. The division rushes onto the roads. It has wings," wrote Leclerc's aide-de-camp, Christian Girard, exuberantly. The scene was one to remember: sixteen thousand soldiers and four thousand vehicles racing at fifty miles an hour in orderly columns. The 2nd DB was flying toward its destiny, one they had awaited for four long years.

PARIS

AUGUST 24, 1944

IN THE SKIES ABOVE PARIS, A PIPER CUB AIRPLANE DROPPED A CANVAS bag that landed in the courtyard of the police prefecture, one of the headquarters of the Resistance. Inside was a message from the 2nd DB. It was written and signed by Alexandre Rosenberg's lieutenant colonel, Jean Crépin. "Hold tight, we're coming."

At the Louvre, Jacques Jaujard finally ordered the French flag to be raised. German tanks, soldiers, and top Nazi officials still surrounded the museum, but Jaujard could tell based on radio reports that the Allies were close. "We lived a moment of intense emotion seeing the three colors rise," Egyptian Art curator Christiane Desroches said of the tricolor flag waving defiantly again above the museum.

Colonel Kurt von Behr was holed up in his headquarters at the avenue d'Iéna, but he was too well-guarded by machine-gun-toting soldiers for Resistance forces to stage any kind of attack on him. "It is not possible to reach him," Rose told Jaujard, adding, "Too bad." What she had in mind was left unsaid. Not long after, von Behr left Paris for good.

In Berlin, Hitler wanted to know if von Choltitz had followed his order to destroy Paris. He radioed over: "Is Paris burning?"

LONGJUMEAU, FRANCE

AUGUST 24, 1944

IN THE PREVIOUS TWENTY-FOUR HOURS, ALEXANDRE ROSENBERG AND his battalion had traveled over 150 miles east toward Paris. At Longjumeau, ten miles south of Paris, Alexandre's artillery unit attacked German anti-aircraft weaponry installations and remained at the ready for the upcoming march to Paris.

Twenty miles north of Longjumeau, a new locomotive finally arrived for the ailing art train at Aulnay-sous-Bois. A handful of German soldiers were ordered to remain inside the train to protect the cargo, and a few reservists guarded the station.

At 2 p.m., Gaston Chauvin, a twenty-four-year-old Resistance fighter from Aulnay-sous-Bois, took a small unit to secure the train.

Gunshots rang out. The Germans were killing civilians across the street from the station. Chauvin cautiously moved forward, gun in hand. Suddenly, a sniper hiding above the train tunnel pulled his trigger. Chauvin fell dead. Another Resistance fighter met the same fate, and three others were injured. The attempt to save the art train had failed.

AT RAMBOUILLET, GENERAL LECLERC REVIEWED his plan for Paris with General de Gaulle. The 2nd DB would enter Paris through three different points. They would pretend to come in from Versailles on the west to distract the enemy with "a big noise," but the main attack would come up from the south through Chevreuse and the Porte d'Orléans. Alexandre and his men were already in Longjumeau awaiting orders. De Gaulle told Leclerc jealously, "How lucky you are! Go quickly."

That night, Leclerc pointed his cane toward the French capital and gave the order. "Head straight to Paris, enter Paris!"

Captain Raymond Dronne's small detachment of three Sherman tanks, sixteen half-tracks, and 150 men would be the first to enter the city.

HÔTEL MEURICE

AUGUST 24, 1944

GENERAL VON CHOLTITZ WAS IN THE MIDDLE OF THE MOST DEPRESSING dinner of his life. Surrounded by his most loyal officers, his chief of staff, and two secretaries, he obsessively thought about his wife and children in Germany.

Through an open window in the small dining room, he suddenly heard the bells of Paris ringing, almost all at once.

Captain Dronne, at the vanguard of the 2nd DB, had not only entered Paris but also made his way into the city center. His detachment took over the Hôtel de Ville, Paris's city hall in the Marais, and broadcast a message over the radio from a secret transmitter: "Rejoice! Rejoice! The Leclerc Division has entered Paris!" The detachment then played a recording of *La Marseillaise*. Parisians opened their windows and let the sound of their national anthem flood the turbid hot summer air.

The announcer then said, "Let the priests ring the bells of their church at full blast."

First came the deep, sonorous bell of Notre-Dame, then the higher-pitched bells of Saint-Sulpice, then the sound of the largest bells in Paris at Sacré-Cœur in Montmartre, which could be heard all throughout Paris, and then the rest. It was exactly 10:10 p.m.

At the Hôtel Meurice, one of von Choltitz's men exclaimed, "*Herr General*, what does that mean?"

"What it means?" von Choltitz responded matter-of-factly. "The American-French army is entering Paris."

From the Jeu de Paume, Rose heard the bells, too. The final battle was coming her way.

JEU DE PAUME

AUGUST 25, 1944

INSIDE THE JEU DE PAUME, ROSE AND HER GUARDS STAYED AWAKE through the night. The clamor and turmoil outside from the Germans preparing loudly for their final stand made it impossible to sleep. She and the two guards observed the chaotic activity through an ajar window.

At 5 a.m., thirteen miles south of Rose, Alexandre Rosenberg and his artillery battalion began to move toward Paris. It was a straight shot north to Porte d'Orléans, but the Germans still resisted with the strength they had left.

Many of Alexandre's soldiers had family in the city whom they had not seen in more than four years. For all the Free French fighters, Paris was the prize they kept before them. It was the goal of all the training, all the battles, the thousands and thousands of miles crossed over land, sea, and air. They had all lost friends and comrades along the way. The Germans coveted Paris for its art, its architecture, its vibrant nightlife, its food, and its sheer beauty. There was no other city like it in the world, no matter how many drawings Hitler sketched or how many models his architects made of future cities in the Reich.

The morning of August 25, 1944, was dazzlingly beautiful, with nary a cloud in sight. At the Jeu de Paume, the German soldier in the watchtower still had his gun aimed at the museum. At 8 a.m., Rose decided to come onto the doorstep to show herself, hoping that the presence of a woman would calm the German suspicions and keep them from attacking the museum. As Rose recounted, "What could the three of us do? Agree to die for nothing . . . or capitulate?" She believed she had one move left: "It was better to show them that no troops were hidden there," she wrote.

She carefully slid open a side door that led to the enclosed garden and deliberately stood in the center of the doorway. The soldier shouldered his rifle and aimed at her. She flashed her expired German *Ausweis* in a Hail Mary. It felt like an eternity, but eventually, the soldier decided not to fire. Her gamble played out, and it seemed that the Germans would leave them alone—for the time being, at least. Reflecting on this juncture later, she wrote, "I truly believe that only my initiative allowed us to choose [our fate]—before it was too late."

Nine miles northeast, at Aulnay-sous-Bois, a fire broke out in one of the art train's railcars, in a possible sabotage attempt. Firefighters extinguished it while the German guards watched. The Resistance, which had not given up on the art train, mounted another attempt to secure it. They derailed two locomotives to block off any possibility that the train could leave the station. The train might still get looted or damaged in the battles around Aulnay-sous-Bois, but it would never disappear into Germany.

At the Jeu de Paume, Rose and her guards waited for the impending arrival of the Free French.

INSIDE PARIS, THE 2ND DB liberated the neighborhoods one by one. At 1 p.m., six Parisian firefighters climbed to the top of the Eiffel Tower, evading bullets from German soldiers at the base, and replaced the Nazi flag with the French one. The tricolor flag also flew from the Arc de Triomphe shortly thereafter.

At 1:30 p.m., while Alexandre was still a few miles from Paris, the tanks of General Leclerc's 2nd DB came up the rue de Rivoli and rue du Faubourg Saint-Honoré and closed in on the Hôtel Meurice. The final battle began right next to the Jeu de Paume, where Rose long predicted it would occur. Another set of tanks barreled through the Tuileries behind the museum, tearing up the grass. The vehicles released their firepower on the Germans, clearing out their machine-gun installations and Panzer tanks.

The Germans responded in force and blew up many of the French tanks heading down the rue de Rivoli. Machine-gun fire and bazooka warheads flew from all directions. Some French infantrymen approaching on foot were killed. An outdated German tank emerged from the Tuileries but was quickly neutralized by the French. Grenades flew out of the windows of the Hôtel Meurice. In the melee, von Choltitz's command cars parked under the arcades of the hotel went up in flames.

In front of the Jeu de Paume, a Panzer at the obelisk in Place de la

Concorde wreaked havoc, shooting at the French tanks and soldiers. The marble lion guarding the museum toppled and shattered onto the sidewalk. Fifteen hundred feet away, a shell strafed Monet's *Water Lilies*, installed inside the Jeu de Paume's sister institution, the Musée de l'Orangerie, and exploded in a side room. A bullet flew through the window of Jacques Jaujard's apartment in the Louvre, narrowly missing him. As German soldiers tried to break into the museum, Jaujard ordered his employees to shoot.

Three hundred and fifty German soldiers, still in the Tuileries, found themselves at the Jeu de Paume with attacks coming from all sides. Inside the museum, Rose watched as the German soldiers hid behind the sandbagged statues in the garden, the very same statues that were too heavy for her to evacuate in 1939. Others cowered behind the iron shutters of the museum to make their last stand. The tanks of Free France surrounded the soldiers from all sides and unleashed their barrage. A young soldier died on the steps of the museum, his blood pooling beneath him. Years after, Rose could still vividly recall the color of his blood, describing the mark it left as "a stubborn brown stain." Up close to the bloodshed, Rose reflected that even the death of an enemy combatant seemed nothing other than an "abominable murder."

The Germans on the terrace surrendered swiftly.

Rose peered out from the museum into the smoky aftermath. The iron shutters were mottled with bullet holes. Nine Germans lay dead in the garden.

Rose watched as Free French soldiers arrested and marched the hundreds of German soldiers across the Tuileries Garden to the courtyard of the Louvre, where they awaited their fate beneath the watchful eyes of the sculptural mythological gods, carved into the pediments of the museum.

In the Hôtel Meurice across the street from the Jeu de Paume, the Allies flushed out the final Nazi stragglers apart from von Choltitz and his staff officers using phosphorous grenades. An FFI leader and a young Leclerc officer climbed upstairs, tossing smoke grenades on the way, and found von Choltitz in one of the rooms overlooking the inner courtyard.

The FFI leader spoke first. "*Sprechen Deutsch?*" he asked the general.

"Probably better than you," von Choltitz answered calmly in his native tongue.

A lieutenant came into the room and realized who they were speaking to. He gave von Choltitz a military salute and asked in French, "*Monsieur le Général*, are you ready to stop the fighting?"

"Yes, I am ready," von Choltitz answered. He was led out of the hotel for the surrender with General Leclerc.

At about the same time, General de Gaulle drove past Alexandre and his battalion at Antony, just under five miles from Paris. Thirty minutes later, a whistle blew, and Alexandre's final push to Paris was on.

Alexandre's battalion drove through the Porte d'Orléans at four in the afternoon to triumphant cheering. A massive crowd swarmed the tanks and jeeps. The women tried to climb up the vehicles to kiss and hug the boys, nearly taking them tumbling down. Parisians of all ages and walks of life wanted to touch the hands of the men who had come to save them. Paris was liberated by the French! They raised their tricolor flags, sang the national anthem, shouted, laughed, and cried. As in Normandy, the people bestowed champagne, wine, food, flowers, and ardent kisses.

Even amid the jubilation, Paris was still an active battlefield, and the combination of joyful celebration and continued gunfire was unsettling. German snipers were everywhere. A few of the 2nd DB were killed this way, including one soldier who had just gotten off the telephone with his parents in Paris. It was a sober reminder of the dangers that remained in a city already deliriously drunk on victory.

General Leclerc drove down the Boulevard du Montparnasse with his famous armored division and saluted the cheering throngs with his sword. The show of military force—armored vehicles, tanks, heavy trucks, and jeeps loaded with ammunition and cannons—dazzled the remaining Germans. Tall, bronzed, and proud Americans rushed into the police prefecture to shake hands and say hello to the speechless Resistance and police forces inside. A lieutenant told a young woman in uniform to write down a statement in French to leave there: "This moment is one of the most joyful for all Americans and we are very happy to arrive here to greet you. With us are 130,000 Americans who are celebrating the liberation of Paris at this moment by brave French people."

General von Choltitz signed the ceasefire and surrender orders with Leclerc at the prefecture. Then, at 4:15 p.m., he formally surrendered to General de Gaulle at Montparnasse train station. Paris was back in the hands of the French.

JEU DE PAUME

AFTERNOON, AUGUST 25, 1944

DESPITE THE GERMAN SURRENDER, A NEW BATTLE WAS ABOUT TO UNFOLD. Outside the Jeu de Paume, civilians celebrated rowdily between the tanks of the Free French, positioned just inside the balustrades of the museum's terrace. The shouts of a growing mob drowned out the singing of *La Marseillaise* as the crowd impatiently waited for the arrival of General Charles de Gaulle. Rose knew that the crowd could act as judge, jury, and executioner on this day. Elation was in the air, but so was the desire for revenge.

Next to the museum, German soldiers still positioned at the headquarters of the German High Command and the headquarters of the German Navy shot into the crowd at Place de la Concorde.

People ducked for cover or threw themselves onto the ground. Others continued walking, blithely unconcerned about the bullets. Resistance fighters and French soldiers on the nearby rooftops shot back at the German snipers. An American journalist reported the dramatic scene on the radio: "The Germans set fire to the Navy Ministry and the Hôtel [de] Crillon and the sky is ablaze. . . . These are the last jerks of the beast receiving the mortal blow."

Rose ordered the Jeu de Paume's two guards to stay inside for their own safety and to continue protecting the art, but one guard disobeyed Rose's orders and climbed up to the rooftop. Rose later recounted, "He wanted to offer himself a privileged position to view the parade, perched at the top of the museum, clearly visible and satisfied to be on the front row." That is, until he was mistaken for a German soldier. Sniper shots came from the Resistance fighters on nearby rooftops, and a cascade of bullets from the tanks hit the museum at close range. He hurried back inside the museum for safety.

Triggered by the sound of gunshots, a nervous and overwrought mob surged up from Place de la Concorde and broke into the museum, forcefully shattering the windows and prying the doors open. They rushed in toward Rose like a "human torrent" demanding justice. Rose herself was hit numerous times by the stock of a gun. The crowd wanted the guard from the roof to be punished, as the "*épuration sauvage*," the "wild purge," had already begun with extrajudicial executions and public shaming of collaborators. "The crowd is often vindictive for no reason," she later described.

Thankfully, an officer from the 2nd DB intervened. Rose defended her guard to him, but the crowd was hungry for vengeance. As she wrote, "A Leclerc army officer was kind enough to listen to my protests and trust me . . . I will always be grateful to him."

Still, the mob shouted in agitation. Who was this woman holding the keys to this known Nazi stronghold? Why was she trying to keep people out of the basement?

Rose felt the barrel of a machine gun dig into her back.

PARIS

EVENING, AUGUST 25, 1944

LIEUTENANT JAMES RORIMER ENTERED PARIS THROUGH THE PORTE d'Orléans, the same gate Alexandre Rosenberg had crossed earlier that day. Rorimer was eager to get inside the city. "Where in the world could a monuments officer be of greater service than in Paris at the moment?" he would write later.

The battle for Paris was far from over, despite von Choltitz's surrender. General Pleas B. Rogers ordered Rorimer and eight other officers to link up with an American combat unit to assist in ousting the last of the German forces. They would bring radio broadcasting equipment to improve communications from inside the city. As Rorimer entered Paris, gunshots and artillery fire continued to ring out in the outskirts, and the streets of the city were still thoroughly barricaded. A military escort led Rorimer's convoy on a meandering route to the Grand Palais to meet General Rogers, who had gone ahead into Paris. The Germans did not surrender their last stronghold until 9 p.m.

Rorimer passed by the Jeu de Paume, where Rose was fending off the mob. "The Tuileries Garden and the Champs-Élysées had seen hideous combat," Rorimer described of the scene surrounding the museum, "The bores of the guns ringing these areas were still hot from the last shells they had fired. . . . The sound of small arms fire kept our nerves jumping."

A fire inside the Chamber of Deputies smoldered. A mysterious "blacked-out" murk hung over Paris. Rorimer found nothing but fire and rubble when he arrived at the Grand Palais. The Germans had ignited the explosives stored in the building. Rorimer was billeted at the Hôtel du Louvre, down the street from the Jeu de Paume, where the sheets of German soldiers still remained on the beds. As Rorimer settled into a hot bath, Rose was fighting to save her life.

JEU DE PAUME

EVENING, AUGUST 25, 1944

ROSE HAD NO CHOICE. SHE DREADED DOING IT, BUT SHE HAD TO LEAD an exploration of the Jeu de Paume's basement. At great personal risk, she had protected the art collection there for four long years. And if there were any Germans hiding there, like the soldier she found cowering in the guard outpost earlier that morning, she would surely be shot. But this was not a crowd that would simply disappear into the night.

If she were killed now, nearly everything she knew about what the Nazis did in Paris and all the intelligence she risked her life to collect over the last four years would die with her. The museum's art that she fought so hard to protect would be looted by this unruly horde. She was a spy—an *art* spy of all things—for France!

Rose walked down the staircase to the basement, gun still held to her back. The first room clearly held nothing but paintings and sculptures. Then there was the men's bathroom, which contained a secure safe room. No lurking Germans were in either place. They found the women's bathroom empty, too, as were the locker room and guard's break room. The last two rooms—the boiler room, holding more art, and the old coal storage room—were clear of human beings.

Luck was on Rose's side. Nothing more was found. No Germans, no weapons. Not a single painting was stolen either. The museum had survived what Rose described as a "last test." Leclerc's 2nd DB soldiers protected her from the crowd, evacuated the museum, and then stood guard in front. It was a close call, but Rose was able to rejoice, knowing she narrowly escaped her own execution.

THE LOUVRE

MORNING, AUGUST 26, 1944

VICTORY CELEBRATIONS UNFOLDED ALL OVER THE CITY, PUNCTUATED by sudden violent reprisals for anyone the crowd believed was a collaborator. The Louvre curators experienced it all.

The Louvre emerged from the last battle relatively intact, but some Resistance fighters wondered how it was possible. One theory circulating was that the Germans and their collaborators had protected the museum during the firefight. Gunshots seemed to have come from the roof during the final battle, which only escalated suspicions that the museum might be a German stronghold. The FFI came to the Louvre to take the elderly curator Marcel Aubert and Gaston Petit, the head of security, for questioning at the local town hall. Then they came for Jacques Jaujard as well.

On the way to the interrogation, the Resistance fighters threatened and insulted Jaujard. "Collaborators! Traitors! Fifth column! Enemies of the people! To death! Shoot them!" they shouted. Some of them were fighters "*de la dernière minute*"—people who picked up arms only at the last minute to cover up their own inaction or collaboration in the war. They were getting ready to execute Jaujard on the spot when Robert Rey, a Louvre curator and a true Resistance operator, revealed Jaujard's identity as not only the director of the Louvre but also a member of the Resistance.

Jaujard, never one to lose an opportunity, asked the mayor to provide him with fifty police guards for surveillance and defense if the Louvre was attacked again. It was a prescient move, as the Germans did, in fact, launch an air attack on Paris that evening. A bomb fell on the Tuileries Garden, but the Louvre, once again, was unscathed.

The art train, however, waited unprotected at Aulnay-sous-Bois. The Allies had not liberated that area of the Paris outskirts yet, and German forces still defended the suburbs north of Paris. Despite everything, Rose had not forgotten the train. She sent Jaujard a terse note of reminder: "The train cars remain with us with 148 crates of art." She dragged a big black suitcase into Jaujard's office, filled with duplicate copies of the departure slips for all the art the ERR had shipped out. She also snatched one of the watchman's logbooks, which contained the names of visitors to the Jeu de Paume. It was a message to Jaujard that she was ready to go after the perpetrators of the thefts in France, and that she would not let them get away with it, if she could help it. It was not enough to simply bask in the present. France's looted art treasures still needed to be tracked down, and the criminals who stole the great artworks brought to account. Rose would keep reminding everyone of that.

CATHEDRAL OF NOTRE-DAME

AFTERNOON, AUGUST 26, 1944

GENERAL CHARLES DE GAULLE PARADED THROUGH PARIS IN VICTORY, led by the tanks of the French 2nd DB. The festivities began at the Arc de Triomphe, where de Gaulle laid a large wreath at the Tomb of the Unknown Soldier. The general then strolled with his entourage down the Champs-Élysées to Place de la Concorde. Tanks rolled alongside and cheering Parisians crammed the sidewalks holding banners that read "*Vive de Gaulle*" and "*Vive la République*." De Gaulle then headed to Notre-Dame in an open-air car flanked by a bevy of motorcycles to attend a service of thanksgiving.

Alexandre Rosenberg also participated in the celebrations. A cousin snapped a candid photograph of him, handsome and heroic, with helmet in hand, giving his shy, sideways smile. He had grown into a confident man since he had last set foot in Paris.

Alexandre's artillery regiment was given the distinction of rendering the honors at Notre-Dame and he was placed in charge of one platoon. Tanks lined the perimeter of the plaza. At about 4 p.m., as General de Gaulle stepped out of his car, gunshots disrupted the celebration. French collaborators and German snipers shot at the crowd from the apartment building next door and from inside the church itself. They still hoped to usher in maximum destruction before they were arrested or killed in action.

Alexandre ordered his men to return fire. A shootout commenced, with Resistance forces, police, gendarmes, and troops joining in. Onlookers screamed and ran for cover. Some threw themselves under and below the tanks, while others lay flat on the plaza, covering their heads. Someone waved a white flag.

De Gaulle remained standing out in the open with a lit cigarette dangling from his mouth. He then walked into the church as snipers shot repeatedly from the upper galleries. Unperturbed, he headed straight down the central aisle. He even repositioned chairs that were knocked over in the panic. The cathedral lit up with flashes of light as the bullets struck the ancient stone walls and ricocheted off. The Resistance and the police shot back. People hid below the church pews, under the chairs, and inside the side chapels. The bullets somehow missed de Gaulle every time. "*Il est vraiment magnifique!*" ("He is truly magnificent!"), marveled a radio journalist broadcasting live from inside the church.

The enemy elements may have been looking to kill de Gaulle but targeted innocent bystanders equally. Men, women, and children lay dead and wounded at what should have been a moment of great jubilation. When the shooters were finally apprehended, along with German officers in hiding, the crowd jeered, punched, and spat on them.

After restoring calm at Notre-Dame, Alexandre and his artillery battalion regrouped for the night in the south of Paris, with their vehicles camouflaged at Parc Montsouris. Danger still loomed, however. An aerial bombardment hit his battalion just before midnight, killing one of the second cannoneers and injuring four others. The Luftwaffe also heavily bombed the northern suburbs of Paris, in the very neighborhood where the art train awaited its own liberation.

AUBERVILLIERS

MORNING, AUGUST 27, 1944

AT ONE IN THE MORNING, ALEXANDRE RECEIVED AN ORDER TO CLEAR the areas north of Paris. He led his unit to Aubervilliers, where the art train had started its meandering journey almost a month before. Alexandre set up his battalion's batteries in front of the nineteenth-century fort in town. He was five miles away from the train's current location in Aulnay-sous-Bois.

Difficult fighting lay ahead. It was also unclear if the Allied forces even knew about the existence of the train yet. German forces shot at Alexandre as his unit happened to move closer and closer to the train. A battle raged all afternoon at Le Bourget, a former Luftwaffe headquarters. Corpses of dead Germans soldiers littered the airfield, killed by shells that burst mid-air. Other Germans, very much alive, hid in deep trenches and emerged unexpectedly from underground tunnels at the airport. "Heavy losses," Alexandre noted morosely in his diary about the troops on his side.

AULNAY-SOUS-BOIS, FRANCE

EVENING, AUGUST 27, 1944

ON AUGUST 27, THE SNCF ALERTED GENERAL LECLERC AND THE 2ND DB that a train at Aulnay-sous-Bois needed to be secured. As he was already nearby, Alexandre received an urgent order to seize the train and arrest any German soldiers still guarding it.

At 4:30 p.m., two American jeeps drove by the train station on a reconnaissance mission. Two hours later, US troops positioned a tank south of the station, next to where the art train was parked. A Piper Cub airplane flew overhead.

With that cover, Alexandre led a detachment of six soldiers to take the station. They quickly secured the station and then approached the train. "Hold your fire," he warned his men, in case there were prisoners inside. The doors of the cattle car, the same kind of train the Nazis had used for many brutal deeds, opened cautiously. A small number of bewildered and weary German soldiers tumbled out. They were easily taken prisoner.

Alexandre moved to examine the cargo cars. The importance of the train quickly became clear: the words "MODERNES PICASSO," "MODERNES BRAQUES," and "MODERNES MATISSE" were stenciled on the crates. One was labeled "MODERNES P.R. PARIS 20," which contained paintings Alexandre had last seen five years earlier on the walls of his family home at 21 rue la Boétie. Among the works was a cubist-style painting of a sleeping woman by André Lhote, a picture of a woman reading on a chair by fauvist artist Jean Puy, and a portrait of a man smoking a pipe by Louis Charlot.

More paintings labeled on the back with "Rosenberg-Bordeaux" came from Le Castel, the last place where Alexandre lived with his family in Floirac. He had carefully inventoried all of those works of art just before the Rosenbergs fled France. Of the approximately one thousand paintings on the train, at least 151 belonged to his father, including sixty-four of them by Picasso, more than a dozen still lifes by Braque, two dozen works by Marie Laurencin, a handful by Matisse, and a portrait by Renoir.

The train contained artwork from dozens of collectors made by the world's most renowned artists, past and present—Manet, Chagall, Degas, Gauguin, Toulouse-Lautrec, Sisley, Modigliani, Masson, de Chirico, Utrillo, Bonnard, Maurice de Vlaminck, and many others. A monumental Cézanne painting, *Bather and Rocks*, belonging to Alphonse Kann, depicted the muscular backside of a swimmer.

Alexandre did not yet know the extent to which his family's art had been looted, but as Rose would describe, it was a "beautiful revelation" for him to rediscover his family treasures in this way. Of all the soldiers in the 2nd DB, what were the chances that Alexandre would be the one ordered to secure this train? Rose called it "marvelously providential." Perhaps Alexandre overcame his fears on the battlefield and was spared in the fierce combat for France precisely for this reason.

Maybe Rose, too, survived to save this train. Later in life, she described the event with great feeling: "I won't hesitate to say that this was one of my greatest joys. To see all these paintings freed at last, found again by my country, a little bit like the soul of Paris that was defending itself, at the time, against the enemy."

Her persistence not only kept the art in France but also saved it from certain destruction. A train was bombed at the station in Czechoslovakia at the exact time the art convoy was due there. The castle where the paintings and sculptures were headed suffered heavy shelling and was gutted by fire. The art on the train, a notable part of the cultural legacy of France and Europe, was spared due to Rose's tenacity and the cunning strategies of the SNCF Resistance operators, then miraculously secured, once and for all, by Alexandre Rosenberg and the brave soldiers of the French 2nd Armored Division.

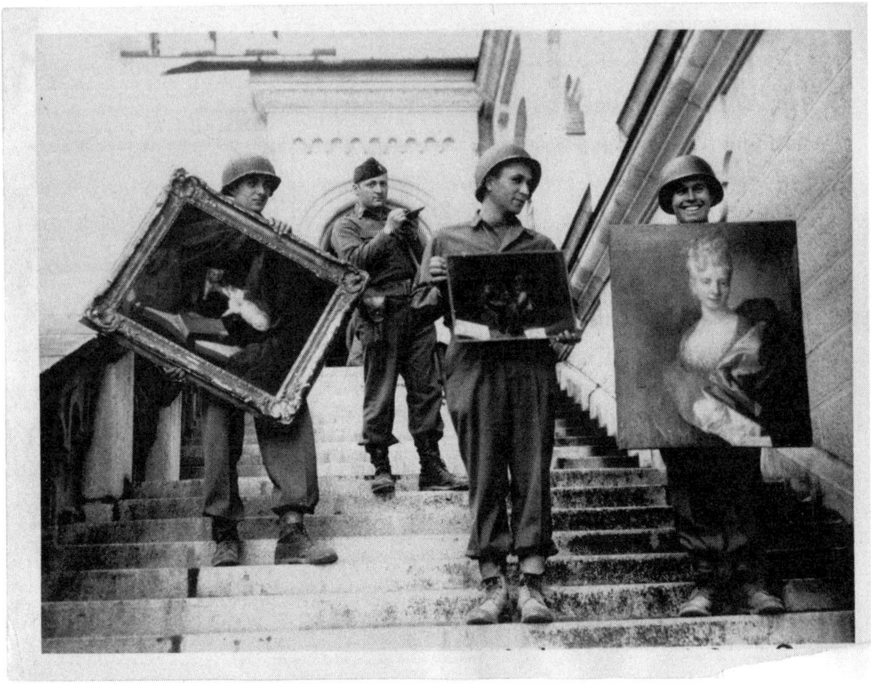

Captain James Rorimer *(second from left)* overseeing removal and restitution of art at Neuschwanstein Castle, May 1945.

PARIS

FALL TO WINTER 1944

IN A WAR WHERE RESISTANCE TOOK MANY FORMS, ROSE AND HER loyal guards at the Jeu de Paume fought to retain the humanity of those whose possessions, family histories, identities, and sometimes their lives were violently stolen from them. She did it all, as she put it, simply "to save a little beauty of the world."

Never once in four years did Rose let any concern for her own safety override her commitment to her mission. Not once did she allow her emotions to get the better of her or cloud her judgment. She played the role the Germans wanted her to, pretending to be a dutiful, timid art historian instead of the determined woman she was. At great risk to her own life, she spied and documented, stole information, was subjected to degrading searches, and was expelled from the museum on multiple occasions. Each time, she returned and skillfully convinced the Germans to let her back in.

After the liberation, Rose's role in the war was far from over. When she heard that the train had been rescued, she rushed to Aulnay-sous-Bois as fast as she could to see it all for herself. She then personally accompanied the repatriated paintings from the train back to the Jeu de Paume.

Rose laid all the paintings flat on the ground, the way she always loved to view art best. For a fleeting moment, she looked at them affectionately, one by one, as if they were hers. She then set her mind to the next important task: returning the artworks to their rightful owners.

Rose felt responsible for the Jewish-owned art collections that transited through the Jeu de Paume. Throughout the war, she hoped that the information she gathered would allow the art to be located and eventually returned.

A period of uncertainty reigned in Paris after Liberation Day. Even though Germany had officially surrendered the city, it took days to get the remaining enemy forces out of buildings and hiding places.

Lieutenant James Rorimer was in Paris to assess the damage to the city's art and architecture, but he found himself cleaning up the "unimaginable disorder" left behind by German authorities. He was also arresting AWOL American soldiers and German soldiers masquerading as French civilians. Rorimer described Paris in the weeks after liberation as "bedlam." Extrajudicial executions of suspected collaborators continued. Women suspected of having romantic relationships with Germans during the war were publicly shamed, often by having their heads shaved. For several months, the Germans continued dropping bombs near the Louvre and on the Tuileries. "If the bombardier had turned them loose just an instant later, the one that landed in the gardens would have demolished a wing of the Louvre. It was a very near miss," Rorimer reported of one incident.

Soon enough, however, he was able to turn his attention back to his actual assignment with the Monuments, Fine Arts, and Archives section. He worked closely with Jacques Jaujard and was able to prevent the Jeu de Paume from being requisitioned by the American Army, which wanted to use the museum as a post office base. He also put a stop to the use of the Tuileries as a jeep and truck parking lot. Primarily, he was focused on assessing what had happened to France's artistic heritage. He wrote later, "Above all we were thinking ahead to the peacemaking days, hoping that restitution and reparations would be more than high-sounding terms. We had not crossed the seas to inflict retribution, but would insist on real justice." So was Rose, but as of the beginning of December 1944, they had yet to meet.

Rose estimated that the Nazis had confiscated one-third of the privately owned art in the country. In total, around one hundred thousand works of art had been looted from France alone. Of those, more than thirty thousand, coming from 203 art collections, were processed at the Jeu de Paume. They were all now in harm's way, secreted inside castles and deep in mines scattered throughout the Third Reich, as the Allies closed in on Germany. Rose was also the only person who knew where they were hidden.

But what if she gave up her information and it just got stuck on a desk somewhere? She was afraid of French bureaucracy. Rose remained so reticent to divulge her secrets that both the Americans and some of her French colleagues began to doubt if she actually knew anything.

Two of Rose's superiors and most staunch supporters knew she held deep knowledge, however. One was, of course, Jacques Jaujard. The other was Albert Henraux, the heroic driver of the Louvre's mass art evacuation and the newly appointed director of the Commission de Récupération Artistique (CRA), which was created at Jaujard's mandate. Rose was appointed as the general secretary. The CRA's headquarters were in the Jeu de Paume, an important symbolic gesture that allowed the looted art to come full circle after it was found.

James Rorimer was eager to know what Rose knew, as it would make the work of the Monuments, Fine Arts, and Archives officers a whole lot easier while the Allies fought through Austria and Germany. On her end, Rose was concerned that the Germans would destroy the artwork seized from France before the Allies arrived. She also harbored no illusions about the priorities of the Allied forces, writing in retrospect, "I became worried as I imagined the immensity of the problems that an army on campaign had to solve. Was the issue of conserving our works of art going to disappear among so many others of primordial importance?"

In mid-December 1944, Henraux sent Rorimer to meet Rose and deliver about a dozen recovered artworks to the CRA. Rose was impressed by Rorimer's knowledge of Paris and his command of French. She also appreciated that he respectfully consulted his French counterparts—not bulldozing in like other Americans—and was sincerely interested in her concerns regarding the looted art now in Germany. She hoped he could locate the art depositories to protect them from the battles to come and German thieves. She would be correct—as the Allies neared, Hermann Göring ordered the Luftwaffe to implode Carinhall, his country estate northeast of Berlin, which housed a portion of the art he looted from France and other nations. The Germans also rigged mines containing looted art for explosion—the schadenfreude that curator Pierre Schommer had feared.

Rose and Rorimer met many more times in the Jeu de Paume. Due to the continuing supply shortage, Rose's office was frigid until she managed to get her hands on a little coal. She would have to stoke the stove constantly just to get enough heat to warm her hands. At the meetings, Rose would tell Rorimer things like, "You must get yourself into some position where you can carry on your usefulness in Germany. You are the only one who is a match for those fellows. I will give you all the information you need. . . . I am sure that you will be the first to be there as you were the first to come to Paris."

Rorimer asked Rose to accompany him to investigate the ERR's Parisian depots and key addresses—including Bruno Lohse's apartment, where they interrogated the current occupants and staff who reported that truckloads of art were taken out just days before the Liberation. Rose also took Rorimer to find the art train, which had been moved several times since Alexandre Rosenberg had found it. Although all the paintings were brought to safety by the end of September 1944, forty-seven train cars full of furniture and household items were still in a freight yard somewhere and needed to be located.

Rose and Rorimer went on an expedition around Paris from one train station to another, with assistance from a stationmaster who had helped delay the train during the liberation. Rose carried her list of train numbers, which she initially copied from the shipping receipts she found at the Jeu de Paume. When they finally found the train at Gare de Pajol, Rose was gratified. She saw again with her own eyes that her information about the rail car numbers was entirely correct.

But Rose was not ready to reveal all her intelligence to Rorimer just yet. From there, Rose played a coy game. This first investigation seemed to show that his heart was in the right place, but she would need more proof of his intentions before handing over her hard-won information. Rorimer found her behavior as "inscrutable as the cat and mouse play." Right before Christmas, Rose sent Rorimer a bottle of champagne. He invited her over to partake in the drinking a few days later. There were no romantic feelings between them—Rorimer was recently married and Rose was living with Joyce—but soon, a warm trust developed that would endure for the rest of their lives. As Rorimer wrote in his memoir, "In the best cloak-and-dagger tradition I uncorked the bottle of champagne and we drank a toast to the success of our mission." She then opened up somewhat, sharing how she had acquired her intelligence in the war, but she did not reveal anything else.

At a dinner together shortly after, in the American officers' mess, she did not share much more. Her years undercover at the Jeu de Paume made her constantly suspicious, and she was afraid of being overheard, telling Rorimer, "There are too many others around. We can talk in quiet at my apartment." Rose invited Rorimer over but said, "I can't ask you for dinner—we just haven't enough food. Why don't you come after dinner?" The "we" indicates that Joyce was present as well, or at the very least, Rose was comfortable enough with Rorimer to allude to her presence. Joyce was now pursuing a master's degree in Greek civilization and writing her thesis on Plato at the Sorbonne.

On a cold evening in December, Rorimer biked over to Rose's place in the Latin Quarter, describing it as so isolated that "if the Gestapo had had any idea that Rose was a member of the Resistance it would have been very easy for them to cart her off at any time without anyone being the wiser." Rose and Joyce had moved to 4 rue de Navarre, just across the street from where they had lived for most of the war. Rorimer climbed up the many flights of stairs and found Rose chain-smoking cigarettes, particularly delighted to get her hands on American brands since the liberation. She also had a small amount of food she took from the German stockpile at the Jeu de Paume and a bottle of cognac. "*Bon soir cher collegue*," she said in greeting.

Rose and Rorimer spoke about the Nazi occupation and the American and British armies, but she took her time to get to the substance of the discussion. It was all very French. Then, when the pleasantries were over, she abruptly said, "You must go to Germany, James. I'll join you as soon as I can, but you must go right away." Rorimer had not received any orders to do so yet, and he told her she needed to give her information to SHAEF, the Supreme Headquarters of the Allied Expeditionary Forces, which would pass it down the proper channels to the forces on the ground.

"Channels?" she pushed back. "I call it bureaucracy. It is nothing more than wheels within wheels. Inefficiency. One fellow is thickheaded and smug, and poof . . . nothing happens." She disappeared into her bedroom and returned with stacks of the photographs developed from the negatives she had stolen. Rorimer described the portraits of the ERR staff as a "rogue's gallery," which she brought to life with her colorful stories. She also had photos of the art that was looted via the Jeu de Paume; images of the castles where the art was taken, including Neuschwanstein, the fairy-tale castle of King Ludwig II in Bavaria, and Hohenschwangau; and piles of documents.

"How can you be so certain?" Rorimer questioned. "You weren't in Germany."

She answered, "Trust me, James. What I tell you is based on more than a woman's intuition. Here, take these two photographs. They will show you where to find what you were asking about."

She insisted that he promise to go to Germany himself to "save our treasures before the SS can destroy them." She felt an immense sense of urgency, which she imparted to Rorimer, and wrote later, "It seemed so obvious to me that the fate of the looted works would depend on what would happen upon the entry of the Allies into Germany."

The level of confidence Rose bestowed on Rorimer was unprecedented for her. As he later recounted, "She had found out that you can trust no one. Even the finest of her colleagues had to play politics during those trying years of occupation and she had suffered too much for her country's welfare to permit anyone to use her or her material for their own gain. She was playing for more than her own personal aggrandizement. Only by keeping complete control of the situation, whether by ruse or stubbornness, could Rose be sure that worthy people . . . would help bring back to France the works of art she had seen taken from their owners."

In April 1945, Rorimer was finally ordered to Germany. In the meantime, Rose enlisted her services with the French Army and received her mission order on May 4, 1945, as a "Beaux-Arts officer" to be stationed in Germany. She held the rank of captain. The French Army had no female uniform for her, so she made a skirt out of a male friend's fatigues. She later attached a button from Hermann Göring's coat on her own as a talisman. In September 1945, she was commissioned as a lieutenant colonel in the US Seventh Army as well. Her job was to hunt down and restitute the art plundered from France and other occupied countries before they could be destroyed or stolen. It was a race against time. Rose's gathered intelligence enabled the recovery of hundreds of thousands of looted artworks stashed in the salt mines of Austria and in German castles.

During the war, Rose Valland did not have the luxury of crying. The Germans were always trying to find ways to dispose of her, and she needed to keep her wits about her. It was not until two decades later that she lost her composure.

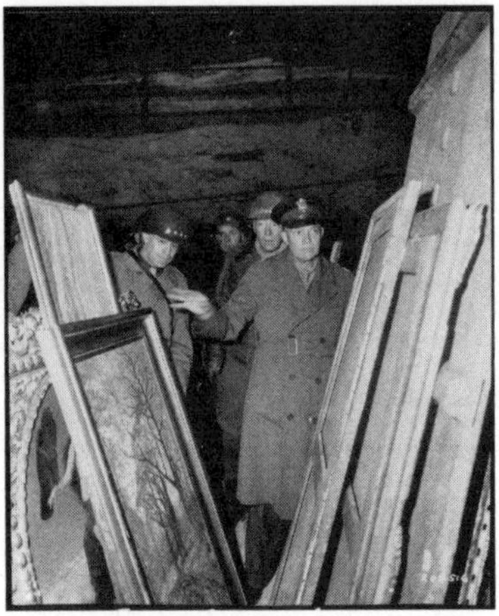

General Dwight D. Eisenhower, accompanied by General Omar N. Bradley and Lieutenant General George S. Patton Jr., inspects art treasures stolen by Germans and hidden in a salt mine in Germany, April 1945.

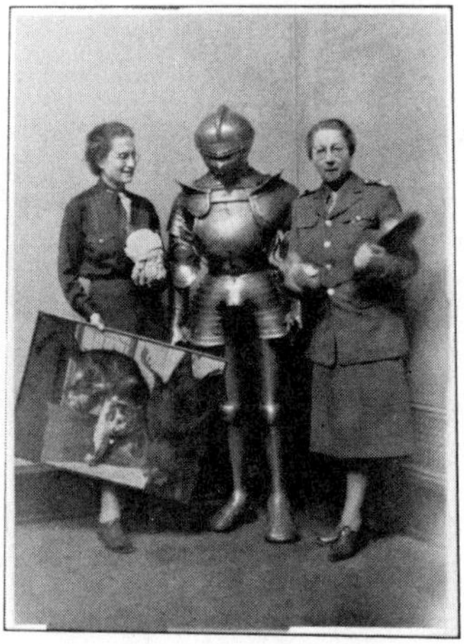

Edith Standen *(left)* and Rose Valland *(right)* at Wiesbaden Collecting Point, May 11, 1946.

On the set of *The Train*, a film optioned off her memoir *Le Front de l'Art*, there were Nazi officers walking around the Jeu de Paume again and sentries out front cocking their rifles. The clip-clop sounds of black boots hitting the floor jolted her back in time. For a few moments, she forgot that the war had ended. Tears flooded her eyes, and in confusion, she fled the museum. "I do not know what happened!" she told a reporter afterward. "I, who am so calm, could not even find the Métro station." At long last, this fierce, independent, unflappable woman finally had to confront the demons she had long pushed aside.

EPILOGUE

ROSE VALLAND SPENT EIGHT YEARS IN GERMANY, DOGGEDLY FIGHTING for the restitution of looted art. She continued to be at the heart of the action—crisscrossing all over the former Third Reich in a requisitioned US Army jeep, tracking down plundered art, and interrogating former ERR employees and associates. Rose's Resistance contact, Pierre-Louis Duchartre, who helped her save the art train, was also commissioned as a Monuments officer and wrote fondly of their time in Germany together under enemy fire. Rose seemed to always be present or nearby when big discoveries were made. She saw Rorimer many more times and was even roommates with him in a military government billet in Wiesbaden.

One of the first missions entrusted to Rose when she arrived in Germany was to locate the Van Eyck altarpiece, *The Adoration of the Mystic Lamb*. It was found in the labyrinthine Altausee mine where Hitler had stored the art intended for his Führermuseum. There, upward of sixty-five hundred works of art—including a sculpture of the Madonna by Michelangelo and paintings by Rubens and Rembrandt, along with Vermeer's *Astronomer*, one of the first paintings to arrive at the Jeu de Paume—were stored vertically one after another, unprotected, on wood scaffolding. The mine had been rigged for explosion but was saved just in time.

At Neuschwanstein Castle, Rose, along with the Monuments officers, found a large portion of the art seized from France, including the jewels of the Rothschild family as well as the meticulously maintained archives and photographs from the ERR in Paris. More ERR files were scattered in other castles, including Schloss Kogl, where ERR director Bruno Lohse was seen digging something up with a shovel in the last days of the war, and at von Behr's castle. Stylish to the bitter end, von Behr and his wife committed suicide together by drinking a 1928 vintage bottle of champagne, laced with cyanide. For his final act, he made sure to wear his Red Cross uniform, just as he did on his first day at the Jeu de Paume. Art historian Hermann Bunjes, who stopped Rose from creating the duplicate inventory on the first day of the ERR's takeover at the Jeu de Paume, also committed suicide shortly after he surrendered to the Allies.

Hitler remained obsessed with the plans for the Führermuseum and the city of Linz until the very end. According to architect Albert Speer, Hitler's

> abiding interest in the plans for the city of his retirement years also gradually assumed an escapist character. . . . When he considered the torment he now had to endure, he would gloomily say that death could only mean a release for him. In keeping with this mood, when he studied the Linz plans, he would repeatedly turn to sketches for his tomb, which was to be located in one of the towers of the Linz complex of party buildings.

Hitler committed suicide on April 30, 1945 in his bunker with his longtime paramour, Eva Braun, whom he married in their final hours. He was buried and reburied secretly several times by the Soviets and was finally burned, in fear that any burial place for Hitler would become a shrine for fascism. In 2009, the head archivist of Russia's Federal Security Service (FSB) stated that all that remained of Hitler were his jaw, which is "kept at the Russian FSB Central Archive as being particularly valuable," and skull fragments, which are in the Russian State Archive.

In February 1946, Rose traveled to the Nuremberg trials as the representative of the CRA to testify about the actions of the ERR. She was disappointed to learn that the judges decided to drop the three days of hearings planned about looted art, but she successfully argued to get one day of the hearing added back to the schedule. She knew how important it was for the future of French art restitution to have a precedent for its litigation at Nuremberg. Rose was also able to interrogate members of the ERR in their jail cells.

Hermann Göring was tried at Nuremberg and found guilty of crimes against humanity and other charges. On October 1, 1946, he was sentenced to death by hanging. Just hours before his scheduled execution he committed suicide in his jail cell by ingesting a potassium cyanide capsule. Alfred Rosenberg, the leader of the German Foreign Office and head of the ERR, was also found guilty at Nuremberg and was executed by hanging.

Rose went to Berchtesgaden in Germany, the site of Hitler's Berghof, as well as the homes of many of his loyal henchmen. In a railway tunnel connecting Berchtesgaden and Salzburg, American soldiers found Göring's private train, which contained thousands of works of art, jewelry, furniture, books, and fine objects. A good portion of the six hundred or so paintings Göring selected for himself at the Jeu de Paume was found, as well as the *Belle Allemande* from the Louvre.

In 1946, Rose was named director of the Beaux-Arts section of the French Control Council Group, a governing body of the Allied Occupation Zone. There, she became directly involved with the legal and moral questions of postwar art restitution and how it should be handled among the Allied powers. In the years to come, she would continue to push passionately and vigorously for French interests in restitution.

In 1946 Rose also became the head of the central post for French artistic restitution in Germany and Austria and in 1949, was named co-director of the Service for the Restoration of Works of Art (SRPOA) at the French Ministry of Foreign Affairs. As part of these efforts, she communicated regularly with the Jewish families in France, who were grateful to have such an advocate.

Rose used her spy craft multiple times to go into the Soviet zone, reportedly using false papers as a journalist and other cover identities to investigate what happened to the looted art in that sector. Although Russia was one of the Allied nations in World War II, it treated cultural patrimony and looted art depositories as war reparations in the countries it liberated. Rose tenaciously confronted Russian officers to demand that French artistic heritage be returned. There was nothing too big or small for Rose to tackle. If it belonged to France, she would try to get it back with everything she could muster.

One of her biggest coups was the restitution of numerous bronze cannons from the Soviet zone taken from the Musée de l'Armée in Les Invalides in Paris. She tracked them down one by one and went clandestinely into postwar Germany's Soviet sector to investigate cannons that ended up in a Russian foundry. Two of those cannons now stand in front of Les Invalides. In an effusive letter of appreciation, General Henry Blanc, the director of the Musée de l'Armée, wrote to Rose, "I know all the difficulties you must encounter, but I also know your big heart and your dedication. I also know that very often you have succeeded where others have failed."

Rose had many a heated exchange with the Russians about French-looted art. She even spotted stolen art on-site in their offices. She came across several hundred flags taken from Les Invalides, but the Russians claimed, using their classic modus operandi, that the flags had disappeared since she saw them. Undeterred, she secretly tracked them down at their new location and had them surreptitiously seized. Rose also reclaimed two stone lions that Göring had purchased in France with Occupation funds, in a sale nullified after the war. In a postwar photograph, Rose posed proudly in front of the lions.

One of the most moving moments of Rose's restitution work after the war happened at Göring's estate, Carinhall, a place Rose was particularly interested in investigating. On Rose's second visit, she came across the burial place of Göring's first wife, Carin, for whom the property was named. A man who worked for Göring told her that the Russians had desecrated the grave, removed the corpse from the burial monument, and smashed Carin's skull against a wall, which caused it to detach from her body. What was left was put into another grave, which was further vandalized. While there, Rose happened to find the back portion of Carin's skull and the rest of her remains. She personally gave Carin a proper burial, an act that earned her the profound respect of those who accompanied her visit.

At Carinhall, Rose found the copy of the Winged Victory of Samothrace that Göring had commissioned from the Rudier Foundry in Paris, still in its box but crumbling from water damage. She also found fragments of the Édouard de Rothschild statues she had been so concerned about at the Jeu de Paume inside Göring's bunker and had numerous bronze statues dredged from the lake.

Rose is one of the most decorated women in French history (if not the most decorated), and among the most decorated women from World War II. She was awarded the US Medal of Freedom, the French Medal of Resistance, and the French Légion d'Honneur, France's highest civil decoration. She was also awarded the Officer's Cross of the Order of Merit from Germany.

She evoked only passionate, extreme emotions in the people she met, both good and bad. One of the French Monuments officers, Captain Elie J. Doubinsky, whom Rose was close with, called her "Saint Rose." Pierre-Louis Duchartre, her Resistance contact who helped stop the art train, called her "Valiant Rose." James Rorimer praised her and devoted a section of his book *Survival* to her. In a draft, he described her as "the heroine of this book." The two remained close after the war. Rose referred to him in her letters as "*Mon cher 'Captain*,'" and he called her "*Ma capitaine*."

It would be several years before Rose would learn how close she had come to death in the last days of the war. Rose traveled back to France in 1948 to participate in Bruno Lohse's French military trial. Determined not to let him get away with his crimes, she served as one of the interrogating witnesses for his trial. In the office of the presiding judge, Captain Harlin, Lohse claimed he had disobeyed von Behr's order to take her to the German border and execute her. He later said he regretted his decision to spare her.

Lohse had succeeded in charming his American interrogators in Germany, James Plaut and Theodore Rousseau, who wanted to provide testimony in Lohse's *defense* at his trial in Paris, arguing that Lohse's compatriots were "certainly far more guilty than he." Rose, of course, knew that he had played what she testified to as a "leading role" and that he had been the "soul of the ERR" who "bears one of the heaviest responsibilities" in the looting, along with von Behr. Rose remained convinced that Lohse had stolen paintings from the ERR and still had them hidden somewhere.

Lohse spent two years in jail awaiting trial in Paris. During the trial, the judge reprimanded him for inconsistent and false statements. Although this supported Rose's long-held convictions of Lohse's duplicity, he was ultimately acquitted and allowed to return to his life in the art world. In an unsent letter to James Plaut, the head of the Office of Strategic Services's Art Looting Investigation Unit (ALIU), James Rorimer tried to express his outrage: "I have practically come to the point where I must refresh your memory about certain letters which you prepared about Dr. Lohse, whom you continue to ask me to whitewash. I believe . . . you will realize that we stand together, not alone as individuals, in this continuation of lies, for which I now have many documents in my possession." Rose had provided Rorimer with the evidence against Lohse.

It could be argued that Lohse's reputation actually increased due to his wartime activities—his network had certainly expanded. He gave lectures at the Louvre and to students from Williams College, invited by S. Lane Faison of the ALIU. He also regularly tried to sell art to the Metropolitan Museum of Art through Theodore Rousseau, who became the museum's curator in chief and vice director, though no direct sales ever came to pass. It is possible he sold art to other American museums and clients through middlemen.

For more than half a century, Lohse continued to rail against Rose and resorted to misogyny in his attacks, claiming that Rose was romantically interested in him and wanted to be in a relationship but that he found her "ugly" ("*hasslich*"). Given her sexual orientation and how much she despised him from the beginning, it seems highly improbable. He also commented pejoratively about the size of her chest and spread rumors she had an affair with ERR co-director Walter Borchers. "Lohse was obsessed with her," says Jonathan Petropoulos, who knew Bruno Lohse after the war and wrote the book *Göring's Man in Paris*, about Lohse's activities in Paris with the ERR. When Lohse died in 2007, dozens of paintings were found in his apartment and his Swiss bank vault, including a looted Pissarro, proving that Rose had been right all along. When asked to reflect on his life not long before he died, Lohse laughed and sang the opening of the well-known song "*Non, je ne regrette rien*" by Edith Piaf. "No, I do not regret anything."

Unfortunately, Rose's dogged determination in art restitution was discomfiting to those who wanted to forget the war or did not want their wartime collaboration with the Nazis known. Others accused her of being a Russian agent, having been a collaborator, or that she was not a real Resistance member. In fact, she made reports and hand-drawn maps for the Allies of the Soviet buildup in Eastern Europe during the Cold War, which can be found in the French National Archives and the Musée de la Résistance et de la Déportation in Grenoble.

Some were jealous of her fame or bristled at her independence. Louvre curator and known anti-Semite Germain Bazin questioned small details of her facts and figures in his book, which he published only after her death. Raymond Schmittlein, head of the French National Education and Fine Art Services wrote in one of Rose's job reviews, "Rose Valland wants a cushy job, free of any control whatsoever, where she will continue to disseminate her self-serving propaganda, with the entire approval of the higher authorities, to whom she extols the virtues of her unruly activities."

Evident in her papers is how difficult a time Rose had on her return to France. She was told there was no way she could keep the title or pay that she had in Germany since her work there was a temporary reassignment of her job in France and not a permanent one. That meant she would work as an assistant curator, the most junior level in the hierarchy, while all her peers had been promoted. In 1954, she took a position as director of the Service for the Protection of Works with the Musées Nationaux. In that role, Rose kept an eye out for artworks in the French museums that might have been acquired through looting, much like what art historian and restitution expert Emmanuelle Polack does at the Louvre today. Rose also worked on plans to protect the French national art collections in case of another war. In 1961, she was made a Commander of the Order of Arts and Letters in France. In the 1960s, she also went to work for the Rothschild Foundation, as head of the department for the protection of works of art.

In 1961, Rose experienced her first brush with fame when she published her wartime memoir, *Le Front de l'Art*. Many newspapers and magazines in both France and the United States covered the book. Then, she sold the film option of the chapter of her book about the art train to Hollywood, which became the fictionalized blockbuster movie *The Train* starring Burt Lancaster. French actress Suzanne Flon played a character based on Rose.

The publishing of *Le Front de l'Art* renewed the attacks on Rose, however. In a letter to a friend, Rose states that "the authorities" blocked her from writing a sequel to *Le Front de l'Art* and warned him not to write a book about his experience either. She stated emphatically, "I never intended to give up writing my second volume of my war memoir, but it was not possible, and I was prevented from doing so." She mentioned that André François-Poncet, the former French ambassador to Germany from 1931 to 1938, advised her not to publish her first memoir. She wrote that *Le Front de l'Art* had been withdrawn from circulation and removed from the stocks of the publishing house. She took back the rest of the inventory and wrote to hundreds of libraries and museums across France, offering the book for their collection. No manuscript or draft of a sequel has been found in her papers to this day.

She was also criticized for the book's account of the incineration of the paintings in the garden of the Jeu de Paume in 1943. Looting by the

Nazis was one thing, but outright destruction of five or six hundred paintings was an accusation on a whole other level. However, the denials came directly from the Nazis in charge at the ERR—notably by Robert Scholz and Walter Borchers—who were directly responsible for the destruction. These disavowals from complicit characters should not be surprising, nor should they be taken seriously. Nevertheless, the doubt was sowed.

Unfortunately, one of the reasons her account of the burning has been questioned was a mistake in the date of the event included in the first edition of her book. It was listed as May 27, 1943, though it took place in July 1943. Rose changed the date in the second printing, but unfortunately, by that time, the incorrect date was circulating in the media and was used as evidence of her unreliability regarding the event. However, this appears to be simply an unintentional error in her book, which she wrote nearly twenty years after the events took place. Her wartime reports remain consistent.

Rose herself took action against the accusations in 1961. She wrote to all the guards and caretakers who were at the Jeu de Paume during the summer of 1943 and asked them to submit their accounts of the event and to have them notarized. It is unclear where she submitted these testimonials, if at all, and they remained hidden deep in her personal files, overlooked for many decades.

Paul Blondel, a Jeu de Paume guard, provided a firsthand account in a notarized and certified written testimony that he was "designated among my comrades by the head of the German services at the Jeu de Paume to burn the canvases and frames coming from the Louvre Museum and of having been under the supervision of a German soldier in the army throughout the operation which lasted from 9 a.m. in the morning until 5 p.m. in the evening." Blondel was a French eyewitness who was forced to actively participate in the burning of the paintings.

Eugène Finitzer, another guard, wrote in his notarized testimony that he certified "that I saw one afternoon in the summer of 1943, burned by the Germans in the garden of the Jeu de Paume museum, which I was guardian, a large number of cut and torn paintings. This fire lasted the afternoon I was at the museum." Finitzer's account shows that not only were the paintings burned, but they had also been viciously cut and torn beforehand.

The guard Develay certified the following and noted that another guard, Louis Deforges, was also present and saw it happen: "I, undersigned, C. Develay, certify that I witnessed the destruction of numerous paintings stored in the rooms of the Louvre by the German occupation service. These gentlemen destroyed the canvases with knives and kicks with unbridled satisfaction. I can affirm this from the fact that I had been assigned to their service in the company of my work friend Mr. Deforges. I also witnessed the destruction of these paintings by fire in the small courtyard of the Jeu de Paume." Develay saw both the knifing and the kicking of the paintings at the Louvre and the burning at the Jeu de Paume, providing additional details.

Paul Moïse, who called Rose at home when suspicious things were happening inside the Jeu de Paume, wrote forcefully, "In my soul and conscience I declare and affirm to have witnessed the destruction of a large number of torn paintings burned in the gardens of the Jeu de Paume one afternoon in the summer of 1943."

Finally, Gaston Petit, the head of security for the Musées Nationaux, wrote on July 23, 1943, in a document labeled "VERY CONFIDENTIAL" on Musées Nationaux letterhead: "The canvases of these lacerated paintings were torn from their frames, transported to the Jeu de Paume, and burned under the supervision of German soldiers. Triage will continue under same conditions."

A small article in the Resistance newspaper *Libération*, dated September 7, 1943, reported on the burning of the paintings. Titled "*Flambez Peintures!*" it stated that "on the grounds of the Tuileries Garden, located behind the Jeu de Paume, next to the gardener's shed, torn master paintings were piled up and burned." It also noted the seizing of Jewish-owned collections in general and that they were brought to the Jeu de Paume.

The silencing of Rose Valland appears to have gone hand in hand with the whitewashing of the dubious wartime pasts of some of France's celebrated civil servants, including Henri Verne, who sold paintings to the ERR. The French art historian and restitution expert Emmanuelle Polack, who is now in charge of provenance inquiries at the Louvre Museum, wrote in her book *Le Marché de l'Art sous l'Occupation* that a photograph of Alfred Rosenberg's arrival at the Jeu de Paume shows Louvre curator Germain Bazin giving a Heil Hitler salute. Polack notes that Rose Valland is in the photo, but only her skirt and folded hands are visible. The rest of Rose is outside of the camera frame. Rose, Polack contends, would not deign to give Rosenberg or anyone a Heil Hitler salute. Polack also writes that this photo, the original of which can be seen today in the diplomatic archives of the French Ministry of Foreign Affairs, was deliberately cropped in Rose's 1961 book *Le Front de l'Art* to omit Bazin. It remained cropped in the 1997 and 2014 reprintings of the book. Polack writes that "this deletion allowed Germain Bazin to pass into posterity, and with honors, without having to answer for this gesture."

Henri Verne, the former director of the Musées Nationaux who would not pay Rose, had a similar reputational resuscitation. Although he was forced to retire early due to several scandals and later served as a middleman selling art to the Nazis, he was widely praised in the memoirs of Louvre curators like Germain Bazin, René Huyghe, and others. Only Pierre Schommer, the arts administrator for the Chambord art depot, detailed Verne's fall from grace in the late 1930s. Schommer's book, *Il faut sauver la Joconde! Carnets (1937–1945)*, was only published posthumously in 2014. His account is corroborated by Verne's retirement files in the French National Archives.

There came a time in France when people no longer wanted to revisit such a painful part of history and only wanted to move forward. The onset of the Cold War drastically changed geopolitical priorities. Art restitution was a pesky, problematic topic that implicated too many powerful families. The sudden, untimely deaths of Rose's two main champions—Albert Henraux in 1953 and Jacques Jaujard in 1967—were detrimental to her career and, undoubtedly, to her personally. Henri Focillon, one of her first advocates, died during the war. As the years went by, Rose continued to fight for Nazi art restitution but was increasingly seen as a peculiar, eccentric presence within the Musées Nationaux.

After the liberation, Jacques Jaujard became the director general of the Order of Arts and Letters in France. He retired in 1959 but was recalled to serve as the secretary general of the French Ministry of Cultural Affairs. He died of a heart attack in 1967 at the age of seventy-one.

Alexandre Rosenberg continued to fight with the 2nd DB as the division moved east through France. About sixty miles to the German border, Alexandre was hospitalized for an illness and given forty-five days leave in Paris for overwork. He returned to service and was demobilized in September 1945.

After the war, Alexandre joined the family business in New York, taking over for his father. He became a preeminent dealer in his own right and a donor to New York City's museums, including the Morgan Library and Museum. He also actively sought to locate and restitute the remainder of the art stolen from his father, working with Rose on the effort. In 1960, Alexandre wrote of Rose, "Mademoiselle Valland is fully committed to our cause and very well disposed towards us." Paul Rosenberg's descendants, including French journalist Anne Sinclair, continue to fight for the restitution of their family's artwork to this day. Many are still unaccounted for, including the Picasso portraits of their family and the Degas painting *Portrait of Gabrielle Diot.*

Curator Agnès Humbert survived four years of imprisonment by the Germans and joined the US counterintelligence corps to identify anti-Nazi individuals in Germany. On June 11, 1945, Humbert returned to France and later published her wartime diary and recollections, *Notre Guerre* (published in the United States as *Résistance: A Woman's Journal of Struggle and Defense in Occupied France*) and joined her Resistance compatriot Jean Cassou at the Musée national d'Art Moderne. Several female Louvre employees, including Lucie Mazauric and Magdeleine Hours, also published their memoirs.

Rose and Joyce stayed together and traveled extensively around Europe until Joyce's death from breast cancer in 1977. Rose buried Joyce in her family vault in Saint-Étienne-de-Saint-Geoirs and had Joyce's PhD thesis on the ancient Greek geographer Pausanias published posthumously. Rose is alluded to anonymously in the preface of the book as a "friend who had taught [Joyce] French and who had loved her for a very long time like a very close relative." Joyce completed her thesis while in and out of treatment for cancer, and her adviser wrote in the preface, "While hospital stays and the very painful treatments for the illness that was to take her away followed one another, she managed, by an extraordinary effort of will, to finish her book in time to be declared a doctor before dying." In a letter shortly after Joyce's death, Rose wrote to her cousin Marguerite, "I know you guess my pain because this event impacts me as directly as if it was me. We have lived together for over fifty years! And if Joyce is in France, it is because of me. . . . My affection for her is coupled with great admiration." She also wrote that Joyce was one of the most admired students at the Sorbonne. In the end, Joyce proved the diplomat Robert Murphy wrong. His assessment of her work at the US embassy—"Her intelligence and general capacity do not qualify her for more than ordinary clerical work"—had been incorrect.

After Joyce's death, Rose lapsed into grief and depression, and never recovered. "You can guess what I have become since Joyce left," Rose wrote to Marguerite. "I don't know how to live anymore." Rose died in obscurity in 1980 at the age of eighty-one, just three years after Joyce died. Only a handful of people attended her funeral at Les Invalides in Paris. One of those was former Louvre art restorer Magdeleine Hours. Two decades later, Jean-Philippe Lecat, the French Minister of Culture at the time of Rose's death, was chagrined to discover he had not been notified of the funeral and that more had not been done to honor the French heroine. He wrote, "I was appalled by . . . the absence of any 'official delegation' at the funeral of this Resistance fighter whose action honors the entire curatorial corps. . . . There is a lesson in humility there that I embrace. The State is too often deaf and blind. It is true that Rose Valland did not serve the state, but an idea that goes beyond it." Rose is buried with Joyce in the Valland family vault in Saint-Étienne-de-Saint-Geoirs.

In the last two decades in France, there has been renewed interest in Rose Valland, led valiantly by the association La Mémoire de Rose Valland and its president, the indefatigable Jacqueline Barthalay, as well as several tenacious French women, including Emmanuelle Polack, Corinne Bouchoux, Ophélie Jouan, Jennifer Lesieur, and filmmaker Bénédicte Delfaut, who have put on exhibitions, written books, and worked on documentaries about Rose. It is due to these collective efforts that a plaque was placed on the Jeu de Paume in Rose's honor in 2005 and the museum's terrace was dedicated in her honor in 2024. In March 2024, a conference on Rose's legacy was held at the Louvre in collaboration with the Rijksmuseum in Amsterdam. In the United States, Rose was a character in the book *The Monuments Men* by Robert Edsel and has appeared in several books since, including *Les Parisiennes*, *Saving Mona Lisa*, and *Paris 1944*. The Monuments Men and Women Foundation released an English translation of *Le Front de l'Art* in 2024.

Rose is perhaps best known in France for her work on art restitution, which continues to have ripple effects today. The Nazis looted approximately 650,000 works of art in Europe during WWII. Rose and her team were responsible for the restitution of more than sixty-one thousand works of art in the decade after World War II. Even when the world moved on, Rose was still fighting. Today, it is believed that over one hundred thousand pieces of Nazi-confiscated artwork, taken from all over Europe, have yet to be recovered.

Rose's meticulously documented information helped prove that Nazi art looting during World War II was not random but systematic and part of a greater racially charged nationalist agenda. Rose's notes and reports, which are located predominantly in the diplomatic archives of the French Ministry of Foreign Affairs, have served as the primary (and sometimes only) evidence that the artworks coming to market today were looted. Her undercover work inside the Soviet zone after the war provides a rare look at the looted art that has not been seen since.

Rose Valland researched, wrote about, and advocated for looted art restitution for the rest of her life. Of all the Monuments officers, she had one of the longest tenures in Germany, locating and returning artworks to their rightful owners. She planted the seed, legally and morally, for what became the practice of art restitution in the modern era. She believed that looted art would continue to resurface long after the war was over, a prediction strongly reflected in the current art market. It is an ideal time to bring Rose Valland to light, the woman who risked her life to protect the world's cultural heritage, fought to restitute Nazi-looted artworks, and predicted where we would be today.

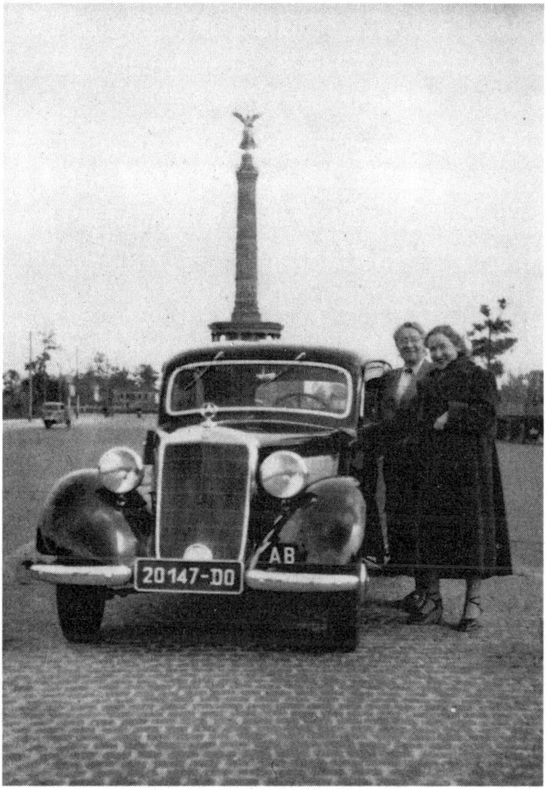

Rose Valland and her partner, Joyce Heer, at the Victory Column in Berlin, circa 1950.

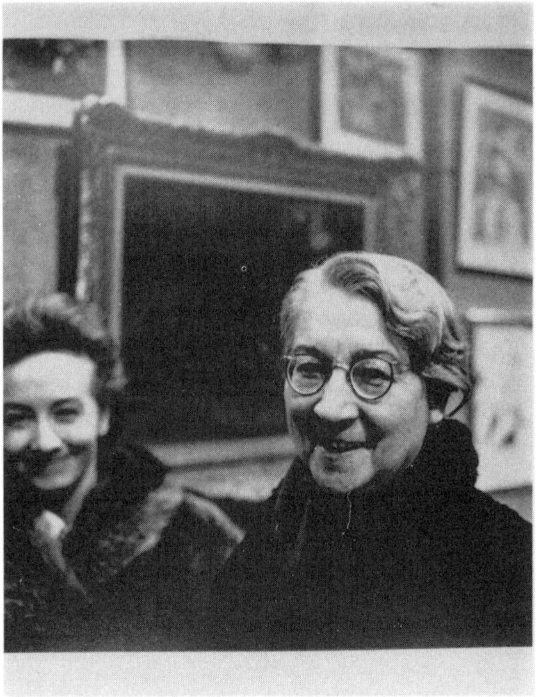

Rose Valland on the set of *The Train* with actress Suzanne Flon, circa 1964.

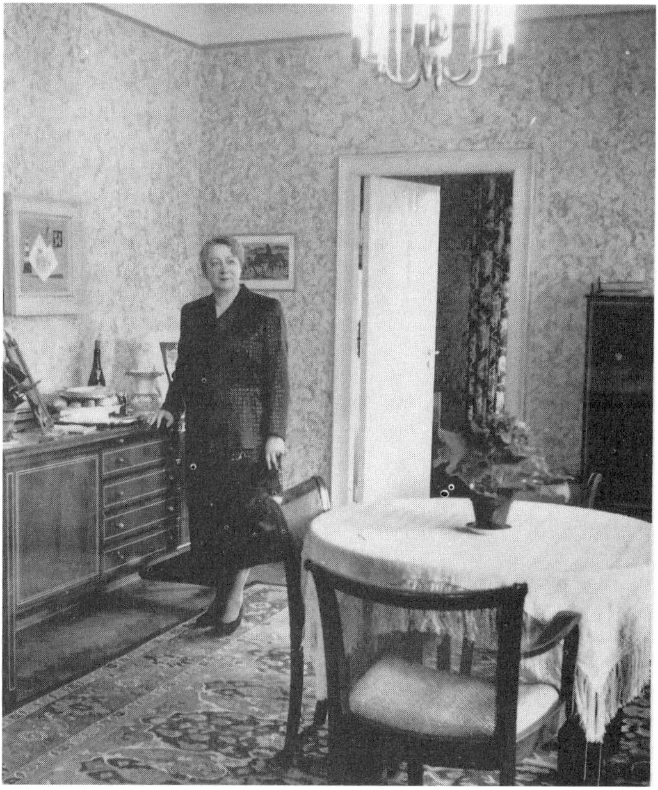

Rose Valland in her apartment.

AUTHOR'S NOTE

I BELIEVE I WAS DESTINED TO COME ACROSS ROSE VALLAND'S STORY. MY initial discovery of her was thanks to the fascinating book *Göring's Man in Paris* by Jonathan Petropoulos. Every time Rose appeared on the page, I was riveted. I was amazed that I had not heard of her, since I almost exclusively read books on female Resistance spies from World War II. My lifelong passion for World War II was sparked by my own family history, which included my grandfather's survival of the atomic bombing in Hiroshima.

I feel a deep kinship with Rose and realized I had been following in her footsteps since I was a child. We both studied art history and were taught to draw and paint in the fine arts tradition. We both learned German—on my end an inexplicable decision I made that seemed to hold little relevance until I wrote this book. When I was ten, I visited one of the salt mines in Austria where the Nazis stashed looted art, and I have been to many of the places Rose went while tracking down plundered art. When I moved to Paris to study architecture, I lived in an apartment just minutes away from Rose's. I was drawn to this part of the city with its narrow twisting streets, crooked buildings, and rich cultural history. Then, I immersed myself in the wartime history of my French in-laws and of France, which led me to discover Rose.

But more than these coincidences, I identified intrinsically with Rose as a woman—with her fight to be acknowledged in a man's world, her fiercely independent spirit, and how she persevered despite being constantly underestimated. The principles she fought for—for equal pay and equal opportunity—are very compelling for the modern reader, but I also loved that there were men in her life like James Rorimer, Albert Henraux, and Jacques Jaujard who saw her for the remarkable talent she was. For many women, war opened up new opportunities and enabled them to reach their full potential. Rose discovered that everything in her life up to that point—her successes and the challenges—put her exactly where she needed to be to change history. And she never ever gave up.

I believed from the start that her story was even more extraordinary than she portrayed in her own book, and that hunch turned out to be correct. She was an incredible art historian but not a self-promoter. In fact, to one reporter, she said "Above all, don't talk too much about me!" To another she said she found the fuss around her "a little astonishing." Her book *Le Front de l'Art* is unfortunately quite dry, and she seemed torn between telling her own exciting story and providing an academic analysis of Nazi art looting. In the end, the latter won out. She even cut out a chapter about her daring escape from Paris, which was one of the most exciting stories for me to write. One thing she did admit in her book was that the daily stress while working under the nose of the Nazis was agonizing and that fear seized her every time she had to show her *Ausweis*. "It was the same thing every day, I never got used to it," she wrote.

Rose was a packrat, and the organization of her documents probably only made sense to her. She left behind everything, including drafts of her work. Occasionally, they are on scraps of paper or on the back of business cards. They are typed and handwritten, sometimes barely legible. These notes and drafts and the deciphering of her scribble gave so much additional color to her accounts that are not in the official record. It was as if she knew someone like me would come later to piece together the breadcrumbs.

Her papers are everywhere, at the French National Archives, in the diplomatic archives of the French Ministry of Foreign Affairs, or left in her apartment and now with her family or at the Musée de la Résistance et de la Déportation in Grenoble, because that is how she operated. It is common to find work papers alongside personal papers. I was told that the diplomatic archives had taken the position that they would rather do a light touch with her papers and keep them in the order she left them rather than try to force a system on them. I respect that and think it honors her method, but it does require unrelenting focus to go through everything.

This all made the research process incredibly exciting.

But in the tens of thousands of papers she left behind, and even in her book, she gives us precious little of her own feelings or thoughts. She was an academic through and through and was used to subsuming her own emotions. This is how she survived as an outsider, as a lesbian, and then as a spy. Only a handful of letters written by Rose to her family before and during World War II were known to remain, but I was honored to have been given access to an incredible stockpile of letters and postcards written to and from Rose that have never been seen before. I believe that if you look deep enough, read someone's words closely enough, and are patient enough, their stories will speak to you through what they left behind.

If Rose Valland has been "forgotten," it has not been due to any lack of effort on her part. In fact, I believe she was acutely concerned with her legacy. She made a point to ensure that notable people like Jacques Jaujard and Gaston Palewski, director of General de Gaulle's cabinet, wrote testimony attesting to her work during the war and for the Resistance. She saved every communication she received, down to the envelopes. She often kept a copy of her own letters. Many letters are from people like the Rothschilds, the Rosenbergs, General Marie-Pierre Koenig, and General Henry Blanc who offered heartfelt gratitude for her work, and there are notes of congratulations from government ministers and her fellow art historians and curators, as well as from notable citizens like David David-Weill when she was awarded the Légion d'Honneur. Letters also came from Germans, like Walter Borchers, who acknowledged the difficulty she faced in the war and apologized for his role in it. She saved every newspaper clipping as it related to her, from the publishing of her book *Le Front de l'Art* to the media surrounding the release of the movie *The Train*.

In addition, there are likely many unknown troves of letters from Rose that have yet to be discovered. There is great potential for future breakthroughs to come.

Of all the research I did for this book, the most exciting discoveries were the numerous pieces of evidence I found that corroborated Rose's story of the fire in July 1943 in the garden of the Jeu de Paume. I discovered her letters to the guards, their replies, and their notarized testimonies buried in the back of an unrelated box in the diplomatic archives of the French Ministry of Foreign Affairs.

I am also very pleased with what I uncovered about Joyce Heer, who Rose understandably kept out of the public eye. I dedicated several months to this quest, tracking down a veritable ghost. Previously, it had been believed Rose and Joyce met in Germany after World War II, but I was able to discover the details of their life together in Paris long before the war. I was able to speak to Joyce's nephew and niece, Andy Heer and Auriel Heer. By phone and by email, they gave me invaluable accounts of her personality and the stories they remembered, although they both admitted they only met her a few times and did not know her well. Inspired by the author and researcher Philippa Langley, I decided to track Joyce down by locating mundane documents that would show she existed. By digging deep into the US National Archives, including scouring every single communication in and out of the US embassy in Paris from the war, and by locating her identification card and job applications, I was able to piece together her early life, her career in the United States and in Paris, the places she lived in, and the horror she experienced while imprisoned by the Germans.

I hope that in *The Art Spy*, I have managed to bring Rose to life and give her the recognition she is due. It was an honor to live in Rose's world, and Alexandre Rosenberg's, for the last four years. It gave me hope that no matter what atrocities take place, there are always those who are willing to fight for what is right, no matter the cost.

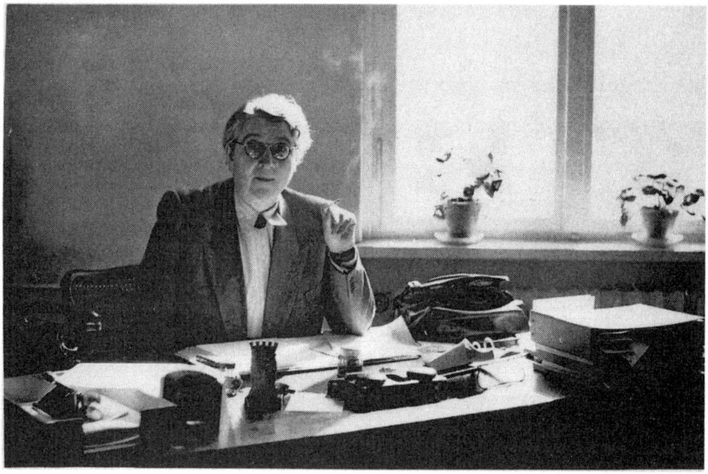

Rose Valland in her office.

ACKNOWLEDGMENTS

THIS BOOK WOULD NOT BE POSSIBLE WITHOUT THE STEADFAST support of my husband, Augustin Pasquet. His excitement, optimism, and dedication got this book off the ground. For four years, Augustin diligently researched in the archives with me, patiently transcribed and translated handwritten letters and old radio interviews, was my first reader for anything I wrote, edited my manuscript, and helped with interviews and phone calls. He also took care of our two young daughters when I traveled for book research. The book is also for my parents, Chiu-Li Young and Shug-Hong Young, my grandmother Kuan-Kuan Lee Su, forever young at ninety-five, and my late grandfather Pei-Pu Su, who have always been so enthusiastic about my projects and instilled in me my love for history and art. To my inquisitive daughters, this book is for you.

The advice and energy of my editor Elizabeth "Biz" Mitchell at HarperOne shaped and perfected the manuscript. Together, Biz and I both believed and knew instinctually that we could give Rose Valland the incredibly brave and exciting story she should be known for. Biz's assistants, Anna Calame and Ghjulia Romiti, were there every step of the way.

Thank you to my agent, Peter Steinberg at United Talent Agency (UTA), for immediately believing in the story and my ability to write it.

The indefatigable Jacqueline Barthalay of the association La Mémoire de Rose Valland based in Saint-Étienne-de-Saint-Geoirs is *the* essential driving force and resource for this book. I am incredibly honored that she agreed to take on my book as her last project before retirement (although one suspects that her devotion to the cause will continue long after this book is published). She opened the doors to the world of Rose Valland in France for me and immediately understood that I was interested in getting Rose's real story down. Jacqueline gave me unparalleled access to her files and trusted me with the information she had carefully collected for three decades.

This book is also for one of my biggest cheerleaders, the author Laurie Gwen Shapiro (*The Aviator and the Showman*; *The Stowaway*), who insisted since the day we met in 2014 that I should write a narrative nonfiction book. Laurie brought me into the book world, coached me, read my pages, and was willing to give me the hard advice I needed to hear at times. Her commitment to getting the story is nothing short of inspirational.

There are so many people who helped with the research for *The Art Spy*, but I must mention a few who went above and beyond. Pascale Riviale, archivist from the French National Archives; Alain Godec at the Fondation de la France Libre, historian Emmanuelle Polack, documentary filmmaker Bénédicte Delfaut, and authors Gerri Chanel (*Saving Mona Lisa*), Jonathan Petropoulous (*Göring's Man in Paris*), Lynne Olson (*Madame Fourcade's Secret War*; *Last Hope Island*), and Louis and Anne Rorimer (*Monuments Man*) for their support and detailed readings of my manuscript. As a scholar in the New York Public Library's Allen Room, I found the library's resources and the incredibly knowledgeable research staff invaluable.

This book would not be possible without the dedicated work of all those who came before me. For essential background on the subjects related to *The Art Spy*, I highly recommend the books *The Rape of Europa* by Lynn H. Nicholas, *Saving Mona Lisa* by Gerri Chanel, *The Lost Museum* by Héctor Feliciano, *Göring's Man in Paris* by Jonathan Petropoulos, *Monuments Man* by James Rorimer (the 2021 reissue of his wartime memoir, *Survival*), *My Grandfather's Gallery* by Anne Sinclair, and *Rose Valland: Resistance at the Museum* by Corinne Bouchoux. For even more on Rose Valland, albeit in French, there are the many books by Emmanuelle Polack, including *Les carnets de Rose Valland* and *Le Marché de l'Art sous l'Occupation (1940–1944)*, as well as *Une vie à l'œuvre* by Ophélie Jouan, *L'Espionne à l'œuvre* by Jennifer Lesieur and *Rose Valland Résistante pour l'Art* by the late Frederic Destremau.

I am also indebted to French journalist Anne Sinclair, the granddaughter of Paul Rosenberg; Antoine Musy at the Musée de la Resistance et de la Déportation in Grenoble; Olivier Cogne at the Musée dauphinois in Grenoble; Alexandra Fleury at Chambord National Estate; Christelle Vaz and Vincent Tristan with the city of Floirac; art historian Guillaume Deprez; architect Pierre-Louis Gerlier. Also, the archivists and researchers at the US National Archives, particularly Kayla Dawkins and Eric Van Slander; Christine Vernay, Rose Valland's grandniece who welcomed me into her home and shared with me the memories and documents she had on Rose; Andy and Auriel Heer, the nephew and niece of Joyce Heer; Sheri Marzaro and Sophie Lagane for research assistance in France; Met Museum archivist Jim Moske; Michael Wolraich (*The Bishop and the Butterfly*) and Jasmine Weber for their skillful manuscript suggestions; Jennifer Lesieur and Ophélie Jouan who gave me their time and expertise on Rose; Vanessa Chan (*The Storm We Made*) for moral support and industry expertise; Julie Satow (*When Women Ran Fifth Avenue*); Hrag Vartanian, cofounder and editor in chief of *Hyperallergic*; and Adam Langer at *The Forward*.

Thank you also to my grandmother-in-law, Monique Delmas, a survivor of World War II, whose incredibly sharp memories of the war lasted until her death at ninety-nine years old in 2023; my parents-in-law, Anne-Claire and Antoine Pasquet; and journalists Christina Horsten, Felix Zeltner, and Mia Kreindler, who answered my many German translation and history questions. Thank you to Stephanie Brown, Pauline Baer de Perignon, Adam Lawrence, Guy Durand-Viel, Stéphane Cousin at Veolia, Conor McCourt, Samantha Schnell, Sophie Seligmann Gosset, Paul-David Regnier, Edward Lewine at Christie's, Michel Morvan, Manon Beulay, Olivia Mattis, Daris

Delins, Carla Gutiérrez, Chris Robinson, Avi Smolen, Jeremy and Caren Kaplan, Charles Berg, Clive Lamming, Scott Selby, Claudine Jeanneney-Duchesne, Sandra Sykora, Victor Plé, Scott and Jane Macdonald, Candice and Alex Wong, and Justin Rivers and Nicole Saraniero at Untapped New York.

To the staff at the many, many archives I consulted and to everyone I was not able to mention individually, thank you for making this book become a reality. Finally, to Nicholas Louvel (*The Uncondemned*) who showed me what real journalism is and what it takes to get the truth out.

IMAGE PERMISSIONS

- Photos on pages v, 67, 68, 76, and 120: Archives nationales, France, 20144792/250
- Photos on pages ii, 6, 13, 321, and 323: Camille Garapont family collection
- Photo on page vi: Archives nationales, France, 20144792/252
- Photo on page viii: US National Archives, 111-SC-193008
- Photo on page 21: Archives nationales, France, 20144707/289
- Photo on page 34: Walter Frentz Collection
- Photos on pages 102 and 142: Anne Sinclair / Rosenberg Family Collection
- Photo on page 133: Bibliothèque nationale de France, QE-1069 (1)-PET FOL
- Photo on page 124: US National Archives, 242-HLB-5073(20)
- Photos on pages 130, 156, and 322: Archives diplomatiques du Ministère de l'Europe et des Affaires étrangères, La Courneuve
- Photos on pages 258 and 306 (right): National Gallery of Art Archives
- Photo on page 298: US National Archives, 239-RC-4-20-23
- Photo on page 306 (left): US National Archives, 111-SC-204516
- Photo on page 329: Association "La Mémoire de Rose Valland"

NOTES

Abbreviations Used in Notes

AAA Archives of American Art, Smithsonian Institution, Washington, DC, USA
AN Archives nationales de France, Pierrefitte-sur-Seine, France
FFL Fondation de la France Libre archives, Paris, France
MAE Diplomatic Archives, Ministère des Affaires étrangères, La Courneuve, France
MD Musée dauphinois, Grenoble, France
ML Morgan Library and Museum archives, New York, USA
MOMA Museum of Modern Art archives, New York, USA
MRD Musée de la Résistance et de la Déportation archives, Grenoble, France
MS Mémorial de la Shoah archives, Paris, France
NARA National Archives and Records Administration, Washington, DC, USA
NARA RG NARA Record Group
NGA National Gallery of Art archives, Washington, DC, USA

SECTION I

1 *peered out from a slightly open window*: Rose Valland, *Le Front de l'Art* (Paris: Réunion des musées nationaux, 2016), 211. All quotes from *Le Front de l'Art* are based on this edition, translated by Augustin Pasquet.

2 *remote-controlled tank*: Dietrich von Choltitz, "Pourquoi en 1944 je n'ai pas détruit Paris," *Le Figaro*, October 8–9, 1949, 5.

2 *"remain at all costs"*: Jacques Jaujard, "Activités dans la Résistance de Mademoiselle Rose Valland Conservateur des Musées Nationaux," AN 20144792/276.

2 *preferred to wear pants*: Letter from Rose Valland to her cousin Marguerite Jacquier-Roux and Marguerite's mother, circa 1920–1930s, MRD.

3 *living for almost a decade*: Joyce Heer's application for *Carte d'identité de travailleur étranger*, November 12, 1936, and application for *Carte d'identité*, March 24, 1934, AN 19940452/2; 1931 French census, Archives of Paris; various documents in AN 20150497/215; the 1934 *carte d'identité* application is the earliest document found where Joyce lists the same home address as Rose, 1ter rue de Navarre, where Rose lived from 1931 until at least December 1943.

3 *as an "unnatural act"*: Michael D. Sibalis, "Homophobia, Vichy France, and the 'Crime of Homosexuality': The Origins of the Ordinance of 6 August 1942," *GLQ (Journal of Lesbian and Gay Studies)* 8, no. 3 (2002): 302. This applied to

both men and women in France but the law against homosexuality in Germany applied only to men.

4 *"A sort of frenzy"*: Valland, *Le Front de l'Art,* 211.

4 *Through the downpour and lightning*: Ibid. Weather records and eyewitness reports indicate the storm occurred the evening of August 18 into 19.

5 *"We were in an entrenched camp!"*: Valland, *Le Front de l'Art,* 211.

5 *just twenty steps away*: Rose Valland, draft of chapter from *Le Front de l'Art,* "Les Combats de la Libération Autour des Musées de Paris," MAE 209SUP/717. In one draft, she notes that this is the entrance on the Place de la Concorde side.

5 *what was to become of her beloved museum*: Valland, *Le Front de l'Art,* 210.

5 *one pistol between them*: Letter from Rose Valland to Jacques Jaujard, November 6, 1941, AN 20144792/65.

5 *if required, "neutralized"*: Valland, *Le Front de l'Art,* 210.

5 *in particular, "disappear"*: Letter from Rose Valland to James Rorimer, June 25, 1957, AN 20150497/215; Valland, *Le Front de l'Art,* 105; Letter from Rose Valland to Captain Harlin, January 31, 1955, AN 20150497/215.

SECTION 2

8 *Life at home was dominated by . . . mostly uninvolved*: Jacqueline Barthalay (president of the association "La Mémoire de Rose Valland"), in conversation with the author, September 24, 2024.

8 *she caught up quickly*: Corinne Bouchoux, *Rose Valland: Resistance at the Museum* (Laurel Publishing, 2013), 13, Kindle edition.

8 *won regional and national awards*: Rose Valland résumés, MRD and AN 20150497/215. At the École des Beaux-Arts in Lyon she won three first prizes, one second prize, and an honorable mention. She also won a medal from the French Ministry of Commerce and Industry.

8 *nearly forty hours*: *Dossier sur l'École des Beaux-Arts,* AN AJ 52/971.

8 *Rose finished sixth*: "Rose Valland, Attachée, Charges de Mission, au Musée du Jeu de Paume. I^{ter}, rue de Navarre, PARIS Veme" (Rose Valland résumé), MRD.

9 *the school barred . . . Rose found a way*: Frédéric Destremau, *Rose Valland Résistante pour l'Art* (Grenoble: Patrimoine en Isère / Musée de la Résistance et de la Déportation, 2008), 11; Frédéric Destremau, *Rose Valland: La Dame du Jeu de Paume,* chapter 1, 9–10, MD.

9 *English language classes*: Identification card, "Société pour de la Propagation des Langues Étrangeres en France, 1929–30," MRD; Destremau, *Rose Valland,* chapter 2, 1, MD.

10 *particularly harshly*: Jacqueline Barthalay, conversation with the author, March 29, 2023.

10 *"the very expression of life"*: Rose Valland, *Essai sur l'Évolution du Mouvement dans l'Art Jusqu'a la Renaissance Italienne*, 1931, École du Louvre-Bibliothèque, Paris.

11 *French poet Guillaume Apollinaire described*: J. Alison Rosenblitt, *The Beauty of Living: E.E. Cummings and the Great War*, W.W. Norton & Company, 2021, iii.

11 *chic blue suit*: Letter from Rose Valland to Marguerite Jacquier-Roux and Marguerite's mother, undated pre-1939, MRD.

11 *lesbian capital of Europe*: Patrick Bade, *Lempicka* (New York: Parkstone International, 2012), 56; "Lifting the Veil on Paris' Lesbian Café Society," Radio France Internationale, January 13, 2011, www.rfi.fr/en/visiting-france/20110113-lifting-veil-pariss-lesbian-cafe-society.

11 *sometimes violently attacked*: Mark Braude (author, *Kiki May Ray*), in conversation with the author November 4, 2024.

12 "Vive Uruguay!": Letter from Rose Valland to Adrien Jacquier-Roux, July 1, 1924, archives of Bénédicte Delfaut.

12 *"One needs time and money"*: Ibid.

12 *"utterly serious"*: Michael Gibson, "How a Timid Curator with a Deadpan Expression Outwitted the Nazis," *ARTNews*, June 1981, 107.

13 *size people up*: James Rorimer, handwritten manuscript draft for *Survival*, James J. Rorimer Papers, AAA, Box 1, Folder 1.20.

13 *even with family*: Christine Vernay (grandniece of Rose Valland), in conversation with the author, August 11, 2022, and September 27, 2022.

13 *The more she felt at ease . . . unfailingly loyal*: Handwritten notes by James Rorimer on Rose Valland, NGA 28MFAA-J2 2–15.

13 *for having a "big heart"*: Letter from General Henry Blanc to Rose Valland, March 21, 1950, MAE 209SUP/706.

13 *"as she was herself"*: James Rorimer, manuscript draft for *Survival*, James J. Rorimer Papers, NGA 28MFAA-J1 4–8, Folder 1 of 3.

14 *full of political intrigue*: Letter from Margaret Scolari Barr to Alfred H. Barr Jr., undated (likely mid-1930s, before 1939), MOMA, Alfred H. Barr Jr. Papers, I.B.36.

14 *He was charming . . . frivolous or insipid*: Magdeleine Hours, *Une vie au Louvre* (Paris: Robert Laffont, 1987), 39; Pierre Schommer, *Il faut sauver la Joconde! Carnets (1937–1945)* (Paris: Éditions du CTHS, 2014), 104.

15 *people were turned away*: Letter from Rosa Valland to Marguerite Jacquier-Roux, January 20, 1931, archives of Bénédicte Delfaut.

16 *"showed no emotion"*: Ibid.

16 *"extreme indulgence of the jury" . . . "would not appear desirable"*: Letter from Henri Verne to Paul Léon, director général Beaux-Arts, May 7, 1932, AN 20150497/215.

17 *who knew how to type*: Extrait du Rapport adressé par M.A.D. ancien Conservateur

du Musée du Jeu de Paume au Conservateur du Musée Nationale d'Art Moderne, AN 20150497/184.

17 *"too late for a brilliant career"*: Ophélie Jouan, *Rose Valland: Une vie a l'œuvre* (Grenoble: Patrimoine en Isère / Musée de la Résistance et de la Déportation de L'Isère–Maison des Droits de l'Homme, 2020), 16.

17 *teaching art history . . . and French*: Letter from Madame H. Pichon, director general of the Collège Féminin, certifying Rose Valland's employment since 1924, June 23, 1930, MRD.

17 *giving tours*: "Au cercle des amis de Marie-Claire," *Marie Claire*, March 31, 1935.

17 *acting as an art broker*: Edward Lewine, vice president of Communications at Christie's, relaying answers from Christie's restitution department, in an email to the author, May 16, 2023.

17 *facilitated the sales of* La Gare: Elizabeth Saluk (Cleveland Museum of Art, Registrar for Exhibitions and Rights and Reproductions), in an email to the author, May 17, 2023; "Albert Gleizes, L'homme dans la ville," *Christie's*, https://www.christies.com/en/lot/lot-6139882; "Fernand Léger, La Gare," *Christie's*, https://www.christies.com/en/lot/lot-6342731.

18 *"is more particularly qualified"*: Letter from Henri Verne to le Directeur général des Beaux-Arts, April 12, 1932, AN 20150497/215.

18 *"most explosive international artistic events"*: Valland, *Le Front de l'Art*, 190.

18 *"most modern museums"*: Alphonse Allard, "L'actualité et la curiosité," *l'Art et les Artistes*, February 1933, 137.

19 *as a "brilliant event"*: Pierre Ladoué, *Bulletin des Musées de France*, 1933, 10.

19 *Over long, indulgent French luncheons*: Letter from Margaret Scolari Barr to Alfred H. Barr Jr.

20 *Severe angina*: Jean René, "Une reception au Musée du Jeu de Paume en l'honneur de Mechtrovitch," *Comœdia*, February 26, 1933, 3.

20 *was "overworked"*: Letter from Rose Valland to Marguerite Jacquier-Roux, around March 1939, archives of Bénédicte Delfaut.

20 *in English and French*: Destremau, *Rose Valland*, chapter 2, 9, MD.

20 *lay all the paintings flat*: Claude Brule, "Si Burt Lancaster tourne à Paris: C'est parce que cette femme a sauvé un trésor," *Elle Magazine France*, September 6, 1963.

20 *"the book would never be published"*: Letter from André Dezarrois to Henri Verne, June 30, 1934, AN 20150497/184.

22 *"I don't believe in war yet"*: Letter from Rose Valland to Marguerite Jacquier-Roux, undated spring 1939, archives of Bénédicte Delfaut.

22 *"turns out to be very tiring"*: Letter from Rose Valland to Marguerite Jacquier-Roux, circa early March 1939, archives of Bénédicte Delfaut.

22 *"one of the first to feel it"*: Letter from Rose Valland to Marguerite Jacquier-Roux, circa Easter 1939, archives of Bénédicte Delfaut.

22 *"And we will win it"*: Janet Flanner (writing as Genêt), "Letter from Paris," *The New Yorker*, July 1939.

23 *securing sculptures*: Letter to André Dezarrois, April 17, 1939; New York's World Fair 1939 and 1940 Incorporated Records, New York Public Library, Mss-Col2233, Box 311.

23 *sun-drenched apartment*: Letter from Rose Valland to Marguerite Jacquier-Roux, May 10, 1942, MRD.

24 *Rose lived with her partner*: Heer's application for *Carte d'identité*, November 12, 1936; Joyce Heer, preface by Fernand Robert, *La personnalité de Pausanias* (Paris: Les Belles Lettres, 1979).

24 *"happy-go-lucky sort of person"*: Auriel Heer (niece of Joyce Heer), in conversation with the author, December 5, 2023.

25 *she always had her sandals on*: Andy Heer (nephew of Joyce Heer), in an email to the author, March 13, 2024; photographs from the collection of Christine Vernay.

25 *attended an all-girls high school*: Joyce Heer's application for appointment, Official Personnel Folder Department of State, St. Louis, Missouri, NARA RG 59.

25 *"getting by on their own in life"*: Advertisement for "Le Collége Féminin de Bouffémont," Ebay (item listing), www.ebay.ph/itm/372800049791.

25 *French-language teacher since 1924*: Notarized letter from Madame H. Pichon, director of the Collège Féminin de Bouffémont, June 23, 1930, MRD.

25 *listed Rose as a reference*: Joyce Heer's application for *Carte d'Identité*, Paris Police Files, March 24, 1934, AN 19940452/2.

25 *"Rosie"*: Postcard from Joyce Heer to Rose Valland, July 1963, MRD.

25 *"Pouchka"*: Letter from Joyce Heer to Rose Valland, October 12, 1948, MAE 209SUP/724.

25 *helped Joyce perfect her French*: Heer, *La personnalité de Pausanias*.

26 *around a thousand other artworks*: Gerri Chanel, *Saving Mona Lisa* (London: Icon Books, 2019), 23; Edmond Pottier, *Le Musée du Louvre pendant la guerre 1914–1918* (France: Lahure, 1919), 19–20.

27 *Red Cross flag visible*: "Protecting the Louvre," September 19, 1914, *American Art News*, 1.

27 *"The Führer would like to see you"*: Diary of Hans Posse, June 18, 1939, Germanisches National Museum, Deutsches Kunstarchiv, NL Posse, Hans, I, B-1.

28 *"that hinders the continuation of the collection"*: Hans Posse, "Vorwort," *Die Staatliche Gemäldegalerie zu Dresden—Katalog der Modernen Galerie* (Dresden; Berlin: Bard, v. Baensch Stiftung, 1930), V.

28 *"bolt from the skies"*: Adolf Hitler, trans. James Murphy, *Mein Kampf*, chapter 2: "Years of Study and Suffering in Vienna," Project Gutenberg Australia, September 2002, https://gutenberg.net.au/ebooks02/0200601.txt.

28 *it would be "child's play" . . . "by far"*: Adolf Hitler, trans. Ralph Manheim, *Mein Kampf* (New York: Mariner, 1999), 19.

29 *"unfit" for painting*: Ibid., 20.

29 *"Artist, no, never as long as I live!"*: Ibid., 9.

29 *"Wherever I now went I saw Jews"* and following quotations: Hitler, trans. Murphy, *Mein Kampf*, chapter 2.

30 *"the greatest German mayor of all times"*: Hitler, trans. Manheim, *Mein Kampf*, 55.

30 *called himself "Führer" and began the use of "Heil"*: Bridgette Hamann, *Hitler's Vienna: A Portrait of the Tyrant as a Young Man* (London: Tauris Parke, 2020), 252.

30 *"from all sections of public life"*: Peter G. J. Pulzer, *The Rise of Political Anti-Semitism in Germany and Austria* (New York: John Wiley & Sons, 1964), 153.

30 *"Release a tornado"*: Herschel Browning Chipp, *Theories of Modern Art* (Los Angeles: University of California Press, 1968), 474.

30 *"German museums and collections"*: Ibid.

30 *"insane asylums or prisons"*: Ibid.

30 *over sixteen thousand modern artworks*: "Entarte Kunst: The Nazis' Inventory of 'Degenerate Art," Victoria and Albert Museum, www.vam.ac.uk/articles/entartete-kunst-the-nazis-inventory-of-degenerate-art; Jonathan Petropoulos, *Art as Politics in the Third Reich* (Chapel Hill: University of North Carolina Press, 1996), 56.

31 *"nothing to do with our German people"*: "Hitler's Speech at the Opening of the House of German Art in Munich (July 18, 1937)," German Historical Institute, Washington, DC, https://germanhistorydocs.org/en/nazi-germany-1933-1945/hitler-s-speech-at-the-opening-of-the-house-of-german-art-in-munich-july-18-1937.

31 *"blather and deception"*: Ibid.

31 *increasingly hysterical speech*: Paul Ortwin Rave, *Kunstdiktatur im Dritten Reich* (Berlin: Argon, 1987), 101.

31 *"cultural decline"*: Hitler, trans. Manheim, *Mein Kampf*, 328.

31 *"come judge for yourselves"*: Neil Levi, "Judge for Yourselves!—The *Degenerate Art* Exhibition as Political Spectacle," *October* 85 (Summer 1998): 41.

31 "Sie hatten vier Jahre Zeit": Stephanie Barron, *"Degenerate Art": The Fate of the Avant-Garde in Nazi Germany* (New York: Harry N. Abrams, 1991), 63.

31 *"Blasphemy!"*: Peter Guenther, "Three Days in Munich, July 1937," in Barron, *"Degenerate Art,"* 36.

31 *"making fun of us"* . . . "dumm": Ibid., 38.

31 *"Aren't they lovely?"*: Ibid., 43.

31 *on the wall were jarring statements*: Barron, *"Degenerate Art,"* 54, 49.

32 *"inmate[s] of a lunatic asylum"*: Barron, *"Degenerate Art,"* 21.

32 *wages of German working* Volk: Levi, "Judge for Yourselves!" 56.

32 *"Revelation of the Jewish racial soul"*: Barron, *"Degenerate Art,"* 54.

32 *on the radio at home*: Gilbert Lupfer and Thomas Rudert, *Kennerschaft zwischen Macht und Moral* (Köln: Böhlau, 2015), 133.

32 *"birthday gift"*: Ernst Kubin, *Sonderauftrag Linz: Die Kunstsammlung Adolf Hitler. Aufbau, Vernichtungsplan, Rettung. Ein Thriller de Kulturgeschischte* (Vienna: Orac, 1989), 15.

33 *"with a local party official"*: Ibid.

33 *"such horrible pictures"*: Frederic Spotts, *Hitler and the Power of Aesthetics* (New York: Abrams, 2021), 191.

33 *"hostile to the state"*: Birgit Schwarz, *Hitler's Museum: Die Fotoalben Gemäldegalerie Linz: Dokumente zum "Führermuseum"* (Vienna: Böhlau, 2004), 35.

33 "Führerpersönlichkeit": Schwarz, *Hitler's Museum*, 34; Lupfer and Rudert, *Kennerschaft zwischen Macht und Moral*, 337.

33 *"at the dissolution of the Louvre"*: Letter from Hans Posse to Wilhelm von Bode, September 14, 1914, quoted by Lupfer and Rudert, *Kennerschaft zwischen Macht und Moral*, 347.

33 *"Linz museum matter"*: Diary of Hans Posse, June 20, 1939, GNM, Deutsches Kunstarchiv, NL Posse, Hans, I,B-1.

35 *"my father's homeland at all times"*: Robert Chenevier, "Un aspect inconnu du Führer: Adolf Hitler Architecte et Urbaniste," *L'Illustration*, December 10, 1938, 508.

35 *"Barely useful" . . . "Not in keeping"*: Kubin, *Sonderauftrag Linz*, 18. Note: Kubin places this anecdote in the Berghof, but Albert Speer says it occurred shortly after in an air-raid shelter in Berlin.

36 *"As was so often the case"*: Albert Speer, *Inside the Third Reich* (New York: Avon, 1970), 245.

36 *"I will give you"*: Kubin, *Sonderauftrag Linz*, 17.

36 *forgotten* and *"left to degenerate"*: Ibid.

36 *"All party and state offices"*: Adolf Hitler to Hans Posse, June 26, 1939, Bundesarchiv Koblenz B 323/163, Nos. 237 and 242 (cited in Schwarz, *Hitler's Museum*, 40).

38 *Theodor Fischer*: Sandra Sykora (external provenance researcher with the Galerie Fischer Archive), in an email to the author, June 26, 2024. Sandra confirms that Fischer is seated at the table and the man standing is his son, Arthur Fischer.

38 *Eagerly put himself forward . . . there were no other dealers. . . . He knew for months*: Barron, *"Degenerate Art,"* 137.

38 *long list of artists' names*: Advertisement, *Beaux-Arts*, April 21, 1939, 7.

38 *"Behind the Fischer Gallery"*: Raymond Escholier, "2 Million un Portrait de Van Gogh par lui-même," *Le Journal*, June 19, 1939.

38 *"Not a cent to the German Reich"*: Anne Sinclair, *My Grandfather's Gallery: A Family Memoir of Art and War* (New York: Picador, 2014), 42.

38 *"would fall back on our heads"*: Ibid.

39 *"Rumors originate from Paris"*: Ibid., 139.

39 *victim of "Jewish propaganda" and wrote:* Letter from Theodor Fischer to Karl Haberstock, Zentrales Staatsarchiv Potsdam 50.01, 1020, Bl. 79 (cited in Georg Kreis, *"Entarte" Kunst für Basel: Die Herausforderung von 1939*, Zurich: NZZ Libro, 2017, 26).

39 *Fischer also sent a letter:* Barron, *"Degenerate Art,"* 146, footnote 17.

39 *Hitler himself announced*: René Barotte, "On vend aux enchères les tableaux proscrits du Reich," *Paris Soir*, July 1, 1939, 7.

39 *"We hope to at least make some money"*: Joseph Goebbels, *Die Tagebücher von Joseph Goebbels: Sämtliche Fragmente*, ed. Elke Fröhlich (Munich: K. G. Saur, 2000), Teil 1, Band 5, December 1937–July 1938, 399.

39 *burned in a conflagration*: Rave, *Kunstdiktatur im Dritten Reich,* 124; Marcel Struwe, "'Nationalsozialitischer Bildersturm.' Function eines Begriffs," *Bildersturm. Die Zerstörung des Kunstwerks*, ed. Martin Warneke (Munich: Carl Hanser, 1973), 135; Wilhelm F. Arntz, introduction by Kurt Fassmann, "Bildersturm in Deutschland," *Das Schönste*, May 1962; Petropoulos, *Art as Politics in the Third Reich*, 56. Rave quotes Goebbels giving consent to the burning of the paintings and that the depot was cleared on March 20, 1939.

40 *"These gentlemen use such means"*: Letter from Theodor Fischer to Karl Haberstock, Zentrales Staatsarchiv Potsdam 50.01, 1020, Bl. 79 (cited in Kreis, *"Entarte" Kunst für Basel*, 27).

41 *fund the war effort*: Letter from Reinheldt at Reich Chamber of Fine Arts to Curt Valentin, November 14, 1936, Jane Wade Papers, AAA, microfilm reel #2322, frame 929; Godula Buchholz, *Karl Buchholz: Buch- und Kunsthändler im 20. Jahrhundert* (Cologne: DuMont, 2005), 64–65.

41 *using funds from the museum trustees*: Alice Goldfarb Marquis, *Alfred H. Barr Jr.: Missionary for the Modern* (Chicago: Contemporary Books, 1989), 178; William D. Cohan, "MoMA's Problematic Provenances," *ArtNews*, November 17, 2011.

41 *"come to the telephone"*: J O K, "Gemalde und Plastiken aus deutschen Museen unter dem Hammer," *Der Bund*, July 6, 1939, 1. Original quote, *"Herr Dr. Frankfurter as Teliphon!,"* is in the Basel dialect of Swiss-German.

41 *"this lady does not please the public"*: "La vente des œuvres d'art 'dégénére à Lucerne," *Beaux-Arts*, July 7, 1939, 1; Kreis, *"Entarte" Kunst für Basel*, 33.

41 *announced triumphantly, "Withdrawn!"*: Ibid.

42 *"Going once, twice"*: J O K, "Gemalde und Plastiken aus deutschen Museen unter dem Hammer," 1; Barotte, "On vend aux enchères les tableaux proscrits du Reich," 7.

42 *"Place your bets!"*: Ibid.

42 *unrest in the free city of Danzig*: "Nazis Pouring into Danzig from Reich to Join 'Army,' Young Poles Also Active," *New York Times*, June 29, 1939. Danzig was not officially occupied in June 1939; German forces and armaments reportedly had been seen being moved into the city.

43 *"German art as 'real money'"*: "'Decadent' Sale Fails," *Daily Herald* (London), July 1, 1939, 2.

43 *"to secure foreign currency"*: "Nazis Sell Works of Art," *Daily News* (London), July 1, 1939, 11.

43 *"I am just as glad not to have"*: Letter from Alfred H. Barr Jr. to T. D. Mabry Jr., July 1, 1939, Roll 2166, MOMA, Alfred H. Barr Jr. Papers; Jonathan Petropoulos, "Bridges from the Reich: The Importance of Émigré Art Dealers Reflected in the Case Studies of Curt Valentin and Otto Kallir-Nirenstein," *Kunstgeschichte*, May 24, 2011.

43 *The newspaper publisher told*: Paul Gardner, "A Bit of Heidelberg Near Harvard Square," *ArtNews* 80, no. 6 (June 1981): 115.

44 *had been added within the previous year*: *Jeu de Paume Inventaire–Tableaux Sculpture Object d'Art*, AN 20144707/528.

45 *the one she preferred*: Hayden Herrera, *Frida: A Biography of Frida Kahlo* (New York: Harper & Row, 1983), 225.

45 *Frida derided "The Frame"*: Letter from Frida Kahlo to Diego Rivera, February 13, 1939, Diego Rivera and Frida Kahlo Archives, Banco de México, trustee in the trust of the Diego Rivera and Frida Kahlo Museum (quoted in Jaime Moreno Villareal, *Frida en París, 1939* [Madrid: Turner Noema, 2021], 71).

45 *"curious and gifted" . . . "the greatest living painter"*: Letter from André Dezarrois to the director général des Beaux-Arts, AN F/21/6743.

45 *Dezarrois told Frida with childlike excitement*: Villareal, *Frida en París*, 30.

46 *"the rich bitches don't want to buy anything"*: Letter from Frida Kahlo to Nickolas Muray, February 27, 1939, Nickolas Muray Papers, 1910–1992, AAA.

46 *"I'm going home"*: Letter from Frida Kahlo to Diego Rivera, reproduced in *El universo Frida Kahlo* (Barcelona: Editorial RM; Mexico: Museo Frida Kahlo, 2022), 131. Also in *Frida* (documentary), Carla Gutiérrez, director, Amazon Studios, 2024.

47 *were about to smuggle*: David Kahn, *Seizing the Enigma: The Race to Break the German U-Boat Codes, 1939–1943* (New York: Barnes & Noble, 1991), 81.

48 *"the dark events ahead"*: *21 rue la Boétie* (documentary film), Virginie Linhart, director, France 5, 2017.

48 *Thirty-two of his Picasso paintings*: "Paintings by Picasso which arrived in New York on the *S.S. Normandie* July 31, 1939, Permanent Exhibition No. 11," MOMA Exhibition Records, 91.5; "Customs Form 7517-A, Treasury Department," August 3, 1939, MOMA Exhibition Records, 91.5; "List of Rosenberg and Helft, London Loans," MOMA Exhibition Records 91.7.

49 *"in the event of war"*: Letter to Rosenberg & Helft, September 8, 1939, MOMA Exhibition Records, 91.3.

49 *something he also offered to Picasso*: Letter from Alfred H. Barr Jr. to T. D. Mabry Jr., July 9, 1939, MOMA Exhibition Records, 91.7; Letter from Dorothy Dudley to

Rosenberg & Helft, September 8, 1939, MOMA Exhibition Records, 91.7; Hugh Eakin, *Picasso's War: How Modern Art Came to America* (New York: Crown, 2022), 344.

49 *personally loaned ninety-five pieces*: Press Release, "Picasso Loans Come to Museum of Modern Art from Every Section of the United States," November 11, 1939, MOMA, https://assets.moma.org/documents/moma_press-release_325143.pdf.

49 *who told Picasso by letter*: Letter from Paul Rosenberg to Pablo Picasso, August 14, 1939, Archive of the Musée national Picasso-Paris, 515AP/C/3473.

49 *Parisians mocked the avant-garde art*: Anne Sinclair, "L'Enchaînement des hasards," *21 rue la Boétie: D'après le livre d'Anne Sinclair* (Vanves: Hazan and Musée Maillol Paris, 2017), 19.

49 *early collector and dealer of Impressionist art*: Veronika Grodzinski, *French Impresssion and German Jews: The Making of Modernist Art Collectors in Imperial Germany, 1896–1914* (University of College London, 2006), 28–29.

50 *"In my view," he once wrote*: Sinclair, *My Grandfather's Gallery*, 25.

50 *"the Rosenberg method"*: *21 rue la Boétie* (documentary film).

50 *countersigning with his famous autograph*: *Acte de naissance* no. 630 from Paris eighth arrondissement, March 8, 1921, Archives of Paris.

50 *he seemed more comfortable*: Sinclair, *My Grandfather's Gallery*, 65, 100.

51 *"shriek with horror"*: Ibid., 80.

51 *a friend of Paul's observed*: André Salmon, "La Peinture," Paris, *La revue de France*, vol. 1, pt. 3, July–August 1921.

51 *wary of its commercialism*: Sinclair, *My Grandfather's Gallery*, 66.

51 *if a painting was authentic or a forgery*: *"Nos enquêtes: Entretien avec Paul Rosenberg,"* supplement to *Cahiers d'art: Bulletin mensuel d'actualité artistique*, Paris, no. 9, 1927, 1.

51 *he responded logically*: Ibid.

51 *"Only Rosenberg has shown . . . allow myself to be forgotten"*: Sinclair, *My Grandfather's Gallery*, 104.

52 *through their kitchen windows*: Ibid.

52 *They were "inseparable"*: Ibid., 119.

52 *Paul would send a note next door*: Ibid., 122.

52 *"an added attraction for you"*: Letter from Paul Rosenberg to Pablo Picasso, August 14, 1939.

SECTION 3

53 *forced to retire early*: Henri Verne, Pension Civiles, AN F/17/24774; Schommer, *Il faut sauver la Joconde!*, 115–121; "Proposition de Pension" for Jacques Jaujard, AN F/17/27852.

53 *he was unwilling to pay her*: Rose was an unpaid attaché until November 29,

1939, when she was paid through a temporary budget. For more details, see official order from Yvon Dellos, Ministre de l'Education Nationale, November 29, 1939, AN 20144792/59.

53 *"seduction itself"*: Gaston Palewski, *Notice sur la vie et les travaux de Jacques Jaujard (1895–1967) . . . lue à l'occasion de son installation comme membre libre . . . séance du mercredi 20 novembre 1968* (Paris: Institut de France, Académie des Beaux-Arts, 1968), 16. From interview with Pierre Schommer.

54 *"sensitivity, courtesy, and kindness"*: Ibid., 23.

54 *As a colleague described admiringly*: Ibid.

54 *A fire in the Berlin Reichstag . . . the first concentration camps for political prisoners*: "Germany 1933: From Democracy to Dictatorship," Anne Frank House, https://www.annefrank.org/en/anne-frank/go-in-depth/germany-1933-democracy-dictatorship/.

54 *an "eventuality that must be anticipated"*: Henri Verne to René Dussard, Conservateur du département des Antiquités Orientales, October 4, 1932, AN 20144792/1.

55 *would minimize the risk*: Chanel, *Saving Mona Lisa*, 27–28.

55 *"limited to the essentials"*: Letter from Henri Verne to André Dezarrois, April 18, 1936, AN 20144792/1.

55 *as inventoried by Rose*: Rose Valland, "Tableaux à Sauvegardes en cas de guerre," May 8, 1936, AN 20144792/1. A draft version is located at MAE 209SUP/317, dated May 7, 1936.

55 *to be added "if necessary"*: Letter from André Dezarrois to Henri Verne, May 8, 1936, AN 20144792/1.

56 *gave credit to the Jeu de Paume's employees, saying*: Ibid.

56 *set up to hold two hundred paintings*: Ibid.

56 *given full command*: Order signed by Jacques Jaujard, September 28, 1938, AN 20150497/215.

56 *was moved back to Paris in a week*: Chanel, *Saving Mona Lisa*, 33.

57 *flew back to England and declared triumphantly*: Neville Chamberlain, "Peace for Our Time" speech, 10 Downing Street, London, UK, September 30, 1938.

57 *"Long live Daladier! Long live peace!"*: "Prague Ayant Accepté L'Accord de Munich," *Le Journal*, October 1, 1938.

57 *"whose anxiety had miraculously disappeared"*: Valland, *Le Front de l'Art*, 39.

57 *"in a delirium of joy"*: Nora Benkorich, ed., *La trahison de Munich. Emmanuel Mounier et la grande débâcle des intellectuels* (Paris: CNRS Editions, 2008), 49.

57 *"we all felt it"*: Lucie Mazauric, *Le Louvre en voyage: 1939–1945* (Paris: Plon, 1978), 14.

57 *"I feel torn"*: "Les Socialistes et l'Accord de Munich," October 2, 1968, *Le Monde*, www.lemonde.fr/archives/article/1968/10/02/les-socialistes-et-l-accord-de-munich_2494613_1819218.html.

57 *"you will have war"*: Benjamin F. Martin, *France in 1938* (Baton Rouge: Louisiana State University Press, 2006), 219.

57 *and evacuation felt "hasty"*: Valland, *Le Front de l'Art*, 39.

57 *Dezarrois wrote in a report*: Report from André Dezarrois to Georges Huisman, transmitted through Henri Verne, "Réponse au questionnaire de M. le Directeur Général des Beaux-Arts transmis par M. le Directeur des Musées Nationaux," October 17, 1938, AN 20150044/28.

58 *"thorniest aspects"*: Report from Pierre Schommer to Henri Verne, August 16, 1938, AN 20144792/1.

58 *"state of complete degradation"*: Report from Pierre Schommer to Henri Verne, November 3, 1938, AN 20144792/1.

59 *In total, 1,845 crates*: "Depots des Œvres d'Art Espagnoles au Palais de la Société," AN 20144792/60.

59 *intense planning and preparation commenced*: Chanel, *Saving Mona Lisa*, 38–39.

60 *such as a family burial vault*: Schommer, *Il faut sauver la Joconde!*, 105–6.

60 *a "serious risk" and "the most"*: Jacques Jaujard, "Rapport à Monsieur le Ministre de l'Education Nationale sur les mesures prises dans les Musées Nationaux en vue de la sauvegarde des collections en temps de guerre," August 5, 1939, AN 20144792/5.

60 *Hitler withdrew from . . . and declared*: "No. 13 Extract from Herr Hitler's speech to the Reichstag on April 28, 1939," *The British War Blue Book* (New York: Farrar & Rinehart, 1939), 29.

60 *"Come home to the Reich"*: Richard Hargreaves, *Blitzkrieg Unleashed* (Mechanicsburg, PA: Stackpole, 2010), 59.

61 *"There will be fighting"*: Lloyd Clark, *Kursk: The Greatest Battle: Eastern Front, 1943* (London: Headline Review, 2011), 25.

61 *able to produce a large quantity of work*: Bureau of Foreign and Domestic Commerce, Foreign Service, Annual, Local Employee Report written by D. J. Reagan, Acting Commercial Attaché, July 1, 1937, and July 1, 1938, Joyce Heer's Official Personnel Folder Department of State, St. Louis, Missouri, NARA RG 59.

61 *she insisted that she wanted to stay*: Joyce Heer's application for Foreign Service, August 1, 1939, Official Personnel Folder Department of State, St. Louis, Missouri, NARA RG 59.

61 *"to kill without pity or mercy"*: Tadeusz Piotrowski, *Poland's Holocaust: Ethnic Strife, Collaboration with Occupying Forces, and Genocide in the Second Republic, 1918–1947* (Jefferson, NC: McFarland, 1998), 115.

61 *"Our strength lies"*: Ibid.

61 *Heinrich Himmler, the head of the SS, announced*: Ibid.

62 *to Cinq-Mars-la-Pile*: Sinclair, *My Grandfather's Gallery*, 43. The family left Hotel Évian between August 19 and 22, 1939.

63 *he planned to escape*: Letter from Georges Braque to Paul Rosenberg, August 22, 1939, ML 3500.24.

63 *Much to the frustration of Alfred H. Barr Jr.*: Letter from Alfred H. Barr Jr. to T. D. Mabry Jr., July 9, 1939.

64 *"Is our continent going to commit suicide"*: Quoted in speech by president of the Belgian Senate, Anne-Marie Lizin, November 15, 2006, www.senate.be/event/20061115-kingsday/speech/2006_11_15_discours_monarchie.doc.

64 *secretly delivered a note to Hitler*: Robert Coulondre, French Ambassador in Berlin, to Georges Bonnet, French Minister for Foreign Affairs, August 22, 1939, *The French Yellow Book* (New York: Reynal & Hitchcock and French Ministry of Foreign Affairs), 288.

65 *prepared for an "instant blackout"*: Ferdinand Kuhn Jr., Special cable to the *New York Times*, "British Less Tense," *New York Times*, August 26, 1939, 4.

65 *"exceptional security measures"*: "Le Conseil des Ministres a approuvé ce matin des mesures exceptionelle de securité," *Ce soir*, August 25, 1939, 1.

65 *calm and collected*: "Ce Matin au Conseil des Ministres," *Ce soir*, August 25, 1939, 2; "A Paris Les Ministres Approuvent Les Mesures de Securité: La France accueille avec un calme magnifique les decisions du gouvernement," *Le Figaro*, August 25, 1939, 1; "Le Visage de Paris? Toujours Calme et Souriant," *Le Petit Journal*, August 26, 1939, 5.

65 *Édouard Daladier gave a radio speech*: "The Text of Premier Daladier's Talk," August 26, 1939, *New York Times*, 7.

66 *"I will not attack France"*: Cable from Robert Coulondre, French Ambassador in Berlin, to Georges Bonnet, French Minister for Foreign Affairs, August 25, 1939, *French Yellow Book*, 302–5.

66 *labor camps and ethnic cleansing*: United States, Office of Chief Counsel for the Persecution of Axis Criminality, Testimony of Hans Fitzche, Head of German Press Division, *Nazi Conspiracy and Aggression, Volume 2* (US Government Printing Office, 1946), 1043; "Das Totenfeld der Volksdeutschen in Polen," Bulmash Family Holocaust Collection, Chalmers Library, Kenyon University, https://digital.kenyon.edu/bulmash/1376.

66 *"I will provide a propagandistic* casus belli*"*: Roy Godson and James J. Wirtz, *Strategic Denial and Deception: The Twenty-First Century Challenge* (New Brunswick: National Strategy-Information Center, Washington, DC, 2002), 100.

66 *"Countless human lives"*: "Roosevelt's Note to Hitler," *New York Times*, August 16, 1939, 6.

66 *that Roosevelt "appears devoted"*: "Inner Circles of Nazis Cool to Roosevelt," *New York Times*, August 26, 1939, 2.

SECTION 4

69 *start packing*: Chanel, *Saving Mona Lisa*, 43.

69 *"continuous slide to the inevitable"*: Valland, *Le Front de l'Art*, 39.

69 *"Whatever the threats"*: Ibid., 43.

70 *tough, independent-minded Corsicans*: Letter from Rose Valland to Henri Verne, May 10, 1939, MAE 209SUP/317 (Rose lists seven guards and two auxiliary guards who can assist with the packing, including Battini, Maestracci, Dhonneur, Basson, and Angeli); "Personnel masculine au 1er Avril 1943" et al., AN 20144792/55.

70 *wrapped in fiber quilt batting*: "L'Évacuation du Louvre," *L'Illustration*, September 16, 1939.

70 *fifty most notable paintings off the walls*: Chanel, *Saving Mona Lisa*, 45.

71 *rustling sounds of paraffin paper*: "Rapport de Robert REY sur l'attitude allemande vis à vis des oeuvres d'art et le vol du RETABLE de l'AGNEAU MYSTIQUE de VAN EYCK, confié a la France par la Ville de Gand," September 1944, AN 20144792/42.

71 *the 5,803 pieces of glass*: "Le Sauvetage de nos Vitraux les Plus Précieux," *L'Illustration*, September 9, 1939.

71 *165 in total*: "Musée de Jeu de Paume (Caisses)," typewritten with Rose's handwritten additions; Rose Valland, "VII depart" and "IX depart," both from AN 20144792/38.

71 *Approximately two-thirds*: Letter from Rose Valland to Henri Verne, September 23, 1939, AN 20144792/21.

72 *Jaujard calmly directed*: Chanel, *Saving Mona Lisa*, 48.

72 *valiantly guided the 1938 art evacuation at top speed*: Pierre Schommer, *Le Cabinet de l'Amateur* (catalogue de l'exposition) (Paris: Éditions des Musées Nationaux, 1956), XI.

73 *During the night on August 31*: "Twenty-Fourth Day, Thursday 20 December 1945, Morning Session," *Nuremberg Trial Proceedings*, Vol. 4 (Nuremberg: International Military Tribunal, 1947), 241–43.

73 *"to oppose force with force"*: "Entre la Paix et la Guerre," *L'Illustration*, September 9, 1939, 35.

74 *Hitler also made a speech at the Reichstag*: "Address by Adolf Hitler, Chancellor of the Reich, before the Reichstag," September 1, 1939, Avalon Project, Documents in Law, History and Diplomacy, Yale Law School, Lillian Goldman Law Library, https://avalon.law.yale.edu/wwii/gp2.asp.

74 *To loud applause, he confirmed*: Message addressed by Albert Lebrun, president of the Republic, to the French Parliament, September 2, 1939, *French Yellow Book*, 384.

74 *followed with an even longer speech*: Declaration read out on September 2, 1939, to the Chamber of Deputies by Édouard Daladier, president of the Coun-

cil of Ministers, and to the Senate by Camille Chautemps, vice president of the Council, *French Yellow Book*, 391–92.

74 *a new study showed*: Chanel, *Saving Mona Lisa*, 54.

75 *Made up of 118 fragile pieces*: Ibid.

75 *"The rope is cracking!"*: René Huyghe, *Une Vie pour l'Art: De Léonard à Picasso* (Paris: Éditions de Fallois, 1994), 116.

75 *"I will not see her return"*: Hours, *Une vie au Louvre*, 44.

75 *"which are known to the German Government"*: Colulondre, French Ambassador in Berlin, to Georges Bonnet, Minister for Foreign Affairs, September 3, 1939, *French Yellow Book*, 400–401.

SECTION 5

77 *were now completely empty*: Letter from Rose Valland to Henri Verne, September 23, 1939.

77 *Rose was retrofitting*: Letter from Rose Valland to Henri Verne, September 23, 1939, AN 20144792/21.

78 *"Consequently, this country is at war"*: Radio address by Neville Chamberlain, September 3, 1939, The Avalon Project, Yale Law School Lillian Goldman Law Library, https://avalon.law.yale.edu/wwii/gb3.asp.

78 "Vive la France!": Appeal to the Nation by Édouard Daladier, president of the Council of Ministers, September 3, 1939, *French Yellow Book*, 403.

78 *"There may be dark days ahead"*: "King George VI First Radio Address—'With God's Help, We Shall Prevail' delivered 3 September 1939, London" (authenticity certified transcript), American Rhetoric Online Speech Bank, https://www.americanrhetoric.com/speeches/kinggeorgevifirstradioaddress.htm.

78 *on a straw mattress*: Letter from André Dezarrois to Henri Verne, September 10, 1939, AN 20150497/184; letter from Rose Valland to Jacques Jaujard, April 12, 1940, AN 20144792/67.

79 *she wrote later that day to her cousin Marguerite*: Letter from Rose Valland to her cousin Marguerite Jacquier-Roux, likely on September 7, 1939, archives of Bénédicte Delfaut.

79 *over five thousand crates*: Chanel, *Saving Mona Lisa*, 58.

79 *a united purpose*: Valland, *Le Front de l'Art*, 40.

80 *for one or two days*: Letter from Henri Matisse to Paul Rosenberg, September 6, 1939, ML MA 3500.310.

80 *his jacket pockets tore*: Janet Flanner, *Men and Monuments: Profiles of Picasso, Matisse, Braque, & Malraux* (New York: De Capo, 1990), 186.

81 *"Picasso has disappeared"*: Letter from Mary Callery to Alfred H. Barr Jr., September 20, 1939, MOMA Exhibition Records, 91.2.

81 *"Nobody has heard from him"*: Letter from Christian Zervos to Alfred H. Barr Jr., October 26, 1939, MOMA Exhibition Records, 91.4.

81 *Rose was overjoyed*: Letter from Rose Valland to Oļģerds Grosvalds, minister plenipotentiary of Latvia in France, September 18, 1939, National Archives of Latvia, fonds 2575, apraksts 7, lieta 2466, lapas 62.

81 *he appealed, asking*: Letter from André Dezarrois to Henri Verne, September 10, 1939, AN 20150497/184.

82 *"I am desperate with nothing to do"*: Letter from Paul Rosenberg to Alfred H. Barr Jr., October 10, 1939, MOMA Exhibition Records, 91.7.

82 *He also encouraged Matisse*: Letter from Paul Rosenberg to Henri Matisse, September 30, 1939, Archives Matisse, Issy-les-Moulineaux, France.

82 *even a Hermès sleeping bag*: H. Brubach, "Survivors," *The New Yorker*, August 1990, 74.

82 *The theaters and the opera reopened . . . and game in abundance*: Janet Flanner, "Letter from Paris," October 28, 1939, *The New Yorker*, 53.

83 *would temporarily be getting 1,250 francs*: Official order from Yvon Dellos, Ministre de l'Éducation Nationale, November 29, 1939, AN 20144792/59.

84 *Verne was like a "king confined"*: Schommer, *Il faut sauver la Joconde!*, 145–46.

84 *"try to overcome my torment"*: Letter from Henri Matisse to Paul Rosenberg, November 29, 1939, ML MA 3500.314.

84 *"Howls from his mother and the housekeeper"*: Letter from Paul Rosenberg to Pablo Picasso, February 1, 1940, Archive of the Musée national Picasso-Paris, cited in Eakin, *Picasso's War*, 365.

84 *strapped onto a gurney and covertly moved*: Schommer, *Il faut sauver la Joconde!*, 182.

84 *The usual suspects for such a high-risk art maneuver were present*: Letter from Pierre Schommer to Henri Verne, November 16, 1939, AN 20144792/39; Chanel, *Saving Mona Lisa*, 72.

85 *caused storage space concerns*: Schwarz, *Hitler's Museum*, 42.

86 *He would regularly grab a pencil*: Speer, *Inside the Third Reich*, 122.

86 *"without any note of protest"*: Ibid.

86 *Hitler envisioned Linz*: Ibid., 147; S. L. Faison Jr., *Consolidated Interrogation Report No. 4, Linz: Hitler's Museum and Library, December 15, 1945,* Office of Strategic Services, Art Looting Investigation Unit, US Army, NARA.

86 *The future Führermuseum*: Zuzanna Stańska, "The Story of Hitler's Unrealized Art Museum in Linz," *Daily Art Magazine*, February 19, 2022, www.dailyartmagazine.com/story-hitlers-art-museum/; Speer, *Inside the Third Reich*, 242, 387.

87 *"What a fine reopening that will be"*: Letter from Paul Rosenberg to Henri Matisse, April 4, 1940, Archives Matisse.

87 *To Picasso, Paul wrote*: Sinclair, *My Grandfather's Gallery*, 189.

88 *"Wonderful mood"*: Diary of Hans Posse, April 9, 1940, cited in Schwarz, *Hitler's Museum*, 48.

89 *she reported their behavior*: Letters from Rose Valland to Jacques Jaujard, May 7, 1940, and May 20, 1940, AN 20144795/46.

90 *Rose stressed in a letter to Marguerite*: Letter from Rose Valland to her cousin Marguerite Jacquier-Roux, May 20, 1940, MRD.

90 *Picasso ran into Matisse on the street in Paris*: André Verdet, *Entretiens notes et écrits sur la peinture* (Paris: Éditions Galilée, 1978), 152.

90 *"Leave the museum"*: Note by Rose Valland, AN 20150497/215.

91 *She had been campaigning to remain for weeks*: Letter from Rose Valland to Georges Huisman, May 25, 1940, AN 20150497/215.

91 *then burning them in huge bonfires*: Jonathan Fenby, *The General: Charles de Gaulle and the France He Saved* (London: Simon & Schuster, 2010), 14.

91 *like a scene from Dante's Inferno*: Robert Murphy, *Diplomat among Warriors* (Garden City, NY: Doubleday, 1964), 40.

91 *William Bullitt, nearly lost his life*: "Une bombe est tombée dans la salle où déjeunaient MM. Bullitt et Laurent Eynac," June 4, 1940, *Le Petit Journal*, 1; William C. Bullitt, Telegram, June 3, 1940, in Orville H. Bullitt, ed., *For the President, Personal and Secret: Correspondence between Franklin D. Roosevelt and William C. Bullitt* (Boston: Houghton Mifflin, 1972), 448–49.

91 *"Somewhere in the north of France"*: Antoine de Saint-Exupéry, trans. Lewis Galantière, *Flight to Arras* (London: Pan Books, 1975), 72.

92 *ran over a sixteen-year-old girl*: Agnès Humbert, trans. Barbara Mellor, *Résistance: A Woman's Journal of Struggle and Defiance in Occupied France* (New York: Bloomsbury, 2008), 4.

93 *unable to find her two young daughters*: Ibid., 5.

93 *stating the terrible truth*: Michel Rayssac, *L'Exode des Musées* (Paris: Éditions Payot & Rivage, 2007), 130.

93 *defiant message to US Secretary of State Cordell Hull that stated*: Telegram from William C. Bullitt to Secretary of State Cordell Hull, June 11, 1940, in Bullitt, ed., *For the President*, 466.

93 *and kept it with her*: "Ordre de Mission" (signed by Jacques Jaujard), June 12, 1940, AN 20144797/215.

93 *done under machine-gun fire*: Christiane Desroches-Noblecourt, *La Grande Nubiade: Le parcours d'une égyptologue* (Paris: Éditions Stock, 1992), 87.

94 *"I will go myself"*: Christiane Desroches-Noblecourt, "Un très grand directeur: Jacques Jaujard," in *Pillages et Restitutions* (Paris: Direction des musées de France, 1997), 24.

94 *Jaujard then personally accompanied*: Germain Bazin, "Journal d'évacuation des dépôts de la Sarthe," July 17, 1940, AN 20144797/179.

94 *used his authority as an army captain*: Germain Bazin, *Souvenirs de l'Exode du Louvre* (Paris: Editions d'art Somogy, 1992), 20.

94 *"I would like my Jewish colleagues"*: Humbert, *Résistance*, 3.

95 *tearfully watched him leave Chambord*: Schommer, *Il faut sauver la Joconde!*, 222; Lucie Mazauric, *Le Louvre en voyage: 1939–1945* (Paris: Plon, 1978), 49.

95 *"thin as sheets of paper"*: Mazauric, *Le Louvre en voyage*, 48.

95 *it was a harebrained decision*: Rose Valland, "Voici quelques details précisant mon attitude et celle de la direction de Musées Nationaux à mon sujet," MAE 209SUP/716.

95 *"As always, in a departure of this importance"*: Rose Valland, draft of chapter "Transfert de personnel pour les depôts," AN 20150497/216.

96 *"dead city; hardly anyone walked abroad"*: Jane Manley, ed., *Mrs. Trewhella's War: 1940–1944*, 2nd ed. (London: Descript, 2011), 24–25.

97 *"catastrophic disorder"*: Valland, "Voici quelques details précisant mon attitude."

98 *she later recounted with conviction*: Valland, "Transfert de personnel pour les depôts."

100 *had decided to abandon the group*: Claude Ferraton, "Etat desavanées faites par la Réunion des Musées Nationaux pour des paiements effectués pour le compte de l'État (Défense Passive) a vue de l'évacuation du personnel de la Direction des Musées Nationaux par péniches le 13 Juin 1940," AN 20144792/67.

SECTION 6

103 *a fervent debate taking place*: Sinclair, *My Grandfather's Gallery*, 50.

103 *"Discreetly examine the genitals"*; *"I've never laughed so much"*: Letter from Henri Matisse to Paul Rosenberg, May 28, 1940, ML MA 3500.327.

104 *The Rosenberg family gathered to discuss their options*: "Testimonial of Jorge Helft," interview by Zachary Donnenfeld in Bordeaux, France, 2016, Sousa Mendes Foundation, Greenlawn, New York, https://vimeo.com/189047352.

104 *Paul was optimistic:* Sinclair, *My Grandfather's Gallery*, 51.

105 *"I would rather stand with God against Man"*: "Aristedes de Sousa Mendes: His Life and Legacy," Sousa Mendes Foundation, Greenlawn, New York, https://sousamendesfoundation.org/aristides-de-sousa-mendes-his-life-and-legacy.

105 *seventy-seven paintings and drawings*: Alexandre Rosenberg, signed, sworn document and notarized document with Charles C. Beeman, Notary Public in the State of New York, June 19, 1947, Paul Rosenberg Archives, MOMA V.A.10.

106 *He hid a few paintings*: "List of paintings from Floirac and their fate," Paul Rosenberg Archives, MOMA V.A.13; Sinclair, *My Grandfather's Gallery*, 203.

107 *Jumping onto one of the trucks*: The following story is recounted in and quotations are from Valland, "Transfert de personnel pour les depôts."

108 *managed to bring one painting with her*: "List of paintings from Floirac and their fate."

108 *Traffic was at a standstill*: Sinclair, *My Grandfather's Gallery*, 52.

108 *a fun family adventure*: The following story is recounted in and quotations are from "Testimonial of Jorge Helft."

110 *"It taught me war, and made me hate it"*: Valland, "Transfert de personnel pour les depôts."

110 *"I will never sign an armistice"*: Fenby, *The General*, 20.

111 *a possible, unprecedented union*: Thomas Rodney Christofferson and Michael Scott Christofferson, *France during World War II: From Defeat to Liberation* (New York: Fordham University Press, 2006), 31.

111 *thought highly of de Gaulle*: John Colville, *The Fringes of Power: Downing Street Diaries, 1939–55* (Weidenfeld & Nicolson, 2004), 153.

111 *"a marriage with a corpse"*: The following quotations and story are recounted in Christofferson and Christofferson, *France during World War II*, 31.

111 *"I tell you today that we must stop fighting"*: "Le discours de maréchal Pétain le 17 juin 1940," *Fondation de la France Libre*, November 20, 2009, www.france-libre.net/discours-petain.

112 *was about to be arrested*: The following story and quotations are from Fenby, *The General*, 28–29.

112 *filled with torment*: Jean Lacouture, *De Gaulle* (Paris: Éditions du Seuil, 1965), 65.

113 *and did not move*: Françoise des Varennes, *Jacques Jaujard: Un Bienfaiteur de la Culture* (Paris: Institut de France, 1984), 10.

113 *hundreds of thousands of starving refugees*: Schommer, *Il faut sauver la Joconde!*, 226.

113 *considered holding a deer hunt:* Bazin, *Souvenirs de l'Exode du Louvre*, 18.

113 *the inexplicable release*: Schommer, *Il faut sauver la Joconde!*, 228.

113 *As Schommer later described*: Ibid., 281.

114 *Speaking of the imminent armistice, he beseeched*: Charles-Henry Groult and Benoît Hopquin, "Uncovering the Not-So-Simple Story Behind de Gaulle's Famed Appeal of June 18," *Le Monde*, January 20, 2023, www.lemonde.fr/en/france/article/2023/01/20/uncovering-the-not-so-simple-story-behind-de-gaulle-s-mythic-appeal-of-june-18_6012361_7.html.

116 *"Do you want to go to England?"*: François Jacob, *La statue intérieure* (Paris: Éditions Odile Jacob, 1987), 142.

116 *government spies in their midst*: Guy Durand-Viel (local historian), in conversation with the author, September 24, 2022.

117 *"I have a lot of people asking me that"*: "Testimonial of Jorge Helft."

117 *words like "Third Company"*: Alain Godec (researcher at Fondation de la France Libre), in an email to the author, August 25, 2024.

117 *The crowd was surprisingly calm*: The following story and quotations are from Jacob, *La statue intérieure*, 143; *1936–1945 Ascain, Ciboure, Saint-Jean-de-Luz, Urrugne* (Urrugne: Jakintza, 2009), 51, 54.

118 *flapping in the wind*: François Jacob, speech at the Sorbonne, June 18, 1940, "Les volontaires de Saint-Jean-de-Luz, juin 1940," *Fondation de la France Libre*, https://www.france-libre.net/les-volontaires-de-saint-jean-de-luz-juin-1940/.

118 *"Winston Churchill"*: Hector Feliciano, *The Lost Museum* (New York: Basic Books, 1998), 69.

SECTION 7

121 *were hunting the duke's exotic animals*: Schommer, *Il faut sauver la Joconde!*, 262.

121 *Schommer watched in disgust*: The following story is recounted in ibid., 250–51.

121 *ran through the courtyard*: Ibid., 238–39.

122 *With a smirk, he said of Hitler*: Ibid., 246–47.

122 *took gold watches for themselves*: "Vol commis par les Autorités Allemandes d'une importante collection de livres et de quelques objets d'art appartenant a Monsieur Guerquin, Secrétaire Général de l'École Nationale Supérieure des Beaux-Arts (Juin à Octobre 1940)"; Letter from Jacques Jaujard to Monsieur l'Intendant beim Befehlshaber Nordwestfrankreich, March 1943; both from NARA RG 260, Entry 55B, Box 326, Folder 248.

123 *"I continued my buffoonery"*: Bazin, *Souvenirs de l'Exode du Louvre*, 22.

123 *He wanted to name a pig*: Letter from Germain Bazin to René Huyghe, July 17, 1940, AN 20200285/2.

123 *the Allies would bring back "triumphantly and arrogantly"*: Ibid.

SECTION 8

125 *The day after the armistice was signed*: Hermann Giesler, *Ein Anderer Hitler: Bericht Seines Architekten Hermann Giesler* (Leono am Starnberger See: Druffel-Verlag, 1977), 386; Arno Breker, *Im Strahlungsfeld der Ereignisse - Leben und Wirken eines Künstlers. Porträts, Begegnungen, Schicksale* (Preussisch Oldendorf: K. W. Schütz, 1972), 155; Speer, *Inside the Third Reich*, 235. Hermann Giesler and Arno Breker put Hitler's visit on June 23, 1940. Speer writes that it was three days after the armistice (June 25). I have opted to go with Giesler and Breker's date, for the detail they provide on what Paris looked like on that day.

125 *"I want to see Paris with my artists"*: Giesler, *Ein Anderer Hitler*, 387.

125 *"Now the gates are open to me"*: Breker, *Im Strahlungsfeld der Ereignisse*, 153.

125 *"what a celebration"*: Giesler, *Ein Anderer Hitler*, 388.

126 *the most beautiful building:* Breker, *Im Strahlungsfeld der Ereignisse*, 156.

126 *he was bewildered not to find one specific detail*: The story and quotations are from Giesler, *Ein Anderer Hitler*, 388.

126 *"you see how well I know my way about"*: Speer, *Inside the Third Reich*, 236.

127 *"You will build my tomb, Giesler"*: Giesler, *Ein Anderer Hitler*, 390.

128 *to be exhumed from Vienna*: Breker, *Im Strahlungsfeld der Ereignisse,* 161.

128 *"Let it be blown up"*: Giesler, *Ein Anderer Hitler*, 390.

128 *Next was a speedy visit to Notre-Dame*: The story and quotations are from Breker, *Im Strahlungsfeld der Ereignisse,* 163, 165.

128 *"I want to make your work easier!"*: Giesler, *Ein Anderer Hitler*, 392.

128 *On the way back to Berlin*: The story and quotations are from Speer, *Inside the Third Reich*, 237.

SECTION 9

131 *nicknamed the* "Ausweis": Schommer, *Il faut sauver la Joconde!*, 263.

131 *"nothing is moving or singing in the trees"*: Jean Guéhenno, trans. David Ball, *Diary of the Dark Years, 1940–1944: Collaboration, Resistance, and Daily Life in Occupied Paris* (Oxford: Oxford University Press, 2014), 20.

132 *"We have known days of immense sadness"*: Letter from Marguerite Jacquier-Roux to Rose Valland, August 5, 1940, MRD.

132 *promptly shot with blank bullets*: Fritz Gubler and Raewyn Glynn, *Great, Grand and Famous Hotels* (Lane Cove: Great, Grand & Famous, 2008), 126.

134 *curator of the Musée national d'Art Moderne*: The Musée national d'Art Moderne (not to be confused with the Musée d'Art Moderne, created by the City of Paris in 1961) opened in 1937 at today's Palais de Tokyo. Jean Cassou was appointed curator of the Musée national d'Art Moderne in 1937, then chief curator in 1940. He was dismissed by Vichy in October 1940.

134 *"I feel I will go mad"*: Humbert, *Résistance*, 11.

134 *"like-minded comrades"*: Ibid.

134 *"secret society"*: Ibid.

134 *to be sent to London*: Desroches-Noblecourt, "Un très grand directeur," 27.

134 *Hitler issued the first directive*: Letter from Wilhelm Keitel to General von Boeckelberg, reproduced in Valland, *Le Front de l'Art*, 234; Jean Cassou, *Le Pillage par les Allemands des Œuvres d'art et des Bibliothèques appartenant à des Juifs en France* (Paris: Éditions du Centre, 1947), 78.

135 *"camouflage of intentions"*: Valland, *Le Front de l'Art, 70.*

135 *the French police provided transportation*: Lynn H. Nicholas, *The Rape of Europa* (New York: Vintage, 1994), 125.

136 *simply hand over his artwork*: Sinclair, *My Grandfather's Gallery*, 32.

136 *curators were held at gunpoint*: Nicholas, *Rape of Europa*, 124.

136 *"commander of the military administration"*: "Nuremberg Trial Proceedings Vol. 7, Fifty-Second Day, Wednesday February 6, 1946, Morning Session," Avalon Project, Documents in Law, History and Diplomacy, Yale Law School, Lillian Goldman Law Library, https://avalon.law.yale.edu/imt/02-06-46.asp.

137 *"Oh, we've seen these"*: Françoise Gilot, *Life with Picasso* (London: Virago, 1990), 37.

137 *This was the main legal founding*: Jonathan Petropoulos, in conversation with the author, September 18, 2024.

137 *Vichy continued to authorize*: Paul Rosenberg Archives, MOMA II.A.19. This box deals with the issues about licenses and getting money out of Paul's accounts in France.

137 *"prepayment and advance for war reparations"*: Feliciano, *Lost Museum*, 35.

137 *"savage expressionism"*: Letter from Carltheo Zeitschel to Ambassador Otto Abetz, November 28, 1940, reproduced in Cassou, *Le Pillage par les Allemands*, 137; Letter from Carltheo Zeitschel to Otto Abetz, November 15, 1940, MS V-105.

138 *"objects valuable to Germany"*: Order from Wilhelm Keitel to the Commander in Chief for the Military Administration of Occupied France, 2 f 28.14 W. Z No 3812/40 g, September 17, 1940, AN 20144792/56.

138 *"Germany will regard the Jewish question"*: United States Office of Chief of Counsel for the Prosecution of Axis Criminality, "International Military Tribunal Indictment No. 1," *Nazi Conspiracy and Aggression*, vol. 1 (Washington, DC: US Government Printing Office, 1946), 20.

138 *behind false doors and inside secret cellars*: "Pillages d'œuvres d'art (du Professur Dr. Wilhelm Treue), Analyse du Chapitre XX, Pillages d'ouevres d'art en Allemagne même et à l'étranger," MAE 209SUP/313.

139 *Hitler expanded the ERR's mandate*: Order from Wilhelm Keitel to the Commander in Chief for the Military Administration of Occupied France, 2 f 28.14 W. Z No 3812/40 g, September 17, 1940, AN 20144792/56.

139 *Jaujard made fake contracts*: Valland, *Le Front de l'Art*, 134; Bazin, *Souvenirs de l'Exode du Louvre*, 93.

140 *"I am happy to greet a senior official"*: Palewski, *Notice sur la vie et les travaux de Jacques Jaujard*, 19.

SECTION 10

143 *a sympathetic hotel receptionist warned them*: "Visas for Life. Episode 1: The Exodus" (Testimonial of Jorge Helft), Sousa Mendes Foundation, Greenlawn, New York, 2016, https://vimeo.com/804385991/39b7619113.

143 *questioning the validity of his enlistment*: Letter from Winnifred Easton to Paul Rosenberg, September 13, 1940, Paul Rosenberg Archives, MOMA II. RR.1.

144 *"It is with the greatest regret"*: Letter from Winnifred Easton to Paul Rosenberg, September 3, 1940, Paul Rosenberg Archives, MOMA II. RR.1.

144 *"just like real British soldiers"*: Letter from Winnifred Easton to Paul Rosenberg, November 6, 1940, Paul Rosenberg Archives, MOMA II. RR.1.

144 *"What a pleasure to breathe"*: Entry from July 12, 1940, personal war diary of Paul Glaoguen, 22nd G.C.F.T.A., FFL.

144 *was named "brigadier of the week"*: Letter from Winnifred Easton to Paul Rosenberg, September 30, 1940, Paul Rosenberg Archives, MOMA II. RR.1.

144 *naturally shy and sensitive*: Letter from Winnifred Easton to Paul Rosenberg, October 16, 1940, Paul Rosenberg Archives, MOMA II. RR.1.

144 *His camp location was kept a secret*: Letter from Winnifred Easton to Paul Rosenberg, January 9, 1941, the Paul Rosenberg Archive, MOMA, II.RR.3.

144 *their "war-time parents"*: Letter from Winnifred Easton to Paul Rosenberg, September 30, 1940, Paul Rosenberg Archives, MOMA II. RR.1.

145 *"What is good enough for the Generalissimo"*: Letter from Winnifred Easton to Paul Rosenberg, February 25, 1941, Paul Rosenberg Archives, MOMA II. RR.1.

146 *telling his friend, the artist Jaime Sabartés, in a letter*: Jaime Sabartés, trans. Angel Flores, *Picasso: An Intimate Portrait* (New York: Prentice-Hall, 1948), 219–20.

146 *"cable news immediately, love"*: Letter from Winnifred Easton to Paul Rosenberg, September 18, 1940, Paul Rosenberg Archives, MOMA II. RR.1

147 *five vans descended on Le Castel*: Letter from Louis Le Gall to Edmond Rosenberg, November 22, 1944, Paul Rosenberg Archives, MOMA V.A.19; Jacky Sanudo, "Paul Rosenberg un printemps en Gironde," *Sod Ouest Le Mag*, January 23, 2016, no. 199, 16; Sinclair, *My Grandfather's Gallery*, 203.

147 *One was Yves Perdoux*: Jacques Helft, *Vive la Chine*: *Mémoires d'un antiquaire* (Monaco: Éditions du Rocher, 1955), 201–2.

148 *remained hidden in the villa*: "List of paintings from Floirac and their fate." Line item 77 reads "Had remained hidden in Floirac."

148 *making derogatory comments about "Israelites"*: Sinclair, *My Grandfather's Gallery*, 203 (based on testimony by Louis Le Gall).

148 *"I couldn't save anything"*: Sanudo, "Paul Rosenberg un printemps en Gironde," 16.

148 *"Remain at all costs at the Jeu de Paume museum"*: Jaujard, "Activités dans la Résistance de Mademoiselle Rose Valland Conservateur des Musées Nationaux."

150 *"these walls accustomed to other echoes"*: Valland, *Le Front de l'Art*, 81.

151 *Rose was seized with trepidation*: Ibid., 106.

151 *Her forty-second birthday was starting out ominously*: Valland, *Le Front de l'Art*, 81. Additional details from this event at the Jeu de Paume come from Chapter 7 of *Le Front de l'Art*.

151 *opening all four hundred cases of art that arrived*: The following story and quotations are from Valland, *Le Front de l'Art*, 82–83.

153 *an almost photographic memory*: Jacqueline Barthalay, in conversation with the author, October 12, 2024. Based on information told to Barthalay from Rose's niece Camille Garapont, about Rose's near photographic memory; "Artful Spy," *Newsweek*, May 22, 1961.

153 *"Everything had to be surveilled and remembered"*: Valland, *Le Front de l'Art*, 102.

153 *believed he had a right to verify*: Letter from André Dezarrois to Jean Cassou, January 27, 1961, AN 20150497/184.

154 *Rose noted of her first impression*: The following story and quotations are from Valland, *Le Front de l'Art*, 84.

154 *we "kept many illusions"*: Ibid., 82.

155 *one of the only French eyewitnesses:* Emmanuelle Polack and Philippe Dagen, *Les carnets de Rose Valland: Le pillage des collections privées d'œuvres d'art en France durant la Seconde Guerre mondiale* (Lyon: FAGE Éditions, 2019), 15.

SECTION II

158 *deriding one man as a "homosexual pig"*: François Kersaudy, *Hermann Goering* (Paris: Perrin, 2013), 190.

158 *was custom-installed for him*: Tilar J. Mazzeo, *The Hotel on Place Vendôme* (New York: Harper Perennial, 2015), 51.

158 *an abundance of towels,* champagne, *and caviar*: Ibid.

159 *"the last Renaissance man"*: Joachim Fest, *Das Gesicht des Dritten Reiches* (Munich: R. Piper, 1963), 103.

159 *"widows and war orphans"*: Hermann Göring, "Order of 5 November 1940," AN 20144792/56.

159 *gave Rosenberg access*: Valland, *Le Front de l'Art*, 87.

160 *"I have brought to light"*: Letter from Hermann Göring to Alfred Rosenberg, November 21, 1940, MAE 209SUP/313.

160 *the visit would be "incognito"*: Letter from Joseph Billiet to Jacques Jaujard, November 9, 1940, AN 20144792/43.

161 *"In addition to this absolutely irregular state"*: Letter from Hermann Bunjes to Dr. Harald Turner and Dr. Franz Albrecht Medicus, November 9, 1940, MAE 209SUP/711.

162 *A long row of books*: Werner Lange, trans. Leonard Rosmarin, *Artists in Nazi-Occupied France: A German Officer's Memoir* (Ontario: Mosaic Press, 2019), 15.

162 *She called him a "passionate amateur"*: Valland, *Le Front de l'Art*, 88.

162 *she later wrote*: Ibid., 91.

163 *to the Jeu de Paume and the Louvre*: Göring, "Order of 5 November 1940."

163 *Jaujard also hoped that he could convince*: Letter from Jacques Jaujard to M. le Sécrétaire Général de l'Industrie et du Commerce Intérieur, November 2, 1940, MS CGQJ-XXI-17; MAE 209SUP/571.

164 *he was unfortunately "duty bound"*: Letter from Jacques Jaujard, November 29, 1940, AN 20144792/59; Laurence Betrand Dorleac and Michel Wincock, interview with Jean Cassou, *Histoire de l'Art, Paris, 1940–1944: Ordre National, Traditions et Modernités* (Paris: Presses de l'Université de Paris-Sorbonne, 1986), 308.

164 *She duplicated the building keys*: Draft notes of Agnès Humbert (likely for a speech), AN 20150497/215; Hours, *Une vie au Louvre*, 62.

164 *On some days*: Philippe Sprang, "Rose Valland, un chef-d'œuvre de Résistance—'Monument Men' relate sa vie," *Paris Match*, February 24, 2014 (based on quote from Jean Rigaud, a fellow Monuments Man who served as her driver in Germany).

164 *relegated to the Jeu de Paume's telephone room*: Cassou, *Le Pillage par les Allemands*, 234; Jeu de Paume floor plans, AN CP/64AJ/594.

164 *She would listen*: Cassou, *Le Pillage par les Allemands*, 234.

165 *discovered it was sometimes easy*: Television interview with Rose Valland, *Les Dossiers de l'écran*, April 9, 1975.

165 *saying things like*: J. S. Plaut, *Consolidated Interrogation Report No. 1: Activity of the Einsatzstab Rosenberg in France*, August 15, 1945, Office of Strategic Services, Art Looting Investigation Unit, US Army, NARA, microfilm M1944 Roll 85.

165 *ERR seized 367 cases*: Letter from le Président de la Délégation Française pour les Affaires Économiques to Monsieur Hemmen, Ministre Plénipotentiaire, Président de la Délegation allemande d'Armistice pour l'Économie, MS CXVII-38.

166 *made their jobs a lot easier*: Robert Scholz, "Rapport intermédiaire sur la saisie d'objets d'art appartenant à des Juifs et devenus biens sans maître, effectuée par l'État-Major Spécial du Reichsleiter Rosenberg dans les territoires occupés de l'Ouest," from Cassou, *Le Pillage par les Allemands*, 117.

166 *Place Vendôme gallery*: Sophie Seligmann Gosset, in conversation with the author, July 28, 2023. This employee was named Lucie Botton.

166 *dubbed ironically as the* "Salle des Martyrs": Rose Valland, "Quelques considerations sur le rapport 32.1.10. Doc VII/RC de la D.G.E.R.," MAE 209SUP/707.

166 *Hitler issued a new order*: "Hitler order ('*Vorbehalt*') signed by Lammers," November 18, 1940, reproduced in Plaut, *Consolidated Interrogation Report No. 1.*

167 *electrical wiring and its fire alarm system*: Valland, *Le Front de l'Art*, 102.

167 *there were at least eight*: Jacques Jaujard, "Activités dans la Résistance de Mademoiselle Rose Valland Conservateur de Musées Nationaux."

167 *She decided that the only way*: "Artful Spy."

167 *"This curiosity was plausible"*: Valland, *Le Front de l'Art*, 102.

167 *Jaujard took the time to write her*: Letter from Jacques Jaujard to Rose Valland, August 17, 1940.

167 *After all she had been through*: Rose Valland, "Voici quelques details précisant mon attitude et celle de la direction de Musées Nationaux à mon sujet," MAE 209SUP/717.

168 *"nearly cost us our lives"*: Ibid.

168 *finally get her appointed officially*: Letter from Jacques Jaujard to Rose Valland, August 27, 1940, AN 20150497/215.

168 *harass lesbian communities*: "Lesbians Under the Nazi Regime," United States Holocaust Memorial Museum, Washington, DC, https://encyclopedia.ushmm.org/content/en/article/lesbians-under-the-nazi-regime?series=200.

169 *The Luftwaffe launched*: Kersaudy, *Hermann Goering*, 455.

169 *He spent evenings with friends*: Letter from Winnifred Easton to Paul Rosenberg, February 4, 1941, Paul Rosenberg Archives, MOMA II.RR.3.

169 *as Winnifred put it*: Letter from Winnifred Easton to Paul Rosenberg, December 17, 1940, Paul Rosenberg Archives, MOMA, II.RR.1.

169 *She had taken to calling herself*: Various letters from Winnifred Easton to Paul Rosenberg, Paul Rosenberg Archives, MOMA, II.RR.2 and II.RR.3.

170 *"I can go no further"*: Hilary Spurling, *Matisse the Master: A Life of Henri Matisse: The Conquest of Colour, 1909–1954* (New York: Alfred A. Knopf, 2005), 397.

171 *"A Spaniard is never cold"*: Jane Fluegel, *Pablo Picasso: A Retrospective*, ed. William Rubin (New York: Museum of Modern Art, 1980), 351.

171 *One soldier asked Picasso . . . "Take it, take it! Souvenir!"*: Flanner, *Men and Monuments*, 194.

171 *her mental state was deteriorating rapidly*: Robert D. Murphy, "Annual Efficiency Report" for Joyce Helene Heer, September 30, 1940, Official Personnel Folder Department of State, St. Louis, Missouri, NARA RG 59.

172 *Her boss, Robert D. Murphy, the American consul, reported*: Ibid.

172 *"to indulge in a little make believe"*: Recap of a telephone call between Maynard B. Barnes, First Secretary of the US embassy in Paris, and Robert D. Murphy; Communication from Robert D. Murphy to US Secretary of State Cordell Hull, August 5, 1940, NARA RG 59, Box 726, 124.516/319.

172 *He wrote in her annual review*: Murphy, "Annual Efficiency Report" for Joyce Helene Heer.

172 *register as "enemy aliens"*: Rosemary Say and Noel Holland, *Rosie's War: An Englishwoman's Escape from Occupied France* (London: Michael O'Mara Books, 2011), 69; Ayshka Sené, "The Orphan Story of British Women and Internment in Occupied France" (PhD diss., Cardiff University, 2018), 101, 155–56.

172 *"prisoners on parole"*: "The 1940 Invasion of Paris / Holocaust Survivor Paulette Shaw," USC Shoah Foundation, June 14, 2023, www.youtube.com/watch?v=blX0G2ZvDss.

172 *suddenly treated like the enemy*: Manley, ed., *Mrs. Trewhella's War*, 40; Say and Holland, *Rosie's War*, 64, 82; Nicholas Shakespeare, *Priscilla: The Hidden Life of an Englishwoman in Wartime France* (London: Harvill Secker, 2013), 177.

173 *were rounded up and interned*: John Henleym, "'They scavenged scraps': The Britons Rounded Up by the Nazis in Occupied France," *The Guardian*, July 10, 2020, www.theguardian.com/world/2020/jul/10/britons-rounded-up-nazis-occupied-france-internees.

173 *All over the city, British women like Joyce*: Katherine Lack, *Frontstalag 142: The Internment Diary of an English Lady* (Stroud: Amberley, 2010), 27, 32

173 *"I must ask you"*: Ibid., 34.

173 *"accompany us to the* mairie": Say and Holland, *Rosie's War*, 87.

173 *storming in:* Lack, *Frontstalag 142*, 27, 36.

174 *"Just a formality"*: Ibid., 35.

174 "Maman, *they've come to arrest me*": "The 1940 Invasion of Paris / Holocaust Survivor Paulette Shaw."

174 *apologetic*: Ibid; Say and Holland, *Rosie's War*, 87–88.

174 "Ayez courage": Say and Holland, *Rosie's War*, 88.

174 *("Move! Move! Out!")*: Sofia Skipwith, *Sofka: The Autobiography of a Princess* (London: Rupert Hart-David, 1968), 190.

174 *could barely see above the windows:* Say and Holland, *Rosie's War*, 89.

174 *around the handles for good measure*: Shakespeare, *Priscilla*, 179.

175 *promptly tossed out the window*: Lack, *Frontstalag 142*, 33.

175 "Bonne chance, bonne chance!": Say and Holland, *Rosie's War*, 89.

175 *Several women gave birth*: Ibid., 90.

175 *A young girl screamed*: Lack, *Frontstalag 142*, 34.

175 *Unprepared and disorganized:* Say and Holland, *Rosie's War*, 93–94.

176 *had a sinister side:* James Rorimer, draft of "Rosenberg Repositories," a chapter of the book *Survival*, James Rorimer Papers, NGA 28MFAA-J1, 4–9.

176 *Rose thought him "deceptively amiable"*: "NOTICES Individuelles sur les membres suivants du Service ROSENBERG (Communiqués par Melle VALLAND)," NARA, microfilm M1944 Roll 85.

177 *Hitler had declared the whole art operation*: J. S. Plaut, *Detailed Interrogation Report No. 6: Bruno Lohse*, August 15, 1945, Office of Strategic Services, Art Looting Investigation Unit, US Army.

177 *"You have been brought here"*: "Testimony of Bruno Lohse taken at Nurnberg [Nuremberg], Germany on 1 November 1945 by Lt. Col. Thomas J. Hinkel, IGD. OUSCC," NARA microfilm M1270 Roll 12.

177 *Composed of over twelve hundred pieces*: Plaut, *Consolidated Interrogation Report No. 1*. At this time, the David-Weill collection, which would consist of 2,687 items, had not been seized yet.

178 *She asked the guards . . . particularly trusted*: Valland, *Le Front de l'Art*, 104.

178 *Rose smuggled out*: James Rorimer, *Survival: The Salvage and Protection of Art in War* (New York: Abelard, 1950), 111. Survival was reissued by Rizzoli Electa in 2022 under the title *Monuments Man*.

178 *had died on that bridge over the Loire*: Valland, "Transfert de personnel pour les depôts." Rose makes a definitive break between her life before her exodus to the Loire Valley and after, that what she saw on the way "definitely took on for me the features of the terror and despair of my country."

178 *"When you're the weakest"*: "Artful Spy."

178 *nothing else seemed to matter*: Rorimer, *Survival*, 111–12.

179 *"My dear Bunjes"*: Letter from Hermann Bunjes to Dr. Harald Turner, Conseiller d'État, MAE 209SUP/313.

179 *"it is we who will decide"*: Note from Hermann Bunjes to the Chef de la Circonscription Militaire de Paris, Service Administratif, February 6, 1941, MAE 209SUP/313.

180 *he brazenly debated Hofer*: Plaut, *Consolidated Interrogation Report No. 1*.

180 *"visibly opposite" . . . Göring responded*: Letter from Hermann Bunjes to Dr. Harald Turner.

180 *whom Rose believed was "terrified"*: Valland, *Le Front de l'Art*, 92.

181 *knowledge of art history and his youthful self-assurance*: Jonathan Petropoulos, *Göring's Man in Paris: The Story of a Nazi Art Plunderer and His World* (New Haven, CT: Yale University Press, 2021), 37.

181 *He folded it*: Ibid., 16.

181 *gave him a personal phone line*: Ibid., 38.

182 *straw mattresses soaked in water*: Say and Holland, *Rosie's War*, 96.

182 *rabbit-sized rats*: Sofka Zinovieff, *Red Princess* (London: Granta, 2007), 220.

183 *"Stand and Deliver"*: Shakespeare, *Priscilla*, 186.

183 *to find what they needed in there*: Lack, *Frontstalag 142*, 42.

183 *was often sprayed with sulfur . . . spoonful of jam and bread*: Say and Holland, *Rosie's War*, 100.

183 *favorite sweets, licorice "allsorts"*: Andy Heer, in an email to the author, March 13, 2024.

183 *died within the first months*: Say and Holland, *Rosie's War*, 105; "Commons Sitting, Oral Answers to Questions, British Internees France" (UK Parliament, May 20, 1942, vol. 380), 205–6, https://api.parliament.uk/historic-hansard/commons/1942/may/20/british-internees-france.

183 *froze to death in their sleep*: Shakespeare, *Priscilla*, 188.

183 *no longer menstruated*: Say and Holland, *Rosie's War*, 102.

183 *"long and delicate treatment"*: Letter from Maynard B. Barnes, First Secretary of US embassy, to Dr. von Roeder, *Regierungsrat*, requesting Joyce Heer's release from Besançon, January 24, 1941, NARA RG 59, Box 1724, 124.513/1559.

184 *"This is not a holiday camp"*: Say and Holland, *Rosie's War*, 108.

184 *raucous party in the middle of January*: Ibid., 111.

184 *set up business bartering sex*: Ibid., 126.

185 *Prewar, her letters were filled*: Letter from Rose Valland to her cousin Adrien Jacquier-Roux, July 1, 1924; letter from Rose Valland to her cousin Marguerite Jacquier-Roux and Marguerite's mother, from the archives of Bénédicte Delfaut.

185 *a "palatial" work lunch*: Letter from Margaret Scolari Barr to Alfred H. Barr Jr..

185 *The writer Jean Guéhenno noted*: Guéhenno, *Diary of the Dark Years*, 51.

185 *skyrocketing, especially among infants*: Ramon F. Minoli, "Food Rationing and Mortality in Paris, 1940–1941," *Millbank Memorial Fund Quarterly* 20, no. 3 (July 1942): 214.

185 *As part of a report to the secretary of state*: Telegram from H. F. Matthews, US Consul in Paris, to Secretary of State Cordell Hull, December 31, 1940, NARA RG 59, Box 1724, 124.513/1448.

186 *interned at Besançon*: Letter from Maynard B. Barnes to US Secretary of State, January 24, 1941, NARA RG 59, Box 1724, 124.513/1559.

186 *formal request for her release*: Letter from Maynard B. Barnes to Dr. Von Roeder, Regierungharat, NARA RG 59, Box 1724, 124.513/1559.

186 *Joyce was released*: Telegram from William Leahy, US Ambassador to France, to Cordell Hull, US Secretary of State, April 26, 1941, NARA RG 59, Box 1724, 124.513/1496. In this letter, Leahy notes Joyce's dates of internment from December 5, 1940, through February 13, 1941.

SECTION 12

188 *he could not wait*: Report by Léonce Labroux, bailiff from the court of Libourne, March 20, 1941, Paul Rosenberg Archives, MOMA V.A.13.

188 *who was likely deliberately sabotaging*: Scott Selby (coauthor of *Flawless: Inside the Largest Diamond Heist in History*), in an email to the author, August 14, 2023.

189 *"We would be obliged"*: Sinclair, *My Grandfather's Gallery*, 47.

190 *Picard had been squirreling*: Ibid., 202. Based on testimony from Madame Picard.

190 *"I will throw him out the door"*: Ibid., 201. Based on trial record of Monsieur Picard.

190 *"I am rather afraid"*: Letter from Paul Rosenberg to Winnifred Easton, April 29, 1941, Paul Rosenberg Archives, MOMA II.RR.2.

190 *"There's nothing left"*: Sinclair, *My Grandfather's Gallery*, 201.

191 *"confiscation factory"*: Valland, *Le Front de l'Art*, 95.

191 *more than ten thousand objects*: Jonathan Petropoulos, in an email to the author, September 16, 2024. In total, approximately thirty thousand art objects were transited through the Jeu de Paume throughout the war. In the first nine months, all of the major Jewish art collections were already looted. Petropoulos estimates that it could have been around 40 percent of the total.

192 *Rose detailed*: Valland, *Le Front de l'Art*, 117, 188–89.

192 *find a way to keep them*: Note from Rose Valland to Jacques Jaujard, September 16, 1941, AN 20144792/276.

193 *near hysterical*; *should be burned*: J. S. Plaut, *Detailed Interrogation Report No. 4: Gustav Rochlitz*, August 15, 1945, Office of Strategic Services, Art Looting Investigation Unit, US Army.

194 *who sold two questionable Rembrandts*: Theodore Rousseau, *Consolidated Interrogation Report No. 2: The Goering Collection*, September 15, 1945, NARA, M1946 Roll 121.

195 *"all you need to know"*: Sinclair, *My Grandfather's Gallery*, 33.

195 *filled Paul Rosenberg's former galleries*: Letter from Paul Sézille to Albert Willm, MS XIg-31.

196 *was offended to discover*: Sinclair, *My Grandfather's Gallery*, 38–39.

196 *"Up to now they have not touched"*: Letter from Paul Rosenberg to Winnifred Easton, June 12, 1941, Paul Rosenberg Archives, MOMA II.RR.1.

196 *"Perhaps it is better"*: Letter from Paul Rosenberg to Winnifred Easton, March 11, 1941, Paul Rosenberg Archives, MOMA II.RR.1.

196 *he had been approached*: Letter from Paul Rosenberg to Monsieur Aglion, Free French Delegation, August 27, 1941, Paul Rosenberg Archives, II.A.1.

196 *Paul wrote Huisman*: Letter from Paul Rosenberg to George Huisman, March 11, 1941, Paul Rosenberg Archives, MOMA II.A.12.

197 *The whole affair made Alexandre sad*: Letter from Winnifred Easton to Paul Rosenberg, April 3, 1941, Paul Rosenberg Archives, MOMA II.RR.2.

197 *"do not help me to get better"*: Letter from Paul Rosenberg to Winnifred Easton, April 17, 1941, Paul Rosenberg Archives, MOMA II.RR.2.

197 *"He does not want to tell us"*: Letter from Winnifred Easton to Paul Rosenberg, March 13, 1941, Paul Rosenberg Archives, MOMA II.RR.2.

198 *Rose purloined the negatives*: Rorimer, *Survival*, 113; "Compte rendu de la 16ème Séance de le comission vaucher Commission Vaucher du 6 Avril 1945," May 28, 1945, AN 20144792/56.

198 *photographed the identity papers*: Draft notes of Agnès Humbert (likely for a speech), AN 20150497/215.

199 *chewed up and swallowed*: Humbert, *Résistance*, 50.

199 *showed him a hidden key*: Dorleac, *Histoire de l'Art, Paris, 1940–44*, 309.

200 *"enjoyed seeing himself"*: Valland, *Le Front de L'Art*, 91.

200 *sold more paintings to Hitler*: Petropoulos, *Göring's Man in Paris, 69.*

200 *Rose found Lohse "unscrupulous"*: "NOTICES Individuelles sur les membres suivants du Service ROSENBERG (Communiqués par Melle VALLAND)."

200 *who were jealous of his special status but fearful*: Plaut, *Detailed Interrogation Report No. 6.*

200 *donned a sweater with the SS insignia*: Petropoulos, *Göring's Man in Paris*, photograph "Lohse and an unknown colleague with two women in occupied Paris."

201 *known to have denounced*: Rose Valland, "Quelques considerations à propos de l'interrogatoire de Bruno Lohse," NARA microfilm M1944 Roll 50.

201 *then secretly moved it*: Petropoulos, *Göring's Man in Paris*, 84.

201 *to join de Gaulle's forces*: Telegram from Winnifred Easton to Paul Rosenberg, May 23, 1941, Paul Rosenberg Archives, MOMA, II.RR.2.

201 *"very hot climate"*: Letter from Alfred Coureau to Paul Rosenberg, June 11, 1941, Paul Rosenberg Archives, MOMA II.RR.2.

202 *"How do you think I can live"*: Letter from Paul Rosenberg to Winnifred Easton, June 12, 1941, Paul Rosenberg Archives, MOMA II.RR.2.

202 *"We have all broken down"*: Ibid.

202 *"with plenty of common sense and good logic"*: Letter from Winnifred Easton to Paul Rosenberg, June 11, 1941, Paul Rosenberg Archives, MOMA II.RR.2.

202 *"apart from the few red flags"*: Letter from Rose Valland to her cousins Marguerite Jacquier-Roux and Adrien Jacquier-Roux, MRD.

202 *The request went up and down the diplomatic hierarchy*: Series of telegrams and notes regarding pay and leave for Joyce Heer during her internment written by State Department employees, NARA RG 59, Box 1724, 124.513/1496.

202 *Joyce continued working*: Letter from US embassy in France to US ambassador in London, October 21, 1941, NARA RG 59, Box 1724, 124.513/1643. Joyce's work was terminated at end of business day July 31, 1941.

203 *Their work inlcuded burning*: Purport Lists and Cards 1940–1944, Entry 124.512/1109 and 1111, NARA RG 59, 124.413/863–124.556/94.

203 *"must not fail in any way" . . . "for how long it will be"*: Marie-Louise Dilkes, *Strong in Will: Working for the American Embassy in Paris during the Nazi Occupation*, Virginia A. Dilkes, ed. (Havertown, PA: Casemate, 2024), 149.

203 *impossible for Joyce to find a job*: Letter from Perry Laukhuff, Third Secretary of the US embassy, to Cordell Hull, US Secretary of State, NARA RG 59, Box 1724, 124.513/1666.

204 *"she has remained at Paris"*: Letter from US embassy in France to US ambassador in London, October 21, 1941.

204 *Joyce made contact*: Ibid.

204 *more than a two-ton load*: Note from Rose Valland to Jacques Jaujard, October 9, 1941, AN 20144792/276.

205 *mostly from the Rosenberg collection*: Note from Rose Valland to Jacques Jaujard, December 3, 1941, AN 20144792/276.

205 *"collection belonging to the Jew Paul Rosenberg"*: Letter from Karl Haberstock to Hermann Göring, quoted in Feliciano, *Lost Museum*, 112.

205 *earmarked for specific people*: Note from Rose Valland to Jacques Jaujard, January 29, 1942, AN 20144792/276.

205 *first and only time in November*: Hans Posse, Fifth Travel Diary, November 9–13, 1941, Germanisches National Museum, Nuremberg, Germany.

205 *"Don't ever mention"*: Plaut, *Consolidated Interrogation Report No. 1.*

205 *He traded Van Gogh's* Starry Night: Letter from Paul Rosenberg to Alfred H. Barr Jr., June 4, 1941, Paul Rosenberg Archives, MOMA, II.A.18.

206 *"I am no newcomer"*: Letter from Paul Rosenberg to Winnifred Easton, September 13, 1941, Paul Rosenberg Archives, MOMA II.RR.3.

206 *"I was a billionaire"*: Letter from Paul Rosenberg to Winnifred Easton, October 3, 1942, Paul Rosenberg Archives, MOMA II.RR.2.

206 *"not behaved as they should have"*: Letter from Paul Rosenberg to Winnifred Easton, June 12, 1941, Paul Rosenberg Archives, MOMA II.RR.2.

206 *"I really do not believe"*: Letter from Paul Rosenberg to Winnifred Easton, May 16, 1941, Paul Rosenberg Archives, MOMA II.RR.2.

207 *arrested on arrival*: Thomas J. Laub, *After the Fall: German Policy in Occupied France, 1940–1944* (Oxford: Oxford University Press, 2010), 217.

207 *"Their wives and children"*: Guéhenno, *Diary of the Dark Years*, 83.

207 *"After all it is the birthplace"*: Letter from Paul Rosenberg to Winnifred Easton, August 20, 1941, Paul Rosenberg Archives, MOMA II.RR.3.

208 *"eat to his heart's content"*: Ibid.

208 *like being on holiday*: Letter from Winnifred Easton to Paul Rosenberg, September 30, 1941, Paul Rosenberg Archives, MOMA, II.RR.3.

208 *planned to send dispatches*: Letter from Winnifred Easton to Paul Rosenberg, October 23, 1941, Paul Rosenberg Archives, MOMA, II.RR.3.

208 *"It is better to be in Africa"*: Letter from Paul Rosenberg to Winnifred Easton, September 13, 1941.

209 *no means of income or subsistence*: Esther Benbassa, *The Jews of France: A History from Antiquity to the Present* (Princeton: Princeton University Press, 2001), 170.

209 *secretary at the Swiss consulate*: Joyce Heer's application for benefits to the United States Civil Service Commission, Bureau of Retirement and Insurance, July 15, 1965, NARA RG 59, St. Louis, Missouri. Joyce worked for the Swiss Consulate from September 1, 1941, to September 3, 1944.

209 *"I am too full of emotion"*: Guéhenno, *Diary of the Dark Years*, 134.

209 *a "major offensive"*: Note from Rose Valland to Jacques Jaujard, January 29, 1942, AN 20144792/276.

209 *"I don't know anything"*: Ibid.

210 *"We are so cold"*: Guéhenno, *Diary of the Dark Years*, 141.

210 *carved big V's for victory*: Ibid., 152.

210 *in only her negligee*: "NOTICES Individuelles sur les membres suivants du Service ROSENBERG (Communiqués par Melle VALLAND)."

210 *"very Prussian cruelty"*: Ibid.

211 *Nazi dishonesty and brutality*: Ibid.

211 *and numerous purchases*: Ibid.

212 *"money seems to have more importance"*: Note from Rose Valland to Jacques Jaujard, June 8, 1942, AN 20144792/276.

212 *Rose reported on the conflict*: Ibid.

212 *a staggering 69,619*: International Military Tribunal (Nuremberg), Judgement of 1 October 1946 (from the Trial of German Major War Criminals), Proceedings of the International Military Tribunal Sitting at Nuremberg, Germany, Part 22 (22nd August, 1946, to 1st October, 1946), Global Institute for the Prevention of Aggression, https://crimeofaggression.info/documents/6/1946_Nuremberg_Judgement.pdf.

212 *"different rumors have circulated"*: Note from Rose Valland to Jacques Jaujard, February 23, 1942, AN 20144792/276.

212 *Behr ran a prison camp*: Plaut, *Consolidated Interrogation Report No. 1*. The Americans described the prison camp as "a little concentration camp."

213 *"Sold? Exchanged?"*: Note from Rose Valland to Jacques Jaujard, July 16, 1942, AN 20144792/276.

213 *hung at least one stolen painting*: Note from Rose Valland to Jacques Jaujard, October 12, 1943, AN 20144792/276.

213 *used what they dubbed* "la valise": Note from Rose Valland, February 2, 1942, MAE 209SUP/716; note from Rose Valland to Jacques Jaujard, June 3, 1942, AN 20144792/276.

213 *the head of the German guards*: Note from Rose Valland to Jacques Jaujard, August 18, 1942, AN 20144792/276.

213 *"this doomed winter has passed"*: Letter from Rose Valland to her cousin Marguerite Jacquier-Roux, March 18, 1942, MRD.

213 *"You know it's not easy"*: Letter from Rose Valland to her cousin Marguerite Jacquier-Roux, May 10, 1942, MRD.

213 *official nine-page report*: Following quotations are from Hermann Bunjes, trans. JA Section, Third US Army, "Safeguarding of works of art belonging to Jews who fled from Occupied France," NARA microfilm M1944 Roll 85.

214 *She called them*: Valland, *Le Front de l'Art*, 64–65.

214 *described the confiscations as "painful"*: Ibid., 110.

214 *"hold on our territory"*: Ibid., 112.

214 *"the persecution against the Jews"*: "Présentation et question" (a Q&A with Rose Valland regarding *Le Front de l'Art* in relation to the release of the movie *The Train*), MAE 209SUP/721.

214 *soon learned of*: Signed testimony of Gaston Palewski (director of General Charles de Gaulle's cabinet in London and in Algiers), April 9, 1955, AN 20150497/215.

214 *also directly informing*: "Note sur les titres de Melle Rose VALLAND assistante des Musées Nationaux," AN 20150497/215; Gibson, "How a Timid Curator with a Deadpan Expression Outwitted the Nazis."

214 *"Due to the possible risks"*: Note from Rose Valland to Jacques Jaujard, March 10, 1942, AN 20144792/276.

215 *because she was French*: Note from Rose Valland to Jacques Jaujard, October 13, 1942, AN 20144792/276.

215 *sheer convenience for the Germans*: Valland, *Le Front de l'Art*, 103.

215 *She also installed a telephone*: Letter from Rose Valland to Jacques Jaujard, January 13, 1943, AN 20144707/97.

215 *bottle of black-market cognac*: Rorimer, *Survival*, 111.

215 *did not allow herself the luxury*: Brule, "Si Burt Lancaster tourne à Paris."

215 *To sabotage the day-to-day work*: Thomas Carr Jr., *Salt Mines and Castles: The Discovery and Restitution of Looted European Art* (Indianapolis: Bobbs-Merrill, 1946), 23.

215 *"Should we believe it?"*: Note from Rose Valland to Jacques Jaujard, October 6, 1942, AN 20144792/276.

216 *"name sounds like 'Von Ingram'"*: Note from Rose Valland to Jacques Jaujard, August 18, 1942, AN 20144792/276.

216 *"The head of the service"*: Note from Rose Valland to Jacques Jaujard, October 13, 1942.

216 *blowing up a brothel*: Guéhenno, *Diary of the Dark Years*, 131–32.

216 *In one notice to Parisian residents*: "Curfew for Paris Imposed by Nazis," September 19, 1941, *New York Times*, 1.

216 *executed twenty of them . . . "accord with the national revolution"*: "Purge of Paris Police: 200 Dropped in Vichy Drive to End Attacks on Nazis," *New York Times*, September 30, 1941, 2.

216 *"Darkness only envelops us"*: Manley, ed., *Mrs. Trewhella's War*, 146.

216 *"How long will this last?"*: Guéhenno, *Diary of the Dark Years*, 136.

217 *to return in time*: Letter from Rose Valland likely to Jacqueline Saupique-Bouchot regarding papers for the pass to the Unoccupied Zone, August 17, 1942, AN 20150497/215.

217 *"I still retain my nationality"*: Letter from Paul Rosenberg to Winnifred Easton, June 12, 1941, Paul Rosenberg Archives, MOMA II.RR.2.

217 *officially "denationalized" Paul*: Sinclair, *My Grandfather's Gallery*, 180.

217 *He sent a telegram directly*: Telegram from Paul Rosenberg to Président Commission cas Déchéances Nationalité, Ministère Justice, Vichy (France), shown in *21 rue la Boétie* (documentary film).

218 *"Given recent events"*: Sinclair, *My Grandfather's Gallery*, 183.

218 *Rose described the "cruel reality" . . . "direct and brutal," she concluded*: Valland, *Le Front de l'Art*, 70–71.

218 *"sterilization of all Jews"*: Letter from Carltheo Zeitschel to Herrn Botschafter Abetz, August 21, 1941, reproduced in Serge Klarsfeld, *Vichy–Auschwitz: Die 'Endlösung der Judenfrage' in Frankreich*, Darmstadt: Wissenschaftliche Buchgesellschaft, 2007, 390.

218 *"as soon as possible"*: Letter from Carltheo Zeitschel to Obersturmfuehrer Dannecker, Otto Abetz, Ambassador Rahn, Darquier de Pellepoix, Pierre Laval, MS VI-176.

218 *almost twenty-eight thousand from Paris*: Claude Lévy and Paul Tillard, *La Grande rafle du Vel d'Hiv (16 juillet 1942)* (Paris: R. Laffont, 1967), 9.

218 *3,625 of whom were children*: "The Vélodrome d'Hiver (Vél d'Hiv) Roundup," United States Holocaust Memorial Museum, https://encyclopedia.ushmm.org/content/en/article/the-velodrome-dhiver-vel-dhiv-roundup.

219 *Some nine thousand French policemen*: Lévy and Tillard, *La Grande rafle du Vel d'Hiv*, 25. This number includes the *gendarmerie*, *garde mobile*, *police judiciare*, *renseigenements généraux*, and *voie publique*.

219 *a few hundred young volunteers*: Ibid., 22. Lévy writes that "three- to four-hundred young people will come lend a hand to the security service" wearing "navy blue shirts, belts, and armbands with the P.P.F. (French Popular Party) logo."

219 *was unbearable*: "The Vel d'Hiv Roundup: 75 Years On, a Survivor Remembers," July 15, 2017, France24, www.france24.com/en/20170712-vel-dhiv-roundup-holocaust-france-survivor-remembers-world-war.

219 *People committed suicide*: "Vel' d'Hiv', 1942. Témoignage d'une infirmière, Rafles israélites à Paris," *Revue d'Histoire de la Shoah* (No. 161(3), 1997), 246–248.

219 *which Paul attributed to*: Letters from Paul Rosenberg to Winnifred Easton, March 6, 1942, March 30, 1942, and others, Paul Rosenberg Archives, MOMA II.RR.2.

220 *"pleased to do his duty"*: Letter from Paul Rosenberg to Winnifred Easton, March 5, 1942, Paul Rosenberg Archives, MOMA II.RR.2.

220 *He told Winnifred*: Letter from Paul Rosenberg to Winnifred Easton, March 30, 1942, Paul Rosenberg Archives, MOMA II.RR.2.

220 *"like a bomb"*: Valland, *Le Front de l'Art*, 139.

221 *"symbolic value" . . . "and to our vigilance"*: Ibid., 140.

221 *"most important work of art"*: "Report on a Visit of Inspection and Depos-

itories of Works of Art in Germany and Austria, 9 May–19 May 1945," AN 20144792/56.

221 *unless three authorizations*: Letter from Joseph Billiet to Jacques Jaujard, August 28, 1942; letter from Jacques Jaujard to Louis Hautecœur, August 31, 1942, AN 20144792/42.

222 *wrote a letter to his boss*: Letter from Jacques Jaujard to Louis Hautecœur, August 31, 1942, AN 20144792/42.

222 *"I will break you"*: Des Varennes, *Jacques Jaujard*, 11.

222 *far more sinister misfortunes*: Robert Rey, "Rapport de Robert REY sur l'attitude allemande vis à vis des oeuvres d'art et le vol du RETABLE de l'AGNEAU MYSTIQUE de VAN EYCK, confié a la France par la Ville de Gand," September 1944, AN 20144792/42.

222 *"It is better to risk your life"*: Des Varennes, *Jacques Jaujard*, 16.

222 *if Jaujard was fired*: Comité des Conservateurs, "Séance Exceptionelle du 26 Novembre 1942," AN 20144792/24.

222 *the fate of the altarpiece*: Valland, *Le Front de l'Art*, 146.

223 *diligently continued to fight*: Summary of letter from Jacques Jaujard to Comte Metternich, March 19, 1942, MAE 209SUP/571; summary of letter from Jacques Jaujard to Dr. Kuetgens, October 21, 1942, MAE 209SUP/571.

223 *"There is only one people"*: Yvon Bizardel, *Sous l'occupation: Souvenirs d'un conservateur de Musée* (Calmann-Lévy, 1964), 156.

224 *"Dangerous character"*: Note from Rose Valland to Jacques Jaujard, November 28, 1943, AN 20144792/276.

224 *Georgian soldiers*: Valland, *Le Front de l'Art*, 106. Many Georgians voluntarily joined the German Army in order to escape inhumane living conditions after they were taken as prisoners of war on the Soviet Eastern Front (more information at www.europeremembers.com/pois/638/the-georgian-uprising).

224 *for explosives and weapons*: Note from Rose Valland to Jacques Jaujard, November 28, 1942, AN 20144792/276.

224 *A search of the museum grounds*: Jeu de Paume guard logbook, entry from November 19–20, 1942, MAE 209SUP/296.

224 *accused of sabotage and of sending*: Valland, *Le Front de l'Art*, 103; Jacques Jaujard, "Rapport de M. Jaujard sur les activités de Rose Valland pendant la guerre," AN 20144792/276.

224 *Rose would later write*: Valland, *Le Front de l'Art*, 104.

225 *"who were asked to account"*: Ibid.

225 *"This is my punishment"*: Note by Rose Valland, August 3, 1943, MAE 209SUP/716; similar quote in Valland, *Le Front de l'Art*, 106.

225 *began discretely eyeing*: Note from Rose Valland to Jacques Jaujard, November 28, 1942, AN 20144792/276.

225 *Starting in February 1941*: Feliciano, *Lost Museum,* 108.

225 *In the middle of the night*: Rose Valland, untitled document about Bruno Lohse, MAE 209SUP/716.

225 *"I find them fully justified"*: Letter from Rose Valland to Jacques Jaujard, October 31, 1942, AN 20144795/44.

226 *he was caught stealing fabric*: Note from Rose Valland to Jacques Jaujard, November 28, 1942, AN 20144792/276; "NOTICES Individuelles sur les membres suivants du Service ROSENBERG (Communiqués par Melle VALLAND).

226 *"Could we not prevent"*: Note from Rose Valland to Jacques Jaujard, December 5, 1942, AN 20144792/276.

227 *"a traitor wants to be paid"*: Interrogation of Bruno Lohse by Henry Delpech, Procurer de la République, November 23, 1945, NARA microfilm M1944 Roll 90.

228 *Nearly 270,000*: "Tunisia Campaign," United States Holocaust Memorial Museum, https://encyclopedia.ushmm.org/content/en/article/tunisia-campaign.

228 *"we will take Paris and Strasbourg"*: Henry Maule, *Out of the Sand: The Epic Story of General Leclerc and the Fighting Free French* (London: Odhams Books, 1966), 163.

228 *"I can rightly say"*: Letter from Paul Rosenberg to Winnifred Easton, May 14, 1943, Paul Rosenberg Archives, MOMA II.RR.4.

228 *"Since my boy"*: Letter from Paul Rosenberg to Winnifred Easton, November 10, 1943, Paul Rosenberg Archives, MOMA II.RR.4.

229 *They got into brawls*: Maule, *Out of the Sand, 163.*

229 *"We are rejoicing"*: Letter from Paul Rosenberg to Winnifred Easton, May 14, 1943.

229 *"what the Jews stole"*: Note by Rose Valland, April 3, 1943, MAE 209SUP/716.

229 *"appreciated the Impressionists"*: Valland, *Le Front de l'Art,* 189; note from Rose Valland to Jacques Jaujard, July 7, 1943, AN 20144792/276.

230 *were packed up*: Note from Rose Valland to Jacques Jaujard, March 18, 1943, AN 20144792/276.

230 *labeled A for* absetzen: Gaston Petit (head of security for the Museés Nationaux), "NOTE sur le séquestre du Louvre," July 23, 1943, MAE 209SUP/707.

230 *"screw everyone" . . . "by Mme von Ingram"*: Note by Rose Valland, July 3, 1943, MAE 209SUP/716.

230 *red with rage*: Jonathan Petropoulos, in conversation with the author, September 18, 2024.

230 *Rose asked Jaujard in her report*: Note from Rose Valland to Jacques Jaujard, March 18, 1943, AN 20144792/276.

230 *"Dr. Lohse warned . . ."*: Note from Rose Valland to Jacques Jaujard, February 10, 1943, AN 20144792/276.

231 *"not having had sufficient control"*: Note by Rose Valland, May 24, 1943, MAE 209SUP/716.

231 *all taken from*: Note from Rose Valland to Jacques Jaujard, February 10, 1943, AN 20144792/276.

231 *did not want to hear*: Note from Rose Valland to Jacques Jaujard, March 31, 1944, AN 20144792/276; account by Rose Valland of what Borchers said he heard from Göring before, which reads, "B. told me that one day he was with Mr. Goering, the latter said that he no longer wanted to hear about v. Behr."

232 *"cannot note without irony"*: Valland, *Le Front de l'Art*, 182.

232 *building a bomb shelter*: Note from Rose Valland to Jacques Jaujard, April 10, 1943, AN 20144792/276.

232 *Rose saw Lohse put*: Note from Rose Valland to Jacques Jaujard, June 23, 1943, AN 20144792/276.

232 *"This will be for us" . . . "saved the whole gang"*: Note from Rose Valland to Jacques Jaujard, April 10, 1943, AN 20144792/276.

233 *"we are always robbed"*: Note by Rose Valland, April 30, 1943, MAE 209SUP/716.

233 *threatened to call the Gestapo*: Note from Rose Valland to Jacques Jaujard, April 10, 1943, AN 20144792/276.

233 *"I was called in the morning"*: Note from Rose Valland to Jacques Jaujard, April 12, 1943, AN 20144792/276.

233 *Tomforde-von Ingram claimed . . . so Lohse demanded*: Note by Rose Valland, August 17, 1943, AN 20144792/276.

233 *was completely undressed*: Note by Rose Valland, August 17, 1943, MAE 209SUP/716.

233 *"difficult for our guards to carry out"*: Note from Rose Valland to Jacques Jaujard, August 29, 1943, AN 20144792/276.

234 *"The slightest infraction will result"*: Note by Rose Valland, June 27, 1943, MAE 209SUP/716.

234 *Lohse specifically accused Rose . . . Lohse told Rose*: Note from Rose Valland to Jacques Jaujard, August 23, 1943, AN 20144792/276.

234 *refused to sign*: Valland, *Le Front de l'Art*, 105.

234 *"I hope this incident"*: Note from Rose Valland to Jacques Jaujard, August 26, 1943, AN 20144792/276.

234 *"Piss off!"*: Note from Rose Valland to Jacques Jaujard, August 18, 1943, MAE 209SUP/716. The text in French reads "dit qu'il nous e_____," for "dit qu'il nous emmerde."

234 *"eliminated" after crossing the border*: Valland, *Le Front de l'Art*, 105; Letter from Rose Valland to Captain Harlin, January 31, 1955, AN 20150497/215; Letter from Rose Valland to James Rorimer, June 25, 1957, AN 20150497/215.

234 *followed her home frequently*: Carr, *Salt Mines and Castles,* 24.

234 *waves of fear*: Valland, *Le Front de l'Art*, 106.

235 *"It went on like this"*: Ibid., 105.

235 *impossible to write*: Jouan, *Rose Valland*, 38.

235 *keep thinking faster*: Brule, "Si Burt Lancaster tourne à Paris."

235 *"to them as well that I belonged"*: Valland, *Le Front de l'Art*, 107.

235 *Lucien sent Henri a telegram*: Testimony of Henri Schloss, James Rorimer Papers, NGA 28MFAA-J1, 1–17.

235 *beat by German policemen*: Testimony of Lucien Schloss, James Rorimer Papers, NGA 28MFAA-J1, 1–17.

235 *hired the Bonny-Lafont gang*: Petropoulos, *Göring's Man in Paris*, 86–87.

236 *"apparent lack of responsibility"*: "Lohse's Statement on the Schloss Affair," in S. L. Faison, *Linz Museum: Consolidated Interrogation Report No. 4*, attachment 26, November 23, 1945, NARA M1946 Roll 139.

236 *described as "off-color"*: Note from Rose Valland to Jacques Jaujard, November 2, 1943, AN 20144792/276.

236 *on behalf of the Germans*: Valland, *Le Front de l'Art*, 128.

237 *hundreds of modern paintings*: Note from Rose Valland to Jacques Jaujard, July 19, 1943, AN 20144792/276.

237 *saw the Germans slash*: Gaston Petit, "NOTE sur le séquestre du Louvre"; note from Rose Valland to Jacques Jaujard, July 23, 1943, AN 20144792/276. Petit writes that this painting is by Kees van Dongen, but Rose, who is correct, writes in her July 23 note that the painting is by Beltran-y-Masses (Spanish Cuban artist Federico Beltrán Masses).

237 *with "unbridled satisfaction"*: Certified and notarized written testimony of Eugène Finitzer (former guard at the Jeu de Paume) in Paris, December 15, 1962; Petit, "NOTE sur le séquestre du Louvre"; letter from C. Develay (former guard at Jeu de Paume) to Rose Valland, December 5, 1962, all from MAE 209SUP/313.

237 *sliced the paintings*: Note by Rose Valland, July 20, 1943, MAE 209SUP/716.

237 *anything deemed Jewish*: Petit, "NOTE sur le séquestre du Louvre."

237 *"In them was a poison"*: Valland, *Le Front de l'Art*, 187.

237 *Hundreds of paintings*: List of artists from both Valland, *Le Front de l'Art*, 187, and Petit, "NOTE sur le sequestre du Louvre"; letter from Rose Valland regarding the burning of the paintings, December 20, 1962, MAE 209SUP/577; "Tableaux détruits a l'incendie du Jeu de Paume" and "Tableaux modernes importants détruits par l'ERR," MAE 209SUP/717; note by Rose Valland, July 20, 1943, MAE 209SUP/716.

238 *"the choice was sumptuous"*: Valland, *Le Front de l'Art*, 187

238 *Almost all the paintings . . . were left in tatters*: Note by Rose Valland, July 20, 1943, AN 20144792/276; "Tableaux détruits a l'incendie du Jeu de Paume."

238 *to set the scraps and frames ablaze*: Certified and notarized written testimony of Paul Blondel in Saint-Pierre-Église (Manché), January 16, 1963; signed written testimony of C. Develay, December 5, 1962; letter from C. Develay to Rose Valland, December 20, 1962; certified and notarized written testimony of Eugène Finitzer, December 15, 1962; certified and notarized written testimony of Paul Moïse, December 12, 1963; certified and notarized written testimony of Eugène Finitzer, December 15, 1962; all from MAE 209SUP/313.

238 *German sentry supervised the destruction*: Valland, *Le Front de l'Art*, 187.

238 *Rose, who saw everything*: Letter from Rose Valland regarding the burning of the paintings, December 20, 1962. The floor plans of the Jeu de Paume from AN 64AJ/594 show that there were doors leading out to the garden of the museum coming out of the central corridor as well as built into some of the arched windows.

238 *"Impossible to save anything"*: Note from Rose Valland to Jacques Jaujard, July 23, 1943.

238 *She made a partial list*: "Tableaux détruits à l'incendie du Jeu de Paume," MAE 209SUP/717.

239 *"verdict pronounced behind closed doors"*: Valland, *Le Front de l'Art*, 189.

239 *kept him informed*: Note by Rose Valland, July 21, 1943, MAE 209SUP/716.

239 *"one of the last bastions"*: Note from Rose Valland to Jacques Jaujard, August 4, 1943, AN 20144792/276.

240 *one unassailable goal*: Maule, *Out of the Sand*, 71.

241 *"Tell Leclerc* always *to keep"*: William Mortimer Moore, *Free France's Lion: The Life of Philippe Leclerc, de Gaulle's Greatest General* (Haverton, PA: Casemate, 2011), 219.

241 *"will be the year of Liberation"*: Moore, *Free France's Lion*, 220.

241 *his first and only visit*: James Rorimer, "Concerning my (Schiedlausky) Report from 22 August 1942 to clear and prove certain doubts and to clarify the responsibilities," MAE 209SUP/893.

242 *"smell of cemeteries"*: Valland, *Le Front de l'Art*, 106.

242 *right arms in a Heil Hitler*: Emmanuelle Polack, *Le Marché de l'Art sous l'Occupation* (Paris: Éditions Tallandier, 2021), 199.

242 *refusing to make such a gesture*: Emmanuelle Polack, in conversation with the author, January 16, 2023, and July 17, 2024. Although only a woman's hand and skirt are visible, Polack stated that she believes the woman to be Rose Valland, whose reports to Jacques Jaujard confirm she was present that day.

242 *over eight hundred cases of art*: Note from Rose Valland to Jacques Jaujard, November 15, 1943, AN 20144792/276.

243 *called Hanesse an "old idiot" . . . to goad a weakened Göring*: Rose Valland, "Le

dernière visite de Goering, amateur d'art," *Arts, beaux-arts, littérature, spectacles*, 13, April 27, 1945.

244 *along with dogged research*: Jacques Jaujard, "Activités dans la Résistance de Mademoiselle Rose Valland Conservateur de Musées Nationaux."

244 *Lohse guarded these addresses*: Note from Rose Valland to Jacques Jaujard, November 27, 1943, AN 20144792/276.

244 *"He takes the opportunity"*: Note from Rose Valland to Jacques Jaujard, February 8, 1944, AN 20144792/276.

244 *"No one here is stupid enough"*: Ibid.

244 *"It would not be good"*: Pierre Dalloz, ed., *Vérités sur la drame du Vercors: Témoinage* (La Thébaïde, 2014), 101.

244 *discreetly hiding people*: Desroches-Noblecourt, "Un très grand directeur," 27.

246 *"they're ambulance drivers"*: Ellen Hampton, *Women of Valor: The Rochambelles on the WWII Front* (New York: Palgrave Macmillan, 2006), 34.

246 *"It's war"*: War diary of Ahmed Abbès-Louslaty, 1/3rd R.A.C., entry from July 27, 1944, FFL.

246 *"touch of wind" . . . "fresh breeze"*: Moore, *Free France's Lion*, 229.

247 *General Leclerc was right there*: Ibid., 231.

247 *directed specifically at Alexandre*: Letter from Paul Rosenberg to Winnifred Easton, July 26, 1944, Paul Rosenberg Archives, MOMA II.RR.5.

247 *"It is not time"*: Harriet and Sidney Janis, "Picasso's Studio" (excerpt from Harriet and Sidney Janis, *Picasso: The Recent Years, 1936–46* [Garden City, NY: 1946], 4–5), *A Picasso Anthology: Documents, Criticism, Reminiscences*, ed., Marilyn McCully (Princeton, NJ: Princeton University Press, 1982), 224.

248 *"heavier stuff is coming down"*: Letter from Winnifred Easton to Paul Rosenberg, March 7, 1944, Paul Rosenberg Archives, MOMA II.RR.5.

248 *"that breathless hush"*: Letter from Winnifred Easton to Paul Rosenberg, April 19, 1944, Paul Rosenberg Archives, MOMA, II.RR.5.

248 *"Only a pimp"*: Karin Hofmeester and Bernd-Stefan Grewe, eds., *Luxury in Global Perspective: Objects and Practices, 1600–2000* (Cambridge: Cambridge University Press, 2016), 254.

248 *"against the will of Göring"*: Petropoulos, *Göring's Man in Paris*, 90.

249 *began taking greater risks*: Note from Rose Valland to Jacques Jaujard, February 18, 1944, AN 20144792/276.

249 *pilfered more than sixty*: Note from Rose Valland to Jacques Jaujard, February 11, 1944, AN 20144792/276.

249 *"How this could happen" . . . "paintings in his briefcase"*: Letter from Robert Scholz to Gerhard Utikal, January 25, 1944, MAE 209SUP/716.

249 *"only one possibility"*: Ibid.

249 *"bites the dust this time"*: Note from Rose Valland to Jacques Jaujard, March 31, 1944, AN 20144792/276.

249 *"one of the most beautiful properties"*: Note from Rose Valland to Jacques Jaujard, January 26, 1944, AN 20144792/276.

250 *removed from the inventory*: Note from Rose Valland to Jacques Jaujard, May 2, 1944, AN 20144792/276.

250 *"very likely . . ."*: Note from Rose Valland to Jacques Jaujard, April 14, 1944, AN 20144792/276.

250 *to a concentration camp*: Günther Haase, *Die Kunstsammlung des Reichsmarschalls Hermann Göring* (Berlin: Edition q, 2000), 37.

250 *"A sort of uncertainty"*: Note from Rose Valland to Jacques Jaujard, June 2, 1944, AN 20144792/276.

250 *"I hope and really believe"*: Letter from Paul Rosenberg to Winnifred Easton, undated circa spring 1944, Paul Rosenberg Archives, MOMA II.RR.5.

251 *to make Rose "disappear"*: Letter from Rose Valland to James Rorimer, June 25, 1957, AN 20150497/215.

251 *"It was unlikely!"*: Valland, *Le Front de l'Art*, 211.

252 *"What a great day!"*: War diary of Ahmed Abbès-Louslaty, 1/3rd R.A.C., June 6, 1944, FFL.

252 *"The beginning of the end"*: War diary of Captain Paul Gloaguen, 22nd G.C.F.T.A., June 6, 1944, FFL.

252 *"I have met his big boss"*: Letter from Paul Rosenberg to Winnifred Easton, July 26, 1944, Paul Rosenberg Archives, MOMA II.RR.5.

253 *"What will we find"*: Christian Girard, *Journal de Guerre, 1939–1945: Témoinage de l'aide de camp du general Leclerc de Hauteclocque* (Paris: L'Harmattan, 2000), 233.

253 *Lieutenant James Rorimer*: According to Rorimer's war record, he was a second lieutenant at this time. He was promoted to first lieutenant on March 1, 1945, and captain on November 1, 1945.

253 regain *their confidence*: Note from Rose Valland to Jacques Jaujard, June 18, 1944, AN 20144792/276.

254 *arrested on espionage charges*: Note from Rose Valland to Jacques Jaujard, June 10, 1944, AN 20144792/276.

254 *in charge of her prison camp*: Humbert, *Résistance*, 112.

254 *using the Jeu de Paume's services*: Note from Rose Valland to Jacques Jaujard, July 26, 1944, and July 27, 1944, AN 20144792/276.

255 *made a melodramatic exit . . . "with great fanfare"*: Note from Rose Valland to Jacques Jaujard, July 28, 1944, AN 20144792/276.

255 *last mass deportation train*: Nils H. Roemer and Shefali Sahu, "Digital Studies: Convoy 77. Digital Studies of the Holocaust / Case Study #3," Summer 2021,

Ackerman Center for Holocaust Studies at the University of Texas at Dallas; "Histoire et composition du convoy," Convoy 77, https://convoi77.org/histoire-et-composition-du-convoi/.

255 *In total, seventy-six thousand*: "The Deportation of the Jews from France," Yad Vashem the World Holocaust Rembrance Center, www.yadvashem.org/holocaust/france/deportation-from-france.html.

255 *One denounced Vichy*: The following quote and descriptions are from Ludivine Broch, "French Railway Workers and the Question of Rescue during the Holocaust," *Diasporas* 25 (2015): 147–67.

256 *its affairs in order*: Note from Rose Valland to Jacques Jaujard, August 4, 1944, AN 20144792/276.

256 *soldiers emptied offices*: Dominique Lormier, *Les Grandes Affaires de la Libération 1944–1945* (Paris: Alisio, 2019), 177.

256 *For good measure, Rose demanded*: Note from Rose Valland to Jacques Jaujard, August 7, 1944, AN 20144792/276.

256 *like a silvery veil*: Personal diary of Lieutenant Robert Salomon of the 1/3rd R.A.C., August 1, 1944, FFL; *La Deuxième Division Blindée Entre dans la Bataille* (Musée de la Libération de Paris—Musée du Général Leclerc—Musée Jean Moulin, 1945).

257 *They raised their hands*: Général Vézinet, *Le général Leclerc* (Paris: Éditions France-Empire, 1997), 142; Maule, *Out of the Sand*, 181.

257 *Leclerc murmured . . . Girard responded*: Girard, *Journal de Guerre*, 245.

257 *"Leave me alone"*: Ibid.

257 *fused to produce a clarity*: Vézinet, *Le général Leclerc*, 143; Maule, *Out of the Sand*, 185.

258 *"I had an idea"*: Rorimer, *Survival*, 3.

259 *"They're a little crazy"*: Girard, *Journal de Guerre*, 249.

259 *"free-wheeling and hard-fighting attitude" . . . "generally just moving"*: Maule, *Out of the Sand*, 185–86.

259 *"We don't know! Just follow us!"*: Ruby Gwin, Testimony of John S. Eberhardt, Headquarters Battery, in *The 250th Field Artillery Men Remember World War II: The 25th Adapted to the Artillery Trademark: Shoot-Move-and-Communicate* (Bloomington, IN: Trafford, 2012).

260 *"We were waiting for you"*: Girard, *Journal de Guerre*, 248.

260 *"liberating and celebrating"*: Maule, *Out of the Sand*, 185.

260 *Leclerc planned troop movements*: Ibid., 186.

260 *forget about them*: Note from Rose Valland to Jacques Jaujard, March 10, 1944, AN 20144792/276.

261 *placed into 148 crates*: Valland, *Le Front de l'Art*, 192; "Inventaire des caisses—train 40-044," AN 20144792/61.

261 *only labeled "Modern paintings"*: Note from Rose Valland to Jacques Jaujard, August 12, 1944, AN 20144792/276.

261 *five Wehrmacht trucks arrived*: Note from Rose Valland to Jacques Jaujard, August 2, 1944, AN 20144792/276; Brule, "Si Burt Lancaster tourne à Paris"; Paul Denarié, "Héroine du 'Train': La Dauphinoise Rose Valland arrache à Gœring en août 44, cinquante-deux wagons d'œuvres d'art," *Dauphiné Libéré*, March 18, 1979.

262 *secretly got ahold of*: Mary Blume, "How French Art Was Saved in War," *New York Herald Tribune* (International Edition), April 22–23, 1961.

262 *the letters and numbers*: Note from Rose Valland to Jacques Jaujard, August 16, 1944, AN 20144792/276.

262 *"with great satisfaction"*: Valland, *Le Front de l'Art*, 192.

262 *She got in touch directly*: Gibson, "How a Timid Curator with a Deadpan Expression Outwitted the Nazis."

263 ways to stall the train: Ibid.

263 *for twenty-five long minutes*: War diary of Ahmed Abbès-Louslaty, 1/3rd R.A.C., Entry from August 8, 1944, FFL.

263 *"black dots in free fall"*: Edith Vézy, *"Gargamelle": Mon ambulance guerrière 2è D.B.* (Clancy: L'Harmattan, 1994), 46.

264 *here is the horrible reality*: Ibid.

264 *he told Göring*: Note from Rose Valland to Jacques Jaujard, August 9, 1944, AN 20144792/276.

264 *"subversive elements"*: "Testimony of Bruno Lohse taken at Nurnberg (Nuremberg), Germany on 1 November 1945 by Lt. Col. Thomas J. Hinkel, IGD. OUSCC," NARA microfilm M1270 Roll 12.

264 *Lohse fled Paris hours after*: Ibid.; Valland, "Quelques considérations à propos de l'interrogatoire de Bruno Lohse."

264 *Rose had long admired*: Note from Rose Valland to Jacques Jaujard, August 5, 1944, AN 20144792/276.

265 *"suppress not only the traces"*: Note from Rose Valland to Jacques Jaujard, August 9, 1944, AN 20144792/276.

265 *"Ouf!" Rose wrote*: Note from Rose Valland to Jacques Jaujard, August 12, 1944.

265 *"Is this really the end?"*: Note from Rose Valland to Jacques Jaujard, August 5, 1944, AN 20144792/276.

265 *"where the heat was on"*: Tristan Rondeau, "Hommage à Guy Lévy, mort pour la Libération de l'Orne le 12 août 1944," March 12, 2008, *Vive la Resistance*, L'Association Vive la Resistance, http://vivelaresistance.unblog.fr/2008/03/19/.

265 *shot near the heart . . . "I am wounded"*: Letter from Winnifred Easton to Paul Rosenberg, August 30, 1944, Paul Rosenberg Archives, MOMA II.RR.5.

265 *cradled the body*: Sinclair, *My Grandfather's Gallery*, 181; Unit war diary for 2nd battery of the 22nd G.C.F.T.A. Entry from 12 August 1944. The 22nd G.C.F.T.A. battalion diary states that Guy's dead body was brought back to camp.

266 *"Gently inform Guy's brother"*: Telegram from Paul Rosenberg to Winnifred Easton, September 1, 1944, Paul Rosenberg Archives, MOMA II.RR.5.

266 *"How terrible it will be"*: Letter from Paul Rosenberg to Winnifred Easton, September 8, 1944, Paul Rosenberg Archives, MOMA II.RR.5.

266 *had been murdered*: Manuela Finaz de Villaine, "Hommage à Gilbert Lévy," *Sévres: Revue de la Sociéte des Amis du musée national de Céramique*, no. 20 (2011): 9; "Eugénie Kahn," Holocaust Survivor and Victims Database, www.ushmm.org/online/hsv/person_view.php?PersonId=4305598. The date of both Gilbert Lévy's and Éugenie Kahn's deaths is April 18, 1944.

266 *he would freeze. Alexandre's condition was known*: Alain Godec (researcher at Fondation de la France Libre), in conversation with the author, September 18, 2023, and August 4, 2024, as well as emails to the author on September 20, 2023, and August 30, 2023. Godec detailed that three Free French veterans—Captain Jean Juif, whom Alexandre Rosenberg trained under; Lieutenant Michel Poinsot, who was in the regiment HQ with Alexandre in Normandy; and Pierre Zécri, who was part of the orientation team commanded by Alexandre at the regiment HQ—all reported to him directly that Alexandre would freeze when he heard gunshots close to him.

267 *Behr asked repeatedly*: Television interview with Rose Valland, *Les Dossiers de l'écran*, April 9, 1975.

267 *rail switches were broken*: Paul Denaire, "Héroine du Train."

267 *"We did it"*: Note from Rose Valland to Jacques Jaujard, August 12, 1944.

267 *The High Command in Berlin*: Chanel, *Saving Mona Lisa*, 269.

268 *for "safety reasons"*: Telegram from German High Command to Dr. Bernhard von Tieschowitz, French Kunstschutz chief, June 18, 1944, cited in Nicholas, *Rape of Europa*, 285.

268 *to "do the impossible"*: Television interview with Rose Valland, *Les Dossiers de l'écran.*

268 *the train broke down*: Valland, *Le Front de l'Art,* 193; Denaire, "Héroine du Train."

269 *"nothing but dead and decaying flesh"*: Maul, *Out of the Sand*, 201–2.

269 *"about medieval walls and boiling pitch"*: Rorimer, *Survival*, 37.

270 *no food or drink left in the whole town*: James Rorimer's typescript war journal, Entry August 18–19, 1944, James Rorimer Papers, NGA 28MFAA-J1.

270 *"indescribable bedlam"*: Rorimer, *Survival*, 39.

270 *said he had no jurisdiction*: James Rorimer's typescript war journal, Entry from August 18–19, 1944, James Rorimer Papers, NGA 28MFAA-J1 1–1.

270 *a German spy*: Rorimer, *Survival*, 41.

271 *"You're crazy!"*: Bazin, *Souvenirs de l'Exode du Louvre*, 113.

271 *called Rorimer a "cow-boy"*: Bazin, *Souvenirs de l'Exode du Louvre*, 113.

271 *"You've got the Paris post"*: Rorimer, *Survival*, 45.

272 *Rose dodged gunshots*: Valland, *Le Front de l'Art*, 209.

272 *"in the bowels of the palace"*: Christiane Desroches-Noblecourt, "La musée du Louvre pendant la libération de Paris," *Images de la libération de Paris* (Paris: Diffusion Paris-Muséees, 1994), 143.

273 *machine-gunned the crowd . . . "Such outbursts of joy"*: Valland, *Le Front de l'Art*, 209.

273 *final support points*: Valland, *Le Front de l'Art*, 210 (footnote).

273 *Soldiers dug bunkers*: Chanel, *Saving Mona Lisa*, 270.

273 *commanding officers sheltered themselves*: Valland, "Les Combats de la Libération Autour des Musées de Paris."

274 *"that had become worrying"*: Valland, *Le Front de l'Art*, 210.

274 *and her guard at gunpoint*: Ibid.

274 *Ten tons of explosives*: Ferdinand Dupuy, *La Le Libération de Paris vue d'un commissariat de Police* (FeniXX réédition numérique, Librairies-imprimeries réunies, April 2023).

274 *he "had to ensure"*: Choltitz, "Pourquoi en 1944 je n'ai pas détruit Paris," 5.

274 *"except as a field of ruins"*: Maul, *Out of the Sand*, 205.

274 *"This gesture"*: Valland, *Le Front de l'Art*, 209.

275 *"Von Behr is back"*: Note from Rose Valland to Jacques Jaujard, August 18, 1944, AN 20144792/276.

275 *he petulantly walked up and down*: Gibson, "How a Timid Curator with a Deadpan Expression Outwitted the Nazis."

276 *did not make good on his threats*: Brule, "Si Burt Lancaster tourne à Paris."

276 *"We had to act quickly"*: J. des C, "Télévision: Le véritable histoire du Train," *Elle*, March 5, 1979.

276 *"alternate between anguish and hope"*: Valland, *Le Front de l'Art*, 193.

276 *would need to be towed*: "Comment les toiles du Jeu de Paume furent sauvées par le SNCF," *Le Figaro*, August 25, 1944. Based on my analysis of the many accounts Rose gave of these events, I believe that the train was held at Le Bourget between August 15 and 17 and left for Aulnay on August 17 or 18 latest.

276 *taken on a slow joy ride*: Arthur R. White, "French Trick Nazis by 'Losing' Treasure Train" (interview with Rose Valland and James Rorimer), *Stars and Stripes*, January 29, 1945; Hours, *Une vie au Louvre*, 62; Clive Lamming (French rail expert), in an email to the author, October 11, 2023. Almost every news report, including the article in the *Stars and Stripes* decades before the release of *The Train*, speaks of a circling around Paris. If the train was indeed taken on a joy

ride, the most logical move would have been to divert it to Le Bourget instead of going to Aulnay; it could get on the Grand Ceinture from there.

276 *standing up in his open-air car*: Maul, *Out of the Sand*, 189.

277 *The Allies killed . . . and took*: Martin Blumenson, *General Bradley's Decision at Argentan (13 August 1944)* (Washington, DC: Center of Military History, US Army, 1960), 417.

277 *He was convinced*: Dietrich von Choltitz, "Pourquoi en 1944 je n'ai pas détruit Paris," October 3, 1949, 5.

277 *high on cocaine and opioids*: Norman Ohler, trans. Shaun Whiteside, *Blitzed: Drugs in Nazi Germany* (Allen Lane, 2016), 202.

277 *soon received his own death sentence . . . will be buried beneath it*: Dietrich von Choltitz, "Pourquoi en 1944 je n'ai pas détruit Paris," October 12, 1949, 5.

278 *Choltitz telephoned his superior*: Ibid.

278 *"irretrievably lost"*: Dietrich von Choltitz, "Pourquoi en 1944 je n'ai pas détruit Paris," October 6, 1949, 5.

279 *"Galloping like crazy to Paris"*: Girard, *Journal de Guerre*, 269.

279 *"Hold tight, we're coming"*: Vézinet, *Le général Leclerc*, 152.

280 *"We lived a moment of intense emotion"*: Desroches-Noblecourt, "La musée du Louvre pendant la libération de Paris," *Images de la liberation de Paris*, 143.

280 *"It is not possible to reach him"*: Note from Rose Valland to Jacques Jaujard, August 18, 1944.

280 *"Is Paris burning?"*: Dietrich von Choltitz, "Pourquoi en 1944 je n'ai pas detruit Paris," *Le Figaro*, October 12, 1949, 5.

281 *Suddenly, a sniper hiding*: "Secrets d'Aulnay: L'attaque du train d'Aulnay // JW N°4—janvier 2018," video by the town hall of Aulnay-sous-Bois, www.youtube.com/watch?v=pMYwbpZNh14.

281 *with "a big noise"*: Maul, *Out of the Sand*, 210.

281 *"How lucky you are"*: Moore, *Free France's Lion*, 294.

281 *"Head straight to Paris"*: Rayssac, *L'Exode des Musées*, 697.

281 *his wife and children in Germany*: Dietrich von Choltitz, "Pourquoi en 1944 je n'ai pas détruit Paris," October 14, 1949, 5.

282 *"The Leclerc Division has entered Paris"*: Maul, *Out of the Sand*, 214.

282 *"Let the priests ring the bells"*: Alain Frerejean and Claire L'Hoër, *Libération: La joie et les larmes. Acteurs et témoins racontent 1944–1945* (Paris: Éditions de l'Archipel, 2019), 181.

282 *It was exactly 10:10 p.m.*: Dupuy, *La Libération de Paris vue d'un commissariat de Police.*

282 *one of von Choltitz's men exclaimed . . . Choltitz responded*: Choltitz, "Pourquoi en 1944 je n'ai pas détruit Paris," October 14, 1949, 5.

283 *As Rose recounted*: Valland, *Le Front de l'Art*, 212.

283 *expired German* Ausweis *in a Hail Mary*: Rose Valland, draft of chapter from *Le Front de l'Art*, "Les Combats de la Libération autour des Musées Paris."

283 *"before it was too late"*: Valland, *Le Front de l'Art*, 212.

283 *a fire broke out*: The story of the fire is told in Rayssac, *L'Exode des Musées*, 699, based on information Rayssac received from SNCF and Resistance eyewitness Maurice Descroix.

284 *blew up many of the French tanks*: Maul, *Out of the Sand*, 219.

284 *quickly neutralized by the French*: Moore, *Free France's Lion*, 307.

284 *went up in flames*: Choltitz, "Pourquoi en 1944 je n'ai pas détruit Paris," October 14, 1949, 5.

285 *a shell strafed Monet's* Water Lilies: Valland, *Le Front de l'Art*, 214.

285 *narrowly missing him*: Desroches-Noblecourt, "Un très grand directeur," 28.

285 *"a stubborn brown stain"*: Valland, *Le Front de l'Art*, 212.

285 *an "abominable murder"*: Valland, "Les Combats de la Libération autour des Musées Paris."

286 *The FFI leader spoke first*: The following exchange is recounted in Choltitz, "Pourquoi en 1944 je n'ai pas détruit Paris," October 15–16, 1949, 5.

286 *just gotten off the telephone*: Vézy, *"Gargamelle,"* 65.

287 *"one of the most joyful"*: Dupuy, *La Libération de Paris vue d'un commissariat de Police*.

288 *"The Germans set fire"*: Matthew Cobb, *Eleven Days in August: The Liberation of Paris in 1944* (London: Simon & Schuster UK, 2013), 297–98.

288 *"He wanted to offer himself"*: Valland, *Le Front de l'Art*, 213.

288 *"human torrent" demanding justice*: Ibid.

288 *was hit numerous times*: Valland, "Les Combats de la Libération autour des Musées Paris."

288 *"The crowd is often vindictive"*: Valland, *Le Front de l'Art*, 213.

288 *"I will always be grateful to him"*: Ibid.

289 *dig into her back*: Ibid.

289 *"Where in the world"*: Rorimer, *Survival*, 47.

289 *"kept our nerves jumping"*: Ibid.

289 *mysterious "blacked-out" murk*: Ibid.

291 *as a "last test"*: Valland, *Le Front de l'Art*, 214.

291 *protected her from the crowd*: Valland, "Les Combats de la Libération autour des Musées Paris."

291 *"Collaborators! Traitors!"*: Rayssac, *L'Exode des Musées*, 706.

291 *getting ready to execute Jaujard*: Desroches-Noblecourt, "Un très grand directeur," 29.

292 *if the Louvre was attacked again*: Valland, *Le Front de l'Art*, 215.

292 *"with 148 crates of art"*: Note from Rose Valland to Jacques Jaujard, August 26, 1944, AN 20144792/276.

292 *dragged a big black suitcase*: Hours, *Une vie au Louvre*, 62.

292 *one of the watchman's logbooks*: Rorimer, *Survival*, 111; a logbook is located in MAE 209SUP/709, Folder D-1, "Cahier de la Surveillance du Musée du Jeu de Paume par les Allemands Mars à Mai 1943."

292 *led by the tanks*; *placed in charge*: Diary of Alexandre Rosenberg, entry from August 26, 1944, in Rayssac, *L'Exode des Musées*, 707; Maul, *Out of the Sand*, 214.

293 *gunshots disrupted the celebration*: Robert Reid's BBC report live from Notre-Dame, August 26, 1944, www.youtube.com/watch?v=FknjLvwm118.

293 *from inside the church itself*: "De Gaulle in Paris: Wild Celebration Interrupted by Snipers' Attack," newsreel by Movietone, www.youtube.com/watch?v=_wiEJoGcCg8; Marc Lancaster, "Paris. Liberated: De Gaulle Under Fire" (account of Helen Kirkpatrick of the *Chicago Daily News*), August 26, 2020, *World War II on Deadline*, https://ww2ondeadline.com/2020/08/26/paris-liberated-charles-de-gaulle-notre-dame-gunfire-audio/.

293 *Alexandre ordered his men*: Diary of Alexandre Rosenberg, entry from August 26, 1944, in Rayssac, *L'Exode des Musées*, 707.

294 *broadcasting live from inside the church*: Live radio report by Raymond Marcillac, "Fusillade à Notre-Dame-de-Paris—Libération de Paris—26 August 1944." https://www.youtube.com/watch?v=OK5xSXlIBM0.

295 *"Heavy losses"*: Diary of Alexandre Rosenberg, entry from August 27, 1944, in Rayssac, *L'Exode des Musées*, 707.

295 *on a reconnaissance mission*: Rayssac, *L'Exode des Musées*, 709. Based on testimony by Maurice Descroix.

295 *"Hold your fire"*: Patricia Cohen and Tom Mashberg, "Family, 'Not Willing to Forget' Pursues Art It Lost to Nazis," *New York Times*, April 26, 2013, Section A, 1.

295 *small number of bewildered*: Sinclair, *My Grandfather's Gallery*, 193.

296 *at least 151 belonged to his father*: "Inventaire des caisses—train 40-044," AN 20144792/61. The number 151 for paintings belonging to Paul Rosenberg is based on counting any painting itemized as "P.R.," "PR," "Rosenberg-Bernstein Bordeaux," "Rosenberg Bernstein," "Rosenberg-Bernstein," "R. B. Bordeaux," "R. Bernstein Bordeaux," "Rosenberg," and two categorized as "G.R" but with Rosenberg and Rosenberg-Bernstein in the title.

296 *it was a "beautiful revelation"*: Television interview with Rose Valland, *Les Dossiers de l'écran*.

296 *"marvelously providential"*: Valland, *Le Front de l'Art*, 193.

296 *"I won't hesitate to say"*: Interview with Rose Valland, 1963, Radio Télévision Française, archives of the association La mémoire de Rose Valland.

297 *A train was bombed*: Blume, "How French Art Was Saved in War."

SECTION 13

299 *"save a little beauty of the world"*: Valland, *Le Front de l'Art*, dedication.

299 *she rushed to Aulnay-sous-Bois*: Brule, "Si Burt Lancaster tourne à Paris."

299 *then personally accompanied*: Television interview with Rose Valland, *Les Dossiers de l'écran.*

300 *"unimaginable disorder" . . . "bedlam"*: James Rorimer, draft of "Paris Monuments Officer," a chapter of the *Survival*, James Rorimer Papers, NGA 28MFAA-J1, 4–10.

300 *"It was a very near miss"*: Rorimer, *Survival*, 64.

301 *"would insist on real justice"*: Rorimer, draft of "Paris Monuments Officer," 4–10.

301 *they had yet to meet*: James Rorimer, handwritten manuscript draft, James J. Rorimer Papers, AAA Smithsonian Institution, Box 1, Folder 1.19; James Rorimer's typescript war journal, Entry from December 18, 1944, James Rorimer Papers, NGA 28MFAA-J11-1.

301 *Rose estimated that one-third*: Rorimer, *Survival*, 108.

301 *around one hundred thousand*: "Mission de recherche et de restitution des biens culturels spoliés entre 1933 et 1945," French Ministry of Culture, www.culture.gouv.fr/en/Nous-connaitre/Organisation-du-ministere/Le-secretariat-general/mission-de-recherche-et-de-restitution-des-biens-culturels-spolies-entre-1933-et-1945/Documentation-historique-et-juridique.

301 *more than thirty thousand*: Jonathan Petropoulos, in an email to the author, September 16, 2024.

301 *afraid of French bureaucracy . . . if she actually knew anything*: Rorimer, *Survival*, 109.

301 *"I became worried"*: Rose Valland, draft of chapter "La Récupération s'organise" in *Le Front de l'Art*, MAE 209SUP /717.

302 *"get yourself into some position"*: James Rorimer, handwritten manuscript draft, James J. Rorimer Papers, AAA Smithsonian Institution, Box 1, Folder 1.20.

303 *was entirely correct*: Rorimer, *Survival*, 110.

303 *"inscrutable as the cat and mouse play"*: Handwritten notes by James Rorimer on Rose Valland, NGA 28MFAA-J2 2-15.

303 *There were no romantic feelings*: Louis Rorimer and Anne Rorimer (son and daughter of James Rorimer), in conversation with the author, June 7, 2022. Jacqueline Barthalay, in conversation with the author, August 16, 2022, May 11, 2024, November 7, 2024.

303 *"the best cloak-and-dagger tradition"*: Rorimer, *Survival*, 110.

303 *"There are too many others"*: James Rorimer, handwritten manuscript draft, James J. Rorimer Papers, AAA Smithsonian Institution, Box 1, Folder 1.20;

James Rorimer, typescript manuscript draft of "Paris Monuments Officer," James J. Rorimer Papers, NGA 28MFAA-J1 4–8 Folder 1 of 3.

304 *"without anyone being the wiser"*: Rorimer, *Survival*, 111.

304 *Rose and Joyce had moved*: Rose and Joyce moved to 4 rue de Navarre between December 1943 and spring of 1944; documents in AN 20150497/215; letter from Mrs. Jeanne Bucher to Louis Carré from the Louis Carré Archives, *Fernand Léger* exhibition catalog, 337, shows that as of May 18, 1944, Rose was living at 4 rue de Navarre.

304 *from the German stockpile*: James Rorimer, handwritten manuscript draft, James J. Rorimer Papers, AAA Smithsonian Institution, Box 1, Folder 1.20.

304 "Bon soir cher collegue": James Rorimer, handwritten manuscript draft, James J. Rorimer Papers, AAA Smithsonian Institution, Box 1, Folder 1.20.

304 *"You must go to Germany"*: Rorimer, *Survival*, 112.

304 *"Channels?" . . . piles of documents*: Ibid., 113.

304 *"How can you be so certain? . . . "before the SS can destroy them"*: Ibid., 114.

305 *"It seemed so obvious"*: Valland, *Le Front de l'Art*, 222.

305 *"you can trust no one"*: Rorimer, typescript manuscript draft of "Paris Monuments Officer."

305 *so she made a skirt*: Draft notes of Agnès Humbert, AN 20150497/215.

305 *later attached a button*: Jouan, *Rose Valland*, 46.

306 *"I do not know what happened"*: Brule, "Si Burt Lancaster tourne à Paris."

EPILOGUE

307 *together under enemy fire*: Letter from Pierre-Louis Duchartre to Rose Valland, September 1946, MAE 209SUP/724.

307 *was even roommates with him*: Rorimer, typescript manuscript draft, James J. Rorimer Papers, NGA 28MFAA-J1 4–8.

307 *but was saved just in time*: Valland, *Le Front de l'Art*, 228–29.

308 *digging something up*: Letter from Edgar Breitenbach to Rose Valland, November 30, 1948, MAE 583-R40.

308 *"Linz complex of party buildings"*: Speer, *Inside the Third Reich*, 387.

308 *all that remained of Hitler*: "Official: KGB chief ordered Hitler's remains destroyed," *CNN*, December 11, 2009, www.cnn.com/2009/WORLD/europe/12/11/russia.hitler.remains/index.html. (archived at https://web.archive.org/web/20240926084234/https://www.cnn.com/2009/WORLD/europe/12/11/russia.hitler.remains/index.html).

310 *using false papers*: Jouan, *Rose Valland*, 52.

310 *and went clandestinely*: Rose Valland, "Restitutions de[s] emportés émportes du Musée de l'Armée à Paris," May 23, 1950, MAE 209SUP/706.

310 *"I know all the difficulties"*: Letter from General Henry Blanc to Rose Valland, March 21, 1950.

310 *had them surreptitiously seized*: Letter from Rose Valland to General Henry Blanc, July 5, 1950, MAE 209SUP/706; letter from Rose Valland to General Carolet, October 9, 1950, and Rose Valland, "Démarches effectuées pour la Restitution des Canons du Musée de l'Armée et des Drapeaux enlevés de France," October 4, 1950, MAE 209SUP/706.

310 *the Russians had desecrated*: Letter from Rose Valland to Monsieur le Chef de la Division Éducation et Affaires Culturelles, November 20, 1947, MAE 209SUP/707.

311 *Rose found the copy*: Ibid.

311 *called her "Saint Rose"*: Letter from Captain Elie J. Doubinsky to Rose Valland, MAE 209SUP/706.

311 *called her "Valiant Rose"*: Letter from Pierre-Louis Duchartre to Rose Valland, September 1946, MAE 209SUP/724.

311 *"heroine of this book"*: James Rorimer, handwritten manuscript draft, James J. Rorimer Papers, AAA Smithsonian Institution, Box 1, Folder 1.19.

311 "Mon cher 'Captain,'" *and he called her* "Ma capitaine": Letter from Rose Valland to James Rorimer, August 17, 1955; letter from James Rorimer to Rose Valland, September 14, 1955, both in Metropolitan Museum of Art Archives, New York, James Rorimer records, Box 8, Folder 2.

311 *claimed he had disobeyed*: Letter from Rose Valland to Captain Harlin, January 31, 1955, AN 20150497/215.

311 *von Behr's order to execute Rose*: Regarding Behr giving the order to make Rose "disappear," see letter from Rose Valland to James Rorimer, June 25, 1957, AN 20150497/215; Valland, *Le Front de l'Art*, 105; Letter from Rose Valland to Captain Harlin, January 31, 1955, AN 20150497/215

312 *regretted his decision to spare her*: Letter from Rose Valland to James Rorimer, June 25, 1957.

312 *"Certainly far more guilty"*: Letter from Theodore Rousseau Jr. to Albert Henraux, March 1, 1949, Metropolitan Museum of Art archives, New York, Theodore Rousseau Papers, Box 26, Folder 4.

312 *a "leading role"*: "Procès—Verbal d'Information," Rose Valland's deposition at Bruno Lohse's military trial in Paris, December 23, 1948, AN 20150497/215.

312 *"soul of the ERR" who "bears"*: Valland, "Quelques considérations à propos de l'interrogatoire de Bruno Lohse."

312 *"practically come to the point"*: Unsent letter from James Rorimer to James Plaut, July 18, 1957, NGA 28MFAA J1 1–17.

312 *no direct sales ever came to pass; however*: Petropoulos, *Göring's Man in Paris*, 173–174.

312 *Lohse continued to rail . . . he also commented*: Ibid., 43.

313 *"Lohse was obsessed with her"*: Jonathan Petropoulos, in an email to the author, August 21, 2022.

313 "Non, je ne regrette rien": *Plunderer the Life and Times of a Nazi Art Thief (Part Two)*, directed by Hugo Macgregor, 2025, Living Memory Productions, PBS.

313 *"Rose Valland wants"*: Bouchoux, *Rose Valland: Resistance at the Museum*, 80.

313 *no way she could keep the title or pay*: "Note pour Monsieur François Poncet" (French ambassador to Germany), March 8, 1950, AN 20150497/215.

314 *worked on plans to protect*: Bouchoux, *Rose Valland: Resistance at the Museum*, 83.

314 *went to work for the Rothschild Foundation*: Véra Volmane, "Rose Valland raconte . . . La Véritable Histoire du 'Train.'" October 1, 1954, *Les Nouvelles Littéraires—Arts—Sciences—Spectacles,* October 1, 1964, 12e année, no. 1935, 12.

314 *Rose states that "the authorities" . . . "I never intended"*: Letter from Rose Valland to Jean Brunon, March 2, 1978, archives of Bénédicte Delfaut.

314 *wrote to hundreds of libraries and museums*: Numerous letters from Rose Valland to libraries, institutions, et al., MAE 209SUP/718.

315 *denials came directly*: Letter from Robert Scholz and Walter Borchers in Kurt Fassmann, "Bildersturm in Frankreich," Das Schönste, December 1962, 75, cited in Petropoulos, *Göring's Man in Paris*, 118.

315 *"designated among"*: Notarized written testimony of Paul Blondel in Saint-Pierre-Église (Manché), January 16, 1963, MAE 209SUP/313.

315 *wrote in his notarized testimony*: Notarized written testimony of Eugène Finitzer, December 15, 1962, MAE 209SUP/313.

316 *"I, undersigned, C. Develay"*: Signed written testimony of C. Develay, December 5, 1962, MAE 209SUP/313.

316 *"In my soul and conscience"*: Notarized written testimony of Paul Moïse, December 12, 1963, MAE 209SUP/313.

316 *"The canvases of these lacerated paintings"*: Gaston Petit, "NOTE sur le séquestre du Louvre"; note from Rose Valland to Jacques Jaujard, July 23, 1943, AN 20144792/276.

316 *"on the grounds of the Tuileries Garden"*: "Flambez Peintures!" *Libération*, September 7, 1943.

317 *"this deletion allowed"*: Polack, *Le Marché de l'Art sous l'Occupation*, 199. Polack also stated to the author that she saw an original photograph in the French archives used in Valland's book *Le Front de l'Art*, where there is tape indicating the crop lines in order to remove Germain Bazin from the photograph. She says the Musées Nationaux would not let Rose publish the full original photograph in her book. She also believes Louvre curator René Huyghe is shaking Alfred Rosenberg's hand, based on photo comparisons. In the days prior, Bazin and Huyghe represented the Musées Nationaux for another meeting with the ERR

for the division of the Schloss Collection (Petropoulos, *Goring's Man in Paris*, 88). I consulted with Conor McCourt, a New York State licensed investigator, forensic image/video analyst and former NYPD detective who compared the high resolution photograph in question with portraits of Germain Bazin from the same time period. McCourt found many similarities including hairline, nose, jowl line, and eyebrows, giving it a 50% probability it is the same person, adding additionally that one should consider "the totality of the evidence" not just the photograph.

318 *hospitalized for an illness*: Alain Godec, ed., *Journal de Marche du 1/3 R.A.C.*, Entries from October 5, 1944, and October 11, 1944 (Paris: Fondation de France Libre), 58, 60.

318 *leave in Paris for overwork*: Letter from Paul Rosenberg to Winnifred Easton, February 10, 1945, Paul Rosenberg Archives, MOMA II.RR.5.

318 *"very well disposed towards us"*: Letter from Alexandre Rosenberg to Maître P. Kraemer-Raine, December 17, 1960, Paul Rosenberg Archives, MOMA V.A.15b.

318 *the US counterintelligence corps*: Humbert, *Résistance*, 252.

319 *to be declared a doctor before dying*: Heer, "Preface," *La personnalité de Pausanias*.

319 *Rose wrote to her cousin Marguerite*: Letter from Rose Valland to her cousin Marguerite Jacquier-Roux, August 24, likely 1977, MRD.

319 *and never recovered*: Jacqueline Barthalay, in conversation with the author, November 16, 2024.

319 *"You can guess"*: Letter from Rose Valland to Marguerite Jacquier-Roux, circa 1977, MRD.

319 *"I was appalled by"*: Letter from Jean-Phillipe Lecat, circa end of October beginning of November 1999, archives of the association La Mémoire de Rose Valland.

320 *more than sixty-one thousand*: "Note concernant Melle Rose Valland, Chef du Service de Remise en Place des Œuvres d'Art en Allemagne," October 25, 1951, AN 20150497/215.

320 *over one hundred thousand*: Dr. Wesley A. Fischer and Dr. Ruth J. Weinberger, "Holocaust-Era Looted Cultural Property: A Current Worldwide Overview" (Washington, DC: World Jewish Restitution Organization; Claims Conference on Jewish Material Claims Against Germany, 2024), 5.

AUTHOR'S NOTE

326 *"don't talk too much about me"*: Volmane, "Rose Valland raconte."

326 *"a little astonishing"*: Blume, "Mostly About People: Liberation Memories."

Additional sources available at michelleyoungwriter.com

INDEX

NOTE: Locators in italics indicate pages with images.